RESTRUCTURING
THE WORLD
ECONOMY

RESTRUCTURING THE WORLD ECONOMY

JOYCE KOLKO

PANTHEON BOOKS · NEW YORK

TO GABY

All rights reserved under
International and Pan-American Copyright Conventions.
Published in the United States by Pantheon Books,
a division of Random House, Inc., New York,
and simultaneously in Canada by
Random House of Canada Limited, Toronto.

Library of Congress Cataloging-in-Publication Data

Kolko, Joyce.
Restructuring the world economy.

Includes index.
1. Economic history—1971–   . 2. Capitalism.
I. Title.
HC59.K5926   1988   330.9   87–46052
ISBN 0–394–55920–7
ISBN 0–394–75900–1 (pbk.)

Manufactured in the United States of America

First Edition

CONTENTS

LIST OF ABBREVIATIONS

ADB	Asian Development Bank
AID	[U.S.] Agency for International Development
ASEAN	Association of Southeast Asian Nations
BEP	break-even point
BIS	Bank of International Settlements
BLS	Bureau of Labor Statistics
BOP	balance of payments
bpd	barrels per day
COMECON	Council for Mutual Economic Assistance
CPE	centrally planned economy
EC	European Community
EEC	European Economic Community
EMS	European Monetary System
FDI	foreign direct investment
FDIC	[U.S.] Federal Deposit Insurance Corporation
FRB	Federal Reserve Board
FRG	Federal Republic of Germany
GATT	General Agreement on Tariffs and Trade
GDP	gross domestic product
GNP	gross national product
Group of Five	informal organization of the five largest industrial nations in the OECD—United States, Federal Republic of Germany, Britain, Japan, and France

Group of Ten   Belgium, Canada, France, Federal Republic of Germany,
                 Italy, Japan, Holland, Sweden, Switzerland, Britain, and
                 United States
IDA   International Development Association
IFC   International Finance Corporation
IMF   International Monetary Fund
LBO   leveraged buyout
LDC   less-developed country
LIBOR   London interbank offered rate
LLR   lender of last resort
M & A   merger and acquisition
NIC   newly industrializing country
NIDL   new international division of labor
NIEO   new international economic order
OECD   Organization of Economic Cooperation and Development;
                 refers both to the organization and to the industrial
                 capitalist countries as a group
OPEC   Organization of Petroleum Exporting Countries
SAL   [World Bank] structural-adjustment loan
SDR   special drawing rights
SEC   Securities and Exchange Commission
TNC   transnational corporation
UNIDO   United Nations Industrial Organization

ACKNOWLEDGMENTS

In addition to all who have shared their thoughts in conversations over the years on the important problems I discuss in this book, I gratefully acknowledge the help of several friends in its completion. One, sadly, is no longer here. Gaston Davoust gave invaluable counsel in the early stages of research and writing. I, like all who knew this extraordinary person, miss him greatly. Ed Herman thoughtfully sent some hard-to-obtain studies early in my research. Saburo Kugai was a constant source of useful materials, and read the manuscript, offering his advice, insights, and knowledge. Ilse Mattick generously read the manuscript several times and was warmly encouraging as well as giving extremely helpful suggestions on both substance and style. I also greatly appreciate the very important part played by Jim Peck, a senior editor at Pantheon.

But most of all, with all my admiration and much more, I happily take this opportunity to thank my husband, Gabriel, a model of serious scholarship, also committed to relating research and analysis to reality and the struggle for a better world. His very special companionship in the totality of my life and the help, thoughtful and perceptive criticism, and sharing in all important ways continuously sustained me at every phase of research and writing in the preparation of this book. While all of the above have been generous with their help, I alone, of course, am responsible for the contents and the analysis.

RESTRUCTURING
THE WORLD
ECONOMY

INTRODUCTION

The question of the survival of mankind mobilizes millions of people in the 1980s. But calamities short of the apocalypse shape the reality of our time. Death and destruction through war, repression, and starvation daily afflict countless persons. More struggle to survive on a subsistence level, millions of others face prolonged unemployment, deprivation, and insecurity.

For over ten years a global economic crisis has been evident to most observers, whether perceived as a series of crises—in energy, the monetary system, debt, trade, food, and the like—or as a general cyclical, structural, or systemic crisis. No aspect of the political economy has escaped the malaise.

All agree that it has been a decade of economic problems, most of them very acute, but some question whether it is a crisis. They equate the word *crisis* with a total breakdown or collapse of the economy. But the term can be used in a more limited economic sense to signify, as *Webster's* defines it, a critical turning point to separate periods, the future from the past. For capitalism, crisis is a condition when and where the problem of accumulation and the form it takes is no longer one of productive expansion—a crisis of accumulation. This crisis over more than a decade may be obscure to a few academics, but it has scarcely been obscure to capitalists or governments in the capitalist nations. Their perceived need to "restructure" the world economy testifies to this. Nor is it obscure to the victims of the breakdown in the productive expansion of capital.

Since 1974, to be sure, there have been periods of cyclical rise and

3

fall of production—recovery and recession—and there are still economists who find satisfaction in observing that the 1975–80 recovery was
longer than any other since that of 1933–37. Yet during the periods
of "recovery," the world economy also hovered on the edge of ruin. One
can point to innumerable trigger points that could have sparked a chain
reaction through this highly integrated system. These points have become more numerous and, in fact, are continually more aggravated. But
a collapse on the order of that of 1929–33 has not occurred. What
countervailing tendencies have prevented it?

Why was this crisis not more clearly foreseen, at least in its broad
dimensions? This myopia is an important part of the problem, for the
whole question of expectations, anticipations, predictions, and assumptions of the future of economic actors, from households to governments,
from private investors to social movements, plays a critical role in
determining their action in the present—which, in turn, partially
shapes the future. Perceptions of the present and the projections based
on them largely determine behavior.

Many critical analyses of the economy continue to focus on particular
structural features—monopoly, international division of labor, debt
crises, hegemonies, and the like—and to extrapolate them into the
future. Studies of this nature have become very influential in shaping
perceptions of the past and the present as well as expectations of the
future. Many became mini-theories and the intellectual frameworks or
paradigms providing the boundaries for new empirical studies. This
was true of "monopoly capital," "neocapitalism," "postindustrial,"
"interdependence," "convergence," "military-industrial complex," the
"miracle economies" (initially meaning those of the Federal Republic
of Germany [FRG] and of Japan but now being extended to the newly
industrialized countries), and similar conceptualizations.

Many studies seized on the structural change of high energy cost and
projected the pattern into the future. Far more significantly, policies of
both capital and states were predicated on this assumption, and these
policies led to new structural changes in the economy. All were an-
chored to factors that were and are transitional and changing.

Perceptions of interests, even inaccurate ones, are elements in the
scenario. Capitalists perceive and respond in the short run even in
developing their long-term strategies. This is a systemic feature that
undermines all efforts of others to reform or regulate the economy.
Important, too, is the speed of change both in the perceptions and in
the objective environment.

There is a fundamental process of interaction between objective
forces, their perception, and the subjective response. The perception

may be based on faulty statistical calculations or on real experience, but perceptions in the capitalist system, true or false, form the basis for action. Hence, throughout this study the question of perception, as distinct from that of objective reality, is crucial, and action based on it, in turn, can influence or shape the objective reality. For example, the perception of the future plays a determining role in plans for investment or the development strategies of states.

PREDICTIONS

The misperception of present forces leads to predictions of the future based on an extrapolation of the observable structural conditions. There is no end to examples.

The Club of Rome, an international gathering of prestigious government and academic economists, was utterly incapable in 1972 of comprehending the forces operating in the industrial economies when it projected perpetual rapid growth into the future, to be hampered only by the potential exhaustion of physical resources. All development strategists for the UN's Second Development Decade of the 1970s also assumed that the growth of the 1960s of the industrial countries in the Organization for Economic Cooperation and Development (OECD) would continue unabated into the future. On the left many predicted that capitalism had essentially solved the problem of crisis with a permanent arms economy, consumerism, or imperialism.

In 1977 thirty-five "experts" from fifteen countries under the auspices of MIT predicted an impending "catastrophe," because of the ever growing demand for and shrinking supply of oil. The Bank for International Settlements (BIS), the central bankers' bank, in 1980 projected an OPEC surplus of $120 billion a year for the foreseeable future. Superseding the predictions about the OPEC countries are forecasts on the future power of the newly industrializing countries (NICs).

Renowned sources predicted in 1979 that the 1980s would see economic and political power shift from Europe to Brazil and Mexico. It is the vogue in the 1980s to view management techniques as the secret of Japan's economic success, just as those of the United States were perceived in the 1960s, in the so-called era of the American challenge. Both perceptions have an impact on the economy as others seek to imitate this "secret" of success.

In a highly integrated world economy, the unspoken assumptions about the future on the part of those holding the reins of power have far-reaching consequences. Among capitalists, predictions relate to the expectation of profit. The daily compulsions of competition—maintaining or expanding market share and reducing costs—shape their actions. Among states, those in the centrally planned economies (CPEs) and in the less-developed countries (LDCs) predicted an expanding world market; they borrowed and built industry to export, distorting their own internal development in the process. Industries invested and borrowed on the assumption that inflation was "forever." The 1980 projections on oil prices had reverberations throughout the world economy, affecting such raw materials as coal. Within two years the situation was reversed, with severe consequences for industry, banks, governments, and those who were forced to pay for these errors—the world's laboring population.

It has been noted that all is predictable in retrospect. But perceptions of the future based on extrapolations of present and past trends, and actions taken on the basis of them, frequently contradict the needs of the future reality.

Needless to say, the very process of living requires behavior based on perceptions of the future, and all institutions must plan for what is to come on the basis of perceptions of the past and present. Pointing to the monumental errors does not absolve some persons from the responsibility of preparing for the future and others from that of anticipating it. It may be that there is no longer any point to analyzing the crisis unless one is able to make some kind of forecast, despite the difficulties and dangers. Obviously, questions relating to the future concern everyone. Although there is no way to predict specific events, it is not enough only to discuss empirically aspects of the crisis or even the general cause and condition. One must also search beyond them and try to ascertain or pinpoint a method for determining the direction of events in order to delineate the probable—and the possible. This requires focusing not on a particular structural condition but on the interaction of many forces and seeing the whole as a process.

The economic problems have more and more a world scope—a world market, world factories, a world system.* Societies have never been closer and more integrated than they are today. This near universality and integration of the world economy exists in dialectical interaction with the fundamental contradiction of national capitalism. Though capitalist states have varied in specific national development—ranging from

*While the concepts of a world system, a totality, and the integration and dialectical interaction of diverse elements in the political economy have for many generations of Marxists been useful analytical tools and conceptualizations of reality, they must now be distinguished from what is now called the "world systems" school.

that of the United States to that of Japan or Sweden, from that of India to that of the Federal Republic of Germany or Chile—the common denominator is approached in times of crisis. The objective integration of the world economy creates limits to national exceptionalism. What is more, whole realms of action that were once part of the state's domain—national finance, money supply, economic policy, trade, even the measurement of these activities—are in large part now beyond national control.

METHOD

This book deals with the crisis in the capitalist system, a system that now prevails with astonishing uniformity throughout the globe; it identifies and examines *horizontally* some of the specifics of that crisis in their linkages and relationships. This is possible because of the de facto integration of the world economy, even in those areas where capitalism is utterly foreign to the traditional social relations and is an external imposition, by way of the imperialism of IMF policies and/or state or corporate manipulation of noncapitalist societies. One can explore the world economy in the same way one can examine, for instance, U.S. foreign policy as it relates to many parts of the world, without necessarily having expertise in each area.

Obviously, one must choose whether to pursue a microscopic examination of a particular problem or to make an effort to grasp the broader relationship of multiple forces in the political economy. A reasonable argument can be made for both approaches, and they both have limits. A specific study may lead to a profound understanding of all aspects of a problem but may not appreciate how it is affected by—and, in turn, affects—others. The alternative approach is open to charges of superficiality on a specific problem. But today all aspects of finance, of production, and of economic policy are so interlaced because of technological change that national frontiers have become abstractions. At the same time, though, nations are strong and struggle in sharpening global competition. These contradictions and changes have *objectively* restructured the economy. How can one deal with questions of trade isolated from the questions of debt and vice versa? The integration of the world economy allows, or even requires, a global focus, even for a full comprehension of the parts. This includes defining the objective factors, both systemic and structural, that interact to form the political and economic environment. The totality is mobile; the interacting parts are dynamic. But while all the disparate elements are linked and interact, they are not susceptible to a coherent global strategy. And the contradictions

that come out of that very objective integration engender a disintegration. What emerges is a dialectic of acts, perceptions, and reactions by
individuals, classes, states—a dynamic of perpetual struggle.

Capitalism is a ubiquitous system; however, since it is not a state of
nature but rather a relationship within and between classes, one must
focus on that relationship as a dynamic process and probe analytically
for the weak points and contradictions. In examining the ingredients
of the contemporary crisis, one may usefully distinguish between the
systemic (intrinsic) and the *structural* (transitional). To overlook the
daily interaction of the systemic features is to risk being misled as to
the probabilities and possibilities of future developments. Because
these terms differ widely in their meaning, some definitions are in
order. They form the crux of the methodology of this study.

THE SYSTEMIC FEATURES

The economic crisis of world capitalism is primarily systemic and
guaranteed in the sense that the contradictions and antagonisms are
intrinsic to the capitalist system itself. I am referring to such basic
features as (1) a society organized for the accumulation of capital for
its own sake, (2) capitalists' decisions based on their perception of
expected profitability for the present and/or future, (3) competition, (4)
relations of production based on exploitation and commodification of
labor and its attendant class struggle, (5) the state as promoter and
protector of the system, and (6) the anarchy of market relations.*

Most would agree that these systemic features serve in part to define
the capitalist system. But to analyze and anticipate future developments, one must see them as predominating and interacting dialectically with the structural features in the political economy. The intrinsic
characteristics will remain constant as long as the system itself exists.
This means the economy cannot be reformed—that is, the intrinsic
features cannot be altered—though it can be, and is being, restructured. Such assertions would indeed be tautological except that the
interactions of these features, essential to understanding the present
and, particularly, anticipating future developments, are often ignored
by economic analysts. Many economists take them for granted and then
proceed to construct their theory or analysis on a structural feature,

---

*Marx used the term *structure* for these features, but for the sake of my
methodological aim in this study and because of the widespread use of the terms
structural and *restructure*, I want to make the distinction between permanent and
transitional features *within* the capitalist economic system, using the term *systemic*
for the former and *structural* for the latter.

ignoring the interaction and tension between the systemic and the structural. Of great importance is the dominance of the systemic, such as the decisions of individual capitalists in their pursuit of profit, in day-to-day activity that mocks all efforts at national, let alone global, reform. Major swings of analytic perception occur by shifts of focus away from the systemic and to only the sometimes rapidly, sometimes slowly, changing structural features.

STRUCTURAL

Structural features are characteristics not intrinsic to the capitalist system but the outcome of the dynamic interaction of economic and political factors. They define particular periods and are always changing.

They may be "restructured" by objective forces or by subjective design, but the outcome is rarely as intended. The structural features of capitalism include colonialism, neocolonialism, the new international division of labor, monopoly, low- or high-cost energy, technological developments, national hegemonies, shifts in industry, monetary and trade structures, inflation, deflation, debt, slow growth, and the like. They also include changes in the working class, state intervention in the economy, the "arms economy," fiscal crisis, and stagnation—all the arrangements in the economy at a particular time that have a major influence on society.

Structural features can be introduced by great events of history— war, revolution, depression—by major developments in science and technology, or by more gradual changes in the political economy. But it is dangerous to build a theory on one structural feature in the economy, because structural features have changed significantly over the decades, often very rapidly, as during the oil crisis. Furthermore, the state's tendency to play a greater role in the economy, widely discussed as a permanent feature, faced contradictions and retrenchment with the fiscal crisis. And the idea of an ever increasing standard of living for certain countries now confronts the retrogression in living standards for the masses and the official acceptance of high levels of unemployment.

In economic analysis one can and should pinpoint tendencies and new structural conditions in the political economy that define the specific character of different periods and crises. In the capitalist system, however, they do not evolve in a straight line; rather, they are changed in their interactions, into something new. For instance, the tendencies toward monopoly, toward a new international division of labor, toward stagnation, and toward inflation or deflation interact dialectically with the systemic characteristics and with the other structural components in the political economy, creating different and new conditions—not in an evolutionary process that one can observe and extrapolate into the future but in a contradictory, zigzag development. The entire process is one of struggle and change—among individuals, classes, sectors, nations, interests, and the objective forces they create on all levels, micro and macro, of the political economy. One must focus primarily on the contradictions that develop. What emerges is a dialectic of permanence and change, but permanent *only* as long as the system endures. One can never say "never" or "forever" in regard to a given structural aspect of the political economy. The systemic features, on the other hand, remain constant and are always present as active agents. One can extrapolate only the systemic features. They alone determine whatever "laws" exist in the capitalist system.

Using a dialectic method—that is, looking for, and expecting, the antagonistic contradictions and interactions between all features in the economic, political, and social process, rather than extrapolating current structural conditions—is very important for prospective analysis, since there is a significant difference between seeing the status quo as fixed and seeing it as dynamic.

The interaction between the systemic and the structural, the objective and the subjective, is of prime importance. For this relationship is a dialectical one with the structural features in the process of perpetual change and the systemic features superseding and persisting, and it mocks the efforts of states to restructure, plan, reform, or manage a system that is intrinsically anarchic. The operations of capitalism are comprehensible but they are not controllable.

We must look for the weaknesses and contradictions behind the appearance of strength and, conversely, for the strengths behind the appearance of weakness, for the systemic that supersedes the structural, and for the dialectic between the subjective policies and the objective process.

RESTRUCTURING

The idea of restructuring the world economy offers a rubric to examine both the objective restructuring of the political economy, as the systemic and structural features interact, and the subjective restructuring strategies of capital and the state in response to their perceptions of crisis. Every government and many important industries now speak of restructuring to adjust to the realities of an "interdependent" world economy in order to resolve the persistent crisis. These plans, reflecting

interests and ideologies, interact, in unintended ways, with the objective features in the economy.

The concept of restructuring lets us explore all the essentials of the
crisis of accumulation, competition, the class struggle, the role of the
state, the dialectic between objective anarchy of the market and subjective planning or strategy. It also captures the social reality of process,
movement and change, that is a dynamic and dialectic interaction.

The notion of restructuring that became in the 1980s a leitmotif
among men of power is relatively new. During the Great Depression,
no one considered restructuring the world economy. Nor was there a
concept of permanent planned reduction or redeployment of industry;
there was only that of recovery. The same was true after World War
II, when the goal was revival, although reconstruction was a direct
antecedent of the process of capitalist planning now known as restructuring. After the war Europe did restructure much of its economy on
the American model. The reasons why the term *restructuring* characterizes the response in the present period are important. I shall explore
the emergence of the concept in the context of the objective developments in the economy in Part I.

It is also important to try to distinguish between ad hoc responses
to immediate perceptions and formulations of strategy. Even among
states, what appeared to be a strategy was usually an improvisation in
the face of perceived immediate threats to interests. States operate in
the real world, but the outcome of their policies is not as intended. Yet
their acts and strategic plans, in turn, do play a role in the objective
process of restructuring. The whole system prevails over the parts.
Nevertheless, there is a consistent strategy of restructuring the world
economy among all the capitalist states.

The restructuring strategies vary and reveal many of the boundaries
and options within the system. They include orthodox policies, which
seek to restore, reinstate, or alter the conditions of the economy and
which range from the OECD, IMF, and traditional development strategies to the cruder monetarist experiments in the United States and
Britain. The strategies span the traditional ideological spectrum, from
full reliance on market forces alone to varying degrees of state intervention to guide the process.

There is also reformist restructuring of international Keynesianism,
embodied in the proposals for a new international economic order and
in those of the social democratic governments of France, Greece, and
Spain. How did they differ, in practice, from their predecessors? What
were the determining systemic and structural boundaries on the reform-

ist restructuring strategies? Moreover, the centrally planned economies are making great strides in integrating themselves into the dominant world capitalist market economy. What have been the motivation and the outcome?

The perceptions of those in power have decidedly influenced state policy over the past years, as one nation after the other has introduced measures to restructure its economy in order to resolve the economic crisis and better compete in the international market. How much room, objectively, is there for maneuver between the various advocates as their efforts lead to conflict?

What substance is there to the popular perception that the developed capitalist economies have entered a "postindustrial" era, one restructured to a service economy, or in the visions of a new international division of labor? Is restructuring a move toward greater reliance on market forces globally? Is it a readjustment of relations with labor or a development of the technological revolution? To what extent can debt and deficit *objectively* restructure the economy and political relations? Hence the overall theme of "restructuring" encompasses a number of crucial questions that may demonstrate the essential relations between capital, the state, and labor in various parts of the world at this time.

Finally, there is restructuring as class struggle. Has it altered fundamentally the objective gains labor achieved in earlier years vis-à-vis capital and the state? Both immediately and ultimately, the crisis crystallizes around the relations of production and between classes. As Marx wrote over a century ago, one must focus on that central social relationship, from which one can see the parts in relation to the whole. It is certainly the primary focus of capital and the state at this time. That relationship alone guarantees crisis. It determines the categories of this essay.

CATEGORIES

The broadest categories—capital, state, labor—remain the most useful for a horizontal analysis of the political economy, since the relationship between them defines the social reality of our world. Each of the basic categories contains systemic and structural features.

This study will seek to underline the relationship of (1) the objective operations of the political economy in crisis, (2) the perceptions that shape the subjective response of those who wield power and rule within the system and of those who must resist or be victimized by the process and policies, and (3) the interaction of these responses in and with the political economy.

In Chapter 1, I shall explore chronologically the interaction of the crucial factors since the beginning of the crisis in 1974. How have they interacted? How have the key actors responded to the crisis at various stages and to the contradictions of state policies with the systemic ad hoc moves by private capital? How have attitudes, policies, and the objective economy been restructured?

After a chronological examination of the dominant developments, the next step is to analyze the relation between the crisis and the primary categories of the system: capital, the state, and labor.

Capital accumulation is the essence of the system. Has the accumulation process itself been put in question by its new forms? Are there true investment strategies in the private sector? How does capital pursue restructuring as a weapon in the class struggle? What is revealed in the state-corporate relationship in this crisis? Who will be winners and who losers and why? Many generalizations have been made about the structural changes in industry, the relocations, the fragmentation, the obsolescence, the effect of the international division of labor, and the shift to a service economy. What are the determining factors? How are they linked to each other and to the crisis? By focusing on a few crucial questions relating to various sectors, one can examine the relationships. Are the changes transitional or permanent? Competition and monopoly are examples of the systemic/structural dichotomy. Which is systemic and which structural? Which is the underlying thrust and motivation in the system? Which tells us most about future developments?

What is the nature of the sectoral crises—in banking, steel, agriculture, resources, and arms—within the general crisis? What special character does each region—the industrial capitalist states (of the OECD), the less-developed countries (LDCs), or the centrally planned economies (CPEs)—hold for private capital?

It is nearly impossible to separate capital and the state in the capitalist nations, especially in their approach toward labor. But the important difference is the extent of strategy. Capital pursues profit and restructures in the process; the state formulates plans and policies of restructuring the economy or segments of it.

The various states are taking their own steps to restructure industrially, technologically, and geographically. They have acted individually and collectively, in cooperation and in conflict. What are the major contradictions in these efforts? What are the mixed motivations and ideologies? How has the state's own need to accumulate (due to debt, deficit, fiscal crisis) contributed to the crisis? What are the means and instruments, such as the IMF, available to individual nations to force restructuring on others? What is the import of the changes in debt, monetary relations, and trade? What is the nature of the international conflict engendered by national restructuring programs? In this volatile period of shifting power relations and resistant economic crisis, in what sense is the economy international and in what sense national? The role of the state is both stronger and weaker in the economy. What are the implications of this contradiction? How has the objective restructuring affected the power of states? After the state's major role in the postwar economy, what is the meaning of the international thrust toward "privatization"?

For the most part, the restructuring strategies of capital and the state are articulated and implemented as an effort to wrest from the working class what they both perceive as lost—an explicit offensive in the class struggle. What are the systemic and structural features in the definition of the working class? How has the very nature of employment been restructured in the industrial countries? Is there a "new" working class? What has been and will be the effect of the high level of unemployment? How much is objective through the operation of the system and how much the result of the states' restructuring strategies? How have labor organizations been restructured in this period of economic crisis? What are the implications of falling living standards? What has been the response?

Critical in this period is the role of science and technology, both as an objective force that reshapes the economic structure and as a strategic tool that capital and the state use in their conscious effort to restructure the economy and/or resolve the crisis. Do new scientific and technological developments represent a revolution (as did the steam engine, railroads, and auto industry, with their expansionary impact on the whole economy) or a continuation of the effort to reduce labor costs and enlarge the area of central control, with contractionary implications for the economy in general? And what are the implications for labor— in industry, the services, and agriculture during this period of crisis?

These questions reveal a process in which each relates to the others, in a state not of harmony but of antagonism, one that is aggravated as the crisis continues and not only eludes a resolution through the subjective restructuring strategies but is worsened thereby. My aim is not to find a precise answer to all these questions but rather to see which features in these relations tell us most about the probabilities regarding the future. Which are structural and will change and which are systemic and will endure? Which impose the boundaries on the restructuring process in the capitalist system?

PART I

CHRONOLOGICAL ANALYSIS

CHAPTER 1

INTERACTION OF EVENTS AND POLICY, 1974–1980

The structural conditions of today differ dramatically from those of 1974. Inflation has given way to disinflation or even deflation. There is a different trend in energy costs, leaving OPEC and other energy-related "growth industries" in shambles, and the volatile changes in currency exchange have had a profound impact on all other features of the economy. There has also occurred an objective and subjective restructuring of a number of basic industries, as continued rapid changes in technology have had swift and unplanned repercussions. To these one must add the evident failure of reformist initiatives, as in France; the political lessons in Poland and Iran; the extent of the consensus on austerity policies among various nations; a famine in Africa in large part the outcome of disastrous policies; the IMF's intrusions in economic policies and its de facto mobilization of populations in the LDCs to resist them; and much more.

Were the current conditions predictable in 1974? Plans were made and executed on the basis of existing realities. Could those who made and implemented them have foreseen and prepared for the new situation? Or were their actions crucial ingredients in the development of the crisis in the world economy? What were the countertendencies to a world depression in the 1970s?

The combination of inflation and recession that confronted the capitalist states in the 1970s led to contradictory imperatives in government policy, restricted as governments are by the boundaries of capitalist economic categories. Traditional anti-inflationary responses had nothing to do with inflation and only worsened the situation. But all the

17

governments chose, in essence, to ascribe the source of inflation to higher labor costs. The new paradigm that emerged in the mid-1970s—the explicit rejection of Keynesianism and the emphasis on the purported dictates of the market—suffused the policies of the international organizations and finally dominated the European socialists and influenced the CPEs during the 1980s.

In this chapter I want to examine the restructuring process as it developed over the past decade, when a consensus emerged that the world economic crisis was not cyclical but structural. Although the emphasis must be on a continual process and interaction, for the sake of convenience, I will here divide the period into four blocks of time: 1968–75, which included years of expansion, recession, boom, recession and the beginnings of the current crisis; 1976–79, the recovery in continued crisis; 1980–82, renewed recession; and the post-1983, recovery.

THE DIMENSIONS OF CRISIS

Vast structural changes have obviously taken place in the world economy since the 1930s, and they give a significantly different character to today's economic crisis. Aside from the vital statistics (a more than doubling of the world's population and an increase in the number of nations from 68 to over 175) has been the shift from colonialism to neocolonialism as the new face of imperialism. Industrial growth in much of the Third World has been accelerated by the developments in science and technology, and the capitalist mode of production has expanded. Moreover, there has been a massive worldwide shift of labor from agriculture to industry to service. Rapid urbanization—or, more precisely, a dislocation of agrarian societies—was an important structural change. By 1980 one-fourth of the Third World population lived in cities.

Another important structural change was the enormous increase in arms production and in expenditure as a percentage of national income in nearly all nations. Economists tend to ignore the impact of war, although they mention the Cold War, in analyzing the decades of economic growth between 1950 and 1973. Yet Keynesian policies and the "golden age" of economic growth were based on the war making of the world's largest economy in the years 1950–53 and 1965–75 and on the economic effects its demand for goods and resources generated around the world. The nature of war has changed, as a war between the great powers is increasingly remote and as local wars, like that between Iran and Iraq, can rage for years without significantly affecting the general economy other than providing a market for the arms industry.

A crucial difference between the stagflation of the first ten years of this economic crisis and the depression of the 1930s was the extent of the state's involvement. The OECD countries showed a vast increase in the state's role both as an employer and as a market and a general intervener in the economy for the thirty-five years following World War II. In the United States roughly half of all new employment after 1950 was created by state expenditures, and a comparable shift occurred in the other OECD nations. Massive government spending kept the economy from collapse and held up profits. Yet government outlays, along with "unduly low" unemployment, were subsequently blamed for inflation.[1] In the 1930s there was no state welfare apparatus; one was introduced as an anticrisis measure. In the 1970s and 1980s the welfare apparatus was progressively reduced in the industrial capitalist countries, because it was perceived as one of the causes of the crisis. And the role of the state as employer began to shift with the fiscal crisis, until by the mid-1980s there was evident a worldwide move to "privatize" various state functions.

Other macro changes include the accelerated concentration and international expansion of capital, intrafirm transfers as a growing proportion of international trade, developments in technology, the new international division of labor, and, concomitantly, the enormous worldwide expansion of competitive industrial capacity within the capitalist world market. The shift from a fixed exchange rate to fluctuating monetary relations had a reverberating impact on all aspects of the world economy.

The major change after 1970 in international lending from individual holdings of government bonds and government-to-government loans, such as existed in the prewar world economy, to commercial banks as the major lenders to sovereign states radically altered the structure of international finance and the domestic economies of borrower and lender alike.

Since the early 1970s the world has become integrated in a unique manner, and this integration is itself an important new structural aspect of the economic condition. If one scrutinizes only regions or specific trends in the world capitalist economy, one risks losing sight of this reality. Events in the world economy can move swiftly and even cataclysmically in a few years, months, or days and change the world decisively—for example, with revolution, war, or the crash in 1929.

Many have noted that the years 1973–74 marked a turning point.

During the first months of many of the years since 1974, government
leaders, such as Takeo Fukuda, Helmut Schmidt, and James Callaghan,
or major capitalists proclaimed that the coming year would be one of
disaster or collapse. It was not alarmist demagoguery; the possibility
was always present. Even the "recovery" in the United States after
1983, loudly proclaimed as the most robust since World War II, was
so riddled with contradictions and the seeds of disaster that only a few
experts were wholly sanguine. At the same time, however, certain
subjective moves of state policy internationally have greatly strengthened and extended the territory for the operation of capitalism. Together, capital and the state have also achieved significant gains in the
perpetual struggle with labor. What are the implications of these contradictory developments?

The specifics of a period of prosperity or crisis are important even
for a theoretical or an analytical understanding of capitalist development. They are not incidental. One cannot examine cycles as if they
were all the same, that is, count the months from peak to trough. But
while a full account of the crisis should not ignore important exogenous
factors, neither is it the outcome of an unrepeatable series of historical
shocks. Recessions are not crises, and recoveries may still be part of
a crisis.

Recovery and recession—the business cycle—hinge on the rise and
fall of production and the accumulation of capital, no matter how slight.
Crisis in the economy includes other factors in its operations. There are,
then, clearly cycles within a crisis like the recoveries of 1933–37,
1975–80, and after 1983. Hence one finds references to recovery
(which means a growing utilization of capital and equipment) when
unemployment is 10 percent, when nations hover on the brink of
bankruptcy, when debt threatens world trade and the largest banks
with collapse, and when there are falling living standards, monetary
disorder, and disastrous deficits. No area has escaped these economic
dilemmas, although they are experienced differently in different areas.
Cycles in this period could not create a new equilibrium but only
deepened the crisis, as there was an important interaction between the
cyclical and the new structural conditions. Although a depression is
always a crisis, a crisis in the operations of the capitalist economy is
not always a depression.

1968–1975

The worst world recession since the 1930s occurred in 1974–75. It
was the culmination of a series of factors. Extremely important was the

organic interplay of the effect of American aggression in Vietnam on the U.S. and the world economy. Had the war ended in 1968, the impact on the economy might have been similar to that of the Korean War. Lasting as long as it did, it had an organic effect on the whole world capitalist system. Many economists recognize that the Vietnam War helped undermine the dollar and the American economy—not just through increased expenditures overseas but also through the intense inflationary impact on the internal economy, increasing imports, over-priced exports, and especially the massive growth in the money supply to pay for the deficit. By 1976, economists were referring to the impact of the war as a problem of "demand management"—of Johnson's refusal to raise taxes to pay for the war or to scrap his "war on poverty." Paul Volcker said, "Our failure to face up to the financing of the Vietnam war [was] one key factor in setting the subsequent inflation."[2]

Other factors behind the recession included the impact of the avalanche of dollars on other world currencies and the 1971 monetary crisis, the mounting costs for industry as world capacity expanded and international competition increased, the simultaneous moves of corporations to expand to the LDCs, and the worldwide scramble for raw materials in 1973–74, further intensified by the rise in oil prices in that year. Private individuals, corporations, banks, and governments—acting separately but in response to the same economic environment within the capitalist system—all played their part in the emerging crisis.

The transnational corporations (TNCs), as we know them today, emerged at the end of the 1960s. Their push toward the LDCs, the periphery of Europe, and, to a lesser degree, the CPEs was a result of the higher cost and, in Europe, of the growing militancy of labor and increasing competition in the industrial capitalist countries. The technology of communication and remote control and new containerized developments in shipping made the establishment of component production in low-wage areas of the world both possible and profitable. One outcome was the partial dissolution of national boundaries, as trade was increasingly between branches of the same corporation. This had many ramifications in the world economy. It greatly affected the fiscal resources of LDC governments, since much of their revenue depended on tariffs and export taxes. Moreover, it allowed real prices, and hence profits, to hide from taxation, and a distorted picture of world trade, especially in commodities, emerged.

In the wake of these objective developments came the ideological handmaidens in the form of the international organizations—IMF,

World Bank, and so on—with their financial leverage, advising the LDCs to adopt export-oriented development strategies compatible with the interests of the expanding corporations, arranging loans for them to build the necessary infrastructure, and, in general, facilitating the profitable new international division of labor. Furthermore, as agribusiness, also dependent on changes in technology, cast its net over wider regions in the Third World, the World Bank abandoned its antirural bias and began to support development for the production of cash crops in demand in Europe and North America and for the export of food. As a consequence the dollar value of LDC food imports to feed their own populations rose, in the aggregate, threefold in the period 1970–74.

Overall growth in the world economy between 1950 and 1970 surpassed all records. There was no growth in the OECD countries in the recession years of 1970–71. In 1972–73 there was rapid growth and an investment boom in the Third World and in industrial Europe. A gigantic steel complex in France, the world's largest shipbuilding center in Britain, and many other projects began—all long-term investments made on the basis of short-term responses to the immediate environment. The banks, already bloated with liquid capital that was an outgrowth of the dollar crisis and then the OPEC surplus, fed the investment boom in both the industrial nations and the Third World. It was an era of great expectations for economic development, as raw materials prices rose more sharply during an eighteen-month period between 1972 and 1974 than during any previous time of such duration over the past two hundred years.[3] The rise in oil prices, of course, was responsible for a large part, but not for all, of this increase. In contrast, until the late 1960s the price ratio between food, energy, and manufactured goods was stable. Prices of manufactured goods led the rise in the 1970s, increasing 3 percent in 1969, 5 percent in 1970, and up to 70 percent by 1975. These rises were followed by those in the price of wheat and oil. Basic materials and fuels, on the average, accounted for 20 percent of the manufacturing cost.

World trade expanded greatly. Between 1972 and 1974 an enormous credit expansion and business demand competed for labor, materials, and capital goods. The tremendous hoarding that pushed prices of commodities to record levels fed the expectations of producers and led to overexpansion and overstocking, preparing the way for a classic overproduction crisis.

The huge accretion of industrial capacity constructed over the preceding decade, and particularly in 1972–74, became an obvious check on further investment. Aggregate investment outlay for the OECD nations as a whole shifted from plus 7.1 percent in 1973 to minus 4.6 percent in 1974.

The expectation of a probable fall in prices with the end of "shortage" was also an incentive to postpone new orders, exactly as earlier expectations of rising prices and fears of scarcity had stimulated hysterical buying and pushed prices higher. Reductions in inventories led to cutbacks in the investment plans that had emerged with the earlier heavy demand.

The massive liquidation of inventories throughout the industrial capitalist states continued through 1975, accompanied by the cancellation of orders. The general collapse of demand directly influenced world trade, the leading industries, development in the Third World (including the OPEC nations), and the deepening recession. There was a domino effect across the international economy, shaping internal political activity and relations between states.

An important dimension of the emerging crisis was the synchronization by 1973 of the business cycle in the industrial nations, the first since the Great Depression. Cycles before the 1930s had been less severe, in large part because they were not synchronized on a world scale. An " 'all-systems go' in many countries simultaneously was the most important mishap in recent economic policy history," concluded the OECD McCracken group on the origins of the crisis.[4]

During 1974–75, governments and capital alike (and even many on the left who denied the existence of crisis) perceived the recession merely as part of a cycle, if more severe and universal. But undermining the calculations of all the capitalist governments was the reality that capital investment never materialized in any of the industrial countries sufficiently to renew the expansion of the economy and end the crisis. Such investment as existed was for the rationalization of industry and for certain exports to the LDCs, OPEC, and the CPEs where there *was* an investment boom, but these moves contained the seeds of new dilemmas. And, supposedly, the government expenditure could sustain the economy only at the cost of higher inflation. Equally alarming was the fact that inflation remained embedded in the system despite the recession and high and rising unemployment.

In July 1974 the OECD governments abandoned negotiations to reestablish comprehensive monetary rules. The members of the IMF could only struggle with a few compromises essentially unsatisfactory to all and aggravate the chaotic condition of international monetary affairs. The monetary authorities in the capitalist states soon became aware that there would be crisis both with and without a formal mone-

tary system, with floats and without. The inability to devise a long-run
solution only heightened their struggle in the short run, since these
questions touched directly on employment, trade, and profits. Monetary
affairs and the movement of capital were objectively outside the control
of states. And foreign-exchange fluctuations are dominated by the capital markets, not, as formerly, by trade. These financial links convey
economic problems from one country to another. Capitalists channeled
liquid capital into financial speculation and other forms of nonproductive investment.

In November 1975 the heads of state of six principal countries in
the industrial world met for their first economic summit to try to reverse
the developing crisis. Since economic realities were beyond diplomacy,
they could only restate their positions and utter some platitudes for
their respective populations in what they frankly declared to be an
exercise in confidence building. The meeting, in fact, reflected their
anxiety that their individual efforts would fail but that at the same time
it was impossible for them to proceed in anything but a national direction. These meetings became an annual tradition, and their significance
remained the same.

While planning for the post–World War II period, government officials had shown great concern about a new depression. No similar
policy alarm existed in the 1970s. Inflation was the focus, and in the
effort to eradicate it, prolonged stagnation, high unemployment, and
austerity were acceptable. Governments increasingly perceived rising
labor costs—undermining profitability, competitiveness, and investment incentives—as the primary cause of the world crisis.

There was also general agreement in the OECD governments and
among economists that one of the principal long-term structural
changes since 1968 was a new international division of labor. The rapid
move of industrial capacity—first by the corporations seeking cheap
labor for the production of consumer goods, and then producer goods,
and subsequently the growth of the state-capitalist sector in the Third
World, effectively competing with the OECD countries' industries in
steel, shipbuilding, mining, forestry, petrochemicals, and, increasingly,
engineering and construction—had structurally transformed the world
economy. Yet these very industries had been expanded only a few years
earlier in the industrial nations in response to a different economic
perception of the Vietnam-War-generated growth of the late 1960s and
early 1970s. This myopia is a systemic feature of the capitalist accumulation process. Competition requires rapid decision making, and the
processes of both expansion and contraction are characterized by a
herdlike response. The industries all entered the world market just as

it contracted. In 1974 each government hoped, because of its payments crisis, to expand exports and reduce imports, as the ultimate means to reactivate its economy. The depression in industrial sectors that emerged in the OECD states from this new competition persisted into the years of "recovery" of the general economy.

DYNAMICS OF THE OIL CRISIS

The oil crisis that emerged with the October 1973 war in the Middle East evolved into a kaleidoscopic series of intersecting forces and aims. Crucial to the bargaining position of OPEC was the general environment of world economic expansion, but, to repeat, its moves only accelerated a process already under way.

The terms of trade for the OPEC states, despite the rise in oil prices, meant that a 75 percent increase in the cost of imports brought only a 40 percent increase in the volume of imported goods. This affected the various members differently, but the grandiose development plans of even the richest began to suffer. The sharp reductions had an effect on those industries anticipating massive orders. By mid-1975 undercutting among the members and production cuts had begun. By the autumn of 1975 Algeria and Iraq had borrowed $1 billion from the Eurobanks. Meanwhile, the development of oil, from the North Sea to Mexico and from China to India, continued.

While OPEC and the rising price of oil did not cause the crisis, a number of structural conditions emerged from the radical change in energy costs: the new liquidity available to the banks, the importing countries' urgent need for foreign exchange to pay for oil, the new demand for industrial plant construction and the expansion of competitive capacity, and the necessity for economies built since World War II on low-cost energy to make a structural shift toward conservation or new sources of energy.

The sharp downturn in the world capitalist economy in mid-1974 hit the nonindustrial states unevenly. After the record rise in the preceding two years, those with raw-materials exports, with the exception of oil, watched the fall in price and volume in 1974–75. At the same time, they were forced to sustain their essential imports of industrial goods and petroleum, whose prices continued to rise despite the recession. The mounting costs of such imports as grains, steel, chemicals, and fertilizer were as important as those of oil in devastating their terms of trade, since the recession caused a decline in both the price and the volume of their exports, particularly commodities.

Yet in a number of the developing countries growth accelerated, primarily as a result of government policy and the recession in the

OECD states. In Asia the aggregate growth figures of 1975–77 exceeded those of 1967–72. Expecting a rapid return to precrisis conditions in the world economy, and actively wooed by banks and other supplier credits from the depressed industrial countries, these LDCs saw fixed investment rise, although they suffered sharp declines in their terms of trade and export earnings. These investments were made possible by foreign borrowing and by a reduction of reserves. This pattern was again evident in the oil-exporting countries, particularly in Mexico, after 1979.

Also with the recession, the continuing trade was channeled to the cheapest source. While world trade contracted, that of some LDCs thus expanded, as their production filled the more limited market.

DEBT

The reality of debt and deficit fueled the international economic expansion but at the same time sharply restricted it. The conditions that existed when the commercial banks began lending to the LDCs in 1974 seemed profitable and relatively prudent for both borrower and lender. A UN study observed in retrospect that "the large increase in the external indebtedness of many countries during the period 1974–1975 was predicated on a speedy return to the buoyant conditions prevailing earlier in the decade."[5]

It is useful to review some of the developments that led to this now well-known condition. In the two decades preceding the 1970s, loans were primarily suppliers' credits and official government loans to the LDCs. Debt service did become an increasing problem for a growing number of countries, bringing about a rescheduling of defaulted debt and usually a change in government by means of a military coup and the direction of the internal economy by the IMF. There was little private-bank lending to the LDCs. In 1971, bank loans accounted for only 13 percent of LDC debt, whereas concessional loans made up over one-third and export credits 25 percent. In 1972–73 the banks aggressively competed for borrowers in high-risk, long-term loans at low interest. The loans financed everything from gangsters to development projects based on the prospect of continued expansion. While oil and other import prices rose, lending in 1974 was increasingly for balance-of-payments (BOP) support as the terms of trade worsened radically. Those nations with a choice preferred to maintain growth and avoid the IMF, with its surveillance and deflationary restrictions. Debt problems became most serious for the richer LDCs. In fact, it must be remembered that nearly all the generalizations on the LDC debt crisis described only eight to twelve countries since the banks did not lend to the poorest countries. Ambitious development strategies were, in part, a response to the availability of cheap credits. Amid high inflation and low interest rates and expectations of continued growth, borrowing appeared nearly cost free, especially for the countries with high growth rates, among them Brazil, Mexico, and Argentina. The rate of growth of their exports was as high as that of their debt in the period 1975–80. But the debt served increasingly to finance their balance of payments and capital flight and, eventually, loans for the repayment of loans.

The debt has been a crucial weapon in the imperialist attempt to secure management control over internal economic policies. The IMF's role in the economic policy of the Third World increased as the debt grew. Its intervention, linking BOP support to economic austerity programs, termed "adjustment," was supervised by its well-paid technicians, who expressed an ideological consensus with a religious fervor. And although over the years it became increasingly clear that, short of a Pinochet-type regime, the political and social costs of the IMF shock economic policies were higher than many governments could sustain, the policy demands never wavered (with the exception of those instances in which the United States considered its security interests at stake). In order to avoid the conditions the fund imposed on the granting of credits, those nations deemed "creditworthy" turned to the commercial banks.

Internationally, debt tended to counter the crisis and at the same time to contribute to it. Budget deficits prevented a depression in 1975, and they also prevented a more than short-range recovery. But the whole problem of debt in the 1970s pales beside the monster that emerged in the 1980s.

1976–1979 RECOVERY

The new environment of economic recovery was marked by the unprecedented combination of inflation and recession, or stagnation, that added new confusion to state policy decisions; by slow growth and continued sectoral depression in the OECD; by historically high and growing unemployment; by the vast expansion of a world debt and credit structure that changed in qualitative terms with the immense increase in quantity; by changes in the structure of world production and trade; by new imperialist relations; by a further integration of the CPEs into the world capitalist economy; by the shifting monetary relations serving as a catalyst within the system; and by a general economic policy orientation and consensus among government officials and economists that reversed that of the preceding thirty years.

Since corporate demand for loans continued to be low in 1975, most

of the banks lent to governments and government institutions throughout the world. Demand was heavy, as a result of the impact the past
boom and then depressed conditions had on their BOP. There was also
an increasing demand from the OPEC countries, supposedly the source
of the world's liquidity. The CPEs of Europe began to borrow in the
Eurocredit markets on a large scale and on advantageous terms once
the banks chose to regard the USSR as the lender of last resort. In
addition, government and suppliers' credits to nations grew over the
year and became an aspect of the intensifying trade competition.

TRADE

Engineering and construction firms as well as the capital goods
industries, bereft of orders in the industrial capitalist countries, built
the most modern plants in the LDCs and the CPEs. Even when they
were reluctant to do so, competition from others willing to sell turnkey
plants compelled them to participate. So, in essence, competition forced
the construction of new competitive capacity in one basic industry after
another. This vast overcapacity, a major inhibition to capital investment in the OECD countries, only further deepened the economic
dilemmas, since the existing or anticipated market could not absorb this
production, given the contraction of markets through austerity policies
everywhere.

World trade, after contracting 10 percent in 1975, expanded 11
percent in 1976. For the OECD countries, imports grew more than
exports, although they all hoped to rely on exports in order to emerge
from their economic crisis. Trade, rather than domestic production, met
the limited demand in the world economy until it began to generate
political opposition and protectionist measures in one market after the
other. As stagnation worsened in such countries as Japan and the
Federal Republic of Germany (FRG), their only strength was in their
export sector. Their own economies were too weak to absorb the production. German exports reflected a few massive orders from Brazil and
OPEC's extravagant development projects. These specialized expensive
items, later curtailed, showed on the trade balance but did little to
stimulate the internal economy. Japan's exports provided low-cost competition in Europe, driving a number of hard-pressed industries like
steel, ball bearings, and shipbuilding to the wall. This was a new
development, which became increasingly important in the following
years. Except in the field of textiles, the Americans and Europeans did
not perceive Japan as a competitor until the late 1960s.

With the recession and inflation in the industrial economies, low-cost
imports of Third World textiles and apparel soared. Between 1972 and

1976 the EEC moved from net exporter to net importer of textiles at a cost of 500,000 jobs, or one-fifth of the total. And the imports swiftly included other consumer goods and then capital goods. The market was shrinking, and relative shares of that market were shifting.

POLICY RESPONSE

The European governments and Japan passed first through policies of individual and then through coordinated programs of expansion, but reduced revenues and higher outlays for unemployment compensation led quickly to higher budget deficits and an objective restraint on expansionary policies. By June 1976 the OECD governments had opted for an economic strategy of "slow growth."

Each set of policies fell victim to its own contradictions. "[B]y the time appropriate policies had been agreed to and acted on, the underlying situation had changed [and] official actions provided reinforcement to new destabilizing tendencies," concluded one UN study.[6]

Equally important, the recovery in 1976 was characterized by a wide variation by sector, high unemployment, inflation, and a low rate of capacity utilization. There were "very few acts of overt reflation" in 1976.[7] That year the European CPEs "scaled down" their national plans because of the "unfavorable external economic environment."[8]

The crisis elicited no shortage of proposed solutions within the framework of bourgeois economics. Their authors ranged from those who advocated the traditional tinkerings with fiscal and monetary policies of the monetarist or Keynesian variety to those who recognized that the new structural problems resisted this type of policy manipulation and who suggested allowing economic market forces to operate to attain a new equilibrium between capital and labor. Others, in response to what they saw as the "structural recessions or depressions" afflicting the industrialized nations, outcomes of the new international division of labor, proposed some type of a state industrial policy. Some advocated a combination of these proposals.

The OECD governments faced several policy alternatives within their system: (1) the vacillating response to pressures from special interests and traditional countercyclical fiscal and monetary measures; (2) protection of threatened industries with subsidies and tariffs, leading to an intensification of trade war; or (3) a state-sponsored development of new products in high technology to compete better in the new international division of labor, supposedly prevented by "rigidities" in the industrial economies. The latter option called for, among other policies, the phasing out of the noncompetitive industries; this involved bankruptcies and increased unemployment. At the same time the

OECD governments supported with guarantees and credits their industries' exporting turnkey plants to build new competition, further contributing to the redundancy of important sectors of their own economies.

There was a growing consensus among OECD governments that they should aid this natural selection by eliminating state subsidies, simultaneously reducing budget deficits and, they hoped, inflation. They would also assist in the rationalization of industry, in order to increase its competitiveness. Above all, however, the state would "restructure" the economy by shifting the national income away from labor and back to capital in order to renew investment incentives.

This strategy was scarcely new. One of the principal founding goals of the EEC was to rationalize European industry through competition and the "survival of the fittest," but the plan was never implemented with the rigor its proponents wanted. Since strong vested interests were involved, efforts at rationalization took precedence over the free operation of market forces. But, unfortunately for the industrial capitalist nations, the structure of the world's industrial capacity had by the 1970s changed significantly, far beyond their control or influence.

To counteract inflation, the OECD governments adopted austerity measures. At the end of 1976 France introduced an austerity program, initially planned to last three years, but in 1978 its prime minister said that restructuring the French economy would require a further "ten-year effort for France to stay abreast of international conditions."[9]

In the United States the "recovery" from 1976 to 1980 never came near to ending the economic crisis, although it lasted longer than any since 1933–37, the other "recovery" in a period of acknowledged world crisis. Significantly, they were the only peacetime expansions since 1834 that rivaled wartime expansions. It has been demonstrated that though the fall in production and employment was steeper in the 1930s, the "recovery" was more vigorous than that of the 1970s. The latter recovery could be so termed only in general aggregates, and such averages say little about the real condition of the economy. Important sectors remained mired in severe depression, so that while the recession ended in 1975, economic crisis continued throughout the 1970s and into the 1980s. As one German economist for the Dresdner Bank observed during the recession, "It would be folly to view the current malaise as just a typical cycle. Our problems are more deeply rooted. . . ."[10]

As the objective developments in the political economy shaped the environment, there was a congruence with the ideological and subjective strategies. Although during the recession of 1974–75 there was no real unanimity on the cause and cure of the crisis, by 1976, during the "recovery," the persistence of a high rate of inflation alongside growing unemployment and investment stagnation had produced a consensus among the bourgeois economists, the men of power in the industrial states, and such international organizations as the IMF and World Bank.

The question of what went wrong led to the formation of many prestigious review committees. It was essential to pinpoint an answer in order to orient the policy response. There was wide agreement that the OECD economies had peaked in the mid-1960s and declined since then and that the crisis was not cyclical but structural. The rise in oil prices only exacerbated a long-term "growth crisis" that began in the late 1960s. The 1970s, in their view, marked a new turning point in the world economy.

While some economists used the term *structural* to apply to the most marginal and irrelevant aspects, such as baby booms (at one moment heralding prosperity; at another, depression), others focused on more real and serious structural problems, such as a *perceived* redistribution of national income away from capital to labor and from profits to wages. Other elements the economists considered important were the end of the process of reconstruction after World War II; the rise in the cost of raw materials, especially energy; inflation; the decline in productivity; the new international division of labor, leading to permanent structural depressions in certain industries that would not respond to recovery in the business cycle; and new developments in science and technology. All these factors, they concluded, created an irreversible shift that would require massive economic, political, and social readjustments, a long-term restructuring of the entire world economy.

The whole concept of restructuring really gathered force after the recession and during the recovery of 1976–80, when the world economy passed into the period of slow growth and stagflation. A new vocabulary emerged to define the illness, the prognosis, and the prescription—*rigidities, imperfections, adjustment, restructure.* [11] And such euphemisms were rapidly translated into policies aimed directly at the working classes in every region of the world.

Within their worldview, the capitalists, as always, perceived the crisis, above all, in the relations of production. Restructuring was essentially one more offensive in the class struggle to alter the *perceived* shift in class relations and shares in the national incomes that was held accountable for inflation, low investment, falling productivity, loss of competitive position, and, finally, unemployment itself.

A shift in the income shares as a prelude to crisis and an emphasis on the primacy of the relations of production is not merely a bourgeois interpretation, of course. Marx asserted, "Crises are always prepared by precisely a period in which wages rise generally and the working class actually gets a larger share of that part of the annual product which is intended for consumption."[12] While the *potential* crisis exists in the chronic underconsumption of the masses—a "tautology" of capitalism—the *immediate* crisis is perceived in shifts away from profit and the costs of and relations with labor. Its resolution is not open to reform, since it cuts into the raison d'être of the system. What is new in the postwar period is the synchronization of these developments on a global scale and the integrated response in many nations.

Monetarist views and "supply side" concepts emerged in the United States more forcefully in 1976, as economists noted that Keynes's ideas were inadequate for dealing with the current problems, particularly with inflation. Governments, they asserted, must try to increase the supply of resources and the factors of production—that is, of capital—through greater incentives and tax concessions, and to decrease the cost of labor by lowering wages and enlarging the reserve of unemployed. High inflation and persistent crisis allowed the monetarists in the universities to supersede the Keynesians as advisers to the men of power.

The bourgeois economists pass from the simple cyclical interpretation and turn to the more profound structural problems, but they cannot go beyond that position and focus on the nature of the system itself. This fundamental limitation keeps them from predicting accurately or understanding the operations of their economic order. Yet the systemic features of capitalism make irrelevant their effort to plan, alter, reform, or resolve this crisis in the system.

Capitalists, on the other hand, respond to their perception of profitability. During the recovery in the last years of the 1970s, capital investment either built new industrial capacity outside the OECD countries, rationalized existing capacity with labor- or energy-saving equipment, shuffled assets with mergers and acquisitions, or expanded in the service sector. During 1979 there was a boom in the oil supply industry; in the new environment, however, those with capital increasingly preferred to use it for speculation rather than for productive investment.

INFLATION

By 1976 "most governments tended to regard inflation as a graver threat to the economy than unemployment," reported the UN survey for 1975.[13] One IMF study held that "a short-term emphasis on growth and employment objectives" characterized the 1950s and 1960s, when inflation averaged 3.5 percent. It then attributed the inflation of the 1970s to the "achievement and maintenance of unduly low unemployment rates."[14] In other words, inflation to the bourgeois economist was equivalent to rising labor costs. The era of Keynesian "fine-tuning" of the economy was perceived as having failed to prevent an economic crisis marked by inflation. The Keynesian stricture that full employment was possible through government spending became an assumption both that full employment could and should no longer be the aim of government and that government spending, in turn, depended on full employment for tax revenue.

In fact, it was not Keynesian policies but war that accounted for the economic conditions of the 1950s and 1960s, just as it subsequently did for the inflation of the 1970s. Nor did the official economists notice the other primary causes of inflation, such as the administered prices and profits of the concentrated industries, or the effect of capital movements on exchange rates. Most analyses focused on the influence of inflation and other "fundamentals" in determining exchange rates. They tended to ignore the influence of the exchange rates on inflation. Rising wages at the end of the 1960s patently reflected an effort to catch up to inflation; they were not its origin. Even the OECD's McCracken group noted that "the synchronized wage explosions and labor market unrest" in 1968–69 were due to "the prior lag in growth of real disposable incomes," yet it then went on to lay the responsibility for inflation on labor.[15] In 1979 the introduction of a value-added tax (VAT) contributed 4 percent to inflation in Britain and 1 percent to that in the FRG. But all capitalist governments chose, in essence, to define inflation as higher labor costs. Ideology and interests, not economic reality, shaped their responses.

Unquestionably, the system could not endure such prolonged and unprecedented international inflation, with its rapid corrosion of social relations as it liquidated debt, reduced real income, impoverished those on fixed incomes, destabilized commercial relations, destroyed confidence in money, undermined investment, and the like. Internationally, there emerged an ideological consensus to put the economy "through the wringer" in order to squeeze inflation out of the system. But capitalism had only one medicine for the inflation virus. Lowering inflation invariably meant squeezing the working class—this was the simple logic behind "wage restraints" and "acceptable minimum" unemployment strategies—and led to the effort to re-create the reserve army of unemployed in the industrial capitalist nations. Finally, pushed to the extreme, it contributed to its success. Inflation receded in the 1980s in this context.

Inflation spreads in only one direction—from the industrial countries outward. Inflation in 1979 in the LDCs had its origin in the industrial nations but was transformed into a much higher rate, being over 20 percent for the majority and hyperinflation for many. Devaluation, usually under external IMF pressure, created higher import prices, pushing inflation even beyond the already inflated import costs.

The recovery in the OECD countries weakened further in 1977, when growth averaged 3.7 percent, compared with 5.2 percent in 1976, and France, the FRG, and Italy had "mini-recessions."[16] This "growth depression" in 1977 "took policy-makers by surprise."[17] And while there was an increasing consensus on a general policy stance, as slow growth threatened to become permanent, both the United States and the OECD in 1977 urged expansionary policies on the FRG and Japan, two nations with relatively low inflation and unemployment, to be the "locomotives" of recovery. The U.S. treasury secretary insisted that these two countries shift their surplus to deficits.[18] Both states set cautious limits on their efforts. Prospects for each depended on external developments, and there was "widespread uncertainty and unease . . . [over] the sluggishness in trade, the exchange instability, the drift toward protectionism," and the high levels of unemployment and underutilization of industrial capacity in the world economy in 1978.[19] Whereas previous recoveries had brought prolonged investment, now no country in the OECD sustained it.

The dollar had been stable in 1976 vis-à-vis the currencies of America's trading partners, but it began to depreciate sharply in mid-1977, as the U.S. monetary policy turned to "talk down the dollar" for trade advantage. In the economic environment of the time, not much effort was required. The money traders unloaded the dollar, which fell 10–20 percent against the leading currencies by the end of the year, while the European and Japanese central banks spent $35 billion to support it in the money markets. In 1978, borrowers moved to prepay their loans and refinance on better terms.

New protectionist techniques emerged in the the industrial capitalist countries in 1978, and there was a consequent deterioration in the trade balance of fifty-two of the sixty-two LDCs. As the size of their deficit grew, so did their indebtedness to, increasingly, the commercial banks.

The slowing growth was centered in the United States in 1978 and spread to the European economies in the second half of 1979, primarily as a result of austerity policies to deal with inflation and the second oil "shock" after the revolution in Iran. Budget deficits worsened as interest rates rose and debt service consumed an ever larger share of the national budget. This reinforced austerity policies. The state has the ability to postpone the day of reckoning by multiplying credit and deficits. But only the United States, whose currency, despite its ups and downs, is the reserve currency acceptable as the medium of international trade, has the privilege of avoiding a final accounting. Inevitably, the fiscal crisis sets a limit to the nation's ability to regenerate the economy. Nevertheless, it can be demonstrated that the enormous deficits prevented the whole economy from sinking into a depression comparable to that of the 1930s.

By 1978 the European governments were beginning to retreat from part of their direct role in the economy. The emerging new lexicon included *denationalization,* and *positive adjustment policies,* which translated into adjustment to high energy costs and a new international division of labor through the elimination of subsidies for noncompetitive industries and a general cutback on social expenditures. The monetarists had attained new credibility with the continued inflation and the fiscal crisis. But while these were their ambitions, the economy showed more prosaic struggles of specific interests, as individual thrusts toward accumulation, albeit in nonproductive forms, and competition in trade objectively altered the economy.

Crucial to the strategy of resolving the structural crisis in the capitalist economies was an effort at a "harmonization" of economic policies among its members, although there was no real possibility of a formal arrangement to accomplish this—apart from the lender's leverage, increasingly exerted by the IMF.

The FRG had been the principal advocate of the deflationary "harmonization" policies in Europe during the last years of the 1970s. The European Monetary System was a part of this much broader strategy to squeeze inflation out of the economies by acquiring increased leverage over national economic decision making. (It was also intended as a response to the American monetary policies.) For many years successive governments in Bonn had rather smugly attributed the FRG's "correct" economic policies to its low inflation rates and surplus in trade and payments. From the time of the "social market" policies of Ludwig Erhard, which got the credit for the German economic miracle in the 1950s, to that of the "island of stability" of the central banker Otmar Emminger, they urged other nations to adopt identical policies. Yet, in reality, the German economic condition has always depended on external factors quite beyond the control of its government policies.

Although self-righteous in dealing with foreigners, the Bonn government was concerned over its internal structural problems of virtual stagnation, which it attributed to the lack of investment in the economy. In defining the origin of the lag, economists focused on a perceived shift in the distribution of the national income between capital and labor. The figures purported to show that the share of profits in the FRG fell from 37.5 percent to 34.8 percent between 1970 and 1977, while the wage share grew from 62.7 percent to 65.2 percent. The profit margin purportedly fell nearly 50 percent in the same period. The government aimed to redistribute this income once again through fiscal measures and "wage restraints." Eventually, they asserted, the traditional, if primitive, formula of "high profits = investment = employment" will resolve the crisis. Meanwhile, the state must encourage "restructuring" in the economy—in favor of new industries, high technology, and the service economy—with wage restraints and a large reserve army of unemployed to help until a new equilibrium between capital and labor is established. Adjustments of this sort are not accomplished quickly, officials assured each other. They will take many difficult years.

Monetarism and high interest rates were the policy tools of most of the industrial countries as inflation mounted and the terms of trade deteriorated. The conservative policies first affected output and unemployment rather than prices. Wages in the OECD countries, on the whole, rose less than prices, and workers took real-income losses; but unit labor costs rose as productivity fell, particularly in the United States, where it dropped by 1.0–1.5 percent in 1979. (Such aggregates give a very misleading picture, as I will discuss later. But the perception was important for policy.) Profits, on the other hand, rose. But, in an inflationary environment, the required rate of profit had to be correspondingly higher to attract investment. The first to implement the rigid monetarist policies was the Thatcher government in Britain. Committed to getting the government out of the economy, the process of a draconian reduction of state expenditures and denationalization began in 1980. Within two and a half years inflation was reduced from 20.0 percent to 5.5 percent, production had fallen 7 percent, and unemployment had risen to 13 percent.

The 1970s brought an "uninterrupted decline" in growth rates for all the country groups—OECD, LDCs, and CPEs—according to a UN study.[20] The slowing growth rates in the CPEs could, in part, be attributed to their greater integration into the world capitalist market. But there were important exceptions. Poland's growth rate in 1975 was 10 percent.

In 1979 the European CPEs experienced the lowest rate of growth since World War II—less than 2 percent—and a sharp deterioration in their terms of trade. In 1980 there was a continued aggregate slowing in the CPE economies and an outright decline in Poland and Hungary. In Poland labor struggles accounted for the fall, of course, and in Hungary it was a deliberate policy to reduce the external deficit. Both situations had a negative impact on their trading partners in the CPEs' trading bloc, Comecon.

OIL: THE SECOND SHOCK

As the revolution in Iran gave OPEC the leverage to raise the price of oil again and to produce the second oil shock of the decade, petroleum prices rose 130 percent between 1978 and 1980. As was wholly predictable, but rarely predicted, these rising prices led to intense exploration efforts everywhere, increasing the supply at a time of a contracting world market. The extravagant prognostications of scarcity made on the basis of the new structural conditions of rising prices led to development plans that exceeded income. With oil reserves as collateral, the exporting countries borrowed to industrialize their economies or for other purposes. Eventually, as we all know, they borrowed to repay debt already incurred. Raw-materials prices began to rise toward the end of 1978, doing so in tandem with oil prices through 1979, as did the world prices of food. Much of the pressure on the price of gold, which rose $250 in six weeks, came from petrodollars following the 1979 rise in the price of oil, as the dollar reached new lows against the German mark and Swiss franc. The new price of oil also stimulated an investment fever among the oil industry's equipment suppliers, eagerly financed by the banks.

IMPACT ON LDCS

The oil shock had the greatest impact on the LDCs. On the average, oil accounted for 63 percent of the energy needs in the 1970s, but for many countries in Southeast Asia and Africa it was 90 percent. World Bank energy loans had been tilted toward oil consumption. For the OECD countries, by contrast, it amounted to 53 percent in 1973 and was substantially reduced over the following decade. Coupled with the new direction of the dollar and the soaring interest rates, BOP deficits forced various governments to take steps to curb imports, impose a ban on certain goods, curtail nonessential imports, limit import licenses, increase tariffs and import deposits, and, sometimes, devalue the currency.

The year 1979 was a turning point, albeit a temporary one, for the IMF/World Bank. With the new rise in oil prices and the turn to positive real interest rates, the IMF staff judged the BOP deficits of the

LDCs to be structural in nature, meaning in this case that the cause was external and beyond their control. Their lending programs were lengthened to three years and the World Bank loan maturities to seven to ten years. In 1981 the fund lent $15 billion, nearly four times as much as in 1979. Two-thirds of the commitment went to sub-Saharan Africa and "poor" Asia. Under pressure in 1980, the IMF set a floor to austerity programs to prevent growth from falling below 3 percent. It had previously squeezed the rates to 1 percent. The World Bank, in its 1980 report, considered growth for the oil-importing LDCs "unacceptably low." Their energy bill had more than doubled since 1978. It then went on frivolously to assert that faster growth "depends heavily on economic management" requiring "efforts to increase exports and investments."[21]

The evolution of the economic crisis in the 1970s had a polarizing effect on various countries in the Third World. The very desperation of their collective position at first reinforced a certain political solidarity vis-à-vis the industrial countries, particularly the United States. From this emerged the demands for a new economic order to alleviate what most saw as the cause of their crisis—namely, their relationship with the industrial countries. The success of OPEC was crucial in this development. At the same time, since substantial bank loans were available principally to twelve of the non-OPEC developing countries, their deepening economic difficulties tended to pull them apart as they competed for the various sources of capital. Most of the economic demands of the Third World bloc at this time—for changes in the terms of trade, indexing of the price of commodities to those of industrial products, price supports and buffer stocks, and a moratorium on debt payments—were impossible to achieve on a multinational, negotiated basis, given the chaotic and unplanned nature of the capitalist market economy.

Since in addition to some modernizing, socially progressive countries, the so-called Third World comprises nations organized on the same class lines as the industrial states and frequently having a more reactionary and repressive character, only the ruling clique would benefit from a redistribution of the world's wealth among nations, even if the realization of such a utopian scheme were possible within the capitalist system. But these countries all share the immensely negative impact of the economic crisis on either their development plans or their profits.

There was also a swift transformation of Third World ideologies and policies under the impact of the objective development of the crisis. North–South confrontations that emerged with the power of OPEC and the strong demand for their export commodities gave way to the IMF-managed debt economies and a trend toward the "privatization" of state industries, and the aspirations and goals of the new nations receded. The escalating demands of the developing countries on the TNCs in the early 1970s also gave way to an intense competition for the limited investment capital, with offers of cheap labor and other costly incentives. In 1977 there took place the last meeting of the Group of 77 that called for controls on the TNCs. Thereafter the competition to attract capital in any form prevailed.[22]

The gigantic projects, funded with the oil revenues in the Middle East, to build the processing industries, awesome military establishments, nuclear facilities, and the like served to nourish the various construction industries in the OECD and further expanded world industrial capacity for the world market, since many of the facilities could be used only for export. The labor shortages in many of these countries set in motion a form of labor recruiting and migration that had a far-reaching effect. But the ambitions were beyond the capacity of many regimes. Many plans for huge projects were abandoned in Indonesia, Iran, Nigeria, Zaire, and other countries. As has been evident for many years, prestige projects that are not integrated into a progressive development plan are merely waste projects. This is, of course, not unique to the LDCs, as the vast abandoned projects in the OECD states prove. It is only that the LDC economies can afford the waste the least.

In other cases, the new industries, incorporating the latest technology, became potent competitors in the international market. The new nomenclature was extended to include the category of newly industrializing countries (NICs).

This new competition was not merely a threat to the industrial states' internal market, which each nation can and will ultimately protect; it is also a threat to their former export markets, especially for those countries heavily dependent on exports. State subsidies to offset higher costs on imports into the United States meet countervailing duties, again giving the advantage to the lowest-cost producer. One instance of the problem is in Sweden, where unemployment is low because of the government subsidies for threatened industries. Nevertheless, new competition made inalterable changes in its trade patterns. For example, Sweden's Arctic iron mines, once the largest in the world, had set European prices. By the end of the 1970s Brazil, where labor costs were only one-fifth as high, was doing so for Europe. Sweden tried to compete with mechanization and increased subsidies, but it could not regain its former role. In many basic industries throughout Europe, the same problem emerged. The conclusion increasingly drawn was that these industries suffered from "structural depression" and would not recover with the so-called cyclical recovery.

OECD trade was sustained in the first half of the 1970s not by its traditional partners but rather by the CPEs and OPEC, with whom there was a 50 percent expansion in the aggregate, usually financed by state export credits, and where it built the capacity and competition that later plagued the OECD industries. But the exceptional demand from the CPEs and OPEC for manufactured-goods exports from the OECD ended in 1979, at which time China became an important factor in world trade, as its imports increased nearly 50 percent, to $5 billion.

The centrally planned economies of Europe had also hoped during the 1970s that the congruence of circumstances in the market economies held out prospects for their own economic development through the international division of labor, as they perceived it. In their eagerness, they overlooked the fact that the mere opening to the east was the outcome of the evolving crisis in the capitalist world market. By orienting their internal development to a changing world capitalist market, they became increasingly vulnerable to its crisis features, as they distorted their own internal economy.

During the 1976–80 "recovery" in the context of a continuing crisis, there emerged a new consensus among various governments to restructure the world economy and its various segments. The congruence of the objective factors, both systemic and structural, with the always present, conservative capitalist designs was to establish the economic condition for the 1980s.

CHAPTER 2

THE 1980s

Politically, the 1980s saw major changes in Europe and the United States. As 1980 began, the United States expanded its military spending, ostensibly in response to the Sandinista victory in Nicaragua, the events in Iran, and the Soviet intervention in Afghanistan. This pushed its budget deficit to $40 billion, awesome at the time, though slight compared with the deficits of subsequent years. Socialists became the governing party in France, Spain, Italy, and Greece, promising full employment and income redistribution and creating expectations of significant political and economic change. In the United Kingdom and the United States, the Right emerged with a determination to reduce the state's role in the economy and to allow market forces to operate unhindered. Policies and ideology differed, but in all of these nations the implementation of such programs soon confronted boundaries imposed by the integration of the world economy.

MONETARY POLICY

An important turning point in the global economy that rested on a subjective policy innovation was the U.S. Federal Reserve Bank's October 1979 decision to increase interest rates sharply and, with them, the cost of loans and dollar-denominated commodities. The dollar had been overvalued in the 1960s and until the devaluation in 1971. It gyrated considerably in the 1970s but was largely undervalued until 1981. The Europeans, rejecting the ravaging effect of the undervalued American dollar, had in 1979 set up the European Monetary System under German sponsorship and with the intent of establishing uniform anti-

41

inflationary policies. At the IMF meeting in October 1979, they threatened that unless Paul Volcker, chairman of the Federal Reserve, acted on the falling dollar, they would retaliate and refuse to accept the dollar's special role in world monetary relations. The turnabout of the dollar's value was swift. Early in 1980 speculative capital continued to flee the dollar, driving the price of gold to record highs. But by March of that year billions were flowing out of the mark and back into the dollar.

This long-demanded reversal of U.S. monetary policy had wide and unanticipated repercussions. Sharp rises in nominal interest rates, part of the struggle against inflation, began in the United States in the end of 1979 and sparked an interest rate "war." By the spring of 1980 the U.S. discount rate was 16 percent, compared with that of 7 percent in the FRG and that of 9 percent in Japan. But the real interest rate did not exceed that prevailing in the FRG and Japan until mid-1981. By then the monetarist stance of the Federal Reserve had forced interest rates to 18 percent, and this interest attracted the dollars outside the United States into American investments. Gold and other currencies plunged, as did other commodities, inflation subsided, and a new recession created a glut in oil and lowered its price, bringing a host of new and interrelated problems in its wake.

Gresham's law prevails in the world economy. As the dollar's value increased, its velocity decreased as it was hoarded. And the "credit crunch," with higher interest rates and shorter maturities, began. And because the dollar is the world's reserve currency and the currency of trade and debt, its massive return to the United States compounded the problems of the earlier period and added many new ones.

1980–1982 RECESSION

The recession in the early 1980s, which began before there was a full recovery from the preceding one, was even more severe than that of 1974–75 and again brought major structural changes. The situation objectively emerged from the crisis of the 1970s, but it took a new political thrust in the 1980s. As all the capitalist nations gravitated toward essentially the same policies, the conservative ideology of capitalism, always present, achieved a uniformity after 1980 it had not had in the postwar era. In 1981, financial markets and trade spread the recession throughout the world. Interest rate pressures emanating from the United States affected capital flows, exchange rates, and the interest rate policies of other nations. Commodity prices in the early 1980s fell below those of any year since the 1950s. The recession began in the United States and moved within three months to Europe, where restrictive monetary policies were already in place. In the OECD countries unemployment rose faster in the 1980s than at any other time since the Great Depression; by 1982 there were twice as many unemployed as in 1975, and the range of occupations affected had broadened. Lower inflation accompanied by near stagnant economic growth followed the recession in the European Community.

INFLATION

Inflation in the OECD states, which the banks and industry had assumed would endure "forever," was finally reduced by draconian austerity policies, high unemployment, international competition, and the impact of the record-high value of the dollar. And then the consequences of disinflation or even deflation became a source of alarm. In the United States the fall in the inflation rate was due not just to increasing misery. The high interest rates, by attracting the world's capital, raised the value of the dollar; this, in turn, greatly increased American imports, whose exchange-determined low cost imposed a competitive restraint on the general level of domestic prices—in particular, those of raw materials and producer goods like steel as well as those of a range of consumer commodities, from clothing to electronics. In Britain, inflation was reduced by maintaining unemployment at over 13 percent and by other deflationary policies. In France, with a combination of controls, de-indexing wages from the general price level, and record high unemployment, the Socialists were able to reduce inflation by several points despite the weakness of the franc. In Europe, notwithstanding the depreciation of the currencies, the general fall of commodity prices was important to the decline in inflation. Crucial also was the de-indexation of wages throughout Europe and the depressing effect of the large reserve army of unemployed on income in general. Inflation was thus finally vulnerable to a combination of factors, including high and prolonged unemployment, vertiginous interest rates, recession, and, in the United States, the competition of imports with domestic products generated primarily by the strength of the dollar, since inflation declined in goods but not in services. But despite the governments' efforts, the major goal of restructuring income distribution had not been fully realized to their satisfaction; as the IMF concluded in its 1983 report: "the major shift . . . from capital to labor that took place in the late 1960s and early 1970s has not been fully reversed and remains an important factor accounting for low profitability and low investment."[1]

But the shift to lower inflation rates created new contradictions in the system. The significant structural shifts of falling oil prices and

general disinflation or deflation—long sought by the banks, corporations, and governments—introduced serious new challenges to their
interests as well. The loans predicated on infinitely rising energy prices
collapsed, causing multiple bankruptcies in the private sector and debt
crises for the oil-exporting countries. And the oil price fell enough to
create a crisis for the oil-exporting states but not enough to ease the
crisis for the importers.

Escalating interest rates aggravated the debt and the foreign-exchange emergencies of many nations. The capital outflow kept European rates high and investment lower. And because oil is priced in
dollars, the rising foreign-exchange burden to oil importers created the
third oil shock.

In December 1981 the Reagan administration had barred U.S. companies from bidding on the Soviet pipeline project, and in June 1982,
at a time when relations were already strained over many other economic issues, it denied U.S. technology to European companies under
contract to build the Soviet gas pipeline. The U.S. embargo backfired,
because it damaged American companies used to profitable licensing
agreements with foreign firms and because even the closest allies of the
United States resisted the blatant encroachment on their sovereignty
and, more important, on their economy. The technology ban was lifted
in November 1982, in return for a delay in subsidized credits, additional energy purchases, and transfers of certain high-tech items to the
USSR.

The cycle of shortage and surplus in production continued. Expansion of capacity based on the momentary perception led to overcapacity;
the high price of oil led to expansion and to glut; inflated real estate
prices led to overbuilding, then to contraction; high prices of food and
commodities resulted in overplanting and falling prices; and so on. In
response to such trends, during the recession of 1980–83 there was a
widespread reduction and destruction of capacity both by the state and
by private capital to lower "the break-even point" of major industries
and to achieve the same profit at lower capacity.

LDCs

For the LDCs the adjustment policies and capital flows contrasted
starkly with those of the mid-1970s, when there was a massive inflow
of OPEC-generated capital and an outflow of capital from the United
States.

The credit flow to non-oil-exporting LDCs in all currencies was
reduced from $30.5 billion in 1981 to less than $2.0 billion in 1983.
Two-thirds of their debt was denominated in dollars and one-half of that

at floating interest rates. By 1985 some 80 percent of the LDC debt was in dollars. Most LDCs experienced a fall in per capita income, and in the aggregate their gross domestic product (GDP) fell in 1982 for the first time in more than forty years. For the first five years of the decade the aggregate LDC growth was 2.5 percent, less than half that of the preceding twenty years. If the newly industrializing countries (NICs) of Asia are excluded, the figure is 0.5 percent a year. For the masses the 1980s were years of falling living standards, if not of outright famine. And in many areas the earlier option of migration was now closed. Such aggregate numbers, of course, hide a wide variety of experiences. The bleak prospects in most regions led a UN study to conclude in 1983 that even "gloom" was too optimistic.[2] The IMF commented on the "declines in real per-capita expenditure in the non-oil developing countries in both 1981 and 1982—an unprecedented development in the postwar period."[3]

Of special importance were the export development strategies that produced a race, particularly among Asian nations, to set up "free trade zones," one of the greatest deceptions of the entire "development" mythology. Such zones incurred great costs for the host countries in building an infrastructure to service them and brought only marginal employment gains; the countries soon learned that the component parts they produced for the TNCs could quickly and easily be relocated elsewhere. The models for this strategy were Singapore and Hong Kong. But their "success" cannot be imitated in this manner, since their initial "development" took place in a different, war-induced, booming economic environment. The later expansion of trade in a number of LDCs was the consequence of the dollar's temporary strength, which drew imports to the U.S. market and at the same time intensified protectionist pressures that will undermine their market in the future.

OIL

The speed of the change in the OPEC position over the first three years of the 1980s is striking. OPEC's surplus fell by three-fourths, as a decline of oil exports of 50 percent occurred between 1979 and 1983. The price declined 10 percent between 1981 and 1984 but was still 90 percent above the 1978 level. The share of oil in energy consumption in the OECD nations fell from 54 percent in 1973 to 45 percent in 1983, and absolute consumption declined 15 percent. In the oil-importing LDCs, by contrast, its share increased by 30 percent, although consumption declined in the recession of the early 1980s. By the end of 1985, OPEC officials admitted they could no longer control prices or output. Only Iraq's bombardment of Iran's export facilities had caused a rise in prices, however temporary. They had reason to fear a peace agreement in the Persian Gulf war since the war had caused a reduction of 2.5 million barrels per day in 1980, and spot prices rose to $40 a barrel in November of that year. The war in Iran and Iraq was beneficial to the trade of a number of arms exporters and kept the oil price from falling further. In other respects this massive slaughter drew little notice in the rest of the world.

By 1982 oil was being traded as an ordinary commodity and was no longer the monopoly of the big-seven oil companies or of OPEC. OPEC's share of the world capitalist market fell from 59 percent in 1979 to 45 percent in 1982 and to 35 percent in 1985. Non-OPEC producers were pumping more oil than OPEC for the first time in twenty years. OPEC managed for a time to stop the falling price, at $29 in 1983, by reducing production to one-half that of 1979. Falling oil prices presented a different threat to the European nations. In mid-1983 France and Britain informed OPEC that a drop in the price below $30 would be unwelcome and unwise. They feared that a lower price would sidetrack their effort to restructure their energy base to nuclear and coal. Their goal was a stable oil price, and they were prepared to impose new taxes on oil if the price fell too sharply. But thanks to the rising dollar, the falling oil price was scarcely felt by the importers. For this reason more and more barter arrangements were made in the 1980s.

By 1984 an open price war between OPEC and non-OPEC producers had begun. Even more detrimental to OPEC's interests was the growing struggle within the organization, as Nigeria joined the North Sea producers in price-cutting in 1985. At the end of that year OPEC dropped its minimum price. The need for capital pushed the producers into intense competition to produce optimally and sell at any price. "If OPEC oil went to $20 a barrel, it would be an out-and-out catastrophe," said Walter Levy, the industry's leading expert.[4] By 1980, costs to discover new reserves had risen to $15–$20 per barrel. In the early 1970s oil had sold at a profit for under $3 per barrel, and production costs in the Middle East were still under $1 per barrel. The ability of some, especially Saudi Arabia, to withstand a price war and eliminate the new competition was formidable.

DEBT

In the context of the renewed recession in 1982, the debt crisis exploded when Mexico was unable to meet its payments in August. Forty countries were in payment default by the end of that year.

The LDC debt, 66 percent of which had in 1971 been owed to official agencies but 70 percent of which was in 1981 owed to private banks, was predicated on a continuation of inflation. But in 1980 the conditions reversed for both borrower and lender. Falling inflation and an interest rate war, the outcome of domestic policy considerations, led to record high real interest rates on short-term or floating-rate debt, and this along with the deepening world recession created the debt disaster of the 1980s. For the commodity exporters there was a sharp drop in the terms of trade as well as in the volume. The new manufactured exports developed over the 1970s faced new protectionist barriers in the OECD countries. With the rise in real interest rates and the fall in prices for their principal exports, countries obviously could not increase foreign earnings at the rate of their growing debt service. In 1983 there emerged the incongruous situation that Brazil, the world's largest debtor, was Poland's sixth-largest creditor.

By mid-1981 the debtor countries had suffered a triple blow: the rise in the oil price, the interest rate war, and the subsequent rise in the value of the dollar, in which both debt and oil were priced.

The LDC debt for the top ten banks was greater than 325 percent of their capital and reserves. The figures were known to be even more serious for many European banks. And as the banks, including the World Bank, insisted that borrowers turn first to the IMF, it became the lender of first resort. There was no option. These contradictions introduced a whole new wave of austerity programs managed by the IMF, compounding the world recession in 1982, and adversely affecting world trade.

The American Right and some members of Congress with a primitive comprehension of U.S. interests had in 1981–82 attacked the new thrust of the IMF and the World Bank as "pinkish," for allegedly aiding the public sector. The Treasury Department, fully appreciating the importance of these institutions to American interests, in 1982 published a report enumerating their benefits to the United States.[5] The report's emphasis embarrassed some at the World Bank, for they do indeed serve more than American interests. At the same time, Washington insisted that the institutions revert to the pre-1979 policies, with the emphasis on linking the conditionality of loans to changes in economic policy. "We want to push IMF's conditionality back to where it was," said Treasury Deputy Secretary Beryl Sprinkel.[6] Under these pressures the IMF cut off loans to fifteen nations by April 1982. After lending to the African nations in the brief years of "liberalization," there was increased toughness in all programs and a cut in new commitments, to one-fifth of those in the preceding years. The United States finally modified its position on the IMF after the debt crisis in Mexico and Brazil at the end of 1982 and again in 1985.

SINCE 1983

The so-called recoveries are riddled with contradictions and structural weaknesses, and the illusions they promote only further endanger the economy. Geographically, the recovery was not general; rather, it was centered in the United States. Did the United States have a stronger economy? It is important to determine why there was a recovery, and why employment grew there and not in the European nations.

Given the extreme contrast between different sectors of the American economy, it is meaningless to lump them together in general growth figures. The tertiary operations are not sufficient for prolonged recovery, and this area played the major part in the "recoveries" during this crisis.

Since U.S. economic policy under the Reagan administration favored government deficit spending for arms expenditures, it in part reduced the duration and impact of the 1981–83 recession. The problems were compounded by the rising real interest rates in the United States and by an overvalued dollar. Reagan lowered taxes for the present while increasing expenditures in a period of high interest rates; this only guaranteed higher debt for the future, because a larger and larger proportion of the budget would be obligated to pay for the debt service.

With the rise in the dollar value came a new shift in the shares of the domestic and world market. The United States lost 23 percent of its export market share between 1980 and 1984 and saw a 20 percent increase in its imports relative to its GNP. Hence the economic recovery and growth was to a significant extent in the retail service industry, which expanded in response to imports although production contracted. Jobs, profits, and inflation declined in production and expanded in services. Unaffected by imports, inflation in the service sector stayed at over 7 percent and that for goods decelerated to less than 1 percent in the aggregate, with even some deflation in the price of producer goods.

The quantity of dollars outside the United States had grown at the rate of 26 percent a year between 1977 and 1981, but its growth virtually ended in 1983, as did lending to the indebted LDCs. Money—dollars and other currencies—now flowed into the United States. By 1984 America was a net importer of capital, for the first time since before World War I, and by 1985 it was a net debtor. In the American banking system alone, the $45 billion net outflow of 1982 became a $24 billion net inflow in 1983. Lending overseas by U.S. banks declined $23 billion in 1983. The U.S. economy drained the world of savings through either U.S. corporate Eurobonds or short-term borrowing, foreign funds seeking higher interest, speculation in foreign exchange, repatriation, debt repayment, or capital flight. Given the instability and contradictions, such developments could only be temporary.

As the Reagan administration's conservative rhetoric of balanced budgets was translated into unprecedented deficits in a period of record-high interest rates, its need for capital imports was overwhelming. Even more than during the Vietnam War, the rest of the world now financed America's arms policy, which accounted for most of the deficit. In 1969, foreigners held less than 5 percent of the U.S. government debt, and by 1984 the capital inflow was financing "40 percent of the budget deficit," according to the *Economic Report of the President.* [7] But also by 1984 the U.S. government securities were being received more cautiously by investors. There was thus a steady shortening of their maturities in order to compete at very high real interest rates. And, according to the IMF, after 1982 "net capital inflows . . . were due more to a decline in U.S. private investment abroad than to a significant increase in . . . foreign investment in the United States."[8] For the time being, however, capital continued to flow into the U.S. dollar since investors perceived no alternative investments. Even as American interest rates fell in 1984 and 1985, the differential with other competitive rates was even higher than earlier, and the dollar continued to rise. Hence, even contradictory signals and trends strengthened the dollar. But it was clear to most observers that the dollar was overvalued and that a shift in the exchange rate would generate an outflow of capital.

Paul Volcker knew it was essential for the world economy to lower interest rates and, with them, the value of the dollar, but he also believed that the consequent outflow would damage America's ability to finance the budget deficit as the state would have to absorb all available savings. U.S. national savings available for private investment had fallen from 7 percent of the GNP in 1979 to 1.5 percent in 1983 because of the U.S. budget deficit. Yet investment in the United States advanced after 1983, as inflows from abroad provided the capital. But profit was increasingly found in speculative and financial instruments rather than in production. The United States, Volcker observed, had become "hostage" to foreign capital.[9]

The reverse of the U.S. situation was the increased capital outflow from Japan. Japanese deregulation of currency controls released Japa-

nese capital, which invested a large proportion of the export earnings
in U.S. government securities. It was estimated in 1984 that the Japanese were purchasing U.S. Treasury bonds at the rate of $1 billion a
month.

Although in the short run the dollar's overvaluation had a serious
negative impact on the economic policies of the European nations and
many of the LDCs, it was beneficial to their export industries. Of the
record volume of world trade in 1984, an increase of 9 percent over
the preceding year, two-thirds were exports to the United States. European exports to America grew 30 percent in 1984 and also gained a
competitive advantage over American exports in other markets. In a
1985 report on the effects on trade, Otmar Emminger concluded that
the strong dollar was not Europe's but America's problem.[10] But the
trade did not lead to the creation of jobs outside the United States. The
dependence on exports would instead leave Europe and Japan vulnerable to the dollar's fall or to protectionist restrictions, since their
domestic economies were too weak to absorb the goods exported to the
United States. By 1987, when the dollar had fallen 85 percent against
the mark in eighteen months, the German government was angrily
demanding action to halt the slide.

The American government had responded to the mounting complaints of the Europeans and others on the effect of the overvalued
dollar with its traditional "benign," or malign, neglect, until its trade
deficit threatened to degenerate into a destructive trade war. The trade
deficit naturally created mounting political pressure for protectionist
legislation in the United States, because it benefited those nations
exporting to it. In 1985, as protectionist demands mounted in the form
of some three hundred congressional bills, Washington began to intervene in the currency markets in coordination with other nations, and
in 1986 the dollar began its inevitable free fall vis-à-vis other currencies, particularly the mark and the yen. A new monetary struggle
ensued, in which earlier demands were reversed.

For too many American interests the strong dollar was a distinct
liability by the end of 1985. Its fall would serve the double purpose
of reducing both the debt and the trade deficit. Objectively, it had been
considered for several years to be overvalued by roughly 30 percent.
The subsequent fall during 1986 had swift, profound, and damaging
effects on the German and Japanese economies. And the aggravation
of the conflict between various interests in the United States made clear
the volatile and dangerous effect of the dollar's central role in the world
economy.

Foreign capital had financed the American recovery after 1982. But capital accumulation, particularly in the United States, had become increasingly ephemeral as money, created by the banks, was channeled into speculation and a shuffling of assets rather than into productive capital. In their effort to compete, the Europeans and Japanese moved swiftly and precipitously to deregulate their capital markets in 1985. In many cases they were only acknowledging what already existed de facto, but the competition pushed most governments beyond what many considered prudent, increasing the chaos and risks in the capital market.

Except for the export industries, there was no recovery in the rest of the OECD countries. The U.S. interest rates until the mid-1980s kept other rates high, and the savings flowed to the United States for investment. By means of austerity policies the Europeans were able to reduce inflation, but unemployment was the most notable feature of the economy of Europe in the 1980s, during both the recession and the weak recovery. Unemployment rose faster than at any other time since World War II, and it was now twice as high as during the recession in 1975. Moreover, the duration had doubled and the range of occupations affected had broadened, the greatest growth being among male heads of families.

As the U.S. economy slowed in 1985 and as the affected sectors of American industry intensified their demands for protection, Washington and the OECD governments called on the Europeans, especially the Germans, and on Japan to adopt expansionary policies, to be again the "locomotives" of the world economy. These governments, however, were reluctant to lower interest rates and claimed that the mammoth American deficit was the origin of the world's economic problems.

The OECD in its *Economic Outlook* of mid-1987, one of the most pessimistic in many years, again called on the Germans to expand demand and the Americans to restrain it. It noted that all the so-called positive signs of higher profits and falling oil prices were undermined by uncertainties in currencies, trade, debt, stagnation, and the like. Clearly the accumulated and unresolved dilemmas in the economy and the policies of states continued to interact and prevent any resolution to the persistent economic crisis in the world system.

DEBT CRISIS

From the 1950s to the early 1970s, the OECD countries were the source of capital flows to the LDCs. Money came as official aid or private investment. Between 1974 and 1981 OPEC was the source of the world capital flow, even though the banks served as intermediaries. After 1982 OPEC was in deficit, and its ability to generate international capital, according to the IMF, disappeared.

Rescheduling debt under the auspices of the IMF gave the illusion of repayment, while a surplus was extracted from the populations of the indebted nations. But, the IMF held, all scenarios to head off a debt disaster posited an early recovery of growth in the world economy.

Pressed on all sides for a change in policy toward the LDC's debt crisis, the United States proposed at the IMF meeting in Seoul in 1985 that private investment could be induced to promote economic growth in the indebted LDCs. The U.S. plan strained credulity. There had been an unrelenting struggle to attract to and hold in the United States the capital imports on which the American "recovery" was based, to the detriment of the other OECD nations, let alone that of the LDCs. And the emergence of the United States as a debtor nation scarcely promised a flow of capital to the LDCs, which were consistently "milked" not only by the banks but also by the TNCs and the capital flight carried out by their own citizens. The inflow of foreign savings to the United States in 1984 dwarfed the inflow to all LDCs combined. The IMF finally admitted that even if the LDCs managed their economies "satisfactorily," they could not compete with America for capital.[11]

The expansion in exports of a few of the indebted LDCs was matched by a reduction of imports, and this had grave implications for their future growth. In turn, it had a negative impact on the OECD countries' export trade, particularly on exports from the United States. Intra-European trade, for its part, was limited by the weak recovery. By the mid-1980s the international situation was characterized by the extremes of austerity on the one hand and profligacy on the other.

One of the most significant changes in the world economy in the 1980s, and certainly the biggest success of the IMF's restructuring program, was the move of China, with its one billion people, toward a capitalist organization of its economy. This bloodless counterrevolution set the pace for the introduction of the market forces in the centrally planned economies. But because nothing in China is certain except change itself, it would be rash to make any predictions about the durability of this move. The contradictions of such planned capitalism materialized immediately and will be put to the test, as some Chinese leaders foresaw, if the structural changes in Chinese agriculture fail to meet any emergency in food production.

Although it is true that the enormous government expenditures in the 1970s created countervailing pressures that kept the world economy from spiraling into a 1930s type of depression, they carried their own contradictions in the widely recognized fiscal crisis of the state. These outlays were soon regarded as "rigidities" to be dismantled in the 1980s as an important part of the "restructuring" process.

Restructuring involved reversing even rhetorical policy goals such as full employment and the state's role in welfare provisions, dictated not only by ideology but also by the fiscal crisis in the context of the economic system. Unemployment was in fact an important backdrop permitting the restructuring of labor relations in the capitalist nations. This policy orientation led to, among other things, denationalization, deregulation, dismantlement of welfare systems, and de-indexation of wages. State expenditures beneficial to capital, on the other hand, continued and in many cases grew substantially. There were frequent government pledges to terminate subsidies to industries threatened by international competition, but these were often postponed or broken. Under the combined pressures of the IMF/World Bank and the general shortage of capital, there was a move toward "privatization" in the LDCs, which had earlier been committed to development through state planning.

An important difference between the contemporary situation and that of the 1930s is that the governments have now tried all the anticrisis measures and they have failed. In fact, they have blamed these very measures for the present crisis. It is now evident that it does not matter whether government economic policymakers call themselves free-market, Keynesian, or socialist. They all consistently pursue the same capitalist economics when in positions of power, and contradictions and failure are built into every effort. In the mid-1980s all of the governments in the OECD were ready to "bite the bullet," to accept ever higher levels of unemployment in order to restructure their economies to compete better in the new international division of labor and for investment capital.

By the mid-1980s the contradictions were ever more intense, aggravated by the very integration of all aspects of the world economy. The efforts to solve the debt problem worsened that of trade and vice versa, and moves on exchange rates threatened to intensify the fiscal crisis and seriously altered trade patterns. A decade of economic crisis had not only changed but had worsened the condition of the economy objectively. And the efforts to restructure were successful primarily in wresting from labor the gains achieved in an earlier era, and in further incorporating into the capitalist market economy those nations previously outside it. The crisis was important to the temporary success of these efforts.

These changes emerged in the interaction of objective development and subjective policies that themselves were the outcome of and response to the economic environment. But there are nevertheless consistent threads that run through the changes and define its direction. In the following chapters I will explore more fully the dimensions of this process of restructuring the economy and what it portends for the rest of the twentieth century.

PART II

CAPITAL

CHAPTER 3

ACCUMULATION, COMPETITION, AND CLASS STRUGGLE

One of the most startling aspects of the current situation is that after over a decade of unresolved challenges in the capitalist economy, of recurrent failures, of constant threats of default and bankruptcy that menace the entire world economy because of its integration, capitalism in its oldest ideological guise—that of Adam Smith—is once more à la mode. It is as if the long succession of failures had heightened its allure. There are reasons for this, of course, and I discuss many of them in the following pages. But, given this current consensus, it is important to look first at how the system itself is functioning and how its operations are *objectively* restructuring the world economy.

To ask what is the origin of recessions, recoveries, or booms is to ask why investment has stalled or why it is expanding. Although there are other incentives to investment—a state may invest for need, self-reliance, an industrialization strategy, or prestige—a capitalist will invest only because he expects to profit or to secure or maintain a market share for expected future profits. Accumulation, not for consumption but for further accumulation, has always been the capitalist compulsion and goal. And capitalists are most acutely aware of three factors in their operations: accumulation (perceived profit opportunities, or the avoidance of loss), competition, and their relations with their workers. It is essentially in the interaction of these three *systemic* features that we find the roots of the contemporary crisis. Here I will explore the form these factors have taken in the period since the mid-1970s and what contradictions have emerged in their interaction that objectively restructure the economy.

57

ACCUMULATION

Traditionally, the accumulation of capital equaled the volume and rate of reinvestment of profits. For some years, however, investment increasingly has depended on debt, not on earnings or equity. And capital accumulation itself is more and more ephemeral, as debt is used to shuffle assets and repay earlier debt and as profits are channeled to, and found in, the financial markets and speculation. What are the implications of this condition? What has the prolonged period of crisis done to the perceptions and actions of capital in the economy? Is capitalism strengthened in the crisis or weakened, or both?

Since capital accumulation is the essential goal of the social system, an exploration of restructuring the political economy should begin with what a bourgeois economist calls the "rational actor seeking gain" on the basis of rational expectations of self-interest, as the capitalist perceives it. While the economist may consider aggregates, the capitalist must look to himself. And on these investment decisions rests the fate of millions of people as well as the operation of the economy.

In general, capital restructures by accretion, not by strategy. Although there is often a tendency to attribute a long-term strategy or at least rationality to capitalists in their investment decisions, in reality there is a surge of capital to where profits are found or expected on the basis of immediate perceptions, and this includes long-range investments. What is perceived is always more important than what is actual in investment decisions. An operational strategy emerges later out of the ad hoc responses to the objective conditions. The closest to a long-range subjective strategy for private capital is its struggle against labor.

Furthermore, the economic environment was *objectively* restructured "behind the backs" of the capitalists through the oil price, inflation, currency uncertainties, interest rates, and other factors. Structurally, there are increasingly a world market, global competition, transnational factories, finance, investment, and disinvestment. The capitalists, too, are vulnerable to these objective operations of the system, and as the international competitive pressures, including shifting exchange rates and developments in technology, increase, they act to cut costs and redress their relations with labor.

Political factors also offer important incentives and disincentives to investment. Trade restrictions stimulate foreign investment to obtain a share in the protected market, state subsidies may reduce the risks, arms contracts may increase production, or currency exchange rates may alter profitability decisively. It has been a period of restructuring on many levels, an interaction of objective developments and decisions.

From the perspective of capital, restructuring is a process of cutting costs by moving to new locations, changes in work organization within the community, and fragmentation of the work process locally, regionally, nationally, and internationally. In some cases it means the destruction of capacity and the perception that whole nations are "getting out of some businesses," as the director of a business consulting firm said, expressing a general view.[1] On an international level it is a process of change to world production and a global market. But this trend is resisted by imperiled interests. Restructuring also means systematically lowering the "break-even point" (profit at a lower operating point and lower sales) in basic industry, primarily by cutting labor costs, closing capacity, and permanently reducing the labor component in production. And in the mid-1980s, restructuring became the goal in the struggle for control in takeovers and the defense against them.

BREAK-EVEN POINT (BEP)

In response to the recession of 1980–82, managers began to reduce the break-even point. According to the business press, "the first move was to slash labor costs" with a concomitant "rush by manufacturing and service companies alike to automate assembly and clerical tasks" and to reduce capacity.[2] Investors "rewarded," by buying its stock, one company that had cut one-third of its labor force and closed three plants in 1982 even before it was able to break even.[3] The automobile companies, for example, are now able to profit on 24 percent less sales than before 1980; and cost cutting, not increased sales, changed losses to profits in other industries. A new break-even point was crucial for the machine tool industry, which acquired it by closing plants and reducing the work force. Employment in the capital goods industry fell 387,000 between 1980 and 1984. The chemical industry in the United States lowered its BEP 10 percent or more, to an operating capacity of 65 percent or lower. Du Pont could profit using only 60 percent capacity, and it was "still dropping" in 1984.[4] Exports of the United States are affected by the Middle East plants' coming into operation as well as by the expanded capacity in Canada and Mexico. Inco Mining lowered its BEP more than 12 percent in one year. Capital spending for all continued to be for further rationalization, not for expansion. GE restructured by cutting employment and products to a point where, with increased sales of only 12 percent, earnings rose by 50 percent.

For some firms the recession was the "great catharsis" to get the "fat" out of the system and make it more competitive, but for others it meant increased indebtedness, greater losses, or bankruptcy.[5] And bankruptcies continued to set postwar records into the "recovery" in the United States. The rate of business failures rose fourfold between 1979 and 1985, while the rate of business startups rose only 25 percent.

For Japanese industry the break-even point is much higher because of the fixed costs of a higher ratio of interest payments and a higher proportion of fixed wage costs. These factors, according to one Japanese economist, have led to a full-capacity policy.

Capital invests not because it has saved, contrary to certain views, but because it expects to profit. If such expectations exist in an era of growth like 1972–74, no interest rate or the cost of commodities, labor, or material is too high to discourage investment. Generally, if the reverse is true, not even a low price is sufficient to encourage it. Savings will be used for other purposes. Of the many crises, the investment or accumulation crisis is the most critical in the operation of the system.[6]

PROFITS

Although the figures for profits are in many cases questionable, that is, inflated for stockholders and deflated for tax purposes, it appears that one may draw several conclusions on the role of profits over this period of generalized crisis.

Aggregate profits for manufacturing in the United States, except for 1974, rose during the recession and subsequent recovery to record highs until 1979. They rose 25.7 percent while production fell, investment declined, and the government deficit boomed. Hyman Minsky attributed this to government deficit spending, which persisted through the crisis, in contrast to what had happened in 1929–33. "[O]ur big government . . . has made it impossible for profits to collapse as in 1929–33. . . . The analysis indicates that stagflation is the price we pay for the success . . . in avoiding . . . depression."[7] Inflation was good for profits for many. During the last half of the 1970s, when inflation stood at 8.1 percent, aggregate pretax profits averaged 13.5 percent a year.

But the distribution of profits among the various sectors of capital has changed radically in recent years. In the 1970s, as would be expected, the fuel industry's share of total profits shot up from 8.5 percent in the 1960s to 22.0 percent in 1979–81, at the expense of the older durable-goods sector, which fell from 49 percent in the 1960s to 28 percent in 1979–81. The defense buildup under Reagan, which absorbed 9 percent of the GNP, is directed toward high-tech electronic warfare and will further undermine the profit share of the durable, nonelectrical industries. There was also an important shift between manufacturing and financial capital. For the bankers the debt crisis was characterized by profits that more than doubled between 1978 and 1983 and tripled between 1974 and 1983. For the first time since records were kept in 1929, in 1981 net interest exceeded profits in the national income statistics. In 1960 the proportion of the national income going to interest was 2.7 percent. It rose to 3.6 percent in 1965, nearly doubled in the following decade, rising to 6.8 percent, and in 1982 reached its all-time high of 10.6 percent, then fell in 1983 to a still historically high 9.3 percent. Profits, on the other hand, were 14 percent of the national income in 1965, fell yearly thereafter—to 8.8 percent in 1970, 8.2 percent in 1980, and 6.7 percent in 1982—rose again to 7.8 percent in 1984, and declined in 1985 and 1986 to 7 percent. Wages and salaries as a percentage of national income rose from 69.2 percent in 1965 to 75.4 percent in 1970, but fell to 68 percent in 1980, and to 61 percent in 1985 and 1986.

Entrepreneurial and property income as a percentage of domestic income purportedly fell for Canada, France, Japan, the United Kingdom, the United States, Australia, and Austria as a group from 34.6 percent in 1960 to 30.3 percent in 1970 and to 24.9 percent in 1980. The situation changed in the next decade. Profits as a share of the GDP rose in the FRG, France, and Britain in the 1980s because of falling wages and unemployment. In Japan the share of profits increased steadily over the years 1980–85, and the wage share declined.

Over the last decade, as I discussed in Chapter 1, many economists have focused on the fall of the profit share of national income as one of the chief causes of the crisis. A number of economists have demonstrated that, *objectively*, neither rising taxes nor rising labor costs were the cause of the falling profit share but that the growing interest payments to the financial sector were.[8] However, when one asks particular questions about why investment falters, aggregate statistics usually do not provide the answer. Rising labor costs were fundamental to the perceptions and the strategies of many basic industries, and the aggregate national picture was of no account. This in no way diminishes the enormous importance of debt on profits, although here, too, the specific may have more meaning than the aggregate in our understanding of what is really happening.

We have to sort out the real profit statistics from the corporate offensive to secure tax and other concessions from the state and labor. On the one hand the corporations have tried to claim that many of their reported profits in the 1970s were illusory, including inventory profits and inadequate depreciation based on the original cost of plants rather than on their replacement cost. In an inflationary period accounting methods can make a difference. Depending on which figures or which methods of inventory evaluation were used, profits soared or fell. But these mythical calculations became dynamic in the real world when dividends and taxes were paid on inventory profits, cutting into working capital and increasing the need to borrow. While the cries of "capital shortage" in the 1970s were, for the most part, contrived, by one 1974 calculation 156 percent of the aggregate after-tax profits of the manufacturing industry were distributed as dividends. And according to the Commerce Department, about three-fourths of the after-tax profits of *all* U.S. corporations in the same year were distributed as dividends. Left short in the recession of 1975, corporations turned in record numbers to the banks. It was estimated in 1978 that one-third of the reported profits were an "illusion" made up of inflationary inventory gains and depreciation reserves, while taxes, dividends, and new growth had to be purchased with "hard cash."[9]

Accounting procedures can make the difference between profit and loss. Some companies, with one-half of the U.S. business inventories, shifted their accounting method in the mid-1970s, reducing their declared profits. Other executives—those of 3M, Chrysler, drug companies, and others—stuck to the old methods, believing they would "be out if the reported earnings [per share] are off."[10] In 1981 a change in the government accounting rules permitted corporations to move profits or losses in currency transactions from income to equity on the balance sheet. This caused a doubling of their involvement in currency speculation by 1983.

In the United States corporations maintain dividends even when profits fall. In the severe recession of 1982, dividends were higher than in 1981, while undistributed profits fell by one-half. In 1983, dividends continued to rise, while retained profits again fell slightly. This is readily understood, despite the accumulation function of capital, given the business climate of "raiders" and takeovers and the leveraged investment discussed below. Managers try to boost the profit statements of corporations to attract investors and protect themselves. They then must borrow at record interest rates for capital expenditure and to meet previous fixed interest payments.

But for investment it is expected profits and not actual profits that count, and for these, of course, there are no statistics. After assessing all the multiple factors that enter into the perception of future profits, based as it is on a response to current conditions, the OECD concluded in 1978 that there was clearly a "downward trend in the expected profitability of capital."[11] The perception of profitability also shaped the *type* of investments that were made during this period of crisis and that have done so much to restructure the economy.

FALLING RATE OF PROFIT

The basic reason for the crisis put forth by bourgeois and Marxist economists alike is the falling rate of profit, even though their conclusions differ radically. Each group is even divided in the same way regarding the causes of the fall—is it one of demand or one of cost, a crisis of production or of consumption? In fact, it is both. The argument among many Marxists is whether the cause of the falling rate is rising constant capital, the rising strength of labor, or the inability to realize profits in adequate sales (underconsumption). They are all important parts of the same totality.

Since the rate of profit (not mass of profits) is calculated by dividing net income by total assets, it is indeed a truism to state that it has a tendency to fall as the cost and complexity of plant and equipment (constant capital) rise.[12] There must be a concomitant destruction or massive depreciation of existing equipment or radical cost cutting and increases in productivity to alter that tendency. The new accelerated depreciation rules enacted in the United States in 1983 substantially increased the rate of profit. Competition and rising costs are the impetus to install new equipment. A marked rise in productivity occurred as capital was substituted for labor at a rate of 3 percent a year for the decade ending in 1983 in the EEC; the rate of profit fell correspondingly, by 1.8 percent a year.

The falling rate may be unclear to many economists, but it is perfectly clear to the capitalists who have made innumerable spontaneous assertions about it. One study prepared for the Committee for Economic Development in Washington concluded in 1979, "It is a widely accepted fact that NFC [nonfinancial companies] profitability has fallen sharply since 1965."[13] According to the OECD, in the aggregate, there was a long-term decline in the rate of profit in Europe after 1974. In 1976 the average rate of return on invested capital was 9.2 percent, compared with 13.4 percent in 1966. In the United States the profit rate for nonfinancial companies has fallen steadily after the early 1960s—from 15.5 percent in 1963–66 to 12.7 percent in 1967–70, 10.1 percent in 1971–74, and 9.7 percent in 1978. But since the end of the recession in 1982, profits, as distinct from rate of profit on investment, have had "a sharp recovery . . . aided by much reduced nominal wage increases and the shedding of excess labor."[14] In the mid-1980s, an analyst for Morgan Guaranty Trust noted, "Fortunately,

the decline in general price inflation in Europe has not squeezed profits.
. . . Indeed, across Europe, profits have surged."[15] But the economy
stagnated. And, according to the OECD, return on capital in 1985 was
still below the 1960s level, and manufacturing industries invested their
profits in the financial markets for the higher return.

But the significant restructuring in the economy lends an ephemeral
aspect to all the figures. In the TNCs profits, like prices, are manipulated among divisions for tax and other purposes. There is frequently
no link between the amount declared as profit in one division and the
amount available for investment.[16]

TYPES OF INVESTMENT

The failure to invest is an obvious source of crisis in the system. But
the *type* of investment is also crucial to the general economy. And now
even the new investment in plant and equipment—taking the form of
overexpansion, automation, and tertiary, or nonproductive, service,
with its intrinsic contradictions with future accumulation—only deepens the crisis. What choices are open for investment in this period, and
how do the decisions objectively restructure the economy?

Capitalists make short- and long-term investment decisions on the
basis of their immediate perceptions, and frequently calamitous errors.
Only their disinvestment decisions become self-fulfilling prophecies.
They move swiftly and competitively to accumulate or minimize losses,
making ad hoc responses to the perceived opportunities. There is never
any time to lose, since the competition within and between companies
is a struggle without respite. This is just as true for the giant as for the
small corporations. The history of mergers, conglomerations, disinvest-
ments, tender offers, redeployment, speculation, and the ebb and flow
of the torrents of capital seeking opportunity obviously bears this out.
The "each for himself" compulsion is a systemic feature of market
capitalism that consistently mocks all efforts at reform and planning.
Every decision made impersonally by many actors on the basis of
immediate perceptions carries consequences—some of them immense—for the entire world economy. This systemic factor provides
the crucial ingredient that shapes or undermines the structural conditions that exist or develop in every economy. This process is under way,
of course, generally without the individual capitalist having any idea
of restructuring. Concepts of this nature emerge as a consequence of
others analyzing the objective conditions that all such factors have
created.

Investment decisions are also influenced by competitors' moves, rising costs (particularly of labor, but also of materials, interest rates, and producers' goods), utilization of existing capacity, currency fluctuations, recession or slow growth, and trade restrictions. These various perceptions lead to different responses and are sometimes both incentives, and disincentives, to investment. Labor militancy and/or rising cost, for example, is an incentive to redeploy with investment in a new area and disinvest in the old or to invest in labor-saving equipment.

Capitalists, to be sure, still have options for the use of capital, depending on where they see a profitable opportunity. The most important for growth in the general economy is in plant and equipment, and the form it takes has great implications. Investment can either expand existing facilities or build new ones; it can replace old plant from its depreciation reserves, rationalize with the introduction of labor-saving equipment, meet pollution control regulations, or relocate within the same nation or outside it. Other choices for the use of capital include the acquisition of existing plant, diversification (particularly into service industries or service functions), speculation in financial assets, repayment of debt, and distribution of capital as dividends to the stockholders. To avoid loss, they may move toward disinvestment or divestiture, repatriation or capital flight.

PLANT AND EQUIPMENT

Investment in new plant and equipment for expansion in North America and Europe has since the mid-1970s been largely confined to certain sectors, with emphasis on labor- and energy-saving equipment rather than on the construction of new productive facilities. This continued a trend that had begun much earlier. In 1960 some 44 percent of all investment in the United States was in buildings, in 1970 the figure was 39 percent, and by 1984 it was 28 percent. Fixed investment as a fraction of the GNP fell by nearly 28 percent from the late 1960s to the end of the 1970s. Important in that trend was the redeployment to other parts of the world. Industries attracting high investment in the 1980s included leisure, real estate, office equipment, and electronics. But the problem of those sectors was that expansion led to overcapacity and falling return.

Costs of capital goods increased more rapidly than the general price index during the high inflationary period of the 1970s, and, most important, costs in general exceeded even the oligopolistic sector's ability to pass the increase on to the buyer in a competitive international market. So the voluntary investment that took place was not for expansion of volume but for labor saving, productivity improvement,

or the building of competitive capacity elsewhere. And by 1985 there
was a further sharp decline in business spending for new plant and
equipment that continued into 1986.

During the "recovery" of 1983–85 in the United States, business
equipment spending in the aggregate grew 39 percent, considerably
faster than in previous recoveries. On the basis of this figure, economists and others have made many generalizations that obscured the
meaning of the statistic. While Reagan's tax changes accounted for
one-fifth of this impetus, it was incomparably less than the advantageous import price of new equipment. Hence the capital invested for
new equipment to modernize industry and attain a lower break-even
point and automate equipment went to foreign suppliers, who had a
decisive price advantage because of the overvalued dollar. Half of every
investment dollar for capital goods went to imports in 1984. And the
U.S. suppliers' former export markets were also lost, primarily as a
result of the shift in the exchange rate. Even imports of computers and
parts rose by more than 66 percent in 1984. Yet, while their former
customers were importing, the machine tool companies themselves,
preferring to buy cheaper foreign steel, resisted protectionist moves by
the steel industry.

During the recovery more of every investment dollar went to computer and related equipment than to traditional machinery. Fifty percent of the investment in equipment, which by the mid-1980s made up
73 percent of all fixed investment, was for microcomputers and telecommunications and other high-tech equipment. A Brookings Institution
study by Barry Bosworth in 1985 found that 93 percent of the rise in
equipment investment between 1979 and 1984 was for office equipment (mainly computers) and automobiles. Even this figure may be
distorted in its economic implications for these years, since the personal
computer, often purchased for video games and household use, was
classified as a business expense. And in 1987 the machine tool industry
was still lamenting, "American industry is not significantly expanding
. . . there is only the replacement business."[17]

Competition, to a point, is a spur to investment, as is the rising cost
of labor. In the United States, imports pressured many manufacturing
companies to invest in more modern equipment in an effort to reduce
costs and raise productivity. "The whole change in the economic environment of the 1980s toward keener competition from both foreign and
domestic competitors puts a higher premium on upgrading capital
equipment," noted a Citibank official.[18] The retail industry expanded
substantially in both employment and new businesses during the so-
called recovery of 1983–85, taking advantage of cheaper imports to

earn higher profits rather than significantly to lower consumer prices.

In contrast to the OECD countries, the Third World and the CPEs underwent an enormous expansion of capacity through investment in plant and equipment of all forms during the 1970s and into the 1980s. To a large extent, it comprised a mixture of state and private ventures that expanded competitive capacity worldwide in both consumer and capital goods manufacture. In some cases it was the outcome of the TNC relocation and in others of the state capitalist ventures characteristic of OPEC and such NICs as South Korea and Taiwan.

Overcapacity, or "output gaps" between potential and actual output, is always a crucial barrier to investment in new plant and equipment. In fact, though, there is not enough capacity, given the vast unfilled needs everywhere. But within the capitalist system overcapacity now takes a worldwide form in most industries, as competitive expansion in the LDCs has enlarged capacity for the limited capitalist world market.

ACQUISITIONS, MERGERS, AND TAKEOVERS

The mergers in the United States at the turn of the century were motivated by the desire to eliminate competition in the same industry; in the second wave, in the 1920s and 1930s, the goal was to create vertical combination corporations extending from supply through production and distribution. It was in response to these trends that theories of monopoly capital emerged. After 1950, acquisition strategies took the form of conglomerates, which accounted for 82 percent of the mergers by 1968. In the 1980s some of the largest mergers occurred within the same industry—particularly in the "troubled" industries of finance and steel, but also of oil. And by the end of 1985 Congress was moving to dismantle some of the legal barriers to monopoly.

Investment in the form of acquisition, mergers, and takeovers rather than in new plant and equipment has been the preferred use of investment funds since 1975, especially because many companies' stock was selling below the replacement cost of their property. By the end of the decade the bulk of the investments in the OECD states were of this nature. Many corporations threatened by competition or losses responded with diversification, branching out from their primary activity.

There was a great reshuffling of assets with no growth and often decline, a "paper entrepreneurialism," as one economist termed it.[19] Capital circulated among corporations, investment bankers, and lawyers, but not in production. A so-called frenzy in 1981 culminated a ten-year merger fever that altogether revealed largely negative results, since many of the combinations broke apart with significant losses over the following years. In the United States in 1981, $82 billion was spent in acquisitions, in large part promoted by the investment banks, which collected monumental fees. Companies paid 50–100 percent over stock market value in certain purchase offers to stockholders. Lacking the cash, the giants then borrowed at record interest rates of nearly 20 percent prime. Fluor borrowed $1 billion to purchase St. Joe Minerals for $2.2 billion, raising its debt fourteenfold; Du Pont borrowed $3.9 billion to buy Conoco for $7.5 billion; and Texaco borrowed $5.5 billion from a consortium of banks. A significant number of these companies were giant oil firms buying into minerals. The takeover targets of 1981 were the big profit earners of 1979 and often the biggest losers in 1982. By 1985 Fluor was seeking to sell St. Joe. Its own market value had fallen to $1.4 billion, $800 million less than it had paid to acquire St. Joe. The oil companies took huge losses in their moves into copper and other diversifications, such as office machinery and retail stores.

Yet the value and number of merger and acquisition transactions continued to increase substantially in the first half of the decade. Mergers over $1 billion were unusual before 1980, numbering only twelve; between 1980 and 1985 there were forty-five—twenty-four in 1985 and over thirty-three in 1986 alone. Between 1981 and 1983 one-half the giant mergers were concentrated in just five industries: oil, banking, insurance, mining and minerals, and food processing. Those in the oil industry accounted for one-fifth of the total merger value of that period. In 1984, $36 billion was paid in oil mergers alone. The increasingly deregulated industries of finance (11 percent), transport, and insurance together made up 25 percent of the mergers. In 1985, in the largest nonoil merger in history, GE purchased RCA for $6.3 billion, making it the seventh-largest U.S. corporation. GE had amassed its funds by way of tax shelters; this allowed it to pay no income tax between 1981 and 1983 on income of $5.5 billion. Others turned to debt. GE also shifted from its traditional, and competitive, core manufacturing to arms. All told, 12,200 companies, valued at $490 billion, changed hands between 1983 and 1987. And 4,000 U.S. firms spent $200 billion restructuring in 1986.

In the 1980s, again reflecting the crisis of accumulation through productive investment, a new ingredient became the decisive element in mergers and acquisitions. The motivation was quick financial profit, and the impetus, increasingly over the decade, came from outside the industry altogether—from independent investors in collaboration with, or at the instigation of, the investment bankers, bidding to take over large corporations on the basis of credit alone. The "raiders" are frequently interested in takeovers in order to dismantle companies to resell their parts. Generally, the last interest they have is production.

The "hostile takeover" is relatively new to the corporate world (and by the mid-1980s was nearly limited to the United States), beginning only in the 1960s. In 1981 such takeovers rose 42 percent over the preceding years. It was scarcely a question of the giants' swallowing smaller companies, as it had been in the era of conglomerates like ITT. One study revealed that 49 percent of the 480 largest corporations feared hostile takeovers and had contingency plans to meet them. Of the 249 takeover attempts between 1980 and 1983, only 52 were successfully resisted.[20] The activities of the "raiders" range from large, speculative stock purchases, financed by mammoth loans or the so-called junk bonds, of great risk but high interest, to offers to the stockholders to purchase their stock at a premium. All corporations are vulnerable, including America's largest. The restructurings generally involve massive layoffs and closures of plants and have a severe impact on the local communities.

"Greenmail" is another technique of the raider. In this case he has no plan to take over but uses the threat as extortion, and the company buys back the stock at a large premium, usually borrowing the capital to do so. Either way the raider wins. CBS, for example, spent $1 billion in "greenmail" and seriously weakened its capital base. This form of extortion is most common in the United States, but it is beginning in Japan as well. The buying back of the company's stock at a premium is the principal line of defense, but the corporations also used others to boost their stock value, amassing a huge debt in the process. These steps included becoming raiders themselves, issuing junk bonds, divesting, or acquiring losing assets or massive debt to make the company unattractive to raiders. Defense against takeovers led many major companies, such as Martin Marietta, Unocal, and FMC, to run their debt to 80 percent of capitalization. Union Carbide doubled its debt and cut employment 20 percent.

The banks, formerly reluctant to finance raids, eagerly joined the fray in the 1980s and became the leading player by the middle of the decade. One Chicago raider noted the change of a few years: "When I started [buying companies] in 1976, no one was really geared up to finance this stuff. Today we could go out and raise probably $1 billion in two days."[21] Citicorp backed the arch-raider Boone Pickens's attack on Gulf Oil. Some raiders set up "shell" companies and issued junk bonds, equal to $15 billion a year in the mid-1980s, using the target company as collateral. Raiders had generally used 80–100 percent

credit for their takeovers until 1986. The Federal Reserve then decided
that the risks of such debt were too high for the system and ruled that
a cash margin of 50 percent should apply.

The struggle between the companies fearing takeovers and the raiders and their Wall Street backers intensified in the mid-1980s. The top
200 corporations had mobilized their forces in 1985 to lobby Congress
to consider legislation to limit the raiders' actions. They strongly favored the Federal Reserve's measure. But the free-market advocates in
the Reagan administration concluded that "extensive research has established that takeovers tend to be beneficial" to the general economy,
primarily because "takeovers substantially increase the wealth of stockholders in target companies."[22] The administration, siding with the
raiders and their financial backers, strongly opposed Volcker's measure, which was modified under pressure to apply only to shell companies and to hostile takeovers.

The conflict between the corporate raiders and the threatened corporate management erupted in 1986 in the Wall Street scandals of insider
trading, an illegal form of profiting on access to confidential information
from investment bankers who counseled corporate clients on their
acquisition strategies. Such information allowed the traders to reap
enormous profits by buying or selling stocks before public announce-
ment of the merger deals. Some of the trading was for their personal
accounts and some for those of the firms. Some stock traders paid a fee;
others swapped information. Such activity was so widespread on Wall
Street that many considered it as illegal as breaking a speed limit on
the highway. Yet prosecution was clearly an opportunity to strike at the
investment bankers—particularly at Drexel Burnham, the most active
firm in the corporate raids and the leading innovator in takeover tactics.
But as those arrested scurried to avoid prosecution by naming their
peers in the other banks, the net widened to include most of the
investment houses. The trading room had become the profit center for
all of them, and naturally no questions were asked of those who created
the profits. The extent of the scandal on Wall Street even led members
of the Reagan administration to call for investigations. Subpoenas were
issued to the leading raiders, and the investigation spread to include
the issuers of junk bonds. But the various indicted traders and bankers
were only at the surface of the affair. The real targets were the hostile
takeovers and the consequent corporate restructuring that had split
American capitalists into warring camps.

About 70 percent of the rise in Standard & Poor's Index since 1984
was due to corporate "restructuring" in the form of takeovers and
buyouts. The average premium for stockholders in takeovers in 1986

was 40 percent above the market value. While enriching the stock-holder is a function of capitalism, accumulation is the primary one, and its neglect carries serious consequences for the entire system. The possibility that a raider can mobilize disgruntled stockholders, particularly the institutional investors, reinforces the short-term perspective of the managers against long-term growth. "If you run a company in a way that penalizes short-term earnings, it weakens your stock and you risk being taken over. So the raiders enhance an already overpowering trend toward the short-term viewpoint," observed a former chairman of the SEC.[23]

Although the merger activity was responsible for 70 percent of the stock market's rally, the immediate losers were the bondholders; as new debt was added, the bonds' ratings dropped, as did their value. Down-gradings of bonds exceeded upgradings by 43 percent in 1985, and a drop from an A to a B rating entailed a 15–20 percent loss in value. Moreover, corporations added $145 billion in new debt in 1985. Investors, especially the pension funds, increasingly shunned long-term corporate bonds. The rash of mergers and the lowering of credit ratings in 1985 affected the U.S. bonds in the Eurobond market as well, and foreign investors shifted to government and World Bank types of issues. In 1986 U.S. corporate bonds worth $3 billion defaulted.

The speculative junk bonds, which made up 21 percent of the U.S. bond market in 1986 and which paid high interest, were the principal debt vehicle for the restructurings, issued either by the raiders or by the existing management. After the LTV steel company, a major issuer of junk bonds, filed for bankruptcy in August 1986, investors began to turn to safer investments. Such events caused some "flight to quality" among more prudent investors, and the interest differential between bonds increased.

In reality, investment was a giant shuffle of assets, with mergers, takeovers, divestitures, diversification, and homogenization frequently being orchestrated by the investment banks. Companies that had earlier become conglomerates began to divest their unrelated subsidiaries, and the buyers of the divestitures in the United States during the crisis, despite the high cost of the U.S. dollar, tended to be Europeans. Their principal motive was "a geographic strategy . . . to spread market and currency risk from one country to another."[24] Europeans have also been active as "raiders" of undervalued U.S. companies.

In Britain mergers multiplied in 1985—totaling a record $10 billion—as 352 companies disappeared. The two leading telecommunications and arms companies (General Electric and Plessey) merged and will probably move to joint ventures with Ericsson of Sweden.

DIVESTITURES

Divestitures by conglomerates of their previously acquired companies made up approximately one-third of the number and the value of mergers and acquisitions between 1981 and 1983. There were 875 in 1982, compared with 666 in 1980, in good part because of the recession. By 1985 one out of three acquisitions was sold or otherwise divested. Between 1980 and 1985 the number of divestitures rose 35 percent, to 900, and had a value of $29.4 billion. Most likely to fail were the gigantic mergers.

In a study of merger failures, one economist distinguished between divestment (sale or closure) and disinvestment (the starving of a subsidiary of funds or the draining off of profits for reinvestment elsewhere). He determined two dynamics in divestment before 1981—international competition and the internal corporate economy—competition among the giants being the more crucial in the cases he studied.[25] The companies competed most intensely in production costs, but it was not many years before prices were also competitive once more. Increasingly during the 1980s, merger and divestiture assumed the character of an investment game of speculation and shuffling of assets.

Companies normally used the threat of divestment as a bargaining tool with labor or as a way to acquire a better "business climate" from the government. If the company could not achieve its goals, disinvestment perhaps followed until the subsidiary failed. Disinvestment is more insidious than divestiture. Barry Bluestone and Bennett Harrison and others gathered much evidence on the conglomerates' efforts to "create the unprofitability of a previously-profitable subsidiary" or simply to move in new, incompetent managers who drain profits for use elsewhere or to create tax losses.[26] "Corporations learned to assess their business as portfolios in the '70s," opined the head of acquisitions at Goldman Sachs. "Divesting a company from the portfolio is not all that different . . . from adding one. . . ."[27]

Even by the end of 1981 a move toward a homogenization of the conglomerates was discernible. Some began to prune businesses that required a lot of capital or were particularly vulnerable to imports, to narrow the range of their activities, to "edit out" companies that did not promise a high return, and to acquire working capital or repay debts.[28] By 1985 a shift back to companies in the same industry and a more indulgent antitrust policy in Washington encouraged these moves.

But Wall Street's response to acquisitions and divestitures also had a major impact. As one conglomerate executive put it, before the 1980s "when we made an acquisition, the stock went up. So we went out and made acquisitions," but since then the stock has responded to divestment.[29] In the mid-1980s the brokers began to rate the "break-up value" of companies whose current price was less than the sum of the parts, and these companies became the prime targets of the raiders. One stockbroker concluded at the end of 1986, "We've reached the point where everything is subject to restructuring."[30] Takeovers and divestment led to a significant shift in management's emphasis. Insecurity turned to panic as the threat of takeovers multiplied and was a spur to taking on greater debt, as an alternative to cutting dividends and risking a proxy fight for control of the company. Raiders targeted companies with the intent of breaking them up and selling their components. Management in scores of the largest corporations, such as Goodyear Tire, USX, and ITT, closed plants, fired employees, sold assets, and terminated research and development in anticipation of these moves. "The average large corporation is at least 50% owned by money managers. We're dealing with investors with very short-term interests," observed the head of one conglomerate.[31] These were essentially investors managing huge institutional portfolios, such as pension funds. At the same time an increase in debt-equity ratio makes the company unattractive to raiders and allows it to acquire property that can be used as a tax write-off. Finally, the tax deduction for interest costs has made debt more advantageous than equity in financing business in the short run.

Companies have also used divestment, or the threat of it, followed by an increase in the filings for reorganization or bankruptcy to wring concessions from labor. Filing for bankruptcy was a successful management "tool" in labor relations from 1982 to 1986. The courts then expanded the implications of bankruptcy beyond labor costs, making the consequences more serious to the company.

CORPORATE DEBT

It is borrowing, not saving or equity, that usually finances investment today, and this has been increasingly true since 1965. In the United States in 1973, external finance as a source of capital formation exceeded internal for the first time since 1950. Debt finances not only investment but also speculation of all types. And over these years of crisis new debt is required to repay old obligations. There are a number of reasons for this condition in the United States, where internal finance has historically been the basis of investment. One is that interest costs are tax deductions. Moreover, the increased pressure from threats of takeovers has encouraged corporations to distribute rather than to invest profits and to rely on debt for working capital. The recent debt has been short-term, whereas in the past it was long-term interest rates in the form of bonds that held the key to investment financing.

"The data for nonfinancial corporations indicate that something changed in the middle of the 1960s," Hyman Minsky told Congress in 1980.

The ratio of debt to internal funds, or liabilities to demand deposits, and of open market paper to total liabilities indicates that the corporate sector not only has greater debt payments to make relative to cash flows but also that the margin of safety for debt in cash on hand has decreased, and the reliance by business on volatile and relatively uncertain sources of financing has increased. The difference between the two indicates that the liability structure of nonfinancial corporations can not only amplify but even initiate a disturbance in the financial markets.[32]

Since then the problem has become considerably more acute. The bankruptcy rate during the recession of 1981–82 neared that of the Great Depression, largely because of a growing reliance on short-term debt, which had accelerated over the 1970s. But compared with the mountain of all-pervasive corporate debt in the second half of the 1980s, such a condition was modest indeed.

Minsky's thesis is that an unstable relation between investment and debt exists in capitalism, both of which bet on an uncertain future. Borrower and lender press for maximum gain, and then each moves to prevent maximum loss. "One bout of successful debt leveraging encourages another . . . toward a state of increasing 'financial fragility,' " another economist concluded.[33]

Inflation had been a major stimulus for the massive reliance on debt for cash flow demands throughout the 1970s, but even when inflation declined and real interest rates were at record levels, the short-term debt of corporations continued to rise, increasing the risk of bankruptcy if their fortunes should change even for what would otherwise be a transitional problem. This was true across the wide spectrum of industries, but disinflation, implying repayment with more valuable dollars, opened new traps.

In the United States profits in airlines, autos, metals and mining, special machinery, and steel in 1983 were inadequate to cover fixed interest and preferred dividend charges. After rising 36 percent between 1975 and 1978, general corporate debt rose 21 percent from 1981 to 1984, when the all-industry average was a debt that stood at

38.4 percent of the invested capital; for some industries, like steel, it was 47 percent in 1984, and in 1986 the second-largest company, LTV, filed for bankruptcy.

Despite the increased risks of overall short-term debt for both the corporations and the banks, there was after 1983 a rash of purchases of underpriced companies by means of borrowed capital. And the megamergers were accomplished with megadebt. The whole thrust of corporate restructuring in the takeover mania added an entirely new dimension to the problem of corporate debt. In 1983 debt rose by around $60 billion and equity by $30 billion. In 1984 new corporate debt soared by $169 billion (and another $145 billion in 1985), and equity plunged $78 billion, as successive corporations, threatened by hostile takeovers, borrowed to repurchase their own stock. According to the head of the Federal Reserve Bank of New York, more equity was retired by companies in 1984–85 than had been issued in all the years since the Korean War.[34] And there was a parallel conversion of debt to equity as the banks were essentially forced to rescue failing debtors. International Harvester converted $350 million in debt to equity, leaving the bankers owning 30 percent of the company.

The question of fixed costs like interest on new productive equipment will cut sharply into profits as the overproduction crisis worsens. Machinery that must produce around the clock for a shrinking market epitomizes an essential contradiction in the system.

The change in corporate debt structure in the United States is striking. In 1950 the average U.S. corporation had $43 for each dollar of interest payment; by the end of 1982 it was $4, and that debt was modest compared with the situation a few years later. Net working capital for all U.S. manufacturing corporations fell 22 percent from 1974 to 1983. During the recession year of 1982 there was no bond market, and considerable short-term distress borrowing occurred as a last resort to avoid bankruptcy. Divestments were also a means of raising capital in emergencies. At no other time since World War II had corporate liquidity been so weak. Debt acquired new significance as inflation fell and real interest rates rose.

Furthermore, there were changes in the type of debt. Short-term debt (under one year) rose steadily over the decade, from less than $40 billion in 1976 to nearly $100 billion in 1984. The high interest rates pushed an increasing number of corporations to short-term debt for their capital needs, even financing five-year capital expenditures with ninety-day borrowing in the hope of lower rates later. In 1984 six industries raised their short-term borrowing by over 100 percent, and some companies by over 500 percent, while reducing long-term debt.

By 1985 some 47 percent of pretax profits went to debt service, and over half the debt was short-term. Many of the gargantuan acquisitions of 1984 were financed with short-term debt. And in 1985, junk bonds made up 25 percent of all new corporate issues. A Federal Reserve governor said in 1984, "The area of corporate lending is experiencing pressure that we have not seen in the postwar period."[35] And the increasing number of bankruptcies in the United States in the 1980s, was, according to the head of the Federal Deposit Insurance Corporation (FDIC), responsible for 62 percent of the increase in bank failures.

To cover their exposure, the companies have relied on some of the recent "innovations" in the credit markets, such as "swaps" of one form of credit to another or investment in the futures market. The larger and most creditworthy companies have begun to bypass the banks, as they find they can raise funds more cheaply by issuing commercial paper or floating-rate notes and by other debt innovations, what the new jargon terms a "securitization" of debt. These innovations only magnify the risks. British Petroleum issued a multimillion-dollar package of short-term Euronotes without the banks' intercession and was shortly followed by Philips NV and others. Finally, according to one bank economist, accounting rules permit companies to hide total debt: "If we could calculate the total of gross liabilities, then the credit structure would be much larger than it is estimated to be at present."[36]

German and Japanese corporations traditionally relied on external finance for investment and operating capital needs, leading to a high percentage of fixed costs. Their difficulties were intensified over the 1975–85 decade. For France, as for the United States, where corporations were customarily self-financing, there was a significant change. French corporations were the least prone to turn to credit before 1965, but they subsequently succumbed to the "investment fever" of the early 1970s and saw their profit margin and self-financing resources shrink. Borrowing, an important part from international finance, increasingly met financial needs. The debts of France's three largest corporations nearly doubled between 1971 and 1974. In some cases nationalization was simply a process of absorbing debt in exchange for equity.

Japanese corporations frequently operated at full capacity, even at a loss, since they were so indebted that they could not risk losing their share of the market. And currency realignments are all the more threatening to their survival. Although there have been significant changes in recent years for the largest companies that have greatly reduced their borrowing, the average is still only 21 percent equity to total assets, much less than in Europe or America, with a heavy reliance on short-term debt, which makes up 25 percent of the total. One New York investment banker expressed his amazement by noting, "You can't have that much leverage and still be a company."[37] But foreign bankers also recognized that the degree of leverage was not the only criterion by which to judge the risks in a Japanese corporation. Nevertheless, Toyota was by the mid-1980s without any debt, and other large manufacturers in general were 100 percent internally financed in 1983, a significant change from the preceding years. And Japanese banks, flush with funds, increasingly turned elsewhere for their lending.

PORTFOLIO INVESTMENT

What is termed portfolio investment, or investment in stocks and bonds, has also been transformed by technology and the innovations in the financial markets. Buyers of stocks now often have no notion of what they are buying; they know only that it is a negotiable instrument they may buy and sell at a profit, or a loss. Because of the new communications technology, computerized services can swiftly survey the globe for an opportunity to buy a stock at the right price and make the transaction at their terminal, bypassing the stock exchanges. In response the various European stock exchanges are belatedly altering their rules and installing new equipment in order better to compete. According to a director of a London merchant bank, "The off-exchange business will continue to grow. The international stock business left behind [to the exchanges] is likely to be minuscule."[38] In order that their nationals face no barriers in their attempt to secure their share of the international business, governments are rapidly dismantling whatever regulations existed. The British took the lead, but the French followed by ending the Bourse's monopoly on trading. The Germans liberalized the deutsche mark bond market, and the Americans eliminated their withholding tax in their effort to hold capital.

For practical purposes, any stock can now be owned, bought, and sold nearly everywhere in the world. Dealing in bonds amounts to the same thing; the question is no longer whose bond it is or whether the issuer is creditworthy, but whether it can be quickly sold or traded at a profit. Once bonds were long-term investments, but in the mid-1980s a U.S. Treasury bond was held for an average of only fifteen days and a Eurobond for thirty days, and then they were sold. The prices were as volatile as the turnover. Securities sales became globalized, as all national barriers crumbled and twenty-four-hour trading was introduced from Europe to Japan. And portfolio investment is, of course, always considerably more volatile than direct investment. During 1984 and 1985 there was a net outflow from the United States, as investors in Europe, the Middle East, and Japan were net sellers of U.S. stocks.

In Europe the mid-1980s stock boom doubled the markets' value in eighteen months. But the flood of privatization offerings of state-owned companies began to overwhelm the markets, bringing the boom to an end.

In the U.S. stock markets, buying and selling has become highly concentrated. Some hundred traders dealing in gargantuan sums are able to push or pull the market in a brief time span with buy or sell orders. Such trading "makes the bull markets more bullish and the bear market more bearish," claimed one major broker.[39] They were responsible for the feverish rise in the early months of 1986 and make the market that much more vulnerable to the inevitable sell-off. Their decisions have nothing to do with the health of a company—in fact, nothing to do with the company at all—it is merely gambling with paper as with interest rates or currency exchange. The "bulk commodity approach to trading stocks makes a joke of their efforts," commented one trader, referring to the brokers' analysis of companies.[40] The massive buying and selling can, however, affect the firm. On the other hand, the tremendous surge in takeovers in the mid-1980s led to a new perspective for the brokers. Some have shifted, according to one institutional money manager, "from picking the best company in an industry to actually choosing the worst," in the belief that it will soon be the subject of a takeover attempt or a defensive restructuring, driving up the value of the stock.[41] Their computers also track the components of the conglomerates to assess the break-up value. Investment managers have financed some of the riskiest buyouts, but when problems become evident they move swiftly to avoid or minimize loss, which can accelerate a downward spiral.

Investment in government securities by nonofficial investors also reached record figures in the 1980s. To hold on to the funds, Washington promised anonymity and special tax concessions, as did other nations in the intense competition for funds. Moreover, the investments in the private sector "indirectly contribute to federal deficit financing by funding competing investments," claimed a study from Data Resources.[42] Foreigners also purchased roughly one-third of all new U.S. corporate bond issues in the U.S. market in 1985, doubling the rate of 1983.

FINANCIAL SPECULATION

By 1985 the U.S. economy had tilted "away from investment toward speculation" or toward what *Business Week*, invoking Keynes, called the "casino society."[43] With deregulation of the financial markets, the inventiveness of capitalists in making money knew no bounds. Since the economy had never fully emerged from the crisis of accumulation through productive investment, money could be made through leveraged speculation, not only on currency exchange and the futures market, as was true in the 1970s, but also through an endless array of arrangements that promised a fast return with no investment of capital, only of credit and risk. The available debt figures do not include the leverage for financial futures and options, on which billions are gambled on whether interest rates or the Dow Jones average will go up or down, and so on. A margin of only 6 percent cash is needed to buy such an option. Stocks and bonds in high-risk companies virtually tripled between 1980 and 1985, and sales of real estate trusts rose sixfold. Internationally, the competition intensified in 1985, to the point that *Euromoney* declared, "It is now almost beyond the wit of man to keep up with the ever-accelerating rate of change . . . in a world gone mad" in the financial markets.[44]

Because of the higher returns in financial speculation, a British executive pointed out that in Europe in the mid-1980s, "nobody is creating new wealth-producing assets for the future."[45] A worried finance director of a German engineering company noted, "[O]ur only sensible alternative [for their DM 800 million in hand] is to put it into government bonds."[46]

When productive investment stalled, currency speculation became an important source of profits. The largest companies along with the banks could change the value of currencies with their dealings and could "force devaluations that national governments are striving to avoid."[47] In France in 1982–83 and in Canada in 1985–86, government policy was oriented to give assurance to the currency market traders, and interest rates, affecting the whole economy, are offered as a kind of sacrifice to the speculating gods. In 1983 the demand for the dollar was from corporate treasurers and speculating blue-chip British and Japanese companies. Currency speculation was the origin of many bankruptcies.

Unlike their American and European counterparts, Japanese non-financial companies before the mid-1980s invested little in the financial markets. They were first and foremost production oriented and had large debt commitments. One large company, Hitachi, had a rule that when cash exceeded debt by 200 billion yen, it could turn to speculation. Although there was some speculation in the mid-1980s, the companies remain relatively conservative. But with the rise of the yen and consequent fall in manufacturing profits, steel traders and others turned to the currency markets and securities speculation for profits.

RELOCATION

The relocation of investment to new sites in search of lower costs or access to a protected market was a major use of investment funds over the last decade. This effort responds to both systemic and structural imperatives.

There is a vast literature on the transnational corporations (TNCs) and the new international division of labor, and many projections have been made on assessments of the current structural conditions. The TNCs as we know them today, in the form of centrally commanded transnational producers of component parts seeking production sites with the lowest costs, really emerged in the 1960s. The TNC in earlier times invested chiefly in the primary sector of commodity production, or for the local market. The growing militancy and cost of labor in the OECD countries in the 1960s and the intensifying international competition in the world market no longer permitted even the oligopolistic industries to pass on their costs to their buyers and created the imperative for lower costs. Developments in technology allowed the process of production to be decentralized while retaining centralized control in the corporate headquarters. The new automated machinery also had the function of deskilling much of the work force, as they replaced the more costly skilled and semiskilled workers who had earlier given the OECD nations a "comparative advantage" in the international division of labor. Despite the introduction of modern technology, the low-wage areas could retain their own so-called comparative advantage as they permitted longer working hours, hence a more rapid return on investment. This situation promised international companies greater absolute as well as greater relative exploitation. The expansion led to crucial structural changes in the world economy—intrafirm trade, transfer pricing, export processing zones, and the like. Profits, the sole justification, were enhanced with an internal division of labor within the firm that controlled the technology and frequently owned all phases of production, transport, and marketing.

The incentives to invest abroad were greatly—"artificially," the OECD insisted—enhanced by the multiple state subsidies, both from the host nation and from the TNCs' home country. This distorted the true cost of capital to the competitive disadvantage of industries in the industrialized countries.[48] Alone, government taxation policies have no role in investment decisions, but they are considered along with other factors. The LDC's comparative advantage in attracting investment was also furthered by the OECD governments' investment guarantees, which reduced the risks of subsidiaries and of building new competitive industries elsewhere. The "offshore assembly provisions" in the OECD, granting tariff-free status to component parts, also facilitated the moves toward the world factory. In the United States intrafirm trade of this nature grew 60 percent between 1964 and 1972, while other LDC imports grew only 12 percent. The equivalent figures for the FRG were 36 percent and 11 percent; for Holland, 29 percent and 2 percent. This myopic systemic impulse to secure immediate profit advantage carried its own contradictions, which emerged in a few years and were characterized by overproduction, idle capacity, competitive struggles, and so on.

Notable shifts in the 1970s in direct foreign investment occurred as European surpassed U.S. new investment in Latin America, as the Americans and Europeans made inroads in the Far East at the expense of Japan, and as the U.S. share of all foreign investment fell from 50 percent in 1970 to 42 percent in 1978.

Compared with only 20–30 percent for the other industrialized countries, over half of Japanese foreign investment was in the LDCs (19 percent in the ASEAN countries) and produced for export. Investment abroad expanded after 1973, rapidly in the mid-1980s, while domestic investment was stagnating. Compared with those of the United States, their investments were on a smaller scale, in both size and profitability. And the trading companies were indispensable to much of that investment, either directly with their own subsidiaries or, much more commonly, with a minority interest jointly with Japanese manufacturers, especially of the smaller- and medium-sized industries, and a local firm. Their motive was generally to secure the trading rights, not direct profits from production. But given their far-reaching network they were able to secure financing, supplies, and distribution to the world market. On the other hand, the giant Japanese manufacturers of autos and electronics generally pursued investment strategies independently of the trading companies, both in foreign investment and in exporting. And to a significant extent in the 1980s these corporations transferred to ASEAN countries the subcontracting relations they had already established in Japan, but now with lower labor costs abroad. Their investments were for production of parts, and they were able to play off these companies in periods of market depression and to encourage competition among them. By 1985, however, Japanese direct investment in the United States had risen to $16 billion, double that of 1981.

Japanese foreign investment in the aggregate in the 1980s was concentrated in the industrial sector, accounting for up to 50–70 percent of the total, and favored chemicals, electronics, machinery, and iron and steel. This was a new departure, for 40 percent of Japan's direct foreign investment had in the past been in the service and trade industries.[49] The rising yen in 1986 was the most important incentive to accelerate foreign investment. New investments in Asia rose 56 percent in the first half of the year. They increased production both for foreign and for domestic sales, leading to sharp cuts in production at home. They have the additional incentive, and the wherewithal, to open or acquire factories in their principal markets in America and Europe.

The FRG also shifted from being a net importer to being an exporter of capital between 1975–80. And during the 1980s there was another major change, as the United States became a net capital importer.

NEW FORMS OF INVESTMENT

There was an important shift in the forms of foreign investment of the U.S. TNCs in the 1970s. They found that whereas earlier they had insisted on 100 percent ownership, such nonequity linkages as subcontracting, buybacks, licensing of technology, servicing of turnkey plants, joint ventures, and international marketing agreements minimized risks and required less capital investment for the same returns. Formal ownership, these TNCs discovered, is not essential to maximize return. These multiple forms are often woven into a complex web of interrelations involving local firms, state corporations, the state directly, local or foreign banks, and multinational agencies. What used to be considered a sale or export of a turnkey plant is now qualified as a "new" form of investment. Or they are directly contracting for either parts or finished products, primarily from Asia, which they then label and package for sale to the world market.[50]

These "new" forms were rather old to the Japanese corporations and trading companies. They had used them as a way of complementing their home industry or in securing access to the crucial raw materials, or products to trade, as well as for the motives described above. They took the forms of joint venture with minority ownership, and usually with a trading company; production sharing, usually for raw materials, the TNC providing technical equipment and financing; and turnkey plants, often with operational responsibility contracts or production sharing.

The trading companies have been called "peculiar to the Japanese economy," but theirs is a form acquiring an ever greater role among other TNCs as the new types of investment and subcontracting arrangements multiply.[51] As the World Bank defined it, subcontracting occurs when "all export sales of articles which are ordered in advance, and where the giver of the order arranges the marketing."[52] On an international level subcontracting may be to an affiliate or an independent company with long- or short-term contracts for assembly, components, or finished products. There are innumerable different types of business ties. The contracting company may be a producer or a retailer. But the subcontractor has no marketing function. Labor costs, of course, were the principal, if not exclusive, impetus for the expansion of these contracts. All American semiconductor companies subcontract assembly work abroad, as do most European firms.

The structural conditions of the 1980s reversed the investment flow. There was even some redeployment of manufacturing, as technological innovation like thick-film printing eliminated hand labor in certain electronic products like radios. General Motors returned one of its subsidiaries to the United States. Other TNCs reduced their investment in such crisis-plagued areas as Latin America by 5 percent in 1983, and there was a fourfold cutback in the Middle East in the 1980s. In 1983 came the first decline in American direct foreign investment since World War II, despite the advantage of the overvalued dollar. Foreign spending plans of U.S. companies again declined sharply for 1986, after an increase in 1984 and 1985. Most investment in affiliates was reinvestment of earnings. But the contracting and purchase from independent companies for distribution continued to grow.

With the record rise of U.S. interest rates and the rise of the dollar vis-à-vis other currencies, the American TNCs in the 1980s began to borrow foreign currencies where lending rates were lower, in many cases monopolizing the foreign credit markets, and to convert to the dollar, not for investment but for repatriation and then repayment of the loans with a stronger dollar. "Our overseas subsidiaries have recently become milk cows," confessed one TNC treasurer.[53] Measures like these were also an important source of the inflow of capital, which further strengthened the dollar. In 1983 the U.S. parent companies borrowed $8.3 billion in the aggregate from their subsidiaries, $3 billion more than they reinvested out of profits. They had many other ways to "milk" the subsidiaries, such as increasing transfer prices, royalty charges, and management and engineering fees to get the money to the parent company. The transfer prices repatriate profits indirectly. These forms of capital drain, as well as capital flight, bled many countries of capital over these years. This is and will always be the reality, despite all the investment incentives designed to attract private capital for development purposes. On the other hand, many TNCs with subsidiaries in the indebted countries had to spend or provide needed materials and equipment to ensure their subsidiaries' survival, since in allocating foreign currencies, the central banks gave preference to the repayment of bank loans. Some TNCs sold out, and nearly all took major losses in Mexico and Brazil.

Profits from subsidiaries are directly affected by currency fluctuations. They provide a high proportion of the total when the dollar is low and a low proportion when the dollar is high for U.S. investors and vice versa for nondollar investors. Despite the currency disadvantage, many foreign companies have continued the pattern of investment in the United States that began in the 1970s. By and large it takes the form of acquisition of existing plant, but there has also been some new direct investment. Between 1974 and 1984 direct foreign investment in the United States increased 600 percent. The peak year for acquisitions (236) was 1979, when foreigners paid twenty-one times profit for U.S. companies (compared with only fourteen by locals) and bought many companies that subsequently suffered severe losses. In 1984 foreigners purchased 151 companies in the United States, for $15 billion, up from $6 billion in 1983. Foreign buyers were then less frenetic and paid about the same as their American counterparts. Many of the takeovers were in the retail industry; there was scarcely any interest in heavy industry, except by Japanese investors, compared with that of the late 1970s. But by 1986 some of the British investors in the service industry were selling their acquisitions for less than they had paid, or they were taking operating losses.

Japanese investments in the United States grew most rapidly, tripling between 1980 and 1985, in a range of manufacturing industries, with around five hundred companies by 1986. In 1984, Japanese capitalists spent $1.7 billion in direct investment, tripling that of the preceding five years. In 1985 the figure was substantially higher, making Japan the third-largest investor in the United States. (Canada, Britain, and the Netherlands still held the bulk of the investment.) And by 1986 Honda and Sony were exporting their U.S.-made products back to Japan. As the auto companies set up or bought plants, they persuaded their Japanese subcontractors to do the same.

Direct foreign investment in the United States averaged $17 billion annually between 1982 and 1985, while U.S. investment abroad was only $9 billion over that period, compared with $19 billion during the preceding four years. Access to the U.S. market remains a principal motive for these investments, and protectionist threats also spur investment. But the other reasons for the foreign investment are clear: despite the recessions, the rate of return in the United States averaged 13.6 percent over the decade 1974–84. Profits from European subsidiaries in the United States when the dollar was high provided some 30 percent

of many parent companies' total when converted into their own currencies. In addition, European investors repeatedly declare, "[T]he real
attraction . . . here is how easy it is to fire someone" or "I can lay people
off and restructure practically from one day to the next. . . ."[54]

According to the *1985 Economic Report of the President,* investment
in the United States during the recovery of 1983–84 depended on
foreign capital. The Council of Economic Advisers chairman Martin
Feldstein in 1984 claimed, "[H]alf of all net investment in the United
States will be financed by the inflow of foreign capital."[55] Foreign
investment in the United States exceeded American foreign investment
for the first time since 1914. And this flow of capital to the United
States kept investment in Europe lower.

Capital can as easily flow the other way. As the buying of U.S.
companies became "more expensive and competitive," investors turned
to countries like Britain, claimed one active American broker in London
in 1986.[56] Direct investment in the United States fell by one-half in
1986 from the previous year.

Many Japanese TNCs began to relocate their Third World production centers, much to the outrage of the ASEAN countries, to the
low-wage areas in the EEC, such as Ireland, Italy, and Spain, as well
as to the regions of high unemployment in the United States. By the
mid-1980s wage rates in Japan were higher than those in Spain and
England and about the same as those in France and Italy. There was
already substantial Japanese investment by some seven hundred companies in the FRG, France, and the United Kingdom to take advantage
of the increasingly protected market, and by the end of 1985 some 12
percent of Japan's foreign investment was in the EEC. But the culture
clash was a significant inhibition. "Numerous difficulties will have to
be resolved before the recipient country finds [Japanese investment]
totally acceptable and the investing companies find them profitable,"
reported one Japanese study.[57]

The TNCs are no longer exclusively from the OECD nations. The
number based in the Third World doubled between 1975 and 1980 and
included 33 of the top 500 outside the United States. Hong Kong is
a major source, but the list also includes state mining and oil companies
with direct investment abroad. Capital from these companies is being
invested in the OECD nations, too, such as the Hyundai auto plant in
Canada. With the high unemployment rates, the OECD countries are
highly receptive to any new investment, and their gain is a loss for
others in the intensive national competition for capital.

As capital moved toward investment in the industrial states, the
LDCs escalated their energetic and mutually destructive competition to

attract investment. Governments increasingly tailored their offerings to order for the TNCs. But such incentives alone will not attract capital, and if profitable opportunities exist, they are not required.

By 1980 the capitalists had easily integrated the CPEs into their worldwide production network; in fact, they claimed they had found their "most stable and profitable relationships with the socialist bloc of Eastern Europe," shattering any illusion that their ideology posed a threat to private profit.[58] But by 1981 one of the many illusions the Polish workers had destroyed was that these same states could guarantee "labor peace."

In addition to foreign investment, there has been significant redeployment within nations toward low-wage regions, accelerating in the 1970s a trend that had already been under way many years earlier in the highly competitive industries like textiles and garments. In the United States those industries beset by international competition were closed or moved abroad in the 1980s. Three million Americans moved to the South and the West during the late 1970s, until the recession in the early 1980s. And as wages in the Northeast fell well below the national average, investment there began to rise once more. Subcontracting, long common in the auto industry, has accelerated within the United States as well, again because of the lower wages in the parts-manufacturing companies.

MANAGEMENT

Within corporations there has over the past decade been a process of internal "restructuring" of management, as an integral aspect of cutting costs in order to compete in the new world environment.

Diverse industries, including 89 of the top 100 U.S. corporations, in the 1980s began to eliminate levels of middle management and redundant top management as a cost-cutting measure. According to a personnel director at Ford, where 20 percent of the planned layoffs were of managers, this trend represented "a total restructuring of American business."[59] Of the planned layoffs in an AT & T division, 30 percent were managers. The threat of raiders accelerated this trend. In the 1970s lawyers and portfolio managers were at the top of the industry, and corporations built "strategic planning" departments that were later charged with major losses; during the restructuring period in the 1980s these were eliminated or sharply reduced in personnel.

Some observers tended to blame the crisis in the banks and industry on "mismanagement." This, of course, was hindsight. Most firms are mismanaged; it is the context of the general economic environment that either obscures this fact or makes it obvious. This misattribution of management skill can also give certain groups an enormous unwarranted dividend—for example, the Americans in the 1960s or the Japanese over the last decade, when a mystique was attached to these nationalities as possessing a special talent.

The new myth that management is the secret of Japanese competitive advantage reached new heights in the early 1980s. Naohito Suzuki, senior management consultant of Nomura Research Institute, was approached by a French company that in the 1950s had studied American management techniques in order to transplant their secrets to France. Suzuki found "that [the Frenchman's] motivation resembles that of Japanese managers who visited the United States and Western Europe decades ago to learn advanced technology and corporate management, in order to modernize and internationalize Japanese firms."[60] "What is most essential," Suzuki concluded, "is for [Western management] to realize that its future depends on its ability to align its employees' wills with corporate goals."[61] In their own foreign investment in the United States, a number of companies introduced an idealized version of the Japanese model adapted to the American culture, featuring a camaraderie between workers and management, and the productivity of the plants improved greatly over what had existed under the former U.S. owners, until the speedups on the assembly line began.

In reality, Japanese industries' success rests on several more materialistic, structural factors that are undergoing change in Japan as the myth of U.S. management in the 1950s and 1960s depended on the hegemony of the American dollar. A primary feature was the attitude of a core of the Japanese workers who accepted much overtime work in return for guaranteed employment. Another crucial reason involves not management skills but the fact that Japanese industry is a decentralized mass of small- and medium-sized subcontractors that produce components for the corporate giants. They are the most indebted and affected by changes in the currency; intensely competitive themselves, they take the brunt of cost-cutting to keep Japan competitive in the world economy. The small (20 employees or fewer) and medium (300 or fewer) firms account for 99.4 percent of all Japanese companies, two-thirds of which are subcontractors for the big-name giants.

Yet the management style of the Japanese and their effort to transplant it to another environment created problems for their European investments, despite the welcome it got in areas of high unemployment. One official study concluded, "Local employees, unlike Japanese employees, do not consider their work to be the center of their lives."[62] The Japanese manager, however, by training, did tend to know more about the "nuts and bolts" of production. The new American manager,

product of the business schools, was oriented toward finance and portfolio management.

The recent developments in the United States vis-à-vis takeovers
have begun to alter radically the security of corporate management.
With the concentration of stock in fewer hands than at any previous
time in fifty years, management has had to consider the desires of stock
owners represented by the institutional investors. In fending off the
raiders with "greenmail" they incurred the wrath of the investors,
particularly managers of pension funds, which hold one-fourth of all
corporate equity. While traditionally the institutional investor buys and
sells stock with no interest in management, and most still replace
60–65 percent of their stocks each year, institutional investors have
taken a more active role in proxy fights. Increasingly they have exerted
pressure on management, accentuating the struggle between the various sectors of capital with each organizing politically to defend its
interests.

In the brouhaha of insider scandals on Wall Street in 1986–87, a
number of American businessmen donated $30 million for a chair of
ethics at the Harvard Business School, a fanciful gesture in light of the
essential ethic, which is to make money. As an article in the school's
prestigious *Review* asserted a decade and a half earlier:

A business that defined "right" and "wrong" in terms that would satisfy a
well-developed contemporary conscience could not survive. No company can
be expected to serve the social interest unless its self-interest is also served.
. . . It is not unusual for company managements to break the law, even when
they expect to get caught, if they calculate that the fine they eventually must
pay represents only a fraction of the profits that the violation will enable them
to collect in the meantime.[63]

The forms of accumulation had by the 1980s shifted away from
productive investment and were increasingly found in speculation and
a shuffling of assets, despite all the generous incentives offered in every
corner of the globe for productive investment. And an ever greater
proportion of the capital used for even this kind of ephemeral accumulation was in the form of debt. This condition of capital accumulation
alone indicated that there was a crisis within the system.

COMPETITION AND THE CONCENTRATION
OF CAPITAL

Competition is an essential systemic feature of capitalism, not merely
of "early" capitalism. A daily reality for all capitalists, along with the

accumulation drive and the relations with their workers, competition is at the core of the system.

There has really been no metamorphosis from competitive capitalism to monopoly capital that would require a new analytic framework. It was never necessary, and in fact was misleading, to oppose the tendency toward concentration to competitive capitalism, as if one superseded the other or as if new laws of motion in the system were involved. The counterpoise can be small-scale and large-scale concentration of wealth and power within an always competitive environment. Concentration of capital, which is a tendency within the system that has altered the political economy structurally over the century, is a more useful concept than monopoly capital.

The problem is that "monopoly capital" became a new paradigm for many individuals. The concept has had an additional disadvantage, because what is intrinsic to the term *monopoly* is not size or concentration of capital but control of supply. It is rather *size,* not monopoly, that is the most relevant, since the large corporations are sometimes concentrated in one industry but are usually diversified in many, the only consistency being the pursuit of profit. For theoretical concepts to be useful, they must explain the larger dynamic of the system. Did the concentration of capital lead to a qualitatively different system, or did this concentration lead to even more intense competition than before? There was no evolution toward harmony, only an occasional transitional truce. Turmoil and struggle between capitalists, large and small, is always the underlying or apparent reality in the capitalist economy.

The imperatives of competition do not preclude cooperation or cartels when they are profitable. There are many instances of licensing and technical joint ventures. For example, the international giants in the rubber and tire industry compete in the market but cooperate in supply and technology. Michelin and Goodyear coproduce synthetic rubber, and Goodyear licenses technology to a Japanese tire builder. GM and Toyota have a coproduction agreement, and U.S. Steel (now USX Corporation) invested in foreign competitors.

The statistics gathered for an industry can be meaningless as the corporation transcends the industry and as profits accrue to the corporation. This is true of U.S. Steel, B. F. Goodrich, the oil companies, and other giant conglomerates that move in and out of different industries. In 1985 GM and the steel companies were making moves to diversify into arms, services, oil, and any area deemed profitable. These firms are not seeking a monopoly position in one industry to control prices. On the contrary, they pursue a quick return by acquiring a wide range of unrelated industries. Their motives are related not to monopolization but to accumulation for its own sake. An analysis of monopoly features tells us little about this economic process. The concentration of wealth and power, however, is patently important in the economy.

The prominence of a world market is clearly a new structural feature, making the forces of competition determinative even for the largest corporations. The giants have been confronted on an international scale by competition as keen as any in the so-called era of competitive capitalism, not only in their export markets but within their own home market as well. But in steel, one of the most crisis-ridden industries, there is an international oligopoly. But what does that tell us about the steel industry?

Competition in the international market means that costs can no longer be routinely absorbed and passed on in the price to the buyer. Industries accustomed to price administration in the past must now compete in price-cutting or cost-cutting, usually in both. Some economists have noted price rises in the concentrated industries during the period of crisis and have made much of this statistic. What they often ignore is that the list price is not the real price. U.S. industry, large and small, is engaged in price-cutting for the world market, whether the items are basic commodities or computers. Virtually no industry is not affected by international competition. The antitrust ideology and regulations that exist to increase domestic competitiveness—primarily in the United States, but in other nations as well—are being dismantled or modified in order to to make national industries large enough to be more competitive in the world market.

Technology is also intensifying competition in industry and has the potential to do so much more in the future. The new flexible automation erodes old "barriers to entry" and brings in competition from sources never before imagined. And the introduction of automation and pace of innovation is determined by competition and labor costs. The one major deterrent to new investment in automation has been the expected decline in the rate of profit.

Competitive forces create surplus capacity on an international scale. The companies and nations in the OECD competed to build the competitive industries that made much of their own capacity surplus. Building their own competition was merely an aspect of the myopic accumulation drive that seeks immediate profit at the expense of long-term interest, and the knowledge that if they do not, their rivals will. International excess capacity is now being systematically destroyed in certain basic industries. It is a force of competition, not monopoly. Competitiveness can be relative, with the fluctuation of currency; and it can be absolute, with obsolete plant.

Although five oil giants and ten chemical companies dominate world production in petrochemicals, they are vulnerable because they built chemical industries in Eastern Europe whose competitive production began to enter the world market in the mid-1980s, and the suppliers' credits, often from those same Western companies, will be repaid with production. The number of petrochemical plants in the world rose by over half between 1973 and 1978 alone, and the bulk of the new capacity became operational in the mid-1980s. Losses and overcapacity in Europe led to closings and to a reduction of capacity by 15 percent in 1983. Capacity was still considered too high before the Middle East production became operational. That production was the greatest threat of all. Producing plastics and fertilizers, Saudi Arabia had completed only two-thirds of its $15 billion program in 1985 when a trade struggle with the EC was under way. Libya, Indonesia, and Canada also vastly expanded their production capacity.

Competition in the engineering and construction industry has been decisive. By 1984 the U.S. construction industry was one-half its size in the 1970s. For large industrial projects, such as an Iraqi power station, a Korean company underbid the American companies by $470 million, and the U.S. firm was not "even close" to a Japanese consortium's bid for the Singapore subway contract.[64] In the new electronics industries there is intense competition to develop and implement innovation.

International competition undermined the oligopolies' power to adjust the rate of output rather than cut prices in response to falling demand. The factor of overcapacity, an outcome and force of competition, must be seen as a worldwide phenomenon until nations close their borders to international trade.

Decisive in the international competition are exchange rates, and as they fluctuate, they evoke tensions among states. The corporate giants' impact on inflation came not only in their pricing power, whether transfer prices or price leaders, but also through their control of international capital movement, which affected the most important price of all, that of foreign exchange, and to which they, too, were vulnerable.

CLASS STRUGGLE

In capitalist ideology the crisis is always attributed to labor, and it is labor that must bear the cost of restructuring the economy for renewed profitability. Capitalists' routine arguments cite labor's strength or full employment as a "rigidity" causing inflation and preventing the necessary "readjustment" of the economy to resolve the crisis. Wages, they claim, take a larger share of national income,

inhibiting investment; labor's militancy prompts relocation and therefore is responsible, along with the minimum wage and unemployment
compensation, for unemployment. Welfare measures cause deficits and
are now expendable, the tax on corporations for social security is a
drain on capital that could otherwise be invested, and so on. These
capitalist postulates are now so widespread that there is a near consensus, extending from the orthodox capitalists to French Socialists and
Italian Communists, that wages are the source of inflation and that
profits must be higher in order to induce investment.

Labor costs increased modestly in the OECD states until around
1968. At that time there was a sharp rise throughout their economies,
both nominal and real, in wages, benefits, and the annual rate of change
in the unit of output until 1975. "[I]t is the rates of change that are
of more interest" in the OECD countries, declared one of its studies in
1978.[65] A precondition to the rise in cost in Europe was a resurgence
of militancy and class conflict during those years and a negligible
reserve army of unemployed.

By 1976 there was unanimity between capital and the state economists that the change in labor cost and a consequent shift in income
share from profits to wages was responsible for the deterioration of the
comparative advantage of the OECD and for the economic crisis.
Higher labor costs both inhibit investment in general and accelerate
labor substitution in such investment as continues. It is rather fruitless
to scrutinize whether there was *objectively* a wage squeeze on profits by
examining the statistics in retrospect. What matters is the capitalist's
perception.

From the beginning of the crisis in 1974, restructuring in the OECD
countries focused on the effort to reverse the post-1968 gains of labor.
The offensive against labor picked up momentum during the recession
of 1980–83. Against the background of record unemployment, industry
after industry demanded concessions, givebacks, reorganization of
work, wage and benefit rollbacks, union smashing, and other measures.
By the mid-1980s labor costs in manufacturing for many industries in
the United States had been reduced to as little as 5 percent and
generally not more than 15 percent of the total cost, depending on the
industry.

In fact, there is always a subjective strategy against labor, but there
are also the objective developments in the world economy of international competition, aggravated by currency exchange rates and the
developments in technology, that will permanently eradicate millions
of jobs.

For the wage worker, wages are what matter most—the only income, on which the worker's life and that of his or her dependents rely. For capital, wages paid to the worker are only part of the labor cost, which also includes fringe benefits paid to the state, currency exchange rates, productivity, and unit labor cost.

The rising unit labor cost in the OECD states developed as the postwar labor surplus turned to scarcity in the capital goods industries that had a high labor content. The labor shortage in the key growth industries led to the strength of the trade unions and the welfare policies of the state. The unit labor cost, which on an average for the OECD countries rose 3.3 percent between 1963 and 1970, jumped to 6.2 percent between 1970 and 1973. This was accompanied by a sharp rise in other costs, particularly those of energy and interest.

Rising labor costs are both an incentive and a deterrent to investment—an incentive to rationalization and redeployment and, in an economic climate of slow growth, a deterrent as they increase costs and reduce profits. As long as increased costs could be passed along in the price and as the market appeared to be expanding, rising costs could be tolerated. For the first two postwar decades many companies absorbed and passed along increased labor costs, because demand was high. "You hated to lose a sale" in labor struggles, claimed one executive, noting that that time was gone.[66]

As competition in the world market challenged the old hegemony of the oligopolistic industries, rising labor costs could no longer be passed along and were resisted. But they were opposed against a background of rising unemployment, debt, losses, intense competition, and falling profits.

There had been a rather sharp variation of labor costs among nations because of restraints on firings in most OECD countries other than the United States. In Europe restraint was legislated; in Japan it was enshrined in lifetime employment policies, which cover only about 25 percent of Japanese workers. This legal or traditional restraint, now called a "rigidity," meant different fixed costs. One Japanese economist estimated that as a result of the widespread layoff policy, only one-third of the general wage costs were fixed in the United States, giving U.S. industry a competitive advantage. And while fixed costs are higher in Japan, the system there depends for full operation on a large reservoir of temporary workers and a system of subcontracting.

Although many economists, some Marxist as well as bourgeois, have focused on market relations or the sphere of distribution, capitalists consistently focus on the sphere of production and the systemic features of accumulation, competition, and the class struggle. They do not seek to expand the market for the realization of their profit; on the contrary, they would rather reduce their costs, principally labor, with the aid of the state. Yet the contradiction remains no less blatant than in Marx's time—one capitalist's worker is another capitalist's customer. The crisis offered capital the opportunity to restructure the relationship with labor. I will discuss further dimensions of this struggle in Part IV.

Yet the outcome of this crisis by the mid-1980s has indeed strengthened capital in these crucial respects. More and more states compete to grant concessions in the form of cheap labor to attract investment, and unemployment has eroded the strength of labor.

DEVELOPMENTS IN ECONOMIC SECTORS

Developments in all of the major economic sectors—service, industrial, and natural resources—reveal the restructuring process in the capitalist economy. The largest changes have occurred in banking, in "basic" industries like steel, and in the development of the industries based on the new technology. The arms industry plays a paramount role in the restructuring of the economies of many nations. The shifting status of raw materials, particularly of oil, has had an obvious impact on the world economy, and changes in agriculture relate to yet other developments. A closer look at these economic sectors brings the contradictions in the process into sharper definition.

CHAPTER 4

THE SERVICE SECTOR

Among the generalizations on the world economy, none are more prevalent than those dealing with the so-called transformation from an industrial to a service economy. This is so because the only growing economic sector in much of the world economy is that diverse group of industries and occupations designated as either "service" or "services-producing sector," or tertiary (raw materials and agriculture being primary and manufacturing secondary). What are the implications of this objective restructuring? Can service industries become core industries? In this and in all other aspects of the economy, generalizations can be very misleading.

Economists have debated the implications of the growth in the service sector. The Japanese government established a committee to examine the implications of what they termed the "softization" of the economy, a trend it actively promotes.[1] Does it imply a postindustrial society or signify a deindustrialization of the economy? What are its implications for income distribution and economic growth? One economist found reassurance that the change could be beneficial in the fact that there is no saturation of demand for services, as there is for durable goods.

A general definition is that a nation has a service economy when more than half of its labor force produces intangibles. This was already true for the United States in 1940. By 1976 more than two-thirds of the work force was so employed, and nearly all the OECD nations were "service economies" by this definition. In terms of their share of the GDP, the service industries accounted for over 60 percent in Britain

95

and nearly that in Japan and France. Statistically, it is under 50 percent
for the FRG since industrial firms primarily perform their own service
functions. In the other OECD nations there is considerable contracting
out for all sorts of service functions. Some LDCs, by the criterion of
employment, are also service economies, or nearly so, having from 30
to over 50 percent of the active labor force engaged in services, which
is often a disguised form of unemployment.

Most who have written on the service sector have recognized that
service is a term difficult to define. Many define it negatively by what
it is not. What it is generally includes the financial services—banking,
insurance, brokerages—trade, transport, communications, maintenance, professions, tourism and leisure, advertising, health, personal,
and business services. Of the world's top 200 corporations, 82 are
classified as service companies. They are primarily banks and trading
companies, 41 percent of them headquartered in Japan and 33 percent
in the United States.

The service industries include industries with the highest rate of
return as well as marginal subsistence occupations. And investment in
the various types of services is important for a realistic analysis of the
economy and its direction. Jobs in the general category of services are
polarized between high-salary professional work, such as that of Wall
Street lawyers, and the lowest-wage labor, such as that of fast-food
kitchen helpers without benefits; the number of middle-income jobs is
very limited. Traditionally, the services are highly labor intensive and
with low productivity. The only one with growing employment, the
service sector, too, is rapidly automating, with everything from the
computer to dispensing machines. In banks like Citicorp one-third of
the new jobs in the mid-1980s were professional or managerial, "a far
cry from five to ten years ago," remarked its chairman.[2]

Government statisticians in the United States believe that the impact
of services on growth, productivity, or trade statistics are neither accurately reported nor accurately analyzed. They have ascertained that the
service industry (excluding finance, communication, transport, and
trade) accounted for 14 percent of all production and 24 percent of all
employment in 1985. Nonprofit services, including public education
and health, accounted for 14 percent of employment in 1977. Producer
services, accounting for 12 percent of the total employment, are much
more important than consumer services, which declined between 1929
and 1977 from 10 percent to 5 percent. According to one study, "the
treatment of the growth of services as a monolithic shift within the
economy is an unwarranted simplification."[3] Some services grew, while
others did not, but the share of manufacturing output in the GNP in

constant prices has remained remarkably steady, at around 21 percent, since 1955.

During recessions the output of goods declines, while service output continues to grow. In the period 1980–84 growth rates in the various services ranged from 4 to 7 percent, figures considerably higher than those for the other sectors of the economy. The highest by far was in "securities, commodities brokers," a sector that showed an annual growth of 16.9 percent. Four mutual funds dealing only in service companies by the mid-1980s indicated the extent of investor interest in the service industries. The president of one claimed that their strength was that service companies were "not exposed to overseas competition."[4]

One of the chief factors in the 1983 recovery and employment growth in the United States was retail trade. The strong dollar created a merchandising bonanza, as consumer prices, but particularly profits, benefited from the sudden shift in import prices. And credit, which in the United States reached the phenomenal figure of 19.6 percent of take-home pay by 1986, financed the consumer expenditures. Attracted by the return, a large proportion of the direct foreign investment in the United States during the 1980s was in the retail trade.

But it is a myth that services could stand alone in anything but a small economy. It was always what its name implies—a service to other sectors. Dieter Ernst makes the important point that the whole postwar restructuring of industry led to the emergence of the service industries as appendages to production, in order to finance and commercialize industrial products.[5] And an appendage cannot exist by itself.

SERVICES IN MANUFACTURING

The major growth in this sector has been in business, not in consumer or household, services. This growth has occurred within industries as well as in the business-servicing industries. The crisis for basic industry would be even more severe except that many are now selling services like the management of facilities, training, and consulting. For arms contractors like Northrup, services accounted for 20 percent of all revenue in 1979, compared with 5 percent in 1974. Lockheed's service revenues grew tenfold in seven years in the 1970s, 90 percent of it through foreign sales. Electric machinery companies, in response to stagnating sales of goods, expanded their service activity. Services account for one-third of the income of General Electric and Borg Warner and for 50 percent of Westinghouse's.

Most important, as more and more U.S. manufacturing companies have shed their production activity under the impact of competition and turned instead to the contracting and distribution of goods produced elsewhere by others, the actual service character of the U.S. economy has intensified. With an "If you can't beat them, join them" mentality, U.S. auto companies are moving to sell Japanese cars. The Commerce Department, until the fall of the dollar, expected 17 percent of Detroit's sales to be made in Japan by as early as 1988. Ford will produce a car in Taiwan, and GM has arranged to sell a Korean car.

Business Week reported, "Companies long identified with making goods of all sorts now often only produce the package and the label.[6] The vice-president of Schwinn bicycles, which contracts out to Asian companies and markets the product under its own name, explained, "When you are a manufacturing company, your mind-set tends to be to sell what you can make. We're market-driven now."[7]

There is, of course, no strategy in these moves in response to the capitalist's perception of profitable action. But this shift from producing to contracting is objectively restructuring the world economy. It is different from the TNC's relocating of production by constructing a plant abroad. And it parallels an agribusiness shift from plantation to contract. The TNCs allocate for themselves the marketing and organizing service function and avoid the labor relations inherent in ownership. For the capitalist the real danger of such a relationship is that the producers can change their buyer. Also, in many cases, the contracting companies have inadvertently created their own competition. In Taiwan, for instance, an American instrument company subsidiary trained technicians who subsequently created eleven competing companies in the area.

In trade, U.S. service exports totaled 40 percent of all goods exports in 1980, and for some years the surplus in this sector offset the deficit in goods. It is also the most difficult form of trade to measure, but estimates are that services accounted for 18 percent of the world trade in 1983. Many nations have set up barriers to protect their own service industry, and the competition in third markets is intense. In "special business services," such as engineering, consulting, and brokerage, France, the FRG, and Britain are in the lead, and the U.S. share fell from 15 percent in 1973 to 8 percent a decade later. Service sales to subsidiaries account for the lion's share of this "foreign" trade. Many services, on the other hand, have prospered in the domestic market, compared with goods producers, thanks to the lack of import competition. But service trade is definitely an arena of mounting international conflict. Gaining access for its nationals in service trade, particularly in the financial services, is one of the main U.S. goals in GATT. The larger LDCs, led by India and Brazil, resist the effort to give open entry to the giants in the service sector; for the most part, they use the infant-industry argument. But now even the service sector, while employing 70 percent of the private sector labor force in the United States, also has begun to relocate in order to get cheaper labor abroad. For instance, market research firms can hire data processors in Barbados for 30 percent of the labor cost in the United States.

Finally, a large part of the service industry is unrecorded statistically, since it is a part of the "underground" economy, whose scale varies from country to country—estimates range from around 8 percent of the GDP in the United Kingdom to the substantial figure of about 30 percent in Italy.[8]

The growth of the financial service sector is the most significant of all over the past decade. It is even credited with having saved New York City from financial disaster in the 1970s. The most prominent industry, and the one most crucial to the general economy, is banking.

CHAPTER 5

BANKING: CHANGES IN A PIVOTAL SECTOR

By the mid-1980s the observation that the banks play a pivotal role in the crisis was banal. The banks have been intimately involved in the restructuring of the economy, but they in no sense planned it. Rather, restructuring was the outcome of their own accumulation drive. Banks are pivotal, but not in the sense of "finance capital" control, for the term suggests that the banks have a strategic aim to control industry. Their aim is not control but profit; only with the greatest reluctance will they turn credit into equity control. In the United States bank control is relatively rare today; whereas in 1900 some 25 percent of the largest 200 corporations were bank controlled, in 1975 only one was. A decade later, owing to their role in financing takeovers, banks were again more prominent in the management of corporations, and conversely, U.S. regulators questioned restrictions on corporate control of banks. But banks are pivotal in their linkage with all other sectors of the economy and because of the impact of their profit-making activity, in a highly competitive environment of ever greater risk, on the entire system.

In this book I will examine how banks have been restructured and what their role, in turn, has been in the restructuring of the economy; I will not chronicle all the picturesque details of their marginally criminal activities. Such details are readily available in a vast literature that has burgeoned alongside the bankers' growing peculations. But one may indeed generalize that the new structural conditions in banking and the economy facilitate, and even invite, criminal or barely legal activities in pursuit of profit.

A U.S. congressional report on insider abuse in American banks

100

shows, according to the committee chairman, "that in 60 percent of the bank failures . . . studied, there was some indication of criminal abuse or activity."[1] But this is comparatively minor in the league of risks. The telex and the computer, the technology that brought structural changes, could transfer hundreds of millions from one bank to another, from one currency to another, in seconds. The access to enormous wholesale deposits from other banks could be mobilized not only for riskier loans but also for currency and interest rate speculation and for an endless array of financial "products" in a highly volatile market. The surprise is not that insolvencies abound but that the banking system survives. It is, after all, a very tenuous and vulnerable activity, resting ultimately on confidence alone. Indeed, the threat of a public loss of confidence in them remains their biggest concern. Banks go to great pains to appear conservative by denying their practices even when it is well known that, increasingly, high risk accompanies all their activities.

Commercial banking has traditionally meant deposits and loans, profit being made on the differential. Investment and merchant banking profits were based on fees for the underwriting of securities. These functions were separated in the United States, with the depression in 1933, and banking was subject to innumerable regulations that did not exist in Europe. The European "universal" banks that deal in securities and can own an unlimited amount of equity were nevertheless subject to an array of regulations, many related to state policy on the control of the money supply.

Several basic changes developed over the past decade have objectively restructured the banks' role in the world economy. National boundaries eroded first with the Eurodollar deposits and then with petrodollars and the interbank network of "wholesale" deposits. The recession in the mid-1970s brought loans to sovereign states for balance-of-payments support. The new information and communications technology, the floating currency exchange, and the floating interest rates had an enormous effect. Banks moved from expanding assets (loans) to "managing" liabilities (deposits) and continuously developing new "products." This trend became especially significant after the debt crisis of 1982. Profits were increasingly gained in trading and fees rather than in loans, as banks began to describe themselves as "financial service industries" or "money centers" rather than as lending institutions. In 1986 some 30 percent of the earnings of the largest banks in the United States was noninterest income. Although stability in the economy was important to lenders, the new money traders had a vested interest in instability.

These changes have also given the banks the power to create money, previously reserved to the state, as an objective outcome of their activity. Debt is now counted as "money," making the problem once perceived as money supply really one of debt. The combination of all of these financial innovations and the mushrooming of new "products" among banks made traditional measurements of money supply irrelevant.

A number of leading economists have emphasized for over a decade the increasing fragility of the financial structure as the commercial banks became de facto more independent of the central banks—to the point where Albert Wojnilower, an economist with First Boston, asserted that the Federal Reserve banks were scarcely more than "branches" of the commercial banks. And David Felix, in his critique of the neoclassical economists who have dominated Washington since 1981, described how the most dangerous trends in financial behavior have actually been celebrated as new efficiency and innovation, as the Reagan administration and Congress proceeded to dismember even wholly inadequate regulations. Yet much of the deregulation of the financial sector in the United States was making de jure what already existed de facto. By mid-1987, the Treasury Department, with the endorsement of the new chairman of the Federal Reserve Board, Alan Greenspan, advocated the creation of five to ten giant banks in order to compete with those of Japan and Europe. It also advocated repeal of the regulation that prevented industrial companies from owning banks.

Competition in the world financial market is also a spur to deregulation internationally. The FRG has progressively dropped its reserve minimums, taxes on foreign deposits, and regulations and bans on "swaps" and other various new "products," to permit "what is possible in the Anglo-Saxon countries."[2] The Bundesbank president, Karl Otto Pöhl, said, "I do think it . . . desirable if Eurobusiness could be repatriated through certain modifications. . . ."[3] The German bankers lost no time in introducing even more exotic financial innovations. London dismantled most of its regulations in 1986 in order to remain the center of financial activity, and under intense pressure from Washington the Japanese government reluctantly dropped many of its regulations.

But most significant for the banks was the shift in the capital flow from bank credit to the capital market. Here again the turning point was the debt crisis of 1982 when the ratio between bank credit and the capital market was 5:1. By 1985 it had fallen to a ratio of 1:2. The big borrowers and depositors turned from the banks to floating-rate notes, which were like loans but tradable securities of "blue-chip" companies or governments, bypassing the banks' CDs and loans. Forty percent of them were issued by nonbanks, and it cut the banks' profit margin from corporate lending significantly as they lost their best loan risks to the capital markets. According to a Deutsche Bank investment specialist, two-thirds of financial activity in the international credit markets in the early 1980s was standard bank lending. By 1985 it represented only 10–15 percent, and bank lending would have fallen even further had it not been for corporate merger and acquisition financing. Sales of securities had quadrupled since 1981.

Like most aspects of the current situation, the banks' new role began in the 1960s. It was linked to every phase of the evolving crisis: the dollar's role, the expansion of transnational industries, monetary crises, inflation of essential commodities and of industrial goods, and other factors. Between 1971 and 1973, lending patterns were transformed in a period of aggressive bank competition to make loans at exceptional risk, compared with the past. The floating-rate loan began in October 1971.

With the vast increase in liquidity at the beginning of the 1970s, particularly during the boom of 1971–73, the banks began aggressively to seek new borrowers, with low margin and great risk. The period is nevertheless referred to as the "good" boom, since the loans were for projects involving production, as opposed to the "bad" boom after 1973, when the loans were for balance-of-payments support and debt service. The vast expansion of liquidity, with the advent of the petrodollar, itself reflected recessionary conditions.

Through the 1970s and until 1982, the banks operated on the assumption that inflation and rising energy costs were "forever," when in fact nothing is forever except contradiction and change. While inflation tended to eradicate debt and frequently led to negative interest rates, disinflation and, in some cases, deflation posed other threats to the banks as corporate borrowers, unable to raise prices, were unable to repay loans, particularly in energy, agriculture, and their supply industries. In the mid-1980s the bulk of nonperforming loans were in energy, real estate, agriculture, utilities, and mining. These loans were the origin of the accelerating number of bank failures, which each year set postdepression records, numbering 79 in 1984 and 136 in 1986 in the United States, compared to 7 in 1981. The contrast between the 1980s and the past is captured by the fact that there were 262 bank failures between 1942 and 1980 but 400 between 1980 and mid-1986. The FDIC list of "problem" banks reached over 1,200 in 1986, up

from 250 in 1983. Yet despite the failures and falling profits of all but
a few banks, new banks continued to open—455 in 1984, more than
twice the number of 1979.

After the crisis in loans to sovereign states, the banks financed every
form of corporate speculation and merger movement, as they cut back
on foreign lending and foreclosed on farm loans. "Corporate balance
sheets revealed extraordinary vulnerabilities for this stage of the business cycle," observed a Morgan Stanley economist.[4]

By the mid-1980s the international capital flow had reached gigantic proportions. It rose 27 percent between 1983 and 1984 and again
24 percent between 1984 and 1985, in large part representing the
refinancing of existing debt. But bank lending grew at a record low
rate of only 5.6 percent in the first half of 1985. Exporters to the
United States, especially those from Asia, deposited their earnings in
U.S. banks during the first half of the 1980s. They had an incentive
to keep their earnings in dollars because of the high interest rates
and dollar appreciation, but on short term because of their perception
of a probable shift in the exchange rates. Foreign deposits in U.S.
banks fell by more than $10 billion in 1986, considerably more than
in 1984 or 1985. Private capital flow into the United States outside
the banking sector was only about one-third of these bank capital
imports. And all this massive capital movement took place while productive economic growth or activity—investment and trade—was declining or stagnating.

TECHNOLOGY

Technology played a leading role in the banks' current position.
Walter Wriston, the former chairman of Citicorp, "would argue that
what one might call the *information standard* has replaced the gold
standard and indeed even the system invented at Bretton Woods.
. . . the expansion of the electromagnetic spectrum up to 300 megahertz
. . . has created an entirely new system of world finance based on the
incredibly rapid flow of information around the world . . . [and] trouble
for governments on all the world's continents."[5] "Money often moves
in response to information," Wriston went on; "unfortunately, there are
very few governments indeed that do not attempt to control the movement of wealth across borders. . . . The air is filled with ideas about
our global market and how to improve it, or repair it, or change it. But
much of the thinking is taking place within a framework that no longer
exists."[6]

The growth of the offshore tax havens also depended on the development of the telex. The $30 billion "parked" in the Grand Cayman or

similar branches of the New York and London banks arrives only in the form of a telex message, and interest earned is tax free. This new technology permits or makes possible the mushrooming of new means of making money and has changed the traders' role in the world of banking and financial speculation in general. But that technology has also greatly increased the competition. In the currency exchange market, for example, within a few years all forms of nonbank institutions as well as an ever increasing number of smaller banks became dealers. Albert Wojnilower, in remarking on technology's role in extending the "crowd" of traders, noted, "It is well known that crowds . . . respond very differently than individuals," but "unlike a casino, the financial markets are inextricably linked with the world outside, the real economy pays the price."[7]

The computer also became an indispensable tool for the traders who devise new means of making money on fractional arbitrage involving hundreds of components. But the ease in buying and selling anywhere in the world also magnifies the risk, since a collapse or default in a remote corner can have instant and vast repercussions. As one investment manager noted in 1986, "Unfounded rumor can travel just as quickly as truth. Traders . . . know that their competitors around the world see [on their computer] exactly what they see when they see it. Hence reaction times [are] always short. . . ."[8]

As fast as new regulations emerged, there appeared ways to evade them. Given pressures from the central banks that examined their balance sheets, the commercial banks simply moved more business off their balance sheets. Their ingenuity knew no bounds. But the risks remained and were often magnified many times. Finally, many governments resolved the issue by what Carl Gewirtz called "throwing in the towel after their fruitless efforts to regulate the Euromarket."[9]

While the banks may support regulation at one period of history, they will oppose it later and even again support it when it suits their interests. One should not look for consistency on these structural questions or expect that what is true of their attitude at one time will be so forever.

INTERBANK

One of the most vulnerable new structural aspects of the banking system since 1966 is the interbank network (termed wholesale banking), which links well over a thousand banks and over two trillion dollars by mid-1987, nearly doubling in two years in a chain whose beginning or end no one knows. Before the Eurocurrency market, international financing was handled by each separate national banking system. There was no linkage between the domestic and international markets. Now all banks put spare funds on deposit by telex, the maturities are short (twenty-four hours to six months), especially for the weakest banks, so the turnover is rapid. There are fewer and bigger "wholesale" depositors, whose deposits are in the multimillions, and they are much less stable than domestic "retail" deposits. Banks depend on rollovers at maturity. Interbank deposits represent two-thirds of the total deposits of many major banks. Hypersensitive to interest rate differentials between banks and countries, the interbank deposits move quickly from one country to another. The whole chain is dependent on the clearing computer in New York, which monitors on a daily basis the interbank accounts; if one bank in the chain fails to meet its commitment, the whole system can break down until the condition is resolved. The London interbank offered rate (LIBOR) is the standard by which loan interest rates are set—ranging from fractions to several percentage points above, depending on the risk.

A bank deposits funds in another, which "onlends" them to other banks, and the process may include many banks in a long chain before the funds are lent to a nonbank borrower or, more likely, used for trading purposes. All banks are both creditors and debtors in the interbank system, but some are more of one than the other. In the United States the small banks are net creditors, and in the Euromarket the reverse is true. The traders gamble on the minute interest rate differential; since they deal in sums in the hundreds of millions, these amount to significant profits or losses.

As two economists pointed out, both the Eurocurrency and interbank market have "a high potential for contagion."[10] They concluded in 1981 that any bank was subject to a run if it had to renegotiate sovereign-risk loans equal to a major part of their capital under conditions of doubt that the country will be able to improve its foreign currency earnings. Although some large depositors from the Middle East, worried about the exposure of the U.S. banks, did move funds in mid-1984 from U.S. banks to the Hong Kong and Shanghai Bank, this did not occur with the major renegotiations over the debt of Brazil, Argentina, and Mexico. Instead, there was a major run on the Continental Illinois National Bank of Chicago, heavily exposed to the private sector and dependent on interbank deposits. Once confidence is lost and the wholesale deposits are not renewed or are withdrawn, the largest banks can be wiped out in a matter of days without a state rescue. As the finance minister of Kuwait stated, "You either have faith in the whole system or you lose faith in the whole system. You cannot say that bank X has better reserves than bank Y. Because if bank Y really goes bust so does bank X, no matter how much better ratios it has maintained."[11]

The number of participants in the interbank network increased in the late 1970s and early 1980s, as the banks in the LDCs and in other nations saw the network as a source of funding in their desire to maximize profits and diversify their loans. With the increase in numbers, the competition intensified. "What is historically unique is the extent to which Euromarkets have become a critical structural element . . . of hundreds of banks around the world," which before the 1970s had no important international business.[12] There is also a sovereign risk associated with interbank deposits in countries with foreign-exchange difficulties and consequent currency controls.

By 1985 the Japanese banks were ready to compete in the international market on a scale equivalent to that of their manufacturing companies. Already in 1982 their 24 banks in the global top 100 banks held 24 percent of the assets and 20 percent of the profits of the total. According to the Bank for International Settlements (BIS), the overseas assets of the Japanese banks rose from $520 billion in September 1984 to $1,190 billion in September 1986, in part because of the value of the yen. A Ministry of Finance official said, "We think they are ready to export financial services, to compete fully with western institutions, and we intend to push them."[13] Their first move to establish a market share will be to cut their margins. "It's part of Japanese bankers' nature—they are very fond of excessive competition," explained the director of Sumitomo Trust and Banking.[14] Many of their world branches are unprofitable, for the present. But the banks have a mass of capital for investment. By September 1986 their market share was 31.5 percent, compared with 23.2 percent in 1984. The U.S. banks' share had fallen over those years from 26.3 percent to 18.6 percent.

In the late 1970s this unprecedented competition and its impact on margins was the chief concern of international bankers. In the 1980s they perceived the interbank market, with its changed composition, to be of even greater risk. "Mismatching" deposits and loans is a high-risk bank management tactic that often yields high profits through the fluctuating rates and narrow spreads, increasing the risk of borrowing short and lending long that characterizes international banking. In 1982, with this perception of greater risk, a tiering developed again among banks, and the smaller banks had to pay more for funds.

The dangers of the interbank relationship, which has long been the chief concern of the BIS, was underlined by the collapse of Continental Illinois. Generally, attention was riveted on the risks of lending, especially of the sovereign-risk loans. But though these risks exist, the real trigger to a liquidity and then to a solvency crisis is a fall of confidence and a withdrawal of deposits, especially the wholesale deposits of other banks, for in a crisis the first area that contracts is the interbank market. Speed is of the essence. The problems for Continental began "in the Far East and then turned into a CD run in London, all while American bankers and regulators were still asleep," one anxious investment banker pointed out.[15] As another banker noted in June 1984, "It took the Fed seven days to get its act together over Continental. By the time they agree to act on a second-tier bank in the Euromarkets, it would all be history."[16]

The interbank links are so all-pervasive that the default of one borrower affects not merely the lenders in a syndicate but also hundreds of other banks in the omnipresent lending system. The threat of an interbank liquidity crisis has alarmed the BIS more than the LDC or CPE debt. And as is well known, when there is trouble along the chain, the whole system is in jeopardy until the lender of last resort picks up the pieces.

The important part of the interbank operation is the art of "liability [deposit] management." Some banks still use the deposits to lend to nonbank borrowers, but they are normally used for short-term gambling in interest rates, exchange rates, swaps, futures, and the like. Profits for banks were increasingly from the "treasury" division specializing in volatile and high-risk currency exchange, interest rate differentials, and other innovative "products" rather than from loans. The swaps of assets among the banks make it unclear who holds what risk. The movement of deposits had reversed, along with the general shift in capital. A significant part of the capital imports into the United States in 1983–84 was the recall of bank, particularly interbank, deposits and U.S. bank borrowing abroad in the context of retrenchment of foreign lending and expansion of domestic credit. The U.S. banks borrowed $17 billion net in the interbank market in 1985, whereas they had deposited $32 billion in 1982. And in 1985 the interbank market contracted, as the capital markets began to absorb an ever growing proportion of the world's liquid capital. These new areas offered new risks, but meanwhile the banks continued to be beset by the problems of their traditional loans. Loan losses rose 30 percent for the top 100 U.S. banks in 1986, to $11 billion, equal to their net earnings.

SECTOR LOANS

As in their concentration in specific countries, the banks have moved as a herd to finance particular industrial sectors, and the problems that developed in each have, in turn, threatened the overexposed banks.

Such areas as shipping, real estate, aerospace, energy, and agriculture have been prominent since the mid-1970s.

After the second oil price "shock" the banks raced to lend to energy-related industries and for exploration. Loans from U.S. banks alone rose from $11.7 billion in 1977 to $32.9 billion in May 1982. Canadian banks made enormous loans to finance Dome petroleum and other moves to Canadianize the oil industry. Loans to oil-exporting countries like Mexico mounted. So confident were the banks (and others) in extrapolating the oil price rise into the future that fifty European and U.S. banks made "nonrecourse" project loans of $10 billion. The nonrecourse loan that some of the largest banks considered a new "product specialty" in a competitive market had no collateral or gua-rantees whatever and would be repaid only out of the earnings of the project. As the loan's name implied, the borrower was not liable if there were no or insufficient earnings. One example was the exploration project off the Australian coast by Woodside Petroleum, a subsidiary of Royal Dutch Shell. Sixty-two banks joined the syndicate led by Citibank and Chase for $1.4 billion. One bank admitted that it had joined on the assumption that oil prices would rise 8 percent a year, to $75 per barrel. The reversal of this perspective came swiftly in 1982, with a fall in the price of petroleum, and was accompanied by a crash in the oil equipment industry. Between 1982 and 1984 the collapse of the oil suppliers industry took with it fifty small U.S. banks. Continen-tal Illinois was the biggest lender to U.S. corporations and the most aggressive in energy loans between 1979 and 1982. When the business collapsed, companies could neither service their loans nor provide the collateral. Nonperforming loans grew to $2.3 billion by April 1984. Only interbank deposits could fill the gap.

Farm loans were another crisis area by the mid-1980s. A U.S. government survey found that farmers together owing 62.5 percent of the farm debt were in danger of default. As foreclosures increased, rural bank failures followed. More than 40 percent of the banks on the problem list of the FDIC were in agricultural regions in 1986, where net loan losses had tripled over the preceding three years. Rural bank-ers received the brunt of the farmers' frustration, in the form of fre-quent assaults and even several murders.

But the biggest area of lending has been in mergers and acquisitions and in loans for hostile takeovers or the defense against them.

LEVERAGED BUYOUTS (LBOs)

By 1984 the pace of LBOs, or purchases of companies by means of borrowed funds alone, was described as "frenzied"; seventy-six of them, valued at $27 billion, were announced in the first nine months, compared with twenty-seven, valued at $4 billion, in 1983. After Continental Illinois's collapse the FRB began to apply pressure, and the bankers were more cautious for several months. However, with slack loan demand and the profitable interest rate differentials of the LBOs, usually 2.5 percent over the LIBOR, their prudence waned. Also important was the fact that the demand came at the time the banks were renegotiating their sovereign loans. In 1986 it was one of the few high-profit loans available. "The flow of LBOs is *created* by lenders. They don't just support the market; they make it happen," reported one participating lender.[17] Banks usually provide 85 percent of the capital for the LBOs. The LBOs at record interest rates are dependent on the conjuncture with a rising stock market. They can be devastated by its fall. As the chairman of the SEC warned, "The more leveraged takeovers and buyouts today, the more bankruptcies tomorrow."[18]

Oblivious to the risks as usual, the investment banks began to buy for their own account by 1986. "We have so much expertise at evaluating and structuring deals that we said, why not take the next step and bet on our own advice," said the LBO managing director of First Boston, explaining its equity participation in nine buyouts.[19]

In 1983–84 the loans to corporations to finance megamergers and takeovers reached new records: $12 billion to Arco for its unsuccessful bid to take over Gulf, $1 billion to Gulf to fight a takeover bid by Pickens, $14 billion to Socal for its merger with Gulf, $650 million to Royal Dutch Shell for full control of U.S. Shell. These corporate loans to prime borrowers were usually ⅜ of a percentage point over the LIBOR.

INVESTMENT BANKS

The investment bankers were active promoters of the mergers and divestitures in the 1980s, acting as the "creative initiator who maps out a new combination for two businesses," as one of them put it.[20] Over the past decade, as *Business Week* noted in 1984, "leading investment banks have evolved from intimate partnerships to huge, diversified enterprises," with thousands of employees and dozens of branches.[21] The bankers also actively promoted international mergers, frequently flying between Europe and America and introducing prospective clients to new opportunities. Their "creative" work was earning "megabuck" fees of $15 to $20 million per transaction. First Boston advised Du Pont and Marathon in their merger problems for a fee of $33 million, and fees for the investment bankers amounted to $100 million in the $1.8 billion takeover of Revlon. Approximately eight investment banks handle the bulk of the mergers over $500 million. These huge fees in the merger and acquisition (M & A) business, "more than 100 percent of profits in the case of some," according to one New York banker, were financing the losses the investment banks were taking to expand in the competitive globalization of the securities market. "The bull market [in M & A] is covering a lot of sins," one American investment banker said. "All this expansion, this headlong rush overseas is being built on the enormous and very profitable domestic corporate business."[22] Certainly, until the next recession, the banks are amassing enormous sums in fees and interest as debt increases for takeovers and for the defense against them and as corporations repurchase their own stock with borrowed funds.

There are no master plans in their "creative" innovations, only the earning of fees and profits and the getting of a "share of the market." From 1980 to 1982 the income of the investment banks doubled and profits were at 30 percent, thanks to their involvement in mortgage banking, commodities, and commercial paper, securities and exchange trading, real estate, equity, and "swaps." By the mid-1980s bankers were even proposing to companies that they issue bonds and offering to put their own capital at risk by buying the issue outright. That and "putting their own capital on the line in takeover situations," claimed the chairman of Credit Suisse bank, was "a risk-taking of a new sort which should be reserved for commercial banks because they are subject to certain restrictions and supervision."[23]

Aside from the insider scandals that were exposed in 1986, the conflict of interest with their traditional advisory role soon became evident, as the investment banks participated for their own account in the deals they were arranging. "If you bare your soul to these people, you're a fool," concluded one senior corporate executive.[24]

The worldwide free market in buying and selling securities made the competition in this area so intense by the mid-1980s, and the eagerness of the investment banks to be part of the globalization of the markets was so great, that most were price-cutting to the point of losses. "Americans have done some pretty crazy things to try to establish their place [in Europe]," commented the vice-president of First Boston, one of the biggest operators.[25] In Japan the securities houses, the equivalent of the investment banks, began in the mid-1980s to sell the new "products" that Merrill Lynch had added in the mid-1970s. These houses want to retain regulations separating and protecting them from the huge commercial banks, much as U.S. investment banks desire to do.

Among the most important new "products" for investment banks since the early 1980s have been the "swaps" of credits, a broker's role of finding those who want to exchange a floating-rate bond for a fixed rate, or any other type of trade. Everything—bonds, equity, loans, options, and so on—became "swapable" into another. They all required expert, and costly, staff and overhead in order to profit on the arbitrage. A few banks were prepared. Morgan Guaranty "saw that to be a global operation you needed to be able to price, trade and sell issues in all markets and all currencies."[26] "The speed of deregulation has forced us to re-assess our position," noted the director of Salomon Brothers International.[27] All these transactions and deals are supposedly recorded as national service trade and play a major role in America's trade negotiations.

The commercial banks must increasingly finance higher-risk ventures, as they struggle to keep borrowers who can now turn to nonloan debt of the types described above. Chafing under the restrictions of the Glass-Steagall Act, the commercial banks were applying to the FRB for permission to handle securities in the United States, which they were already dealing with in the Euromarket. Morgan Guaranty, Citicorp, and Chase reportedly warned that unless they were able to deal in securities, they would give up their commercial bank licenses. Branch banks, they held, were becoming "white elephants."

In Britain merchant banks have been excluded from the stock exchange and deal primarily in the underwriting of bonds, but with the growing deregulation they are increasingly merging with stockbrokers.

CURRENCY EXCHANGE

Some of the larger banks had the power to "make markets" in their enormous currency dealings. In 1979 the Justice Department opened an investigation of a conspiracy among the banks to manipulate the dollar for their own profit. One of Citibank's currency traders had accused the bank of violating the currency controls and tax laws of several countries in 1978 and also confirmed that the currency traders of the large banks met and agreed to drive down a particular currency (in this case the dollar) by selling simultaneously. The process usually involved borrowing, selling, rebuying at a lower rate, and then repaying the loan. The profit was considerable, since they were dealing in colossal sums, and the impact on national currencies was also great. During the dollar crises of 1978 and 1979, the foreign-exchange earnings for Citibank went from $18 million in 1976 to $105 million in 1978, and those of the other large banks rose proportionately. The big change in the currency markets in the 1980s was the increase in the share of the yen in all transactions; its share more than doubled between 1980 and 1983.

The competition in foreign exchange intensified as the number of domestic banks engaged in trading rose from eleven to fifty-nine between 1980 and 1983 and as the number of foreign banks in the United States rose from forty-two to sixty over those years. The foreign-exchange trading of nonbank financial institutions like securities and brokerage houses, commodity traders, and insurance companies rose sixfold (from $7.4 to $42.6 billion) between 1980 and 1983. But operating a full-fledged currency exchange trading department is extremely expensive, requiring computers and staff that have access to all the variables and that process the huge volume of transactions on a daily basis. By 1984 some banks were beginning to question the risks of such rapid trading in such huge volume. Because of the costs, many smaller banks began to turn to brokers for their dealings. Other banks, pressed by competition, offered more and ever riskier services in foreign exchange as well as loans.

By 1986 about 90 percent of all currency exchange was in the hands of traders, primarily in the banks. They deal in million-dollar blocks, exchanging some $200 billion a day. Traders can buy or sell within minutes rather than within days or weeks, as in the past. This tremendous power has effectively eroded the ability of states to control their own economic policies.

Interacting with and overriding the structural changes were the primary compulsions of accumulation and competition. "We do not want to be No. 1 in assets; we want to be No. 1 in profits and profitability. . . . Our strategy is not one of making loans; our strategy is one of making money," emphasized the chairman of Citicorp in 1983.[28]

Some studies have shown that there is a national difference in bank management styles. While in general the European and Japanese banks have a committee type of collective decision making, the American style concentrates decisions in individuals. In Japan salaries are low, and the bankers' style is minutely meticulous. In dealing with a Japanese bank over a swap, one American banker reported, "They call me up in the evening to point out spelling errors we've made in the English text" of the document.[29] The German banks have traditionally had closer links with German industry, which has used bank credit for expansion. The largest, Deutsche Bank, has holdings in forty or fifty sectors of the economy. It is on 140 supervisory boards, but again this is often the result of invitations from executives who would like access to the bank and its funding; it should not be assumed to mean managerial control.

In the largest American banks the intense interbank competition is replicated internally. In Citibank, for example, managers are on com-

mission and compete with one another. Salaries of the successful traders are reportedly in six and seven figures. As individual decision
makers, bankers must calculate in the short term. The final outcome
of their risks may come after they have been promoted or have moved
on to another firm. "You have to perform or you're out," reported one
insider.[30] There is little time to weigh the risks. "If there's an opportunity, take advantage, don't analyze it to death," insisted the Citibank
vice-chairman Thomas Theobald, the quintessence of the international
banker.[31] And in times of trouble it is each for himself! A German
banker noted, "All the U.S. banks operate on a short-term horizon, but
Citibank['s] . . . philosophy is confined entirely to a quarter."[32] Lehman
Brothers was ripped apart in a well-publicized struggle for power between the traditional investment bankers and the traders, which Lewis
Glucksman, the trader who fought his way to the top, attributed to an
exceptional "level of greed . . . and personal selfishness that was
disgraceful."[33]

The maximizing of profits became increasingly dependent on the
money market trading room dealing in foreign exchange and on the
interest rate movements of wholesale deposits. These activities took
precedence over the lending function and were often at variance with
it. The traders have a vested interest in instability, oriented as they are
to the momentary opportunity, and are able to shift huge deposits for
fractional differences in interest. They became the dominant players in
the brokerages and investment banks, increasingly playing with their
own account for profit rather than for commissions for others; they were
sometimes caught, as was Kidder Peabody, for using $145 million of
the capital of customers for its own account, and as were those in the
subsequent scandals of insider trading on Wall Street.

The banks also introduced activities such as offering "commitments"
to customers to make loans, deal in currency exchange, guarantee the
obligations of creditors, and the like that were "off balance sheet," and
hence not examined by regulators. These arrangements amounted to
$800 billion for the fifteen largest U.S. banks in 1986, according to
a conservative estimate by the FDIC. The banks themselves have come
to prefer securities, finding them more profitable than loans. The question of what is a "security" and the definition of "underwriting" are
being fought out in the American courts, as the commercial banks try
to extend their turf.

Marketing short-term securities over a five-year period is an "off—
balance sheet" activity. Banks charge a fee for these services, which
do not get listed as loans and thus are not scrutinized by the examiners.
A bank gives a standby commitment for a loan to a company issuing

short-term notes in the Euromarket. The bank collects a fee, but the loan is not operative unless the notes cannot be sold. Such "underwriting by another name" reached $20 billion in 1984. The bank's risk comes if it cannot market the notes. This activity rose 285 percent between 1983 and 1985. With their new "products" the banks replace one risk on loans with even greater dangers and also undermine their long-run profitability.

By the end of 1985 the BIS was warning about the excessive risks in the off–balance sheet lending—in this case, borrowing in exchange for special issues of securities, which internationally was nearly double the traditional lending. The securities, unlike loans, fluctuate with the market.

The increasing number of American bank failures put a brake on the process of financial deregulation in the United States, particularly on that allowing them to underwrite securities again. But the failures have also encouraged states to eliminate barriers to interstate banking, as they seek rescues from the largest banks for those failing regionally.

The purpose of all the new "products," according to Alexandre Lamfalussy, manager of the BIS, was "to hedge against the uncertainty [of exchange and interest rates], to circumvent regulations or to avoid taxes, to take up opportunities offered by deregulation or new technology."[34] They were made possible by the objective and then official deregulation that occurred as one nation after the other competed for international capital. Increasing the network of financial risk was the fact that other corporations, such as J.C. Penney, Sears, Roebuck, and American Express, entered the banking activity of deposit and loans. Moreover, the "nonbank banks" slipped through the ever more porous regulatory net, as the U.S. courts decided they were not to be regulated by the FRB.

SOVEREIGN RISK

In the mid-1970s the banks, like corporations, turned to the LDCs and CPEs when OECD business was slack, and they were sanguine concerning the risk of lending to states, which is termed sovereign risk. In 1978 they cited sovereign loans, called "evergreens," as a justification for their low reserves against international-loan losses. The reserves, they argued, were necessary only to secure their private loans. Until 1978 international-loan losses were only a fraction of all domestic-loan losses, and these were concentrated in the private sector. On the list of the countries in which the losses occurred, the United Kingdom, the FRG, and Japan were second, third, and fourth; only Brazil was higher. A mere three countries were in arrears to the commercial banks in 1974, and then only in the amount of $500 million. As late as 1978 the banks feared, and were forced to succumb to, the LDC "threat" to prepay their loans in order to secure new loans at a lower rate. Throughout the 1970s the unsophisticated LDC central bankers had deposited roughly $90 billion in non-interest-bearing accounts in U.S. banks. The banks reaped a bonanza in profits by relending these sums, sometimes to the depositors. This profitable anomaly ended in 1981.

Sovereign-loan losses ranked a distant third in the concerns of bankers in 1978. In 1980 David Rockefeller noted with satisfaction, "Whereas five or 10 years ago our earnings from Europe were greater than Latin America and Asia, now Latin America has become the most important contributor. It's really very exciting. . . . We really are a major factor in the Brazilian economy."[35] Rockefeller and Walter Wriston not only granted major loans but also praised Chile as a model for the Third World. The international banks also concentrated their loans; only eight to twelve LDC countries received 70 percent of the loans. Lending to the LDCs increased 20–25 percent annually throughout the 1970s and beyond, until it abruptly halted with the Mexican moratorium in 1982. By then Citicorp had 231 percent, or $10.4 billion, of its equity in five Latin American countries alone. Even as the situation was crumbling in the first quarter of 1982, Mexico and Brazil accounted for 60 percent of new U.S. bank lending. Brazil alone provided 20 percent of Citicorp's earnings. Yet by the end of 1982 twenty-five countries were in arrears for a total of $6.5 billion, and sovereign exposure appeared the most immediate threat to bankers. Many banks, in response, tried to emphasize corporate loans. But some bankers, after the shock of their Latin American loans in 1982, were "rushing into the Far East like lemmings," Euromoney ironically noted.[36] Although the risks were great, the most important factor for the banks in sovereign lending was that the profits were correspondingly high. In the midst of the 1982 debt crisis, a banker at Manufacturers Hanover made this comment on the reschedulings: "to the extent to which [they] have broadened spreads, they're going to have a beneficial effect upon bank earnings."[37]

From the borrower's point of view in the 1970s, the inflation and fluctuating currency values appeared to make commercial bank borrowing a prudent course, especially for the oil exporters but also for those with balance-of-payments problems. So long as their interest rates were fixed and their export prices rising, they could repay their loans with a cheaper dollar. They could also avoid the strictures of the IMF by seeking commercial loans for existing debt service. The cheap dollar and inflation made the average *real* interest rate 0.85 percent between 1973 and 1980. The strategies all hinged on the various parties' perception of the future.

As changes in U.S. monetary policy after 1979 raised interest rates to unprecedented highs—to 10.7 percent in 1981 and 16 percent in 1982— interest rates on new loans were no longer fixed. In addition, real interest rates continued to rise, banks began to make only short-term loans, the dollar skyrocketed in value, and the ability to earn foreign exchange fell with the recession, trade restrictions, and declining commodity prices, including that of oil. The country debt problem was compounded in the early 1980s, as nations moved to short-term credits to avoid being locked into the extremely high long-term rates. The banks joined with the IMF and made the implementation of austerity programs the precondition for rescheduling loans. In addition to the generalized rise of the dollar, the debts were multiplied many times by the imposed devaluations. In Mexico, for instance, the peso was devalued 85 percent in 1982, increasing the debt servicing costs in local currencies five- or sixfold. By 1984 some 80–85 percent of the loans to the LDCs were denominated in dollars, for which the LIBOR was 12 percent, in contrast to the 6 percent rate for the mark and yen.

RESCHEDULING

When the rescheduling of sovereign loans began in the late 1970s, the banks began to hire political-risk analysts—political scientists and, especially, former CIA analysts. Henry Kissinger was an adviser for eight hours a year to both Chase and Goldman Sachs. In practice such precautions were of little help. During the first quarter of 1982, the banks made huge loans to Mexico. Pemex borrowed $2 billion, and thirty banks eagerly sought to participate. One New York banker recalled, "They had oil and that was all many of us thought mattered."[38] Some bankers became skeptical of their ability to evaluate the security of loans to countries and relied instead on diversification as the prime risk control mechanism. But even when the repayment of the principal was in doubt, the loans to the LDCs continued to be highly profitable in the short term. The long term was another story.

The banks have charged fees, margin spreads, and "miscellaneous expenses" when granting the original loan, already providing for much of the risk of trouble in repayment. The additional forms of income in rescheduling the debt—penalty charges and new fees—are "superprofits," as one writer pointed out.[39] In their insatiable quest for profit, they passed on to the borrowers the risks normally borne by the banks, and find they have probably lost the principal. As the head of the BIS observed in 1985, "some of the banks looking back, would have preferred to have lost on their interest margin but find themselves today with a less damaged loan portfolio."[40] By the beginning of 1983 the banks were demanding 2.25 percent over the LIBOR from Mexico and Brazil, in addition to huge "signing fees" for new loans.

The Group of Thirty's 1983 report, *Commercial Banks and the Restructuring of Cross-Border Debt,* held, "If arrangement fees are taken into account, the restructured debt is yielding banks about 2 percent a year more than the terms on which most of that debt was originally contracted . . . about an extra $1.75 billion a year on the $90 billion . . . renegotiated."[41] Given the drastic cuts in the standard of living of the population to repay the loan, the added profits were "not reasonable," added the chairman, the former IMF director Johannes Witteveen.[42]

By the end of 1983, under pressure from both the FRB and the IMF, the banks modified their spread by one-eighth and reduced their fees from 1.5 to 1 percent. The banks' aim was to make money, and frequent reschedulings increased their profits, even if they can scarcely expect to be repaid. They counted their front-end fees as profits as soon as the loan was signed. While there was a contraction in new lending in 1983, for the first time in twenty years, the profits of the world's major banks grew 10 percent or more.

THE LOAN MARKET

The banks developed a market among themselves in trading and selling loans in the 1980s. "We're now told we should sell loan participation just like we sell bonds or foreign exchange . . . just another product to be sold. . . . [T]he buzzword is asset management," said a New York loan officer in October 1983.[43] By 1985 most of the biggest banks in the United States were selling their "top-quality" loans, whereas they had sold none three years earlier. "Loan selling is at the core of our strategy as a bank," said Bankers Trust's senior vice-president.[44] The loan's worth depends on its price in the capital market, as banks discount them 25–30 percent. By mid-1986 the discount price on the dollar was 45 for Polish loans, 56 for Mexican loans, and 76 for Brazilian loans. Soon the market for the sales comprised not only other banks, as with the syndicated loans, but also mutual funds, pension funds, and nonfinancial corporations. Most of the sales were for loans with a maturity of less than one year. By 1984 more common than cash sales among banks were "swaps," a form of countertrade, such as the exchanging of Brazilian and Argentine debt for Polish and Nigerian debt.

In their endless array of innovations, the bankers with the various indebted states created a scheme whereby interested corporations could buy the discounted loans and trade them for local currency investment. Banks both unload their "value impaired" loans and collect fees. The country offers a discount on the exchange, but one not as great as the banks' in selling the loan. For example, if a company bought a loan for 65 cents per dollar, the government would offer to buy it for 90 cents in local currency or more if the investment was of high priority. But by the end of 1986 it seemed evident that the sale of loans to corporations would retire only $3 to $4 billion of Mexico's massive debt of $92 billion. The government feared hyperinflationary pressure if the process became too extensive.

In the wake of the capitalization program, political conditions were attached. "The whole capitalization issue is bound up with making Latin America more open to market forces," said the head of the Latin American division of one of the largest New York banks.[45] The indebted country must dismantle its nationalist regulations on foreign investment.

The sovereign-risk loans were originally for three to five years, then increasingly for one year or less; finally, with rescheduling, they have been stretched out to "forever." "Lending new money will allow us the pleasant illusion that we are getting repaid," claimed one banker.[46]

"The principal is not going to get repaid," the treasurer of the World Bank announced flatly in November 1984, regarding the bank loans to the LDCs. He advised the banks to stop "pretending" that it would be.[47] Yet the U.S. comptroller of the currency in mid-1985 classified as "value impaired" (meaning the banks had to have special reserves) only loans to Poland, Zaire, Bolivia, Nicaragua, and Sudan, countries where the U.S. bank exposure was low.

But when Brazil announced a temporary moratorium on debt service, Citibank moved in mid-1987 to create a $3 billion reserve against loan defaults, taking the largest loss on earnings—$2.5 billion—in the banking industry's history, and prompted the other large banks to do the same. This move made them less dependent on interest repayment and reduced their incentive to continue lending.

The investment bankers, on the other hand, acted as financial advisers to many countries that were rescheduling their debt. This led to considerable conflict with the commercial banks, which in some cases told the borrowers to go elsewhere for loans if they hired the bank advisers. The first banks to offer advice for a fee were the "Troika"— Lehman Brothers, Lazard Frères, and S. G. Warburg—which restructured Pertamina's finances and then continued as the financial adviser to Indonesia's central bank. This profitable business grew over the following years, until by August 1982 the Troika could count a dozen clients. During negotiations with the commercial banks, the advisers often sit in the next room ready to be consulted; at times they negotiate directly. The commercial bankers hold that the advisers charge useless and exorbitant fees, steal the bankers' ideas, and then "sell them to the borrower. Basically they're a kind of blood suckers" a "spoiler" in the negotiation.[48] But the Troika was unable to warn its clients of the impending debt crisis in 1982. The rescheduling activities led the investment banks into additional profitable advisory roles for their clients, incorporating new borrowing strategies, attracting foreign investment, reorganizing state enterprises, financing government projects, and managing reserves.

THE BANKS AND THE IMF/WB

The loans to sovereign states led the commercial banks to an explicit relationship with the IMF, creating an unprecedented leverage on the political and economic policies within the developing countries. In 1976 the banks tried unilaterally to impose economic policies on the debtor nation of Peru, which had borrowed $2 billion. Hit with falling copper prices and an exceptional disappearance of its school of anchovies, a major export, Peru was unable to meet its payments. The banks, led by Citibank, tried to impose devaluation and higher taxes. Riots and attacks on the bankers followed. The banks learned their lesson and never directly tried again. Thereafter, they insisted that the debtor apply to the IMF before renegotiating a loan. Argentina's request for rescheduling in 1976 was the first such demand, which set the pattern over the subsequent years.

The banks have orchestrated their lending policies for other political changes or to participate in destabilization campaigns, as in Jamaica in 1979 when they refused to reschedule the government loans although the government was conforming to an IMF agreement. Indeed, they even discussed new credits with the opposition leader.

But because of conflicting interests—short-term for the banks, and longer-term for the United States and the IMF—there was frequently a struggle between the banks, the debtor nations of Latin America, the FRB, and the IMF during the debt crisis of 1982–83. The banks, again led by Citibank (which had the largest LDC exposure), took the offensive in rescheduling debts, pushed for the highest fees and the widest spreads, and cared nothing about the political and economic circumstances of the borrower or the international financial structure. Everything they did was "perfectly legal but as unethical as can be," reported one U.S. banker.[49] Citibank's net income rose 36 percent in 1982, and three-fifths of it was generated abroad.

Paul Volcker, alarmed by the wider implications of the Latin American debt crisis, moved at the end of 1983 to reduce LDC interest rates. He told the U.S. bankers involved that higher rates would trigger massive defaults, and he encouraged the Mexicans to hold out for easier terms. Citibank read Volcker the riot act, one U.S. banker later reported, adding, "It's a very dangerous move, he shouldn't politicize things unless he is willing to go the whole way and nationalize the banks."[50]

Yet in 1982 the IMF for the first time insisted that the banks increase their loans to Brazil and Mexico as part of a package. The package included IMF loans and surveillance of their austerity programs. An important part of that package was to persuade the banks to keep the interbank lines open to the commercial and central banks of those countries. The transfer risk in interbank lending had been highlighted by the Mexican crisis. The government could not allocate foreign exchange to the banks while there was a national crisis.

One banker, who had lent more than $50 billion, anonymously expressed his remorse and admitted he had "rushed blindly along chasing a rainbow we thought would lead to easy profits." He resented the pressures of the IMF and the U.S. government to continue lending: "In order to rectify earlier mistakes we bankers are called to make new ones. . . . The disastrous record of private financing for economic development shows that this is no place for banks."[51] The LDCs accounted for only 5 percent of new bank lending in 1986, compared with 21 percent in 1982.

LENDER OF LAST RESORT (LLR)

The protection of the American and German economies from the financial disasters implicit in the bankruptcies of the Franklin National and Herstatt banks in 1974 led to the perception that governments as lenders of last resort had become institutionalized, and bankers, according to one, grew "more reckless than ever."[52] It became taken for granted that no government would allow the collapse of a crucial company.

Yet the LLR criteria dissolve in the maze of international banking. In fact, despite the issuance of reassurances by the Group of Ten in the BIS, there is no LLR in international banking activity, where the vast bulk of the risks are contracted. Any action in an emergency would ultimately be an improvisation. A clear example of the absence of any agreement was the refusal of both the Bank of England and the Israeli central bank to assume responsibility for the Israel-British Bank, a London subsidiary of an Israeli bank.

The central bankers' 1975 agreement on responsibility for their national banks never determined which central bank would be responsible in case of the collapse of a foreign subsidiary, a key factor in international lending. The $400 million collapse of Bank Ambrosiano in Luxembourg in August 1982 exposed the loophole in this 1975 agreement. The Italian central bank guaranteed only the parent bank's commitment and allowed the foreign auxiliary to sink. The next near collapse of a subsidiary was also in Luxembourg. It involved the German Schroder Bank, which used its Luxembourg branch to avoid the German reporting regulations and which had made loans to a single borrower in excess of the legal limit. Schroder was rescued at the end of 1983 when the Bundesbank forced the twenty other German banks linked to it in interbank lending to absorb the loss.

In 1983 there was a sharp curtailment in Euromarket lending and a "flight to quality" in lending to such countries as Japan and Canada. As in 1974 after the collapse of Herstatt and Franklin National, the interbank network also contracted, from $14 billion in the first quarter to $4 billion in the second. "Everyone is pruning his deposit-takers list," noted one investment banker.[53] The interbank market contracted again in 1985. The consortium banks are the least secure in terms of an LLR and became increasingly less popular in the 1980s. That confidence is at the core of the banks' relations to each other is the crucial difference between banks and nonbank corporations. If one bank fails through insolvency, that can lead to the fall of solvent banks. This is generally avoided by an LLR, unless other crisis characteristics define the situation. Given the nature of today's wholesale banking, confidence is more precious than ever.

Continental Illinois, America's fifth-largest bank before 1984, "went from being the prime example of everything that was right to the prime example of everything that was wrong with US banking. . . . in 1981 it was the biggest commercial and industrial lender in the nation," according to a *Business Week* report.[54] The difference between it and the other money center banks was simply one of degree. At Continental, dependent on short-term interbank funding, the response of other banks to rumor and an increase in yields nearly emptied the coffers, by telex, in less than a week. Large investors had stopped buying its certificates of deposit (CDs) in 1982, because, as one of them put it, "they were lending to the rust bowl."[55] Continental then began to pay higher rates on its CDs, which served as a clue to the interbank market that the bank was in serious trouble.

Once confidence fails, solvency can be restored only by larger banks' absorbing the smaller or by nationalization. When Continental Illinois collapsed, in May 1984, the government failed to arrange a rescue by other banks, and even the Federal Reserve's injection of $7.5 billion in June did not restore confidence. The run on deposits also threatened to spread to other giant banks "despite the full faith and credit of the US government," observed *The Banker* in August.[56] The U.S. government, looking into the abyss, swallowed its ideology and all precedent and, in effect, nationalized the bank on July 26. Some 2,400 banks had $3 billion worth of uninsured deposits in Continental, and only nationalization, guaranteeing all deposits and creditors, prevented "hundreds of bank failures," according to the chairman of the FDIC.[57]

With the nationalization and the Federal Reserve Board's assurance that, effectively, it would print all the money necessary to save the biggest banks and the world monetary system—then, and only then, was confidence restored. The Fed would, according to one of its members, "lend, lend boldly, and keep on lending" if the other large banks had liquidity problems.[58] The implications of this radical departure from precedent are great. The move asserted that there was an LLR for the largest banks in the United States, if not for the others. This message was to encourage the biggest banks in even more reckless policies. Internationally as well, the size and importance of certain financial institutions and nonfinancial corporations gave them the confidence that no matter what risks they took, governments could not permit them to collapse.

The LLR role of the U.S. government is being increasingly tested, as traders in brokerage houses and investment banks reach for the marginal interest rate differentials in the "troubled" banks. Merrill Lynch alone had $9.5 billion in such banks in 1984. Insured losses were costing the FDIC "hundreds of millions of dollars." "[T]he customer's not at risk—the FDIC is at risk. . . . It's a life or death issue with us," noted its chairman, William Isaac.[59]

A new BIS agreement, however, was like the old in that it merely tried to camouflage the continuing reality that the central banks would not accept general or binding responsibilities in the matter of defaults of subsidiaries in other countries. Many nations, including the FRG and Luxembourg, do not even claim to have an LLR. And many banks in London are headquartered in countries without convertible currencies. Given that so much banking rests on the intangible of confidence, the vague assurance of the BIS reflects little that is concrete; rather, it is an effort to minimize the fears of the world's depositors. Added to the fears is the new prominence of the nonbank banks, the elaborate

international web of companies that do not fall under the jurisdiction
of banking regulators. One Japanese banker said, "It is easy to see how
the lines of responsibility can get blurred. The question in a crisis is:
will there be time to sort out each regulator's role?"[60] The worst of all
worlds is in fact the present situation: it gives the impression that there
is a reliable LLR internationally when there is none.[61]

What are the implications of all these changes in the process of
restructuring the economy? One can list the details of an endless array
of expanding risks which may explode or which may continue to be
contained by improvisation, as over the past decade. Finance capital is
tied to the fates of industries and of states. In turn, it is an active agent
in the fate of others. Technology has greatly magnified the risks. And
as the very nature of banking has been objectively restructured and as
the race for profit leads to deeper, untested waters, even the very
amplitude of the risks is not fully known. Not only the lenders but also
the depositors have turned into traders. State power is objectively
weakened. But the changes that are the outcome of the pursuit of
individual profit indicate that there is still no incentive for the productive investment that is crucial if the world is to emerge from the crisis.

CHAPTER 6

THE INDUSTRIAL SECTOR: STEEL

Some economists refer to the "sunset" and "sunrise" industries in the OECD countries to describe those sectors of the economy that are depressed or expanding as the economy is restructured. Three components of the industrial sector—steel, the "new" industries of high technology, and the arms industry—illustrate dramatically the most salient features of this process.

Steel, perhaps more than any other industry, remains in the minds of many the industry that is the sine qua non of economic power. But one observer has noted that in certain industrialized countries it has been transformed from a symbol of "economic might to a symptom of economic blight," or the "rust belt."[1] Steel is also an industry that today reveals the multiple aspects of "restructuring"—economic, technological, and political—in the capitalist system. But from the capitalist's viewpoint, of course, the problem is strictly one of profit and loss. "You cannot expect a corporation to continue in an industry because someone thinks it's necessary," asserted the chairman of one American company.[2]

Many generalizations and projections are made on the basis of the steel industry's relationship to the rest of the economy. Steel presents an informative example of the interactions of perceptions, plans, and actions in a swiftly changing economic environment, especially given the enormity of the investment required to make shifts in strategy. Both the private corporations and the state are vulnerable to these myopic perceptions and decisions. It is therefore useful to trace briefly the fluctuations in the industry over the past fifteen years. Most noteworthy has been the rapid change in the locus of production, technology, and ownership.

LOCALE OF PRODUCTION

A few statistics capture the essential shifts. In 1955 the United States produced 39.3 percent of the world's steel; in 1975, 16.4 percent; and in 1984, 7.8 percent. Between 1973 and 1983 U.S. steel production fell 44 percent, and it has continued to decline. It dropped 22 percent in 1986 alone. The giant U.S. integrated steel companies supplied more than 95 percent of the American market at the end of the 1950s, but by 1982 their share had fallen to 60 percent. In 1956 Japan produced 5 million tons; two decades later, 118 million tons. It had three times the FRG's capacity and was nearly equal to that of the USSR and the United States.

The LDCs produced 17 percent of the world's crude steel in 1982, compared with 7 percent in 1970. Their productive capacity doubled between 1973 and 1982, from 34.0 to 68.9 million tons. In 1981 South Korea opened the world's largest and most modern steel plant, with an 8.5 million ton capacity. Only three years earlier, in 1979, South Korea's capacity had been 2.9 million tons. Its production between 1973 and 1983 grew nearly ten times.

In contrast, in the OECD nations capacity fell from 457 to 328 million tons, and it continues to be reduced. By 1984 the International Iron and Steel Institute had concluded that even excluding the CPEs, the world steel capacity of 640 million tons was 200 million more than the current demand or that anticipated in 1995. It concluded that capacity had to be cut by 30 to 70 million tons over the next decade and that no new capacity should be built anywhere. In fact, between 1979 and 1984 the industrial countries cut world capacity 50 million tons. In the United States capacity was reduced by 16 percent between 1981 and the end of 1986. Yet the UNIDO conference of May–June 1977, in contrast, called for an increase in LDC steel production to 370 million tons by the year 2000.

For the major steel user, that is, the auto industry, there was also a parallel geographic shift of production. The United States's share of the total world auto output dropped from 50.4 percent in 1960 to 24.5 percent in 1980. Japan's rose over the same years from 4.9 percent to 28.8 percent, and the Japanese steel industry benefited from this expansion.

TECHNOLOGY

After over a century of very little technological change, both the scale and the method of steel production changed radically in just a couple of decades, rendering inefficient and obsolete much of the existing capacity and giving a great competitive advantage to the new facilities. A significant portion of these were located in the new plant going up in the LDCs. But in the OECD countries themselves new minimills, with their new technology, offered major competition. New technology undermined the economy of scale, whose "epoch" was "now past," according to a European industry executive.[3] New production techniques also require less labor. Certain technological factors, such as the capital intensity of investment, were important in giving the large integrated mills an advantage and in providing barriers to new entry in the past. Only the chemical and nuclear energy industries rivaled steel in the proportion of capital to labor in production. The cost of changes in technology is gargantuan for the large integrated mills, giving the competitive advantage to those building new, rather than replacing old, plant. Only between 1965 and 1976 was there a rapid change from the old to the new technologies for the large mills.

The new steel technology is owned and licensed by a small number of OECD steel corporations, but this has not prevented their extending it worldwide, ultimately to their own disadvantage. The most significant technological change was the emergence of the minimills in the 1960s. Operating with scrap and electric furnaces, usually in nonunion plants, they increased their share of the U.S. market from 3 percent in 1968 to 18 percent in 1983, and it continues to grow. In many cases they were unaffected by the chronic crisis in the steel industry, although they were hit by the recession in 1982. In Europe there were sixty-one minimills by 1983, with a 20-million-ton capacity. While of growing importance in the FRG and in Sweden, the majority are in Italy, which has been at the forefront of the new technology. Beginning in the mid-1950s in the region around Brescia, and using hydroelectric power and scrap, these small mills have been constantly upgraded technologically and by the early 1990s will be fully automated, computerized plants with virtually no work force. At present they are highly automated and the most modern in Europe.

Among the integrated giants the United States has had the slowest rate of replacement of equipment of any major nation. Investments in the 1950s did not modernize but only expanded capacity. By the time it began to modernize, American steel had lost its competitive advantage. In 1980 the U.S. steel industry still relied on the open-hearth process for 30 percent of its production. In an assessment of the 140-million-ton U.S. steel capacity at the end of 1983, one expert concluded that 50 million tons of it was very competitive, 25 million tons only somewhat, and the rest obsolete.

The modern, continuous-casting method was only 26–30 percent of the U.S. industry in 1983, and that mainly in the minimills, compared with 86 percent for Japan and 61 percent for Europe. The American giants were in the greatest danger, because their antiquated technology would require an estimated $60 billion investment to bring it up to world standards, according to the the Iron and Steel Institute. Even if we allow for some exaggeration of figures for political purposes, the costs are gigantic. New technological developments in the United States for sheet steel require less capital investment than the old process does and only 10 percent of the energy cost. They will further increase the competition in the domestic industry. Nevertheless, the government will aid a U.S. Steel–Bethlehem combine with the initial investment. In the CPEs of Europe, the majority of the facilities are open-hearth. Only 4 percent of the Soviet capacity is continuous-casting. Brazil, on the other hand, moved swiftly into the new technology. In 1975 continuous casting made up 6 percent of its capacity, but five years later it made up 34 percent.

In addition, important technological changes in the steel market had a major impact on the steel industry. The new industries in high technology required less steel than the declining industries did, and there were important substitutes in other steel-using industries.

OWNERSHIP

The ownership of the world steel industry altered radically over the thirty years between 1950, when 77 percent was private, and the 1980s, when around 30 percent remained in private hands and that was largely concentrated in North America, Japan, the FRG, and Australia. Britain nationalized 91 percent of the industry in 1967; after converting the industry's debt to the state into equity in 1978, France nationalized the industry formally in 1981. Smaller private companies existed in some LDCs and in Europe as well, but most of the steel industry in the EEC and the LDCs, as in the CPEs, was owned by the government.

These changes in ownership in the OECD increasingly were the outcome of the industry's crisis of profitability. Nationalization in the capitalist context did not alter the crisis in the industry but only sustained productive facilities by absorbing its losses until it could become profitable once more.

CYCLES—THE FLUCTUATION IN THE MARKET

Sharp cyclical swings have always been characteristic of the steel industry, but the situation in the 1970s differed significantly from that of the past. The rapid and extreme shifts in both government and private industry strategy were the outcome of a myopic perception of the economy and its direction. Changes occurred in response to the gyrations of the business cycle, which objectively restructured the terrain. A brief survey of these fluctuations in the 1970s and 1980s will underline the point.

Like all wars, the Vietnam War was initially a boon to the world steel industry, but by October 1971 the situation had changed drastically. The last half of 1971, in the wake of the recession, was the worst for profits since World War II, and American steel faced its lowest demand since the 1930s. The Germans began to curtail production, and the largest British corporation was in the red for the second consecutive year. A number of Japanese companies were also in serious financial difficulty, and the new dependence of a number of them on exports was heightened in 1972, when Japan exported 30 percent of its production, compared with only 10 percent in 1967.

The economic boom that began toward the end of 1972 and lasted into 1974 increased demand to a point where the industry worldwide was operating at full capacity and had a backlog of unfilled orders. Expansion of facilities began once more with plans for new iron ore mines and the construction of plants everywhere, especially in Brazil and Indonesia. The immense demand more than tripled prices between 1972 and 1974, pushing expansion plans further. British Steel built the largest complex, committing $8.7 billion in 1974 in order to raise capacity to 30 million tons by 1985. Such capacity far exceeded even the most optimistic anticipated domestic demand and was destined for export.

Italy in 1970 started a great expansion of capacity in the south, assuming that consumption would reach 30 million tons by 1980. In France the industry constructed the first phase of an enormous new facility at Fos, on the Mediterranean, in 1974. (The second phase was abandoned in 1975.) In 1974 profits peaked for German steel, production reaching 53-million-ton capacity, and preparations for expansion were also under way. The International Iron and Steel Institute in Brussels predicted in 1974 that demand would grow rapidly, and the entire industry looked forward to a large increase in capacity by 1985. In the United States the steel industry operated at full capacity in August 1974, and since it was unable to meet domestic demand, imports increased. As late as September 1974 the business press reflected the myopia when it predicted, "[T]he U.S. steel industries will be operating at full capacity for most of the next five years."[4] Global production of 709 million tons was more than double that of 1960. Canada, in contrast to other countries, had built its industry under the level of domestic demand and had always operated at near capacity until the expansion of the 1970s. Since that time it, too, has suffered from overcapacity.

As the economic conditions had reversed by the end of 1974, orders were canceled and pressures mounted to curb imports. Only the Japanese did not abandon their 1973–74 expansion plans, but they had no incentive for further investment after 1977. Yet they did not begin to reduce capacity until 1982. All dimensions of the recession hit the European industry; the collapse of domestic demand and the loss of export markets merged with the high cost of borrowing and aging plant. Structurally, the market declined as the use of steel in production fell. Normally, the capital goods industry, the first casualty in a recession, consumes two-thirds of the steel output. There was an immediate crisis of overproduction, as prices fell in 1975 by 30 percent and capacity utilization dropped to less than 60 percent of the preceding year's. The vast expansion of capacity worldwide made "yesterday's customer into today's competitor." Nevertheless, with the fall in demand in the OECD states, some of their steel industries, along with engineering firms, competed for orders to build yet more capacity in the LDCs and the CPEs.

The collapse of the steel market in 1975 was the worst since World War II. Between the end of the war and 1974, *world* production had declined from the preceding years only in 1954, 1958, and 1971. There were, however, many more cyclical gyrations in the United States.

Fluctuations of demand continued, followed by increases and contraction of production. In early 1976 there was an increase in demand, primarily from the auto industry, and some inventory accumulation. Prices rose, and the steel industry in the United States operated at 90 percent of capacity in May and June and then sputtered to 72 percent in November. Again in May 1977 the industry operated at 88 percent and dropped to 75 percent in September. In March 1979, mainly to meet the demand of the oil industry suppliers, rigs, and the like, output was again high, and industry worked at peak capacity, producing the largest volume in five years, as delivery time tripled and users again turned to imports, paying a premium to build inventories. By September shipments and profits were falling, and at the end of the year U.S. Steel closed thirteen facilities, eliminating 12,500 jobs. In 1980 it reported the biggest loss in U.S. business history. After closing down 11 percent of its capacity between 1977 and 1981, the U.S. industry increased its profits on less production. There was again much optimism in the first half of 1981. U.S. Steel increased its capital spending, and minimills went on a general "building spree." But in September 1982 the U.S. industry was operating at an average of 39.8 percent of capacity. Republic Steel, however, dropped to 26 percent for the last quarter.

PROFIT AND LOSS

Losses in the European industry set records in 1977–78. British Steel lost $1 billion in 1977. Most of the industries not already state owned received enormous subsidies from their government. Japanese integrated mills are profitable at 70 percent of capacity, but must export 25 million tons or more. But in 1986, as an outcome of the rising yen, all five of Japan's largest companies recorded major losses.

Compared with the rest of the world, *in the aggregate,* the U.S. industry was profitable in the 1970s. Only in 1977 was there no profit. Despite all the closures, losses, and restructuring, distributed profits were maintained at the same average percentage of earnings of 49 percent for U.S. Steel and at 53 percent for Bethlehem throughout the 1970s. Maintaining high profits and dividends at all costs is considerably more important to U.S. firms than to others. In the first half of 1981, profits were second only to those of 1974, as the industry operated at 89 percent, although, significantly, the profit was chiefly from the sale of assets like coal. Since that time there have been severe losses. The record $4 billion losses in 1986 led to the bankruptcy of the second-largest company and to threats of bankruptcy from the third-largest. But such aggregates hide the fact that it was the minimills and specialized steel companies that profited as the large integrated mills lost more than $6 billion in 1982–83. And, increasingly, profits were from their nonsteel assets.

PRICE COMPETITION

The giant losses of the 1980s led the president of U.S. Steel to assert, "We have to recognize the new, competitive forces in the marketplace. . . . The test is adapting to a competitive environment."[5] In the United States competition began in the late 1960s, both from imports and from the increasing number of domestic minimills. Until then the American industry had been quintessentially the oligopolistic model and had grown unaccustomed to price competition. In 1982 there was sharp price-cutting through discounts of up to $100 a ton, and domestic price competition was the rule in 1982. In fact, one study concluded that domestic competition "may be more important than competition from foreign steelmakers."[6] Price competition took the form of discounts when the list price was stable or even rising. Companies raised their price 6–7 percent in an act of desperation, but the real price was falling. By 1985 discounts, or real prices, were 20 percent off the list price. Too often economists overlook this reality when generalizing on statistical data. By 1983 competition had objectively eroded the oligopolistic character of the industry. And an open price war developed in 1987.

The recession in the early 1980s intensified the competition from the minimills. As an example of the minimill advantage in the United States, in 1984 the Raritan River minimill in New Jersey forced U.S. Steel to close its wire rod production. "They blame imports, but it was us," claimed the minimill's president.[7] Raritan sold rods with a profit at $300, while the integrated mill sold them at $450 with no profit. These nonunion, largely scrap-dependent companies (ten of the sixty are partly or wholly foreign owned) have objectively restructured the American steel industry independently of foreign competition.

The Italian minimills followed their own, independent strategy and added 4 million tons capacity between 1974 and 1981, while the EEC was calling for reductions. But the minimills were not immune to the recession and were badly affected throughout the world in 1982.

THE NEW INTERNATIONAL DIVISION OF
LABOR IN STEEL

The LDCs' "comparative advantage" was magnified and distorted, according to one OECD report, by the forms of investment guarantees, long-term credits, tax "relief," export aids, a state-financed infrastructure, and other incentives. Thanks to all these assets, the usual investment risk was greatly reduced.

Since 1975 the European, American, and Japanese steel industries have competed to build turnkey plants, and hence their own competition, in the LDCs in order to offset their lack of business during the crisis in the OECD countries. And since 1973 six LDCs—Brazil, Argentina, Mexico, Taiwan, South Korea, and Venezuela—have become exporters of steel. Brazil was the world's eighth-largest producer in the 1980s. The old adage "Yesterday's customer, today's competitor" had been realized with a vengeance.

Financing LDC steel projects, many in the billion-dollar class, were the banks, the World Bank for many years, and official export credits. These export credits for steel plants amounted to $857 million during the period 1966–69 and grew to $3,593 million in 1976–77. About 15 percent was official government aid. Loans for steel plants were made in Venezuela, whose products would cost twice as much as the Japanese competition's. Money was also often diverted from the loans into capital flight.

By the 1980s the OECD steel industries had begun to recognize the obvious—that the world industry and market had been objectively changed "probably forever." "But we're going to have to learn to live with it," admitted one German executive.[8] Referring to the giant turn-key plants built in the 1970s, OECD executives sheepishly proclaim that they did not expect the shift in trade; rather, they believed that the production of the new plants was destined for internal consumption. After building their own competition while in many cases dismantling their own facilities, they decided they had to adapt by establishing a two-tier world system in which OECD firms would be restructured to produce specialty steels while the LDCs, ideally, could produce the crude. In the United States it was not until 1982 that most of the steel companies recognized the necessity of specialization. U.S. Steel, whose share of the national market had by 1983 been reduced to 16 percent, was the last to do so.

With their traditional myopia, industry executives as late as 1983 claimed that the LDCs could continue as "commodity suppliers," but the commodity would be basic, unsophisticated steel products. "Of the 2,000 steel products we have, you can safely let the Third World make the products it can manufacture more cheaply," opined an official at the German Klöckner-Werke.[9] The Japanese, too, encouraged the high-polluting first phase of production in the LDCs to send the product to Japan to be upgraded.

In that illusory international division of labor, high-technology speciality products were reserved for the OECD. At the same time, they continued to build the world's most modern plant, capable of the most sophisticated production, in South Korea, China, and elsewhere. Mexico in 1979 had the most modern direct reduction mill and planned to sell its technology worldwide. Both the state and the private corporations build their own competition. Nippon Steel constructed plants for

South Korea, Brazil, Mexico, and China. By 1983 the Japanese were building an integrated modern mill in the Philippines and selling steel plant and technology to Malaysia and Thailand. In 1983 the Korean plant ran at full capacity, while the Japanese were forced to cut back production. Competition was the spur as the OECD continued to bid for projects to expand the capacity worldwide even while there was a crisis of overcapacity. The Japanese industry did not bid on a South Korean project to expand their capacity with a second integrated mill in 1984 until the European industry made bids first. The builders finally included Austrian, German, British, and Japanese companies. U.S. Steel's Engineers and Consultants Division, which constructs turn-key steel plants and steel-making technology, grew 30 percent a year between 1969 and 1978. The U.S. Export-Import Bank eventually declined to provide financing because of world overcapacity in December 1983. In the past, $4.5 billion in U.S. foreign aid had gone to develop the steel industries in forty-six countries since World War II. Such subsidies came to an end in 1977, when Congress, at the instigation of the companies and the steelworkers' union, acted to stop them.

TRADE

These changes had their impact on trade in steel, which became increasingly important in the postwar years and whose volume increased ninefold between 1950 and 1979. The usual notions of "comparative advantage" in trade, access to raw materials and energy, have little relevance. If it operated, noted one expert, Japan would have abandoned steel production in the 1950s. Japan lacked raw materials but was able to purchase iron ore and coal at a lower price than U.S. companies paid. The lower shipping costs in the 1960s were crucial to their expansion in the world market.

By 1979, imports were 20 percent of the British market, compared with 11 percent in 1967; in the United States, the world's largest importer of steel, imports were 22 percent of the total by 1982, and imports from the LDCs had more than doubled in a decade. In fact, in the six years between 1973 and 1979 the exports of the NICs plus Canada and Australia increased from 7.6 million tons to 18.0 million tons. The U.S. industry lost its pricing power through the competition of imports. Imports reached 40 percent in the FRG despite its gigantic modern facilities. And by 1982 the tables had turned on the Japanese, as imports filled 10 percent of the Japanese market and the LDCs competed with the Japanese companies in third markets.

The reverse was equally true as the Third World moved from being an importer to being an exporter. In 1974 Brazil produced 7.5 million tons and imported 1.6 million tons from Japan. By 1980 it was producing 15.3 million tons and importing 160,000 tons, a decline of 90 percent. In 1983 Taiwan became self-sufficient and had a surplus for export. Between 1977 and 1980 South Korea imported 2 million tons a year. The government-owned Pohang Steel Company, having grown from 500,000 tons in 1970 to 10.7 million tons in 1981, swiftly altered Korea's position as producer and market.

China in the mid-1980s was considered the brightest outlet for the coming years and was Japan's number two market for steel. But it was the German-led consortium with French and Swiss partners that finally won the contract for DM 1.4 billion to expand China's plant. Their willingness to transfer the most modern technology was the decisive factor in the competition.

The capacity of European companies far exceeds domestic demand and always has. For profitable production, they are required to export. The Japanese industry depends on direct exports of around 39 percent of its production. Moreover, much of Japan's domestic sales is exported in autos, ships, and other products; that means the Japanese export at least 50 percent of their steel production. While the five largest companies produced 77 percent of the crude steel, dozens of small steel producers operate on capital that is over 80 percent debt. Called "bicycle operators"—if they stop peddling they fall—they are the most aggressive exporters, for sales are their only alternative to bankruptcy. Their efforts posed the real conflict between the EEC and Japan in steel, since the quotas on Japanese exports covered only the six integrated producers. But the figures on the Japanese percentage of the European market, which tripled between 1973 and 1976 (after the United States began restrictions in 1972), reflected a shrinking market rather than an expansion of Japanese exports. The volume in 1976 was similar to that in 1973. The restrictions on exports to the U.S. market have led other producers to present the Japanese companies with "stiffer competition" on their turf in Southeast Asia, complained an official of Nippon Steel.[10]

Steel exports are absolutely crucial for many developing countries. The Korean integrated mill must export one-third of its production just to pay its debts and import its raw materials. Likewise, steel exports to the United States are critical to Mexico and Brazil in order to service their bank debt. Some $7.7 billion of Brazil's debt was incurred for its steel works. In 1982 the United States agreed to an export tax levied in Brazil but in 1984 decided to renew the import duty. In response to the U.S. demands, Brazil's industry minister said with exasperation, "How can our creditors expect us to pay our debt by reducing production . . . ? Brazil can in no way accept export limitations. We are expanding our exports and will continue to do so."[11] In 1986 production expanded 7 percent while falling drastically in the United States, Europe, and Japan. Although an IMF-imposed devaluation and the rise of the dollar had caused the competitive price, in February 1984 the United States imposed a 27.7 percent tariff on Brazilian steel in order to make it too expensive for the U.S. market.

The crisis in steel again exposed the contradictions in interests among various powerful industries. The bankers had considered their loans to build steel plants to be the most secure, since the output would generate the profits and the exports would earn the foreign exchange to repay the loans. But the power of the domestic steel industry to restrict imports undermined the calculations of the banks as well. In turn, the fierce struggle for import quotas on steel aroused the agriculture industry, which then became the target of European retaliation. Import quotas that raised the price of steel made steel-using industries less competitive, especially the machine tool and metalworking industries.

As the crisis worsened, steel became the focal point of international tension between Europe, the United States, and Japan, within Europe, and between the OECD states and the Third World exporters. Dumping, trigger prices, export restraint, quotas, and retaliation were the key terms in the international steel trade. The United States imposed its first antidumping ruling on Japan in mid-1977, and the first suit against the Europeans was, ironically, brought by an American subsidiary of Willy Korf, the German TNC. As "agreements" to limit exports were reached with successive countries, by 1985 covering 75 percent of all imports, there were new contestants. U.S. Steel filed complaints against most of Eastern Europe, Austria, Sweden, and Venezuela, some of whom were repaying with production the credits that built the industry.

The OECD tried to incorporate four LDC producers (Brazil, India, South Korea, and Mexico) into its steel committee when it was organized in November 1978, but these countries proved suspicious and hostile to the effort. The EEC filed complaints against Brazil and Romania, the Americans levied penalty duties on debt-ridden Brazil, the Japanese industry took measures against South Korea, the Europeans fought over production quotas, and the Americans demanded new quotas from the Europeans, a demand that brought instant threats of retaliation. The Europeans with justification pointed to the rising dollar as the origin of their new competitive position. In 1980, for example, German steel cost $525 and U.S. steel $510. Less than one year later German steel was $365 and U.S. steel $580. In the successive years the difference was even greater, as the dollar continued to rise. The Korean steel price, set in dollars, fell from $426 to $291 between 1981 and 1983. In general, all steel exports sell below the domestic price—"it is just part of free trade," asserted a director of British Steel.[12] But in no way could the shift in dollar price be attributed to subsidies or dumping. The steel importers claimed that if the price was the same, they preferred a domestic source, but that if the difference was more than 5 percent, they would buy an import. While the U.S. companies were demanding protection from imported steel, the American steel companies were, in turn, demanding price discounts of 2–10 percent from their suppliers and were, ironically, turning to the German, Swiss, and Italians for equipment, particularly to those with state-subsidized export credits. Consequently, there were dozens of bankruptcies among the U.S. suppliers to the steel industry.

By the end of 1983 Japanese steel, which long claimed to be the victim of such action, petitioned against South Korean and Taiwanese imports, claiming they were being "dumped" in the Japanese market. They also accused their competitors of dumping in the markets of Southeast Asia. In 1982, imports had indeed captured 10 percent of Japan's internal market and were disturbing the market sharing agreement between the five major Japanese companies that had controlled production to fit market demand since 1976.

LABOR

Despite the rhetoric that has colored the steel industry's struggle with labor, rising labor costs were the lesser part of the increased expenses. Energy makes up more than one-half the costs. Iron and transport are also important, and their price rises exceeded those of labor. Nevertheless, cheap labor along with the new technology and currency exchange rates remained a crucial "comparative advantage" for LDC steel producers. The labor cost differential, which also reflects the currency exchange, was expressed in 1982 Korean hourly wages of $2.60, compared with $14.30 in Canada and $23.00 in the United States. Labor costs remained around 33 percent of steel production costs in the United States in the mid-1980s. Wage increases had been greater in the FRG and Japan than in America since the mid-1970s. Steelworkers have been in the top ranks of their respective countries in wages and benefits, which rose along with layoffs. In the United States labor rates are estimated to be 66 percent above the manufacturing average.

Between 1974 and 1983, as part of the restructuring process, steel employment in the OECD countries fell by 34 percent, and the industry in both Europe and the United States continues to reduce capacity. The French agreed in March 1984 to cut subsidies and eliminate another 30,000 of the remaining 93,000 jobs. The Germans also announced they would "shed" an additional 30,000 workers, and the Spanish Socialists declared that they would shut down state-owned blast furnaces in 1984. Steel employment in Britain fell 60 percent between 1974 and 1982.

As unemployment has grown, many workers have conceded or been deprived of the wage gains won over many years. Armco, on the border of bankruptcy in 1985, after having cut employment 34 percent since 1980, planned to cut again by that figure and obtain further labor concessions from those who remained. The union traded wage and benefit cuts of 20 percent from the giant Bethlehem Steel for preferred stock in order to save jobs in the industry. A union official noted that the companies had only two sources of capital—their workers or the Japanese companies that wanted to invest.

Labor costs were 28 percent of U.S. Steel's production costs after its restructuring. Diversification into other areas gave U.S. Steel the power to resist strike threats, according to a union president. U.S. Steel, the president of one union local said, "wants to get out of steel and blame it on the union."[13] In August 1986 its intransigence led to a six-month strike, the longest in its history. Within days of the settlement in which it gained further concessions, the company announced closures and reduction of union employment by 25 percent. The union was at an obvious disadvantage. The company expects only 15–20 percent of its sales to be in steel in 1990.

LTV Steel introduced "new" labor relations modeled on the Japanese system in its new electrogalvanizing plant. Along with the high technology, workers receive salaries rather than hourly wages, at wage and benefits $5–$10 lower than previously, overtime pay only after forty hours, bonuses beginning in 1987, job security, teamwork in production, and no cost-of-living adjustment. Months after arranging the concessions, the company declared bankruptcy. By 1986 industry-wide bargaining had been changed to company bargaining, with the aim that each firm would lower wages by about one-fifth. Again, months after acquiring the concessions, the company filed for bankruptcy and was demanding yet more.

RESTRUCTURING POLICY

What are the implications of such gyrations in demand and the effort to reduce capacity? There was a consensus in Europe and, to a lesser extent, in the United States that the industry must be restructured in order to compete in the new international division of labor. In Europe restructuring the industry has meant cutting physical capacity and labor force and retaining only specialized production in modern plants. The state restructures by organizing cartels, nationalization, closures, channeling investment, and encouraging mergers. Abstractly, state bureaucrats and the company executives agree on this goal. In reality, it was, and is, an intense struggle.

In the early years of the crisis, the various governments in the OECD believed the problem to be of only temporary duration and turned first to traditional stopgap measures. In Europe, in order to avoid an all-out price war, the EEC in 1975 encouraged an effort to organize a cartel (Eurofer) to establish production quotas, capacity shares, a minimum import price, and allocation of the market. From the beginning, participants described the meetings of Eurofer as involving terrible infighting and sharing the misery. Almost immediately the German industry undermined it by ignoring the rules. Later an executive at Willy Korf called it "a failure" because the Italians consistently underpriced despite the threat of fines. In fact, the EEC agreements were geared to protect the older, less efficient plants and penalized the more competitive, modern minimills of Italy.

To avoid a price war, the first move of the EEC, which had the authority to regulate prices and assign quotas for production, was to cut production. The market was then filled by imports from Japan and the LDCs. In 1976, for example, the Swiss bought two-thirds of their steel from Japan. The German industry began to reduce capacity in 1976 and at first opposed protectionism, but as the Japanese doubled their exports to the FRG in the last months of the year, it demanded urgent action against imports. In 1978 the EEC introduced a price rise of 15 percent and called for further cutbacks in production. The price rise, however, spurred additional output. In July 1980 the EEC ordered production cuts of 18 percent. In October it invoked the Treaty of Rome provision and declared the obvious—"a state of crisis" in the European steel industry—and demanded mandatory cutbacks and the power to impose a levy on the excess. The French steel federation had called for such a declaration in 1975.

In 1980 the Germans resisted what they termed the "bureaucratic, statist" measures of the EEC, insisting they had already restructured more than other nations.[14] The FRG, with its modern plants, protested that the other EEC members were subsidizing obsolete plant and equipment and proposed a systematic capacity reduction, the elimination of state subsidies, and the termination of 100,000 jobs for others in the EEC. It opposed quotas and protectionist measures proposed by the

French and British. The latter threatened to flood the German market with cheap steel if the Germans did not cooperate. In fact, there was a price war in 1980, and Eurofer virtually collapsed in that year. By March 1981 the Germans threatened to restrict the importation of subsidized steel even though their threat contravened the EEC treaty guaranteeing a unified steel market. De facto prices were 15 percent below list. Given the crisis conditions, the EEC organized Eurofer II, which set voluntary quotas and fines for noncompliance. Restructuring, therefore, was agreed to in principle by the EEC members, but in practice it remained a volatile political question. As the *Economist* noted in January 1982, a cartel works only "when the market [is] either halfway down from a boom or halfway up from a recession."[15] At the top and the bottom, the industry ignores the regulations.

The more modern and competitive Italian minimills were again penalized by the plan's minimum-price rules. But the giant obsolete integrated mills could not compete with the new technology, even if labor costs were equivalent. The states' role in the restructuring was to close the obsolete plants and channel capital into the modern ones, but not into the minimills. As the earlier cuts had not resolved the problem, the EEC in 1983 demanded further reductions, which exceeded by 50 percent those its members had already agreed upon. It demanded the largest cuts from the FRG and Italy, since the Italians had not reduced capacity earlier. At the end of 1983 the EEC ministers agreed that minimum prices were needed and that sales had to be "in conformity with the traditional patterns of trade."[16] As the demand for steel increased in the spring of 1984, Krupp and Thyssen again challenged in court the EEC plan for a cutback of an additional 6-million-ton capacity, insisting they had already "streamlined" before 1980.[17]

The EEC sought to achieve its goal of a subsidy-free industry and a capacity reduction of 30 million tons by 1985. The governments had doubled their subsidies to industry since 1973. Steel received 10 percent of the German industrial subsidies and in France steel and shipbuilding obtained 40 percent of the total industrial subsidies. Large portions of the subventions were wasted, such as 10 billion francs to build and never open obsolete plants, or diverted to profits, or for dumping to secure market shares. The subsidies were originally meant to tide the industry over a "temporary" slump but were soon an enormous tax on revenue in a period of acute fiscal crisis. In January 1986 the EEC, save for Greece and Spain, abolished all subsidies except those for research, environment protection, and closures. It had planned to terminate production quotas by the end of 1986, but the situation for the industry was so grave that it considered allowing quotas indefinitely for 45 percent of all steel products. During 1980–85 the European members had spent $40 billion in restructuring the steel industry, and since the early 1970s they had reduced capacity by 20 percent and eliminated 400,000 jobs.

In the United States the government plays a role by means of fiscal policy—tax write-offs, depreciation allowances, changes in regulations on environment protection and antitrust, federal aid for research, and, most important, trade negotiations and restrictions. In 1977 it established a $250 million revolving-loan guarantee to provide capital for restructuring the industry. But while the industry benefited from these measures, its restructuring took forms other than modernization. Ten years later the government was working on a plan for "an orderly contraction" of the American steel industry and Congress was debating relief for additional huge shutdowns.

MERGERS

Mergers were another dimension of the European restructuring effort. Krupp and Estel Hoesch, numbers two and three in the FRG, merged at the end of 1982, forming Ruhrstahl, and the state provided the "restructuring" funds. The move cut capacity and eliminated 13,-000 of 24,000 jobs. When, in 1983, Krupp again proposed a merger with Thyssen, the state refused more than DM 500 million to implement it, and the discussion ended.

Mergers were also a means for American companies to respond to the crisis and avoid bankruptcy. "Mergers are a wonderful survival option," noted one business analyst.[18] But it took nearly one year for the government to waive the antitrust regulations when in February 1984, America's fourth-largest producer, Republic Steel, merged with Jones & Laughlin, a subsidiary of LTV and the third-largest American steel producer. After U.S. Steel failed in its attempt to acquire National Steel, Nippon Kokan bought a half interest in the company and is now financing its modernization. These mergers did not resolve the problems, however. The new LTV Steel had losses on operations, enormous write-offs of idle plant, and debt that reached 72 percent of capitalization in 1985, and bankruptcy in 1986. The number of integrated companies in the United States continued to decline through bankruptcies and mergers. There were twenty-three in 1968, fourteen in 1981, and ten in 1984, compared with sixty minimills.

DEBT

Debt, partly caused by the diversification, mounted for the U.S. companies in the 1980s. It was 32 percent of invested capital in 1980 and 47 percent in 1983, and for U.S. Steel it rose to 67 percent in 1984. Debt to equity was 24 percent in 1960, 38 percent in 1970, and 50 percent in 1980—and it has mounted sharply since then. European steel has traditionally been debt ridden. The French government extended loans to the industry in the early 1970s, rolled over the debt at the end of the decade, and finally absorbed the debt with nationalization in the 1980s. Belgium also converted debt to state equity at the end of the 1970s.

Corporations restructured with closures and divestments, relocations, diversification, cost cutting in their struggle with labor, and mergers. Disinvestment—the decision to make no capital improvements and to provide only the barest upkeep—was an alternative to closure. The principal goal of the U.S. industry was to reduce the profitable capacity-utilization point. By the mid-1980s the U.S. industry had reduced its capacity to 127 million tons, from 144 million tons in 1970. Capacity must be destroyed if the industry is to become profitable once more.

In other words, restructuring the industry in the United States means single-mindedly reducing the "break-even point" (BEP) in management, marketing, and, especially, labor policies. Together, the American companies had pushed their BEP down 10 percent by 1983 to be able to profit at 65 percent capacity utilization. Although traditionally many of the giant industries kept their unused capacity to preserve their market share in boom times, between 1974 and 1982 the companies closed down 199 facilities and cut their salaried workers' payrolls by 30 percent.

DIVERSIFICATION

Diversification is an increasingly important form of restructuring the industry. U.S. Steel moved to diversify between 1976 and 1979, and its nonsteel assets grew 80 percent. The company's president decided "to concentrate on only those things that make money." "Return on investment will dictate where money goes," he said.[19] Since this less and less meant steel, nonsteel assets were expected to provide an ever greater share of its revenue in the 1980s, up from 27 percent in 1978. In 1984 steel accounted for only 32 percent of its income, compared with 73 percent in 1979. In line with these plans, the company in 1982 borrowed $6.3 billion to purchase Marathon Oil. And it continued to divest its steel property in order to pay its Marathon debt. Between 1979 and 1985 the company had closed 150 plants, reducing steelmaking capacity by 30 percent, eliminated the jobs of 100,000 steelworkers and of 54 percent of the white-collar staff, and sold $3 billion in other assets. The company continued its expansion into energy by purchasing the Texas Oil and Gas Corporation in 1985, to the dismay of its stockholders. At the end of that year, U.S. Steel was again one of America's largest corporations, with assets of around $23 billion. But by 1986 a mere 31 percent of its revenue was derived from steel; oil and gas provided 58 percent. In July of that year U.S. Steel formally became a conglomerate by changing its name to the USX Corporation; only a subsidiary, one of four, in steel production, was henceforth called the USS Corporation.

National Steel invested $6.9 billion in savings and loan companies, a part of which it later sold to General Motors, and Republic Steel acquired an insurance company. Armco dropped the word *steel* from its name, and in 1983 National Steel changed its name to National Intergroup, to emphasize both the diversification and the shift away from steel. National then cut its steel capacity in half and sold 50 percent of the remainder to Nippon Steel. By the end of 1984 it was arranging a merger with a drug distribution firm, Bergen Brunswig. Diversification was successful for Armco in the period 1978–81, when it had record profits, but the recession hit all of its acquisitions, and in 1984 it suffered a loss of nearly $300 million. A renegotiating of bank credit forced it to divest its more profitable sectors in order to reduce its gigantic debt. The LTV Corporation, which was a merger of Jones & Laughlin and Republic Steel, had also diversified into the aerospace arms business, which was its major source of profit as a contractor for the Pentagon. In July 1986 the company declared bankruptcy.

Rather than modernize, for which it took subsidies and concessions from labor and the government, the U.S. steel industry in the 1980s stressed acquisition, diversification, closures, and a policy that provided a continued high level of dividends in the 1980s. German steel also began to diversify out of steel—in the case of Krupp, into aircraft and energy conversion, engineering, and trading divisions. And by the end of 1984 the Japanese steel corporations were planning to diversify into other, nonferrous metals and to reduce the percentage of steel in their total activity over the subsequent ten years to 50 percent.[20]

CONCLUSION

What do these trends in the world steel industry signify? Is steel production an anachronism in the OECD nations? The forces of competition and capitalists' traditional behavior vis-à-vis perceived profitability *objectively* restructured the industry. And the state-owned industry followed the same "laws" of accumulation, responding to the same "signals." The myopia that allowed the vast overexpansion in the early 1970s and then the systematic elimination of capacity within one decade is striking, involving investment and destruction worth many billions of dollars, and additional billions in subsidies to underwrite losses and for the construction of competitive capacity elsewhere.

Overcapacity is worldwide and a perennial source of crisis in the system, despite the obvious need for steel everywhere for construction, urgent repair of infrastructure, and the like. Destruction of plant and reorganization are traditional measures in dealing with overcapacity. Restructuring in the steel industry has left hundreds of thousands of workers unemployed and hundreds of communities in America and Europe in shambles.

This is not a process leading to a transformation in the OECD countries to a new "postindustrial" society. It is rather the forces of competitive capitalism in the world market. Steel, allegedly the quintessence of monopoly capital, could not compete after, it had, in part, built its own competition. It is an industry for economic expansion and the first casualty of contraction. And the new capacity, built for export, in other areas of the globe faces the same contradictions in the world market. Most important, steel is only one industry among many that are no longer "competitive" in the OECD states. Other manufacturing industries, including automobile production, and even the new-technology industries are threatened as corporations struggle to compete by obtaining the lowest costs. Only the state could provide a respite with tariffs, but at what risk in the highly integrated world economy, where all nations are export oriented? Competition is intense, and threats of retaliation lead to conflict in other areas. This core industry of the industrial nations is in a "state of crisis." It is the other, "new" industries that many hoped would offer the alternative for industrial growth and a "comparative advantage" in trade.

CHAPTER 7

THE
NEW-TECHNOLOGY
INDUSTRIES

For capital, technological innovation continues to be stimulated by the systemic features of competition and by the drive to reduce the role of labor in the production process. Even in the area of research and development, these factors and the capitalists' perception of the market often determine what is investigated. Important discoveries and developments, if not obvious sources of commercial profit, are often neglected.

Especially relevant to this study are three factors among the crucial dimensions of the new industries based on recent developments in science and technology: the expectations on the part of the state that these industries will resolve the crisis in its economy, the economic impact of the new technology on other industries, and the manner in which the high-tech new industries themselves relate to and interact with the crisis.

Some have likened the far-reaching social implications of the new technology to those of the industrial revolution in the nineteenth century. But while the new technology does have revolutionary implications for the general economy, the industry has not had a new-product breakthrough with an expansionary, multiplying economic impact, as did the railroad, automobile, and airplane. On the contrary, the new technology has the potential to contract the economy greatly. As Wassily Leontief noted, the industrial revolution increased labor's role as an indispensable factor of production, but with the new technology "not only the physical but also the controlling 'mental' functions . . . can be performed without the participation of human labor."[1] And its potential in changing the demand for inputs like raw materials can affect that sector significantly.

As an alternative to traditional industries in the industrial nations, "new-product development" is a mirage. In the past, as new technology replaced old with new products, the locale of production remained the same. Now new products are as vulnerable as the old, to the extent that labor is an important component of cost. The transistor industries are a case in point, as the producers of the components sought the cheapest labor. And to the extent that new technology is capital intensive, it will simply further displace labor. The automation of skilled machinists' work is proceeding more rapidly than that of assembly line work.

Although technological developments have produced a revolutionary change, automation was certainly conceivable thirty or more years ago, but it required a conjuncture of conditions to make it profitable. Technological efficiency has no value to business unless it enhances profits. At present, the trend toward automation in capitalism aggravates its contradictions and tendency to overproduction on a world scale as never before. The new technology contains the seeds of new crisis.

While the new technology, particularly the reprogrammable robots, greatly increases productivity, the ultimate question remains, as the president of the world's leading robot producer queried, "Why have a robot working round the clock twice as fast as humans if already you can't sell what the humans are producing on a single shift working?"[2] But twenty-four-hour production and full utilization are essential in order to amortize the expensive equipment and to achieve an acceptable return. With the labor-saving capital equipment, the constant capital is greatly increased and the return significantly lower, contributing to the falling rate of profit. Since a major purpose of science and technology in capitalism is to reduce the labor cost of production or to increase productivity, it is linked to the shifting capital-labor relationship. The rise in wages was leading toward the installation of ever newer fixed capital. The trend to automate, driven by competition and costs, is clearly in evidence today. It can change just as swiftly if labor costs appear to be falling in a recessionary environment, the trend toward investment in expensive equipment may also lessen.

FLEXIBLE AUTOMATION

The great innovation in the recent technology is "flexible automation." Its importance lies in its capacity to automate small-volume production and shift from one type of product to another without retooling; it can produce any number economically, from many thousands to one. Its maxim is "Nothing will be produced without an order in hand."[3] It introduces economies on a wide range of scales, or what is now termed economy of scope. Flexible automation can make obsolete large plants, with their large-scale investments, and hence reduces its expansionary economic impact. There is a move away from size and a recognition with the new technology of the "diseconomies of scale."[4] By 1985 AT & T was closing its large assembly plants to build a smaller automated plant. Manufacturers with the new equipment can also quickly produce in new fields. "Some companies will find themselves blind-sided by competitors they never imagined existed," noted an American management consultant in 1983.[5] The equipment is expensive and must therefore operate full-time to be amortized, but as the prices fall with growing competition, as they have over the past decades, incorporating the new technology and all its accompanying contradictions into the economic system will accelerate. While the automated modern plant's profitable operating capacity exceeded that of national markets earlier, a question now is, How can capacity be measured with flexible automation? Or what effect will it have on the tendency toward overproduction?[6] In theory, it is possible someday with the new technology to restrict production to demand. But in reality, how likely is such restraint? It is not today's *technology* that forces GM to produce a vast surplus in excess of demand.

Fully automated plants have existed so far primarily in Japan. There were only about two dozen in the United States in the mid-1980s. Their costs are great, but once the investment is made, their advantages are obvious: a reduction of working capital, since companies can avoid large inventories; a reduction of machinery, as new machines are reprogrammable for multiple tasks formerly performed by different machines; less depreciation, with a higher intensity of operation; and the obvious reduction of labor costs. Because of the rapid developments and great cost of this form of technology, companies also have the incentive to wait for the even more modern devices at the lowest cost, and also for a "shakeout" in the industry in order to ensure future servicing.[7]

Although, according to the OECD, the United States did have "undeniable superiority in component technology" in the mid-1970s, it has been slower than other industrial countries to invest in new equipment.[8] By 1983 only 125 out of 42,000 factories in the country had introduced computerized systems of information technology to control inventory and schedule production. Increasingly, it is the small, so-called job shops—the subcontractors—that build the metal parts for the giant firms and employ the bulk of the blue-collar workers in the United States, and a large proportion of the skilled machinists, which are automating. In 1986 one-quarter of the robot sales were to such companies.[9] Finally, in 1987 General Motors started production in its fully automated, computer-controlled plants in Kansas and Georgia.

In 1983 more than 34 percent of machine tools in the United States were more than twenty years old (and only 4 percent were numerically controlled), compared with 24 percent in the United Kingdom and 18 percent in Japan. Even so, there has occurred since the 1930s a general reduction of one-third in the physical life of machines. A computer's life expectancy is around five years. These calculations were made in the early 1970s. Since 1981 the accelerated depreciation of capital has been much more rapid in the United States.

There has been a comparative decline in U.S. competitiveness in R & D. Spending fell by one-half between 1960 and 1974, and the percentage of patents issued to scientists in other nations rose from 13 percent in 1966 to 28 percent in 1975. The U.S. lead in high technology is essentially a spin-off of the government-subsidized arms research, where man's ingenuity is given full scope and endless funds to develop "appropriate" technologies to kill. In fact, one of the most modern factories in the United States is LTV Aerospace and Defense, where a fully automatic factory has run twenty-four hours a day, six days a week, since July 1984, making parts for the B-1 bomber. The U.S. Air Force set up a three-year-guarantee project to persuade subcontractors to switch to computer-controlled manufacturing and robots.

The United States has been less successful in translating this technology into nonmilitary products. New-product failure rates were 80 percent in some industries in the mid-1970s. The Japanese, by contrast, sought out the latest innovations worldwide and adapted them to commercial use. By 1985 there were 67,300 robots operating in Japan, over four times those in the United States and three times those in Europe.

COMPETITION

The high-technology industry, rather than being immune to crisis features, as many had hoped, was as vulnerable as any other to the developments in the general economy. In January 1982 the semiconductor industry announced a decline in profits of 70 percent in 1981, caused by reduced demand and by Japanese competition, which contributed to a fall in prices. After the industry's previous recession and cutbacks in 1976, the Japanese were able to take a larger share of the market. The rising dollar also had its impact on the American electronics industry, which ran up a trade deficit (of $6.8 billion) for the first time in 1984, and the deficit doubled in 1985. The deficit with Japan in the electronics industry exceeded that in autos. Some have concluded that the U.S. industry is increasingly a distribution business, as ever greater numbers of components are imported rather than produced.

The illusion of a recession-free electronics industry was also shattered in 1981 in Europe when, according to one industrialist, "there was a drastic change in profitability for all of us."[10] Amid a "no holds barred" price war in integrated circuits, no one made any profit, and Texas Instruments, then the biggest foreign company in Europe, suffered the heaviest losses. Some electronic component prices were 30 percent below those in the United States. It was a disastrous year for U.S. high-tech producers in Europe, as sales fell by one-third or more while the Japanese firms struggled to secure a market share. By 1982 Europe was reportedly "a smaller but also a bloodier arena."[11] The European companies then turned to the export markets in order to develop economies of scale. Several companies made the decision to produce products they could "sell at international volumes and stop the rest."[12] Their strategy shifted from diversification in all areas of electronics to cooperation on a select few.

Since the Japanese and the Americans were far ahead in the fields of the new technology, a dozen European companies in June 1982 felt forced to support a collaborative R & D program, called ESPRIT, funded with $42.5 million from the EEC. Past European efforts had been dismal failures because of rivalries. There were higher hopes for this project because the Japanese had "everyone scared rigid," according to one EEC official.[13] Yet, by mid-1983, little had been accomplished, and the EEC deficit in high technology had reached $15 billion. Protectionism, links to foreign firms, and government incentives had all failed to reverse the trend.

While inter-European cooperation is an affirmed goal, for the short run the various companies are making alliances with IBM or AT & T to gain access both to U.S. technology and to the U.S. market. European companies like Olivetti continue to invest in the United States with the precise purpose of acquiring the latest technology. But the Japanese are still the most active and enterprising in buying the most advanced science and technology in the United States, even before the commercialization has been realized.

The economic cycle persisted. The year 1984 was a "boom" time again for the high-tech electronics industry; orders were backlogged, particularly for personal computers, as the U.S. industry worked at capacity. The industry expected a 37 percent worldwide expansion of investment. By 1985 there was overproduction, retrenchment, and sharp price competition among the biggest firms like IBM and Apple.

In the robot industry, as well, the recession took its toll, as it did in all of the capital goods industry. Employment fell 10 percent in the United States, with the first-ever layoffs in some computer industries.

The high-technology industry has also been rapidly automating its own production processes. In Japan robots make robots, and for the labor-intensive aspects relocation is still an option. In March 1983 Atari moved 1,700 jobs abroad, and Hewlett-Packard was building major plants in Mexico and Britain despite the extensive inducements to locate in their area that various U.S. cities and states offered.

THE NEW INTERNATIONAL DIVISION OF LABOR

The developments in technology were never meant to create a new international division of labor, but they provided the preconditions for it. The critical motivation on the part of the TNCs was competition and resurgent class conflict, with the consequent rising labor costs. There was a race to be in a position to capture a greater share of a world market that was expected to expand but that was, in fact, contracting. The profit margins would be greatest for those TNCs that could produce at the lowest cost, which meant relocation and rationalization. The essentials of the system had not changed, only the structural circumstances.

The world factory was made feasible by this congruence of factors that, in part, restructured the global economy. The new technology that fractured and segmented the work process and further eliminated skills and that made possible the low-cost, efficient containerized transport system, the new breakthroughs in communication and control, and the seemingly inexhaustible supply of cheap labor in various parts of the globe were the preconditions for the new international division of labor. The banks reinforced the corporate moves to exploit these factors, and such institutions as the IMF sustained them politically. The TNCs also exported the machinery that the latest labor-saving innovations in the OECD countries had made obsolete. Relative to the labor supply, industry in the LDCs is always capital intensive.

When investment for capital goods plant construction stagnated in the OECD nations, the huge engineering companies competed for the demand in the CPEs and in OPEC and other Third World countries, which increased their debt to expand their industrial base. GE was the leading exporter from the United States in the late 1970s, when 38 percent of its sales, primarily giant industrial complexes and turnkey plants, and 42 percent of its profits were foreign.

Turnkey plants are usually technology "packages" that entail a long-term dependent relationship to the seller in terms of maintenance, repair, and technology updates. Because of this relationship, the plants are increasingly classified as "new forms of investment" rather than as sales. Technology transfer, *Business Week* noted in 1976, includes "formulas, processing, worker training, executive development, financial expertise, and organizational techniques. It embraces the skills transmitted by retailers as well as industrial concerns. . . . the sale of technology itself is becoming a big business overseas."[14] In addition, there is a built-in obsolescence of limited life expectancy. Development of agricultural technology was very important in building so-called agribusiness in many parts of the world, including control of seed, fertilizer, insecticides, machinery, and other inputs as part of a package.

The information technologies provide new forms of centralized control through computer communication. These transborder data flows provide superior inventory control, economies of scale with international decentralization and specialization of production, purchasing economies, and coordination of financial flows to avoid exchange rate risks. Yet, as technology changes certain industries, such as textiles, from labor to capital intensive, and as it automates other labor-intensive tasks, the LDCs' "comparative advantage" is lessened if not removed, perpetuating the need continually to lower wages further.

The technological dominance of the OECD countries, on which the restructuring of the world economy strategies are based, has been rapidly eroding. The OECD secretariat acknowledged in 1978 that new centers would provide competition both in third markets and in the OECD itself.

It is evident that there are no frontiers in production techniques—no geographical boundaries between low-labor-cost regions, which would specialize in low-technology, low-skill industries, and the OECD countries, which would concentrate on high-skill, high-tech industry. There was scarcely even a transition period; before the OECD plans for a rational restructuring of its economies had advanced beyond rhetoric, the NICs had moved into the sophisticated technologies. The oversimplified notions of the international division of labor were made obsolete, as the NICs successfully installed the most modern plants in capital goods and moved swiftly, as was said of South Korea, "to get out of yesterday's industries [45 percent of their textiles encounter high tariffs] and into tomorrow's," meaning computer services, telecommunications, and electronic control machines, and even to go beyond "today's industries" of steel, shipbuilding, autos, and the like. The NICs began to supply their own semiconductors and chips industry for their economy and henceforth could compete in the export markets.

CONCLUSION

Science and technology are objectively restructuring the economy in their traditional form of reducing and deskilling the labor component in production and white-collar functions. In addition, the new high-tech industries require less material inputs than previous technological revolutions did and so are deflationary in relation to other industries, and the developments in communications permit centralized control of world production and have transformed the global financial structure. Subjectively, governments have aspired to resolve their crisis and restructure the economy by encouraging the growth of the new-technology industries, only to confront new contradictions and to find that competition in the NICs is developing apace.

There is, of course, no limit to the benefits for humanity if science and technology were consciously directed toward its needs. The question of appropriate technology is one not just for the Third World but for the entire globe. But now, as in the past and in all areas, it is capitalism that sets the rules. Technology is therefore often used for purposes distinctly alien to human needs—for the military, to create unemployment, for the refinement of control and manipulation of others, and for innumerable other antisocial activities. Even when the purpose is beneficial, such as increasing the production of food, the technology is frequently perverted and the social outcome often calamitous.

CHAPTER 8

THE ARMS INDUSTRY AND THE ECONOMY

With a seemingly limitless market, the arms industry is being restructured as the major export industry in many nations. The world's total arms expenditures had reached $1 trillion by 1984, up from $300 billion in 1972. And in constant prices there was an 80 percent increase between 1960 and 1980 internationally. In today's intense competition in the world market, the arms industry has a primary economic significance as a major factor in world trade.

In the United States after 1975, when the Vietnam War ended, the prime emphasis of the arms industry was placed on exports. Foreign sales for the aerospace industry were two and a half times more profitable than domestic sales to the Defense Department. Even during the Vietnam War, from 1970 to 1976 the top twenty-five defense contractors increased their exports by 45 percent while their U.S. business fell 23 percent, so one-fifth of their sales were foreign, compared with 4 percent in 1970. To counter the competition, the U.S. government plays an active role as salesman. When a foreign government places an order, the Pentagon makes the procurement, often providing huge direct subsidies. By 1977 arms sales had reached $10 billion, or 8 percent of all U.S. exports, and they more than doubled in value between 1980 and 1984. Thereafter, weapons were one of the few strong sectors in the U.S. trade balance.

As in other industries, the trend in the arms industry internationally is also increasingly toward coproduction in the purchasing country, transfer of technology, and the like. Recent sales have stressed technological transfers, turnkey plants, and the most advanced equipment. In

153

the export of arms there is often a link with nonmilitary sales and a package arranged between governments. The French linked a Renault car plant to a tank factory sale to Argentina and included an air control system in its sale of Mirages to Brazil. The British linked a steel mill to Brazil to the construction of navy ships.

In France there had been a demilitarization of the economy between 1958 (the end of the Algerian war) and 1970. With the generalized economic crisis, however, the state has steadily increased its emphasis on arms as its most significant competitive sector in international trade. Since 1970 the aviation industry has been the "motor of growth" of the French economy.[1] Before that year the arms industry depended on the state for 75 percent of its sales and on exports for the remainder. During this phase its growth was less than the average of all industrial sectors combined. In the first half of the 1970s exports accounted for 50 percent, and the arms industry became *the* growth industry, expanding twice as fast as the national average, and three times as fast by the end of the 1970s. The French aircraft industry, now nationalized, is dependent on exports of military products. In 1979 three-fourths of Dassault's total business was foreign arms sales. For Matra, a producer of guided missiles, the figures are the same. This demand quickly determined the industry's specialization. The aerospace industry accounted for 80 percent of all military sales, and the Paris Air Show is now the world's most important marketplace for arms sales.

Arms became increasingly important for the French economy, as moves to restructure the basic industries increased unemployment and no new industry emerged as an alternative in trade. Between 1976 and 1982 the French share of the LDC arms market rose from 9 percent to 15 percent. But because of the pressures of the debt crisis and intensifying competition in the Third World, military orders dropped from over 41 billion francs to 30 billion francs between 1982 and 1983. "There is little demand right now . . . it is a worldwide crisis," lamented the director of export sales for the French government's arms agency.[2] Nevertheless, in 1984 France was number two in arms sales to the LDCs, with orders of $9.1 billion, compared with $10.4 billion for the USSR and $7.3 billion for the United States. About 80 percent of France's arms exports are destined for the Middle East. The Persian Gulf war was particularly important; France had sold Iraq $11.5 billion of equipment by the end of 1986 and hundreds of millions to Iran. Matra was also able to secure a Pentagon contract for the first time in 1983, for $83 million for a so-called superbomb. "The key is having the superior technology and being able to sell it," according to a Matra executive.[3] The Pentagon then made a $1 billion order to a joint

French-German Euromissile group. All the arms sales were expected to "help the French order book in 1984" when nothing else was possible.[4] In 1985 the Pentagon again awarded the French Thomson CSF in partnership with a U.S. company a $4.5 billion contract for a battlefield communications system. It was expected to lead to an even larger contract from South Korea. Yet there was an obvious danger to the French economy in its becoming so heavily dependent on the export of arms to a highly competitive and volatile world market.

Joint ventures as a means of reducing costs are important among the European countries, especially in aircraft. The French and Germans also cooperated on a new helicopter of which each country will order 200 for 30 billion francs, and both cooperated with the British in several multibillion-dollar projects, ostensibly to fill Europe's military needs in the 1990s. The success of the Exocet missile in wars in the Falkland Islands and the Persian Gulf did much to promote French expertise. By contrast, the Soviet Union's arms sales, one of its chief hard-currency earners, suffered a setback in the competition when Israeli aircraft destroyed its most modern missiles in Syria in 1982.

Competition has been keen. When in 1977 Carter called for a reduction in U.S. arms transfers, the French, Swedes, and British moved quickly to pick up the contracts in Argentina, India, and Bolivia. In 1984 intense competition raged for a Greek order of a hundred planes for its air force, worth $3 billion, the largest weapons purchase in the country's history. Competing were the French, America's General Dynamics, and a joint venture of the FRG, Italy, and Britain. The French used their Socialist party ties and offered the fledgling Hellenic Aerospace Industry participation in building a new European combat fighter for export. The Greeks compromised by buying forty each from Dassault and General Dynamics.

Since sales are to governments, bribery became a major factor in the competition, often to persuade governments to buy goods they did not originally want. Northrop, the producer of the F-5 fighter planes, paid $30 million in bribes over three years—equal to its net earnings for the period.

ARMS AND THE U.S. ECONOMY

The U.S. arms industry, despite its guaranteed profit from the state, had a low rating in the financial markets until the 1980s. Its bond ratings were one-half those of their civilian counterparts, its funding from the commercial banks was always short term, and investment houses were reluctant to invest in the arms sector. Nevertheless, under the Reagan administration profits in the arms industry significantly surpassed those of other manufacturers, and with its emphasis on high technology and electronics, it began to attract capital because it was the one area in the internal economy not threatened by intense international competition. The ten largest arms contractors in 1984 had an average of 25.0 percent after tax return on equity, twice the average of all manufacturers. Profits declined during the recession but not as sharply as in the civilian sector. A number of companies diversified into or acquired electronics companies to obtain a share of these benefits. The Pentagon's leading electronic warfare (EW) contractor, with $8.4 billion, was GM after acquiring Hughes in 1985. By 1986 GE had merged with Raytheon and became number two in these contracts.

The majority of employees in the arms industry are technicians; depending on the sector, only 28 percent (guided missiles) to 54 percent (aircraft) are production workers, compared with the average of 90 percent in 1981 for U.S. manufacturing. Although the prime contractors in 1984 employed only 2.86 million persons, the arms industry absorbs up to one-third of all American scientists and engineers. It also absorbs an inordinate proportion of skilled workers. Of the 300,000 machinists, nearly one-third work in the arms industry. Per dollar, the arms industry produces one-half as many jobs at 20 percent higher salaries than civilian expenditures do. There is, perhaps, a multiplier effect producing a maximum of an additional million jobs. But as the weapons become more sophisticated, their costs rise and the multiplier effect is reduced. It has very little impact on unemployment. In fact, the arms industry, like the rest of the industrial sector, has been eliminating jobs over the past decade through the introduction of robots and computer-controlled manufacturing. Its mammoth budget is primarily for development, not production, and excess production capacity exists among all the prime contractors.

In the mid-1980s, 35 percent of all U.S. arms contracts involve no bidding whatsoever, 60 percent are "competitively negotiated" with a few companies the Department of Defense deems "qualified," and 5 percent are open to competitive bidding.[5] And the military sector is not subject to the normal profit-and-loss criteria. The recent scandals brought some increase in competitive bidding in the 1980s, leading to a number of foreign contracts. Periodically, scandals of fraud in weapons procurement are made public. Recently, it was estimated that $16.2 billion a year in frivolous personal expenses are added to the costs as Pentagon "allowable" expenses. While General Dynamics was being investigated for fraud and corruption, the Defense Department awarded the company a $5 billion contract as the only supplier of one of its major weapons. These make colorful headlines but are less significant than the billions for research and development in fiascoes of new weapons systems. Congress is also responsible for adding "at least $10 billion a year, [for] things we don't want . . . but are in there to protect vested interests," according to a Pentagon official.[6]

Military procurement in the American aircraft industry has since World War II been shifting steadily from quantity to sophistication and complexity. The Pentagon purchased 3,000 aircraft per year during the Korean War, 1,000 per year in the mid-1960s, and 300 high-tech aircraft in 1980 for U.S. use and slightly more for export. The industry, as a consequence, was operating at 55 percent capacity of one shift and had made insignificant capital investment since 1968, although it had contracted heavy debts. Pentagon procurement fell from $17 billion in 1968 to $7 billion in the mid-1970s (in real terms). Exports of military aircraft grew over this period from 10 percent to 60 percent of total sales.

Electronic weaponry has top priority in the Pentagon, which anticipates that by 1991 the electronic component will be 47 percent of the cost of all U.S. hardware. EW research and procurement are the fastest-growing expenditure in the military budget. By 1986 their cost amounted to $57 billion. The electronics companies have lost no time in their effort to cultivate their market in the Pentagon. In 1982, representatives of fifty companies began "top secret" biweekly meetings to help shape "the basic structure for planning and building U.S. EW devices over the next 20 years," confided the Defense Department's director of electronic war R & D.[7] The billions for "Star Wars" R & D form part of this intimate linkage of weapons and industry.

Various economists, such as Lester Thurow and Wassily Leontief, in 1981 predicted that an escalation of military spending would cause a sharp rise in inflation. While the budget produced other disasters, inflation was not one of them. The vertical nature of "peacetime" military spending in the economy differs radically from the inflation-inducing expenditure for war, with its horizontal impact across the economy.[8]

The U.S. Star Wars budget of $26 billion to 1989 has enticed a number of European companies even as their governments have rejected the proposal. The European governments want to devote their own resources to their own research programs like Eureka, the French-sponsored, largely civilian space program, backed by the Germans and the EC. The Germans also proposed a European Defense Initiative. But European companies, such as Fiat, need immediate research funding and hope to benefit from commercial spin-offs. Their illusion ignores, however, the primacy of U.S. interests, which ties the results of European participation to U.S. control and its interest in, as an assistant secretary of defense put it, "making sure that information is passed to nonporous recipients."9 But most important to the European arms industry, employing an estimated 750,000, in the 1980s has been the war between Iran and Iraq. Those two nations have spent some $70 billion since the war began in 1980, a good proportion of it in Europe.

In Japan the role of arms in the economy accelerated under Nakasone, rising from 6.5 to 7.9 percent a year. As Saburo Kugai pointed out, much of the expenditure has in any case been hidden in other budgetary divisions in order not to exceed the budget ceiling of 1 percent of the GNP. Officially, it was about $21 billion, but in fact it stood near $28 to $30 billion, and its impact was greater because of the rise of the yen vis-à-vis the dollar and the enormous size of the GNP.

In the OECD countries only the military is permitted the massive state expenditures that have kept the world economy out of deep depression. War, or its preparation, is institutionalized and used as a Keynesian economic prop and stimulus. If there is an acceptable substitute in capitalism, it has yet to be found. Fundamental structural changes have been made in the world economy as a result of these massive "peacetime" arms expenditures, and they have introduced new contradictions in the system.

ARMS AND DEVELOPMENT

Forty-eight of the LDCs are administered by the military, and in nearly all the others the army plays an important role in politics. Hence it is not so surprising that Third World arms expenditures rose fourfold between 1960 and 1980. In the aggregate the LDCs increased their arms expenditures from $72.6 billion in 1970 to $118.7 billion in 1979, in constant prices. Although there was a cutback in 1983 because of the pressures of debt and austerity, in 1984, led by the Middle East and Africa, the LDCs increased their arms spending twice as fast as the rest of the world did. This change has had great economic and political implications for the entire globe.

In the 1950s the United States sent its obsolete weapons as military aid to the LDCs as part of the Cold War. From the 1960s international competition in the LDC arms trade began, and commercial criteria dominated trade, especially among the European countries. Arms account for an important part of the LDCs' balance-of-payments deficit but have the highest priority and are usually purchased with suppliers' credits arranged by aggressive and highly competitive arms exporters. Global arms trade grew from $3–$4 billion in the beginning of the 1960s to $30–$35 billion two decades later, and transfers to the LDCs increased from $1–$2 billion to $25–$30 billion. About 81 percent of the total arms imports were in the LDCs and primarily to the Middle East. That area, awash in petrodollars, accounted for 32 percent during the 1970s and for 40 percent thereafter. Since the mid-1960s both the United States (over one half) and the USSR sold the bulk of their arms exports to that war-torn region.

Arms production in the LDCs is also a new phenomenon. In 1960 there was none, and production grew fivefold between 1970 and 1981. By 1980 Brazil, North and South Korea, Israel, India, Pakistan, Turkey, China, and others were active exporters, but insignificant compared with the USSR (30.1 percent of the market in 1982), the United States (26.2 percent), France, the United Kingdom, the FRG, and Italy. These six accounted for 84 percent of all sales to the LDCs. The figures vary according to the source. If military services, which make up 40 percent in some cases, are included, the United States leads in sales. But the rapidity of the change is significant. In 1975 Brazil had no exports. In 1980 it ranked above Israel, and its arms exports amounted to $800 million, primarily to Iraq, surpassed only by its soybeans and coffee in export value. Brazil became very competitive quickly since it specialized in arms of intermediate technology, those that did not require sophisticated training and maintenance, suitable for the sort of fighting that occurs in much of the Third World. The general in charge of sales declared, "We look toward the Third World, and we will sell to the right, to the left, and to the center."[10] As one writer noted, it was a concrete example of South-South cooperation.[11] Israel, which is always, if questionably, ranked as an LDC, was the number two arms exporter among them, exporting primarily to Central America, South Africa, Uruguay, and Argentina. For military expenditures per inhabitant, it ranks number three in the world.

There is a considerable literature on the costs of arms expenditures to economic development, in terms both of allocation of scarce resources and of their impact on the orientation of many nations' industrialization. The IMF calculated that the average military expenditure of the oil-importing LDCs was 14 percent of the budget and that together they accounted for 22.5 percent of the total world military expenditure in 1979.

Weapons production is capital and import intensive. This unproductive waste expenditure for imports and production alike, plus the dependence on suppliers for spare parts, maintenance, and debt service, is a major restriction on economic development. Other negative effects on development include the diversion of scarce resources, including skilled manpower, from civilian needs and the inherently inflationary bias of such unproductive expenditures.[12]

CHAPTER 9

NEW DEVELOPMENTS IN RAW MATERIALS AND AGRICULTURE

The world commodity sector, comprising all raw-materials and agricultural production, has undergone sustained restructuring since the world economic crisis began in the 1970s. There has been an intensification of the traditional surplus-shortage cycles as well as a shift in the structure of ownership and trade of, and demand for, many key commodities.

Many LDCs remain dependent on the fate of one raw material, or of a few, for their well-being and economic development. And there is a direct link between their debts and the constantly shifting revenues they obtain from their commodity exports, since rising prices stimulate greater production, expanded capacity, and increased borrowing, whereas falling prices aggravate the debt crisis and lead to increased output, which further depresses prices, to repay debt. Debt generally replaced equity in financing mining operations in the 1970s and became part of the cumulative debt crisis in the 1980s.

But factors like the terms of trade or the health of the national economy are of no concern to the companies dealing in the materials. Prices are fixed by the TNCs, usually dealing in several commodities, that market the produce. Intrafirm trade of vertically linked corporations also controls the prices of certain commodities. Oligopsony, market control by a few buyers, has become increasingly characteristic of world commodity trade, with its corollary of contracting out to small independent producers or of joint ventures with the state rather than direct production by the world's giant TNCs. An OECD study noted in 1984:

161

Joint ventures, production-sharing arrangements, and service and management contracts had largely replaced FDI [foreign direct investment] by the late
1970s. . . . [T]here seems to be a consensus among students of the mining
industry that . . . the multinational mining corporations are tending to transform their role from that of equity investors to one of mobilizers of international loan capital (from public and private sources), innovators and suppliers
of production and processing technology and management, and above all
providers of access to world-market outlets for many developing-country minerals producers.[1]

The Japanese, especially, have perfected an advanced form of oligopsony over the years of acquiring access to their raw-materials supplies.
The trading companies organize the financing and marketing and coordinate production. They arrange long-term loans to joint venture na-
tional-Japanese mining companies. The Japanese minority share operate at a loss or break even at the production end; profits come largely
from the interest on loans and, primarily, the marketing.

Reportedly, "only rarely do most commodity prices move down-
wards in unison, and almost never do they all drop at the same time."[2]
Commodity prices fell in 1975 and collapsed in the recession of 1981–
82, the steepest and longest fall since the 1930s, primarily because of
overproduction that was the outcome of the expansion and the rising
prices in the late 1970s. By the end of 1985, commodities were again
falling sharply—tin, rubber, vegetable oils, sugar, cocoa, and petroleum. Prices fell 13 percent in the aggregate that year, well below the
point reached in the preceding recession. In the years 1980–85 metals
prices fell 30 percent and the overall index by 24 percent, and they
continued to fall, along with the price of oil. While prices of commodities also are subject to manipulation by speculators and vulnerable to
capricious rumor, political events, and, in the case of agricultural products, the weather, the falling prices were again due to overproduction,
as supplies increased more during 1984–85 than at any other time
since 1960. Given the rampant speculation in the other areas of the
economy, the slowing world trade, and the colossal debt, the price
deflation in raw materials was especially ominous. Supply and demand
always determine the extent of the intercapitalist conflicts and international rivalries over raw materials, and the importance of raw materials
in U.S. foreign policy, and these in turn reflect the general condition
of the world economy.[3]

RESTRUCTURING IN THE OIL INDUSTRY

Oil, of all the commodities, has had the most profound impact on
the general economy and has had the sharpest swings in boom and bust

since the early 1970s. This process objectively restructured the economy in many ways. One major structural change in the industry was that by the end of the 1970s all foreign-owned oil production in the LDCs had been replaced by some form of production sharing or service contract. Predictions of future developments are most common and most risky in the area of raw materials and commodities. By the mid-1980s everyone was familiar with the roller coaster of oil prices, but this did not inhibit further sweeping, policy-orienting prognostications.

Demand for oil began to fall in 1979, but its price continued to rise, to a peak of $34.70 in 1981, 170 percent above the 1978 price and a 1,200 percent rise since 1973. A combination of factors gave OPEC the leverage to raise the price from $13 at the end of 1978 to $34 in 1981 although demand had already begun to decline. OPEC was able to adjust supply to the level of demand by controlling production, which dropped from 31 million barrels per day in 1979 to 17 million in 1985.

After 1979, billions were invested in the OECD energy industry, on the expectation of continually rising oil prices. As the revenues of the oil field suppliers industry doubled between 1979 and 1981, orders backlogged, and with the expectation of rising profits many new entrants sought financing, which the banks were eager to provide. The repercussions of this development were widespread. It was a major element in the rapid regional economic growth of the American Southwest.

But as the recession in 1982 reversed the perceptions of the future, oil-related stocks dropped sharply on Wall Street. Stocks in new oil exploration fell 31 percent between January and June 1982. Backlogged orders turned into massive cancellations, and thousands of workers were laid off. There were cash flow problems for dozens of companies, and bankruptcy for others in oil service, exploration, and supply. The oil industry borrowed $40 billion in 1982, as the price of oil began to fall. The collapse of Penn Square Bank in Oklahoma was linked to its energy-related loans, which in turn undermined the solvency of Continental Illinois. Astonishingly, the whole scenario was repeated as soon as 1985–86.

Fields discovered in the early 1970s in Mexico, the North Sea, and Alaska came into production at the end of that decade. OPEC's share of the OECD/LDC market fell from 59 percent in 1979 to 45 percent in 1982, and it continued to drop. Its volume of exports fell 50 percent between 1979 and 1985. Non-OPEC producers were pumping more oil than OPEC for the first time in twenty years. OPEC had managed to stop the falling price, at $29 in 1983, by reducing production to one-half that of 1979. The fall in price reverberated across the whole economy of the oil-exporting countries, affecting profoundly their ability to service their debt. In 1986 Indonesia's budget contracted for the first time in two decades.

Saudi Arabia had borne nearly all of OPEC's cuts in production to support the price until August 1985, at which time it was producing only 2 million barrels per day, or less than one-fourth as much as in 1980. The Saudis then decided to drop the official price and to regain their market share, and they effectively pursued a price war against OPEC and non-OPEC producers alike. With production costs of $1–$2 per barrel and with their vast reserves and small population, the Saudis were in the best position to win such a struggle. And they retained the option of again restricting supplies at a future time, assuring that the price of oil would remain a volatile variable in the world economy.

At the end of 1985 OPEC dropped its minimum price. The need for capital had pushed the producers into intense competition to pump and sell at any price. Its share of the non-CPE world market had fallen to 35 percent, from 60 percent in 1979. As the price tumbled over the following months, falling 55 percent in real terms in 1986, both the high-cost competitors and alternative energy investments were threatened. The new high-cost producers, especially among the indebted LDCs, suffered a loss of income of 50 percent in the first few months of 1986.

By 1986 the falling price was again threatening the regional domestic American oil producers along with their banks and suppliers. The U.S. oil industry regarded it as "worldscale predatory price-cutting and a war of attrition," the Unocal chairman informed Congress.[4] The oil and gas industrial sector in the United States accounts for nearly 13 percent of the GNP. The negative effect on the economy, including additional unemployment in the tens of thousands, became apparent much sooner than any beneficial effects to the rest of the economy, especially because only three years had elapsed since the last depression in the oil patch. A reflection of this slump came when Vice-President George Bush unsuccessfully tried to persuade the Saudis to halt the price war and to curtail production, arguing that the United States desired "the lowest possible prices consistent with the fact that we need a strong domestic oil industry for our national security."[5]

THE COMPANIES

In the past the oil companies relied most on exploration and production for their profits. Even for Exxon, the least dependent, exploration and production provided four-fifths of net income. OPEC's contribution to the oil companies was the impact on their profits, which for the big-five companies rose 200 percent between 1972 and 1979, all along the line, from the wellhead to consumer sales. Although getting less per barrel on OPEC oil, the companies enjoyed higher profits on their non-OPEC holdings. For the companies less dependent on OPEC oil, profits rose 440 percent.

But as the price falls toward the cost of locating new oil, there is a significant reduction in exploration. Production costs in oil vary sharply, from $10–$20 per barrel in North America and the North Sea to $1–$2 in the Middle East. In 1983, industry consultants asserted that the U.S. companies were paying $12–$18 per barrel and that with assorted charges it could easily reach $20 or more. And the price of oil had fallen below $10 by 1986. Debts the industry had incurred through mergers and stock buybacks before the price fall had cut into capital expenditure plans.

In some cases the oil companies accepted the service role of technical expertise. In Venezuela, after nationalization, Exxon stayed on as technology supplier and marketer of a million barrels per day. An executive remarked of the new relationship, "I think both sides are satisfied. The government has gained control of the oil industry without risk, and we have found an attractive income for technology we would have to develop anyway. That is the way the world is going and it is, in itself, a profitable business."[6] The oil companies, according to an OECD study, "are increasingly concentrating on supplying technology, certain key managerial functions, and international marketing with the host country assuming ownership. . . ."[7]

DIVERSIFICATION

Mineral prices had risen in tandem with energy, as coal was increasingly considered a possible substitute for oil. And in 1981 the oil giants moved as a herd to diversify into other minerals, such as copper, and many analysts perceived a trend in 1979 toward concentration of minerals production. Sohio bought Kennecott for $1.8 billion. Social paid $4 billion for Amax. "They had a tremendous cash flow. They had to put that cash into something," noted a vice-president of Arthur D. Little.[8]

By May 1982 the oil companies owned 55 percent of the U.S. copper interests, and they wanted out. They had bought at the high price and had to sell at the low. Arco began to diversify Anaconda out of copper, and falling profits led Cities Service and Exxon to sell off or reduce their copper interests. Sohio admitted, "We just aren't going to take [Kennecott's] losses indefinitely."[9] A reverse scenario emerged as well. The

Hanna Mining Company had acquired energy companies in the halcyon days of the late 1970s, and these were by 1984 producing 85 percent of its $28.8 million loss.

By the mid-1980s diversification in many areas had proven too costly for big oil. Exxon, which had ventured into electronic office equipment, was preparing to write off hundreds of millions of dollars as losses, having already absorbed a loss of $1 billion on other diversification efforts. Mobil was ready to sell its retail Montgomery Ward, which it had purchased in 1977 for $1.8 billion. And Texaco, in November 1984, wrote off $765 million in land, supertanker, and refinery losses.

The oil companies turned first to diversification and then, failing in their divestment strategies, to merging with each other. Although the principals had enormous reserves, most of the megamergers of the oil companies involved borrowed funds. During a two-week period in July 1981, six oil companies arranged lines of credit for $28 billion just for merger and takeover bids. Texaco acquired Getty for $10 billion, Occidental swallowed Cities Service, Mobil merged with Superior Oil for $5.7 billion, and Standard Oil of California purchased Gulf for over $13 billion. As Michael Tanzer and Stephen Zorn added it up, "All told, from 1979 to mid-1984, oil companies spent more than $35 billion to acquire each other."[10] But these giant companies were also targets of individual raiders like Boone Pickens, because their stock was underpriced, selling for less than half the cost of finding new oil. Pickens continued his raids, forcing such oil companies as Unoco to borrow in order to repurchase their own stock. "It will trigger a wave of restructuring," noted an oil consultant.[11] Arco borrowed $4 billion to buy its own stock in anticipation of a raid and restructured the company by reducing its labor force by 20 percent, cutting operating costs by $500 million, raising its dividend by one-third, and selling a refinery. It also raised its debt ratio to 60 percent of capital. Even Exxon and Amoco started to buy their own stock in 1985 to defend themselves against raiders.

The characteristics of the oil market have changed as well. High oil prices after 1973 led to basic changes and technological adaptations in the energy consumption of other industries. By the 1980s the utilities industry was burning 50 percent less than in 1973; the chemical industry consumed 26 percent less than in 1972, while increasing its output by 40 percent. New steel technology uses 40–60 percent less energy, and seventy of the seventy-eight Italian cement companies had by 1985 shifted to coal. Nuclear energy accounted for 5–6 percent of the European energy consumption in 1983.[12]

MINERALS

The linkages of the various minerals to each other and to other developments in the economy are significant. For example, with the second rise in the oil price, in 1979, the fortunes of coal as the alternative energy source soared. In 1980, economists from governments and companies of seventeen nations produced a world coal study that typically projected world demand by projecting from existing conditions. Producers around the world stepped up production. There was a race to build export terminals along all the coasts of the United States, as a record quantity of coal was exported in 1980. The huge demand was due not merely to rising oil prices but to the strikes in Poland, which reduced that supply of coal by 12 million tons. Four years later the demand for coal was estimated to be about half the projected figure. With the recession, U.S. coal exports fell one-third between 1981 and 1983 and continued to fall thereafter. By 1985 excess capacity and low or nonexistent profits was prevalent in the industry in both the United States and Australia, the world's leading exporters.

Mining in other minerals in the OECD countries also declined sharply in the 1980s, after a brief and costly rise. An $8.9 billion industry in 1980, mining saw its value fall to $5.9 billion in 1983. Employment dropped from 109,000 in 1981 to 44,800 at the beginning of 1984. The ten largest American mining companies took losses of $1.8 billion in 1982–84. Debt reached 41 percent of capitalization in 1984. Some 25 million tons of iron ore capacity was "permanently" closed in North America after 1980, and the economic "recovery" in the United States did not touch the mining industry.[13] The crisis in steel affected the demand for the primary metals, since that industry was the biggest customer for iron ore, nickel, and molybdenum.

Throughout the recovery, the mining industry in general suffered enormous overcapacity, as the LDCs continued to open new mines with the latest technology, driven by the urgent need for capital and usually pressured to do so by the World Bank and the IMF, which also insisted on devaluation in order to give them a competitive advantage. Brazil's Carajás iron mine, which opened in 1985, is the world's largest, with 20 billion tons of the richest ore. Its output in 1988 was expected to equal the total U.S. production. In a significant structural change over the past decade, the TNCs that had formerly owned the mines now sold the technology to the LDCs at exorbitant prices, shifting their profits from the output of the mines to the sale of inputs and turnkey projects.

Although there has been a diffusion of production and expansion of capacity worldwide, the marketing of raw materials remains in the hands of the giant traders, and there is both oligopoly and, now primarily, oligopsony as TNCs control the marketing of 70–80 percent of the world's commodity trade. The Brazilian government offered joint ventures to some of them to ensure marketing and financing. According to an OECD report, the same companies control "not only one material but also its substitutes, and not just at the mining stage" but vertically through the semifinished product.[14]

Discussing the question of availability and access, the OECD concluded that supplies of any of the critical materials were not hindered by physical shortages. But it went on to show that giant U.S. TNCs had restricted access to nickel for Japan and Europe during the Vietnam War. It also noted, "The question of preferential intramultinational-company supplies in a critical situation might well be much more than just academic."[15] The danger of such interference was underlined by Reagan's restrictions on U.S. technology to the Soviet pipeline. These inhibitions or restrictions on access are much more important than any imagined threat from a radical regime in an LDC whose compulsion to sell its commodity anywhere is its paramount consideration.

COMMODITY CARTELS

Commodity cartels other than OPEC have never achieved much success. In boom times producers scarcely want a ceiling on prices, since their development plans, profits, or debt repayment depend on maximizing them. To succeed, a cartel must control an essential material that is not easily substituted, it must have means to support an embargo, the number of producers must be limited and have common interests, and the market must be such that a considerable price rise is possible.

The International Tin Council (ITC), organized in the mid-1950s, is the oldest producers' cartel but also includes consumer nations with sharply differing interests. It collapsed in October 1985 with $1 billion in debts, dragging down the London metals dealers who were committed to purchasing tin for the cartel's buffer stock. The manager of the buffer stock had exceeded his authority and bought 50,000 tons in excess of the authorized maximum. But it was only this measure that had kept the price within the agreed range. The banks had financed the excess with loans collateralized at 110–125 percent in tin. Involved with the twenty-two governments and the ITC were many banks and the London Metal Exchange, and they were all required to divide the losses. Suspecting corrupt dealings between the unsupervised ITC, the banks, and the London Metal Exchange that had led to windfall speculators' profits, the member governments, themselves in financial straits, refused to provide the promised funds for the purchase of the tin for the ITC. The cartel members, a Southeast Asian metals expert said, are "simply not speaking the same language. They're all going their own ways."[16] Trading on the London Metal Exchange was discontinued. The banks, holding loans of $1.3 billion with 40,000 tons of tin as collateral, could paper over their plight for the moment only by extending more credit. Some banks began to break ranks and sold supplies, causing the price to fall further. By the time the dust had settled, losses amounted to $800 million and the brokers and banks were snarled in litigation. The collapse had widespread repercussions in banking and weakened confidence in government agreements. Parent companies acted in panic and disclaimed responsibility for their subsidiaries on the metal exchange, thereby undermining a perception of cross-border responsibility for the liabilities of affiliates. Metal prices in general, as a consequence, fell 6 percent in the last months of 1985.

Other producer cartels—in sugar, rubber, and cocoa—fared no better, for they all succumbed to the same capital shortages, leading to oversupply and falling prices. But while they were still in a better position than those commodities with no cartel at all, the fact remains that the rapid fluctuations that characterize the entire commodity sector has produced an endemic instability. Subject, too, to the larger fluctuations of a global economy under pressure from innumerable interacting factors, commodities only increase the fragility of the world economy. But in 1986 an even more serious condition threatened the producing countries. As the secretary-general of the United Nations Conference on Trade and Development (UNCTAD) reported, "The traditional link between cyclical fluctuations in economic activity and demand for raw materials has been broken . . . [and will] profoundly affect development prospects in very many developing countries."[17] Such commodities as rubber, tin, copper, and palm oil were becoming technologically passé with the development of more efficient and less costly substitutes like glass and optical fibers in the communications industry. Reading the writing on the wall, nations like Malaysia and Indonesia are furtively diversifying to cocoa, guaranteeing a future oversupply in that commodity.

CONTRADICTIONS IN AGRICULTURE

Agriculture is yet another sector of the world economy that has been profoundly altered since the early 1970s. Although the new developments in science and technology have vastly increased productivity, disasters have nevertheless multiplied for the world's people as the capitalist mode of production has further penetrated and restructured global agriculture.

In 1985, the year of the famine in Africa, world output of food rose 11 percent, the largest increase since 1960, and a record 200 million metric tons of grain were stored. Nowhere are the contradictions of the system more vivid, and there now exist a multitude of studies describing them. Much has also been written on the transformation of the peasant in both the developing and the industrial nations. The generalized economic crisis over the past years further accelerated these developments, which took specific forms in the OECD and the developing countries.

OECD

Except for Japan and Britain, the OECD countries are dependent on the export of food, not on imports. In 1985 even Britain was a net exporter of wheat. The European Common Agricultural Policy, providing high domestic prices and a protected market while subsidizing exports, remains the essential ingredient of the EEC, consuming 70 percent of its budget and supporting huge surpluses in grain (17 million tons), dairy products, wine (over one billion liters), meat, and sugar by the end of 1986. By 1984 it was close to exhausting its allocated funds, but the policy continued. The subsidy amounted to around $23 billion in 1986. Some 8 million farmers, three out of four of them farming only part-time, make up a powerful political lobby, resisting all government efforts to restructure agriculture in the EC. Although now only half the number of those who farmed in 1945, they still make up nearly 8 percent of the total civilian employment. In 1985 the EEC reiterated its determination to maintain that percentage of the population on the farms. The price support policies enriched the largest, most efficient farms and provided a barely adequate living for the great majority. Within the EEC there was division on how to scale down the cost; reduction on export subsidies and production quotas were advocated by the Germans and free market in the EC and continued export supports, by the French, reflecting their position of strength in EC agriculture.

In 1980 about 9 percent of all workers were in agriculture in Japan, compared with 3.6 percent in the United States. The average farm size is less than 3 acres in Japan, compared with 431 in the United States and 163 in Britain. Japanese agriculture is marked by high cost and great political power. The government spent $15 billion in agricultural subsidies in 1986. Japan, while highly protectionist (it even imposes tariffs on bananas, which it does not produce) is the largest agricultural market for the United States.

Trade conflict between the OECD nations in agriculture has always been acute. While the European and Japanese have been primarily protectionist, the United States has been both protectionist and expansionist and has used its agricultural surplus as an imperialist arm, especially in the form of food aid, to penetrate and create new commercial markets for the huge American surplus. Until the 1980s nearly all the American efforts in GATT focused on agricultural questions. In the context of the vast overproduction worldwide and of the struggle between nations of subsidized exports, the under secretary for economic affairs declared in early 1987, "I'd say clearly that [agriculture] is the most important economic problem today—more than trade, debt, and so on."[18]

With the investment in monoculture, once an important characteristic of colonialism but now described as a "comparative advantage" in the international division of labor, nations previously self-sufficient must now import food, chiefly from the United States. American government officials have been candid regarding their aims. The U.S. secretary of agriculture, after a trip to Brazil in 1983, reported that he was "appalled by Brazil's huge agricultural potential and advised the country to grow less food."[19] Until the food crisis reached famine proportions, the United States had aimed to create total "interdependence" in agriculture on a world scale dominated by both exporting and importing U.S. enterprises.

RESTRUCTURING U.S. AGRICULTURE

Trade has always been an overwhelming concern of U.S. agriculture. But since 1974 it has taken a particularly critical turn, making sharp gyrations as it interacted with all the other aspects of the generalized economic crisis and affected both the transformation of the American farm and farmer and the intense international rivalry. Exports rose nearly six times from 1970 to 1980. In 1976 the United States exported three-fourths of the grain in international commerce. And in 1979 some 42 percent of all U.S. *crops* were exported. Yet, by 1986, farm products were less than 14 percent of the value of all U.S. exports, the lowest percentage since 1940.[20]

After the export boom of 1974, land prices rose an average of 10 percent a year until 1981, and speculation in land typified U.S. agriculture in the 1970s. Capital gains in land exceeded farm income by a ratio of 3:1. As farmers acquired extravagant loans from eager bankers, they invested in expensive machinery and speculated on land value, as farm indebtedness tripled in the 1970s. The land boom in the last years of the decade also attracted outside investors, to the point that twenty-four states passed laws to prevent the sale of land to nonresidents or non-farm corporations. Yet during 1980–82 small foreclosed farms were acquired by nonfarm buyers for industrial farming or to collect government storage subsidies. This speculative agricultural boom also caused considerable erosion and water loss, as trees were cut and marginal land—suitable for grazing but unable to sustain crops for more than a few years—was plowed for corn. For speculators, however, it did not matter; there was immediate profit from either sales or subsidies. And with the rising prices, U.S. agriculture had become inflation, as well as export, dependent.

Linked to the farm prosperity, of course, were the farm equipment and other ancillary industries, which enjoyed a boom in the late 1970s and suffered near bankruptcy a few years later. In part, the Federal Reserve's monetary policy of the early 1980s was aimed at curbing such speculative investment. Combined with other factors, particularly the embargo on the USSR in 1980 and the rising dollar and interest rates, the boom deflated swiftly in the 1980s. Depression in the farm sector has had widespread reverberations in employment and related businesses. A Midwest agriculture official claimed that one business disappeared for each ten farm closures and three nonfarm jobs for every farm. In the aggregate, property values had by 1985 fallen 19 percent from their 1981 peak, and in some states value dropped by another 20 percent in 1985. Falling land values reduced the farmers' collateral for new loans.

One-third of the farmers held two-thirds of the farm debt of $214 billion in 1985, and it was concentrated among the middle family farmers. Six percent ($12.8 billion) was owed by insolvent farmers, leading to dozens of failures of regional banks and, cumulatively, to severe losses for the giants like Continental Illinois, Bank of America, and Crocker.

While encouraging the small farmer in the LDCs, Washington's strategy has been to restructure U.S. agriculture further toward "larger farms and fewer farmers." It counts on the survival of the most efficient large-scale farms "to return farming to a freer market," allowing the government to cut the farm support program by two-thirds.[21] Budget Director David Stockman even planned to cut farm subsidies of all sorts to zero. But the farmers' political power forced the Reagan administration instead to provide record farm subsidies, especially in the election year of 1986, when the price support program reached the phenomenal figure of nearly $26 billion, compared with less than $1 billion in 1975.

The largest farms, those with sales over $100,000, account for 14 percent of the farms but earn 70 percent of farm income. They also receive 66 percent of the direct government payments. Indeed, only 30 percent of the American farms collect anything at all. The largest 50,000 farms, around 3 percent of the total, in 1981 produced 38 percent of total cash sales. According to the *1986 Economic Report of the President,* "on average these farms [with sales over $500,000 and net worth over $2 million] receive about $33,000 annually in direct government payments."[22] But the larger farms also faced serious debt problems by mid-1985. Farms with sales over $500,000 had the highest debt-to-asset ratio, by far.

At the end of 1985 the government moved further to concentrate the farms, terminating its twenty-five-month moratorium on foreclosures in order to collect $6 billion in arrears, lower the price supports, and even more "aggressively" compete in the world market with its surplus. The value of farmland fell for the fifth consecutive year, by 12 percent. By 1987 an economist at the Federal Reserve was able to say, "The [agricultural] sector's improved because the weak people have been bankrupted."[23]

The export market changed for the farm sector as well as for industry during the 1980s. Indebted and needy nations could less afford to buy, and some former buyers either had found alternative suppliers or were now self-sufficient—at least for the moment, which is all that matters in capitalist agriculture. Others, such as India and China, were exporting competitively. Thailand became a major competitor in corn in the Middle East. And the Europeans, Australians, and Canadians had moved into the Soviet market. Competitive prices reduced the U.S. share of Algeria's wheat market from 41 percent in 1979–80 to 16 percent in 1984–85. U.S. imports of food, meanwhile, were setting records and roughly balanced exports in 1986. Until protests by American farmers stopped it, Cargill, the giant American trading company, even tried to import Argentine wheat into the United States in early 1985 in order to reap a higher profit.

In 1985 Congress introduced a record farm price subsidy bill, expected to cost a minimum of $52 billion over the first three years in order to offer a low competitive world price while guaranteeing the farmer a minimum direct-transfer income. The subsidy that existed until 1986 was a complicated and costly mechanism whereby the government made a loan to the farmer, taking the crops as collateral. The loan would be repaid if the market price was equal to or exceeded the value of the loan, which was in effect a minimum price for the farmer. If the market price was lower, the government collected the collateral and built its huge surplus stocks. By 1986, surplus stockpiles in corn and wheat amounted to 31 percent and 62 percent, respectively, of the total U.S. yearly demand. Most of the year's harvest goes into government storage, and the traders like Cargill and Continental Grain buy it at subsidized prices. Washington decided that in the past its loan rate had served as a minimum world price under which the other nations could price their products. In 1985, in order to counter the mounting competition in the world market, the U.S. Congress launched a subsidy war that provided U.S. exporters with $2 billion worth of U.S. surplus to sell at competitive prices, supposedly to force other exporting nations to discontinue their subsidies. The ultimate contradiction occurred in 1986 when the Reagan administration offered subsidized wheat to the Soviet Union, undercutting both Canada and Australia, to the benefit of only the USSR, as it was simultaneously trying to undermine the Soviet economy in other ways. It was a classic example of the triumph of politics and economic interests over ideology.

A major force behind the new policy of embarking on a price war in the world market was the giant, family-owned trading company and processor Cargill Inc., along with other leading export agribusinesses. Cargill is the leading grain exporter (with 20 percent of U.S. exports) and egg producer; it is also at the top in meat packing, in grain milling, and in seed, feed, and fertilizer production, as well as the world's largest cotton trader. The trading company has diversified into fifty businesses, nearly all related to bulk commodities, in forty-six countries. Most of the company's growth occurred in the 1970s, its sales rising from just over $2 billion in 1971 to nearly $29 billion in 1981. Its success, resembling that of the Japanese trading companies, is in part attributed to its global system for gathering information on any factor likely to change the price of a commodity.

The American price war accelerated the deflation in grain, much as the Saudis were doing in oil. While the administration itself considered this an unworkable and undesirable war, in which only the buyers would benefit, the political power of the agricultural interests was, as usual, decisive. And the government turned instead to confront rivals in foreign trade.[24]

LDCs

While in the agrarian developing countries the age-old class struggle for land remains the fundamental economic, political, and social question, there have been significant changes that are, at least in part, restructuring aspects of the agricultural system and the forms of exploitation. And the most profound form of restructuring agriculture in the

LDCs has been the extension of export agriculture, with disastrous consequences in the lives of millions. Here I want merely to refer briefly to some of the tendencies in this period of economic crisis. The primary factors are the recent appearance of transnational agribusinesses, the emergence of the contract system, and the development of food for export to pay for the monumental debt of many countries.

Agribusiness is usually a multicorporate consortium that generally desires some government participation both to get money from international finance organizations and to build the infrastructure. The agricultural TNCs have increasingly concentrated the sale of inputs, shipping, processing, and marketing. For instance, six TNCs control the distribution of 60 percent of the world's coffee, three TNCs sell 75 percent of the bananas, fifteen control more than half of the world's sugar trade, two TNCs control half the wheat trade, and two companies produce more than half of the farm machinery.

Formerly, ownership of the land and large plantations with hired labor were characteristic of agricultural TNCs like United Fruit, but the 1970s and 1980s brought a shift to contracting out to nominally independent peasants and marketing their produce. This often takes the form of a "nuclear estate" based on a central processing plant and including "packages" dealing with all aspects of production, from planning, building the infrastructure, contracting to peasants, supplying the inputs of seeds and fertilizers, transport, storage, processing, and marketing. Costs are deducted from the payment the peasant gets for his produce.

Exploitation of the peasant occurred under these contracts, as it had under the plantation system. In fact, agribusinesses find it considerably more profitable to buy the product from independent peasants or cooperatives under contract than to produce it on their own land, just as contracting has increasingly appealed to many manufacturing and mineral TNCs. The companies no longer have to invest in the supplies, seeds, pesticides, or such expenditures as irrigation and flood control, much less absorb the losses in case of natural calamities like typhoons. But they were able through the contract clauses to force the peasant to do so, and the companies generally sell the supplies to them. And since oligopsony has prevailed, companies have controlled the prices and imposed the "quality control" in contracts allowing them to reject produce at the peasant's expense. When demand for the produce declines, it is usually the small peasant who is cut back; this again parallels what is occurring increasingly in industry. The peasant rarely has a marketing alternative. There were instances, as in Honduras, in which peasants tried to turn to a cooperative distribution organization.

In this case Standard Fruit asked the Honduran army to intervene on its behalf. In effect, the economic risks in the contract system are always transferred to the peasant.

This new organization of contracting to the independent peasant is a growing trend, but by the 1980s it was restricted to certain regions and crops. In other areas, wage labor, particularly seasonal, on large plantations continued to prevail. In Central America 70 percent of the agricultural labor force consists of seasonal migrants. Mechanization has sharply reduced the need for workers, except during brief, seasonal periods. Many of the agricultural workers migrate between the rural and urban areas in Latin America. And the amount of labor required, given the mechanization, is vastly smaller, and the alternatives for the displaced peasant are rapidly declining. In addition to the large plantations, cattle farming for export, absorbing 45 percent of the arable land in Central America, continues to push the small peasant onto the most inferior lands, where, lacking alternatives, the peasant families cling to their land for marginal subsistence.

Agribusiness investment was principally attracted to high-growth environments like Brazil during the early 1970s. But agriculture elsewhere continued to compete with industry and other profit-producing activities in attracting investment capital. In response to the increased private investment in agriculture and the development of agribusiness, the World Bank shifted its emphasis in the early 1970s to aid it. In harmony with the interests of agribusiness, the World Bank, too, decided it was more efficient to retain the small farmer under the contract system than to set up large farms with hired labor. In the Philippines, the Bank in 1987 criticized the hesitant government program and advocated a radical land reform of immediate expropriation and rapid distribution.

The governments of the LDCs have played an important part in the shift to food for export. For example, while malnutrition is rife in Brazil, affecting what the UN's Food and Agriculture Organization estimated to be 86 million of a total population of 120 million in 1984, the government and its economic advisers have decided to exploit the country's enormous agricultural potential to help pay the foreign debt. Although one government institute warned that agriculture was being oriented toward exports, half the trade surplus in 1984 was provided by soybeans, orange juice, and chickens. Soybeans, which got their start during Nixon's ban on U.S. exports in 1971, now make up 25 percent of Brazil's exports, surpassing coffee. Basic food supplies for internal consumption have been neglected; their prices were increased up to 400 percent as part of the IMF-imposed austerity program in

1984. In that year Brazil had to import such basic foodstuffs as corn, black beans, and rice.

The advances in shipping and transport have permitted cash crops in Africa in many cases to fill the luxury food shops in Europe, displacing the indigenous food of the local population, and the orientation toward the export of food has helped create famine and death on a monumental scale. Periods of drought were not unusual historically in the Sahel of Africa. One expert noted, "The farmers would grow a variety of crops, not high yielding but they were tough and they survived. . . . [T]he rapid shift to cash crops, without enough variety, has contributed to the disaster. The West has institutionalized famine."[25] Yet it is irrelevant to blame the situation on "the West."

CHAPTER 10

CONCLUSION TO PART II: CAPITAL

The past decade has seen innumerable changes in the structures of capital. But its systemic features—most notably the compulsion to accumulate, goaded by competition and the struggle to reduce labor costs, using any and all means to achieve this end—have remained unchanged. But what conclusion can we draw from these descriptions and case studies at this stage in history? Do they allow us to judge what is to come? Do they form a pattern?

The laws of capitalism, or the operation of the systemic features, proceed as always. Without adequate incentive for productive investment, money flows into speculative financial assets and gambling reaches precarious extremes, banks undermine stability, and basic industry succumbs to competition. The "new" industries are also intensely competitive and equally prone to overproduction and recession. The only significant growth is in the increasingly competitive armaments industry, the products of which, in turn, threaten the future of all mankind. Commodity prices gyrate widely, affecting all other sectors of the economy. As capitalism has penetrated agriculture in the LDCs, famine or new dislocations have followed, and in the developed nations abundance appears to menace prosperity.

Capital continues to flow in quest of profit, and this process itself objectively restructures the economy—through accretion, not as a consequence of a strategy or a plan. But profit since the 1970s is found primarily in financial speculation and commercial parasitism, and in other ephemeral services, rather than in production. All the expansion in finance and service cannot alone sustain the economy. In fact, it

178

undermines it, for only production creates tangible growth and wealth in society.

The phenomenal growth of financial "product innovations" in the 1980s, the internationalization of equity markets, the stampedes of currency speculations by banks and corporations gambling for a quick return at the expense of their long-term interests and that of their collective system—all follow the laws of capitalism that encompass and make irrelevant the successive measures to restructure the economy for future growth and development. For fundamental to the very operation of the system is the imperative for each capitalist to look to his own profit or loss. It is a question of survival for many individual capitalists, and they act accordingly.

The banks themselves have been transformed from being lending units to being financial speculators, as their sources of profits shift and as other industries seek different sources of finance outside the banks. But the banks create most of the money for the speculation, or it does not exist at all, as in buying stock or new financial "products" on margin. Debt continues to finance the turmoil in the financial market, as industries buy and sell each other with mergers, takeovers, and divestitures, shuffling assets like cards from one hand to another in brief spans of time. And as insecure managers distribute working capital as dividends, debt finances operations. All these developments interact in a chaotic and anarchic fashion.

In response to falling profits in productive investment, capitalists try to reverse this situation by cutting costs and lowering the break-even point in production in order to profit at ever lower capacity. Invariably, labor costs are the capitalists' primary concern. Hence today's structural conditions are the outcome of the perpetual struggle under the pressure of competition to reduce labor costs with new machinery, foreign labor, or, increasingly, the contracting out of production.

At the same time that capital is being concentrated in huge conglomerates and trading companies, the components of both industry and agriculture are breaking up. In all areas—agriculture, mining, and industry—there is an increasing trend toward contracting out for production to small producers, as large manufacturing companies turn toward packaging and labeling the products of others. Yet that trend is, in turn, undermined by robotization, as competition promotes new technology and reduces the costs of production.

Technology first made possible the component production in the world factory and the immediate flow of capital from one state to another on the basis of the instantaneous transfer of information about where a profitable opportunity existed. The new technology further transformed the production process in the direction of robotics and automated factories. But it also introduced new competition from unexpected and multiple sources and permanently reduced employment.

Growing competition in the capitalist world economy has created overcapacity in all sectors—finance, basic industry, and commodities— inhibiting investment and encouraging nonproductive financial speculation. The ability to produce limitless supplies exists and continues to grow in step with the inability to realize satisfactory profits through sales. The capitalist crisis is, once more, one of overcapacity and overproduction. There is, of course, nothing necessary about this condition, for, as always, massive and desperate unfilled needs prevail. But it remains an essential contradiction of capitalism. And the traditional solution for such a crisis within the system, is not to use the capacity or the surplus to fill the needs but rather, if possible, to destroy the surplus, as states are systematically doing in the European steel industry. But since there is no worldwide control, competitive capacity nonetheless continues to expand.

There is no logic whatever to private investment beyond the pursuit of profit. Growth or development may be an incidental outcome of the process, but only if it is part of the path to profit, and it rarely occurs when or where it is most needed. The capitalists' daily actions, fraught with implications for the general economy, are sometimes, as in financial trading, measured in minutes. And the attempt to secure sufficient profit by shrinking the market through unemployment and lower wage costs remains a fundamental contradiction of the system.

Contradictions are ubiquitous in capitalism, making it unwise to project what seem to be current "trends." Constant contradictions reverse the trends of a particular period, as inflation turns to deflation, economic growth to stagnation, shortage to surplus, market demand to saturation, industry to service, in a short time. All these changes continually transform the environment. The lessons in these developments are obvious to capitalist decision makers, yet they are, as always, irrelevant to the drive for profit.

The capitalists, too, are vulnerable to these objective operations of the system, and as the international competitive pressures, including shifting exchange rates and developments in technology, increase, they act to cut costs. But there has not been an investment "strike," implying a conscious conspiracy, as a subjective strategy to force the state to bring about the appropriate business climate. The closest to a longrange subjective strategy for private capital is its struggle against labor, and it is now using the crisis to force new conditions in that relationship.

Despite overcapacity and overproduction in all sectors, competition forces the building of new capacity and the destruction of old. Rationalization, lower wages, and unemployment shrink the market. The interaction of these structural developments in the capitalist economy is, as always, chaotic, dynamic, and dialectic.

The current structural developments have revealed both the impossibility of extrapolating from observed trends and the persistence of most capitalists and decision makers in power, and also of economic analysts, to continue to do so. If there has been any linear or sequential trend, or movement in the economy, it is the spread of the capitalist mode of production throughout the globe and the formation of a world market. It also reveals the dominance of the systemic—accumulation, competition, and the offensive against labor—which assures the antisocial outcome of the entire process. These systemic features of capitalism would once have scarcely needed recapitulation. But given the current political response to the crisis of accumulation, as states are entreating capital everywhere to provide the investment to renew productive growth in the world economy, it is necessary continually to reiterate the intrinsic threat in this economic system.

Capital moves in the pursuit of profit, and this process restructures the economy. It is the state in the capitalist system that formulates the strategy or plans, and each state responds to and affects the moves of capital. In Part III, I shall explore some of the efforts of the various states to restructure their own and the world economy.

THE STATE

CHAPTER 11

THE ROLE OF THE STATE IN RESTRUCTURING THE ECONOMY

THE NATURE OF THE STATE

Nearly everyone has assumptions about the state and its role in society, and it may reflect anything from profound consideration to brutal experience to false consciousness. The citizen or subject may respond to the state with support, acquiescence, opposition, hostility, or fear. There is also a large literature in which scholars assess the nature of the state from various viewpoints. Pluralists regard the state as an independent entity that in a democracy is open to influence from competing classes and groups in society of which none is dominant. Others consider the state as wholly autonomous of and above any external class or force, as acting strictly in its own interest. Most exotic today is the prominence of the neoliberal view of those on the Right who choose to attack the state as encroaching on the terrain of the free market and as a force hostile to capital, even though they support a strong state whenever it involves the military and the maintenance of internal order. Marxists usually view the state as subordinate to the ruling class, if not as the direct instrument of that class. Within the Marxist perspective there is now a wide discussion on the nature of the state and Marx's concept of it, particularly its connection with the ruling class. The perceptions range from the state as the instrument or the servant of the capitalists on every issue to the state as a "partnership" with that class or to the state as being relatively autonomous within structural constraints. Whether explicit or not, assumptions concerning the state—including my own, evident in the following pages—are unquestionably central in every analysis of the political economy, especially at a time when the state plays a crucial and shifting role in the economic crisis.

The nation-state, though an integral part of the capitalist system, is subordinate to it. In those areas where capitalism is not yet dominant, there may be other, sometimes rival, feudal and military interests influencing the state. But the capitalist system is increasingly ascendant throughout the globe, and in the process of restructuring that is being imposed on many states, the old social orders are forced into a mold shaped primarily by capitalist considerations.

In the capitalist nations, capital is always politically organized and capitalists form the class that rules in the broadest sense of the term. The state in capitalist societies is neither autonomous nor even relatively autonomous of that class. Governments, on the other hand, having multiple forms, may *appear* to be independent as long as the objective economic conditions permit differing approaches to managing the economy.

Applying the systemic-structural dichotomy that I discussed in the Introduction, one may regard the state as systemic, a composite of institutions, and an integral part of the capitalist system, while the governments are structural and may be liberal, Keynesian, conservative, social democratic, and so on. In parliamentary politics, governments change, but the state, intrinsically linked to the system, does not.

The ultimate bases of the state, of course, are the instruments of coercion—the police and military force. Without absolute control of these, the Left in government power will remain the "guests in power."[1] And the instances in which the "guests" were rudely evicted cast a pall over future efforts in many countries to attempt any fundamental changes in the class basis of the state. Yet, important though this inhibition has been in countries like Spain, Greece, or Italy, far more crucial are other reasons, discussed in the following chapters, why the socialists and even the communists have adapted to the current uniformity of conservative economic policy.

It would appear in the present period that, far from being autonomous, the state is barely even separable from capital as a category of analysis. The linkage is multifaceted, with an overwhelming unanimity in the struggle against labor. The state is not autonomous even when it owns the means of production through state industries and nationalizations. Ownership is less and less important as nationalizations serve as recuperative stages for bankrupt capital and the state then tries to forestall its own bankruptcy by selling its property in whole or in part to private investors. The crucial point is that the systemic features define the relation between classes or, put simply, that the goal of the society is profit. Nevertheless, capital and the state embrace different aspects of the effort to restructure the political economy.

Government *ideologies* may vary from conservative to socialist, but there is a uniformity in practice determined by the boundaries of the capitalist paradigm. Although the forces discussed in Part II objectively restructure the economy, regardless of the political coloration of governments, the goal of "restructuring" for the industrial capitalist state in the present period is renewed national growth, which means investment and increased competitiveness in the world market. When investment stalls in response to the economic process and the capitalists' perceptions of profitability, it is the function of the state to try to create conditions that will stimulate its revival. Profits and accumulation become its prime consideration and responsibility. The state's own accumulation is also an important goal. The state is for capital and for itself. Who is to pay for the process, and how, and what the outcome will be are critical questions.

Since 1945 the capitalist state could play a role in a period of prosperity that differs from that in this time of economic crisis, although its basis remains the same. The welfare programs that depended on a structural condition of rapid growth and labor shortage, in turn often dependent on war, during economic crisis were stripped away even by their leading advocates—the various socialist parties of Europe. But since the whole social organization is geared to the generation of profit rather than the fulfillment of the needs of the citizenry, such an outcome could be expected. Every introduction of welfare was the result of struggle, but when conceded in a period of full employment, rather than taken, it is expendable.

It is wholly in the interests of the bourgeoisie that the state appear to be autonomous of economic class relations and to represent a "national interest." Significant now is the eclipse of this posture among the bourgeoisie and the readiness, under the condition of crisis, to discard even the rhetoric of full employment and welfare, even as an abstract goal. Curiously, academics and many on the left picked up a variant of this theme that the state is semi-autonomous at the very moment when empirically it is the most exposed as fallacious and abandoned by its principal advocates.

In the capitalist democracies workers have been able to get concessions from the state, as from capital, when their bargaining position is strong; they lose from both when it is weak. As the corporation yields to labor demands in the oligopolistic sector during periods of growth, so the state in some nations may, under political pressure, yield welfare measures to strengthen the social consensus when it can afford to do so—that is, in periods of prosperity. Because the workers are at certain times able to wrest from industries concessions in the form of wages and benefits, does that imply that the capitalists are somehow relatively independent of their class interests? As with capital, so it may be with the state. The welfare state and the Keynesian perspective operated only as long as it was affordable during times of relatively full employment and of adequate revenue. Labor gains come in a period of prosperity and givebacks in periods of fiscal crisis, now rationalized with "restructuring" policies. The state's role is to serve in the accumulation process, and what it grants to the working class also depends on the condition of the economy. During periods of prolonged crisis, when revenues decline and expenses mount, the so-called compromise with the working class is swept aside as the state, like the corporation, takes back from labor, while granting further concessions to capital, in the interest of profit. This is being repeatedly demonstrated today internationally, regardless of the party in power.

Capitalists, however, need an arbiter as they struggle among themselves. But the results usually depend on the relative power of the factions, not on the arbitration of a neutral state. While it is absurd to look for orders from capitalist factions on every issue—perception and understanding of reality must avoid such simplistic views—in many concrete cases, when there is no equal and rival claimant, the state serves as the instrument of specific capitalist interests. History, which repeatedly demonstrates this reality, cannot be forced to fit some preconceived theory.

Capitalists' interests shift over time, and with them so does the role of the state. What was relevant in one epoch may not be in another. Apart from specific cases, the state's role can swing from laissez-faire to interventionism and back, or to a mix, depending on the needs of capital at the time. The state was more and more interventionist in the industrial capitalist economies after World War II, but it could not manage or rationally plan the system. Now, increasingly, states everywhere are tending to withdraw and let the market forces operate "freely" once more. Superseding these abstractions was the conviction among men of power in the capitalist democracies that the state's primary function, beyond public order, was to renew the conditions for capital accumulation in a process of restructuring the world economy and the national segments of it.

Since the beginning of capitalism the state has served in the accumulation process; in fact, it was usually indispensable in building the infrastructure, as the instrument of various interests, for repression in the class struggle, providing protection from foreign competition, imperialist adventures, and the like. Postwar governments, many assert, accepted a responsibility for economic activity and employment that was "unthinkable" before the war in many industrialized nations.[2] Yet this form of state intervention with macroeconomic policy in the area of social security and management of aggregate demand was not the cause but rather the effect of the over two decades of relative prosperity in the general world economy that resulted from the U.S. war making in Korea and Vietnam. Only a military rationale has permitted Keynesian economics in America, and then only until the inherent contradictions of inflation, fiscal crisis, and so on changed the context. When examined closely, orthodox deflationary policies were prominent even in Keynesian policies like the European Recovery Program, unless linked to expenditures for the military or for the Korean War. It is important, too, that the Keynesian recovery technique of a massive increase in spending and the public deficit was conceived and applied when the real interest rates were close to zero.

THE CAPITALIST STATE IN THE ECONOMY AT THE END OF THE CENTURY

The state is now both stronger and weaker in the economy. It is weaker in the sense that whole areas once under its control—money creation, exchange rates, international capital flows, foreign trade, and the like—are are now outside the control of any state (a process immeasurably enhanced by the new technology I discussed earlier). Those areas in turn affect all other aspects of state policy, such as trade and domestic fiscal and monetary policies. This situation came about not through design but through objective processes. State sovereignty is undermined by the free flow of capital, not only in relation to each other but internally as well. The industrial economies objectively are both integrated and interdependent; at the same time they are incompatible.

The de facto privatization of economic functions that once were the purview of the state was noted in the OECD's McCracken report in 1977:

[T]he limits of reserve-creation have become ill-defined and fluid, being set now by the private market's judgement of the credit-worthiness of individual countries rather than by official multilateral evaluation of the needs of the system as a whole. In this sense the private market has taken over functions and responsibilities that used to be thought more appropriate to national and international authorities, and the international monetary system has taken on some of the characteristics of a domestic credit system without a central bank. Today, it is often private institutions which effectively make the crucial decisions regarding access to liquidity and the financing of payments imbalances. The terms attached to this liquidity tend to be those associated with standard banking practices.[3]

Concomitantly with these developments, the ideology of those in power has advocated the state's retreat from some of its economic activities. In response to the realities of a fiscal crisis, the state in Britain, France, Italy, Canada, and other nations has moved to "privatize" state companies. In the LDCs as well, under the impact of the objective factors of crisis and the financial and ideological pressure from the IMF and other foreign-aid organizations, particularly the American AID, many states are trying to privatize large segments of the economy under their control. Of course, private interests are attracted only to the profitable segments, to those very areas that could relieve the state's fiscal crisis.

Yet, clearly, the state remains strong in other respects. Aside from its obvious military prowess, the state continues to be responsible for economic policy, social order, a context for international competition and rivalry, and assurance of access to markets and materials. It offers subsidies and protectionism, a market and employment. For the United States the imperialist role exists. The budgetary decisions of the strongest states have an enormous impact on the objective economy both internally and internationally. The state has a direct role in the accumulation process through state industries, the financing of private corporations, and fiscal policies. But the outcome of state action is scarcely what they intend, since the policies interact with other economic and political developments. And the state always can reintroduce new regulations or close its borders to trade and capital flow, though not without serious costs and new contradictions, especially if it involves a major economic power like the United States, which could trigger a trade war and a global depression.

A fundamental contradiction in the world today is that economies remain national in key aspects yet are fundamentally linked internationally by capital movements, investment, and trade and by the powerful transnational operations of their various corporations. This international integration led to the discussion of "interdependence" in the world economy. Interdependence now has more meaning for the United States because it is no longer as dominant and independent as during the period from the end of World War II to the 1970s. However, its national policies still have an effect on international trade, and its domestic monetary and fiscal policies affect those of other states. Capitalism remains national, and rivalries can develop into conflict. Interdependence exists but is more akin to the interdependence of scorpions in a bottle than to a harmonious interaction. As various interests are adversely affected, there is a constant contradiction between nationalism and the integration of the world economy. The most intense rivalry between states since the beginning of the crisis, and intensifying in the 1980s, has been to attract and hold the world's investment capital within their national boundaries. At the same time capital flow is more international than ever before.

Faced with the objective conditions of crisis—inflation, recession, monetary disorder, trade rivalries, deficits, unemployment, armed conflict, and so on—states frequently respond to each in an ad hoc manner and then develop a strategy. The ad hoc response may be protectionism, subsidies, devaluations, investment incentives, loans, imperialist coercion, repression, or an arms race. Their strategies pertain to restructuring the domestic economy for a strong competitive position in the world market or for economic development. Finally, the state itself has become the object of the restructuring policies in an effort to reverse its perceived encroachments on the terrain of private capital and to relieve its fiscal crisis. Formulating the policies to restructure the world economy and its national sectors has been the role of the supranational organizations, such as the IMF and the OECD, which have orchestrated increasingly uniform ideological and policy responses to the developments in the economies of their member nations.

Developments in the world economy in the areas of money, debt, and trade, in large part beyond the control of states but to which they must relate, set the context for the competition between nations and for their restructuring policies. These policies, similar in essence, are introduced with varying degrees of success in the different regions of the world, depending on the power of the various interests involved. In the succeeding chapters, I will examine the policies in the industrial capitalist nations, the less developed countries, and the centrally planned economies. Depending on its relative power, the state restructures the economy or is restructured by others to change its role in society.

CHAPTER 12

MONETARY RELATIONS

It is significant that Johannes Witteveen, former director of the IMF, confided that *"nobody* really understands the international monetary system."[1] And in 1985 Denmark's central bank governor observed that it is evident, with the increasing multiplicity of financial transactions, that the central bankers "to a large extent . . . don't understand what's happening. Contracts are now so complicated that ordinary people—among them central bankers—don't understand them."[2] What do these professions of ignorance by those at the highest levels dealing with monetary questions imply for the world monetary system, or nonsystem? Today, money itself is put in question.

CURRENCIES

The partial free market in currency exchange—the float—since its beginnings in 1971 had a severe impact on all economies in many unanticipated ways. First proposed by Milton Friedman in 1952 as a means of stabilizing the international monetary system, it was, after years in operation, a major source of instability in trade and economic policy; it also encouraged speculation and perpetual monetary turmoil. Helmut Schmidt said, "There were people who put high hopes on floating. These high hopes were absolutely futile."[3] Many Europeans like Schmidt believed that the interdependence of the national economies was so great that governments had to coordinate their policies and consider the effect of their domestic monetary moves on other nations. Others, such as President Valéry Giscard d'Estaing of France, understood that this was "not realistic," since the problems were in great part the result of the U.S. deficit and military expenditures and since Washington would in no way consider other nations when formulating its policies.[4] The Europeans could not coordinate their policies with each other, let alone with the United States and Japan.

Monetary questions are first and foremost power struggles. The floating exchange rates were increasingly viewed as devastating to all economies, but by the mid-1980s no one could agree on an alternative policy. The American administration was split into advocates of a range of policies, from free market to a gold standard, but effectively it was moving toward an expanded European Monetary System (EMS) linked to a consensus on an American-directed economic policy.

The role of exchange rates in the world economy cannot be overemphasized. The price of the national currency is indeed the most important single price in each nation, and this certainly became true of the U.S. dollar when currencies began to fluctuate. It directly affects capital flows, competitiveness, trade, employment, profits, and debt, and the speed of the changes can be devastating. Daily foreign-exchange trading in the United States rose from less than $1 billion in 1969 to $23 billion in 1980 and $34 billion in 1983. Worldwide it doubled between 1979 and 1984, from $75 billion to $150 billion, then rose to over $200 billion in 1986. Of the huge volume of foreign exchange in the United States, only 16 percent financed trade or other customer accounts. The rest was speculative transactions, and it has been estimated that, worldwide 90 percent of currency exchanges are in the hands of dealers, primarily in the banks.

Banks, the TNCs, and even the central banks have been the chief speculators in currencies. For the banks, as was discussed above, speculation has been a major source of profits and of a number of failures as well. Corporations have set up trading divisions and shifted massive funds in herdlike moves. State companies gambled against the national currency—Renault conducting its operations through a subsidiary in Switzerland. British Petroleum's director of money transactions stated modestly, "Our currency dealing is at least as important as our oil trading."[5] Its turnover was reportedly bigger than that of the Bank of England. The central banks themselves were accused, by one investment banker handling their accounts, of "wild and ill-informed trading in currencies and commodities."[6] This was especially true of the Singapore bank, which in its activity in foreign exchange and in the scope of its speculation was akin to a commercial bank The Soviet bank is said to be particularly adept at trading, making huge profits with timely sales of the dollar and mark. The professional traders consider the British able and the U.S. Federal Reserve the most clumsy and out of control. On the other hand, by 1985 central bank reserves as a proportion of currencies traded worldwide were insignificant, compared with those of only a few years earlier. The former trader for the New York Federal Reserve noted, "Central bank decisions used to bring instant profits or losses. Now traders are not concerned about what a central bank is doing, but what their clients are doing."[7] This was especially evident when the dollar was in free-fall in 1986–87. The Japanese government made an attempt to halt the slide, but its buying of $9 billion in one day was feeble in the scale of trading. This change has been important in reducing the power and status of the central banks.

The innovation of "swaps" subvert currency regulations between different national markets. By 1983, exchange rates, noted an official American report, had become "an asset market, like the stock and bond market."[8] But economic policy was forced to respond in the real world to the staggering exchange rate fluctuations that speculators are able to create in a short time. The sharp shift in the exchange between the yen and the dollar in less than a year had severe consequences in all aspects of the Japanese economy.

The German central banker in 1984 was pleased by the de facto and growing de jure deregulation internationally: "I welcome any form of deregulation . . . it promotes the impact of market forces, both in national and international markets."[9] Another European central banker was less sanguine and confessed in part to "being terrified of the consequences." He added, "I just hope that, whatever happens, every national monetary authority retains some form of control within its jurisdiction."[10] Governments have little choice but to deregulate their financial systems de jure, since technology and the surging numbers of new financial devices have conspired to undermine or eliminate their power to control their domestic money and capital markets.

A concerted effort of the largest economies to control the value of currencies could still have an effect in the exchange markets, because by September 1985 such a fall had been anticipated for some months, and it was the traders who picked up the cue and had the greatest impact. The day following the Group of Five's decision for joint action to lower the dollar's value, it suffered the greatest single-day fall since the beginning of the floating exchange. But the collaborative effort had other serious repercussions and contradictions, as it pushed the Japanese and German economies toward recession.

After a policy of "neglect" for one and a half decades, U.S. Treasury officials in the spring of 1986 concluded the float should be replaced by "reference zones" similar to those of the EMS and linked to the coordination of internal economic policies. The other OECD countries had no interest in orienting their own policies to American leadership—proposed at the moment of the Iran-contra scandal and criminal brouhaha on Wall Street—and disagreed on the proper parity of their currencies. The American government itself was divided on the question. But it continued to encourage the fall of the dollar and threatened protectionism to force the others to change their economic policies.

The flow of capital has doubtless undermined the economic policies of governments. Their intervention in the money markets demanded huge reserves in order to have any impact, and after wiping out reserves, it often required them to borrow heavily at high interest. They later had to repay these debts by intensifying the austerity measures for the population, which, in part, were intended to be a "signal" to the financial world of conservative economic policy that would support the value of the currency. France, for instance, borrowed $4 billion in order to support the franc in 1983; despite all the cost to prevent it, the currency was devalued anyway. Speculators remain poised to profit and incidentally devastate whole economies, which remain highly vulnerable.

Although the dollar's rise in value in the 1980s was the largest in history, the United States as the world's biggest single market could absorb the inflow of an immense proportion of the world's savings—needed, in any case, to finance record budget deficits after 1982. Rather than have an inflationary impact, as earlier inflows of dollars had had on other nations, and as the Germans feared with the shift in rates in 1986, the competitive price of imports curtailed any significant growth in domestic prices and sometimes forced them down. With its rise vis-à-vis other currencies in the 1980s, the dollar reemerged as the world's standard of value. But since the United States has become a debtor nation, the fall in the dollar not only was important for trade but also substantially reduced the debt.

For the rest of the world, and for many Americans, the dollar's low value during much of the 1970s was intolerable, because it spread inflation and offered stiff trade competition. The high value was also intolerable, since the dollar, as the currency of essential imports and of debt, had a deleterious effect on the economic policy of others when the U.S. interest rates peaked in the 1980s. In order to try to stem the hemorrhage of capital, the European nations were forced to raise their own interest rates, and they thereby prolonged the recession in their economies. "To get the dollar down, we would have to raise rates to an absurd level," complained one Dutch economist as early as 1981, when the dollar began its spectacular rise from its trough.[11] Five years later the process reversed. The outcry again was that the free-fall of the dollar was creating havoc in other economies. But while the instability created chaos, it meant profit for the traders.

In the first half of the 1980s, attracted by the record interest rates, the capital flow of the preceding decade reversed. By 1984 "half of all net investment in the United States [was] financed by the inflow of foreign capital," according to Martin Feldstein, chairman of the president's Council of Economic Advisers, and the rates had to remain historically high in order to retain that capital.[12] But given the size of the U.S. deficit, without the enormous inflow of capital, interest rates in the United States would have to be considerably higher.

Yet by 1984 the inflow of investment capital had begun to slow, and, most important, anticipating the inevitable fall, the capital imports tended to be highly liquid short-term investments, many of them in the form of interbank deposits. As they were portfolio investment or interbank loans, the dollar remained highly vulnerable to a sudden withdrawal, which would swiftly accelerate its decline. Into 1985, though, the alternative investments in other currencies were less attractive. The dollar rose at every contradictory signal—rising inflation (implying higher interest rates), falling inflation, higher and lower growth figures, rise or fall in oil price, easing or worsening of the debt crisis, and so on. Conversely, after the dollar started its fall, with the prompting of the central bankers and finance ministers in the autumn of 1985, even "good news" on the American economy was leading by February 1986 to further decline. Speculating traders who buy and sell billions every day react to the same imputs, and they are always short-term gamblers, although the sum of their moves has long-term consequences. But the decline of the dollar in 1986 affected only Japan and Europe, not Canada, Brazil, Taiwan, or South Korea. Overall, on a trade-weighted basis, the fall was only 6–7 percent for these countries.

In the context of economic crisis, where financial profits rather than production attracted capital, funds flowed to the highest return while remaining highly liquid. Japan's financial deregulation released a vast wealth for foreign investment. Since investment opportunities internally were less than the savings accumulated, Japan "recycled" its enormous export earnings in the 1980s by purchasing foreign bonds and securities, primarily in the United States, and this pushed the dollar yet higher. Japan had replaced Saudi Arabia as the principal source of foreign capital to finance the U.S. deficit. The U.S. government was keenly aware of this important fact and assigned the same individual who had advised the Saudis on the investment of their surplus petrodollars in the 1970s to deal with Japan. By 1984 the

Japanese were investing $1 billion a month in U.S. Treasury bonds. But after the dollar began its fall, the Japanese in 1986 let it be known that they would no longer purchase these bonds in such quantities, and a large part of their funds went instead to real estate. This was a serious "threat" for the United States since foreign sale of the bonds directly affected general interest rates and raised the cost to the United States of financing its deficit. It is one of the primary reasons the U.S. government applied so much pressure on Japan and the FRG to lower their rates. But by 1987 official government investors were again buying U.S. Treasury bonds with the dollars purchased to support its value in the currency exchange market. The Japanese banks also competed to increase their interest rates in order to hold the funds at home, but they succeeded only in putting severe strains on the domestic economy and the government budget.

There was a shift in the standing of Japan and the United States in foreign investment after 1980. While American foreign assets dropped from $100 billion to around $20 billion in 1984, the Japanese assets grew from $7 billion to $74 billion, as Japan invested its trade surplus abroad. In 1985 Japan was the world's leading capital exporter, or creditor nation. And after sixty-five years as the world's creditor, the United States in 1985 became its largest debtor.

As usual, the raising of real interest rates to record levels had a number of consequences, intended and unintended. As part of an anti-inflationary strategy in the United States, it contributed to the recession, and the rising dollar made imports cheaper and more competitive; in this sense the policy was successful. U.S. inflation fell from a high of 18 percent in March 1980 to 7 percent in 1982. On the other hand, the policy had important negative consequences for U.S. exports, leaving many domestic industries unable to compete, producing the consequent gigantic trade deficit. For the American TNCs the rising dollar meant smaller overseas profits.

On the other hand, the overvalued dollar was a boon to the exports and profits of America's trading partners, and although this offered no increase in jobs, it may have saved some that were later lost when the exchange rate shifted. The other effect of the currency fluctuations on trade was to increase protectionist pressures. But the indebted LDCs bore the greatest negative brunt of the floating-exchange system, especially the rise of the dollar in the 1980s.[13]

LIQUIDITY

As with most things in a capitalist society—famine in Africa while granaries are gorged in other parts of the world, billions of dollars in

bank credits for gambling at high risk in the futures markets while the
extremes of penury prevail elsewhere, capital flight to Swiss banks and
Florida real estate while the working population is being further impoverished to pay off the ever growing debt—there is too much liquidity
for some and far too little for others. Capital-short countries are net
exporters of capital, as the world's richest nation became a net importer
in 1985. And monetary relations are also always a story of the effort
of those with too much to force those with too little to pay for the
problems of having too much on both a national and an international
level.

In 1981 the IMF, primarily at U.S. insistence, claiming that too
much liquidity would offer an "inflationary signal" to the world economy, once more rejected appeals to increase its special drawing rights
(SDRs). While still a form of credit, the increasing of drawing rights
for the borrower is less onerous than loans, since it was free of the
conditionality linked to the IMF loans. The United States continued to
oppose an increase in such liquidity over the following years, as did the
Germans. The conclusion of the Group of Ten on the functioning of the
monetary system in 1985 was that during most of the 1970s and 1980s
the supply of international liquidity was "ample, if not excessive."[14]
Indeed, billions of dollars or its equivalent is being transferred around
the world in speculative investment and arbitrage. For others, penury
was required both to restrain inflationary "signals" and to enforce
particular IMF-imposed policy adjustments.

Central bank reserves rose and fell with the effect of speculation in
currencies and gold. According to economist Robert Triffen, world
monetary reserves grew eleven times more in eleven years than in all
the "centuries since Adam and Eve."[15] At the beginning of 1970 the
total world reserves were $79 billion. By September 1980, with
the spectacular rise in the price of gold, they were $1.046 trillion. The
subsequent fall in the price of gold cut the reserves by one-half.

There is at the same time an obvious shortage as all nations, including the richest, desperately compete for capital. This competition
among the LDCs has led them to restructure their economies to attract
investment capital and become ensnared in the debt trap and succumb
to IMF restructuring. One important source of capital for many LDCs,
the remittances of the migrant workers, was ending with the recession
in the OECD nations and the contraction in OPEC revenues. At the
same time, the industrialized countries struggle with interest rate wars,
dismantle regulations in the financial system, and offer investment
incentives and subsidies to reluctant capitalists with too many suitors.

Money creation, which is really debt creation, is now in the hands of private banks and other private issuers of credit. As one economist pointed out, both Keynes and the monetarists ignored the financial structure in their theory and analyses and used only the concept of "money," whereas in reality the financial structure is lenders and borrowers.[16] The IMF's 1985 assessment of the monetary system addressed this point: "Countries can obtain reserves from financial markets provided they maintain their creditworthiness, which is mainly a function of their own domestic policies and performance."[17]

It was the monetarists' tenet that an increase in the money supply would bring an immediate rise in the GNP, but they made a major error on the question of the velocity of money, or its use as a demand for production. In 1986 the Federal Reserve increased the money supply by roughly 13 percent, and the GNP barely grew and inflation continued to fall. The added money was concentrated in the hands of those who used it for the feverish speculation in the financial markets that provided no impetus to production. Among their serious errors was the assumption of a closed economy. Instead, the dollar was held as a store of value internationally. It is important that as currencies are freely exchangeable, there is no way to measure monetary aggregates. Even more important, money itself, as it was known in the past, now has many rivals in the form of other liquid assets. As the head of the Federal Reserve branch of Boston wrote in 1986, "It is one of the ironies of economic history that monetarist doctrine found its most widespread support at the very time that it became impossible to measure the money stock."[18] The whole academic debate bordered on the ridiculous. If money in whatever form it takes cannot be controlled by the central authority, there can be no monetary policy. And the central banks by the 1980s had no control over money. By then both the United States and the United Kingdom, the most ideological monetarists, had largely abandoned their effort to measure the money supply and were giving more attention to the exchange rate as a basis for their monetary "policy." As one economist anxiously noted, it is important to determine if "money" is even the key variable in the world economy.[19] In the real world vast sums, or the illusion of such, were flowing across borders. I say "illusion" for much of it was really bank or brokerage credit, an enormous bubble waiting to burst. But the monetarist policies did have real effects on a large portion of the world's population. Economists have been given increasingly powerful positions, and their decisions often become real ingredients in the economy, affecting millions. Their arcane theories have left the academy and are introduced into the real world, to the detriment of all. As always, the deceptively dry and neutral economic language, the pretense of being scientific, masks the most pernicious plans.

When the U.S. Federal Reserve shifted in October 1979 to a monetarist stance, interest rates soared, with the incidental effect of devastating the financial markets that were attuned to fixed rates. Since that time rates have fluctuated like commodity prices but remained historically high in real terms, as inflation declined and deflation in commodities began and soon spread to other parts of the economy. A futures market in interest rates, gambling on the rate at a future date, became an important instrument of speculative investment. Treasury bond futures are the most heavily traded of the interest rate futures.

These innumerable "innovations" in the private market by 1986 were the cause of increasing alarm among the world's central bankers. Given the global integration of the capital markets and the deregulation of finance, the Bank for International Settlements and the Group of Ten issued an exceptional report warning of (1) the trend of commercial banks to substitute securities operations for direct lending, (2) the "spectacular" growth of their off–balance sheet business, (3) the indistinct line between bank lending and the capital markets, (4) the integration of the various national economies through the capital markets and the instant spread of trouble from one to the other, and (5) the effect on monetary policies of changes in the exchange rate. Moreover, by the mid-1980s a new context existed for these developments—in 1986 deflation of an average 0.1 percent occurred in the OECD countries as a whole.[20]

All the evidence has shown that money and monetary policy, once the prerogatives of states, have to an important extent been privatized and tied to debt. Borrowing provides the basis for money creation and for the operations of states. Money is primarily debt, and increasingly debt is money.

CHAPTER 13

THE DILEMMAS OF WORLD DEBT

As money is increasingly debt and debt is considered money, economic activity of all sorts takes place through borrowing and lending. When the economy is growing, it is the great lubricant of the system. When the economy stagnates or declines, as everyone now agrees, the dimensions of the debt burden are magnified many times and portend disaster—for individuals, corporations, and states. Yet without continued debt the entire world economy would collapse.

It is the debt of states, both external and internal, that interests us here. Particularly important are its linkages with all the other aspects of the international economy. Nearly all nations face enormous debts to one degree or another. But it is in the context of total debt, public and private, that state debt has the greatest implications. The only solution to the "debt crisis" until now has been more debt—and a restructuring of the political economy of numerous countries.

So familiar is the debt crisis that it scarcely needs statistical proof. The debt figures alone, in any case, are of little analytic value and must be seen in the general context. Debt may be used to provide the wherewithal for capital formation, to expand production, or to service old debts. For an LDC, development and growth imply a deficit, and most development strategies have produced indebted industrialization. A nation's balance or surplus in international accounts, in fact, may also mean a stagnating economy. State debt is not new, of course; what is new is its current form and extent. In the contemporary situation sheer quantity has for once been transformed into a qualitative structural change, and the speed of the change is noteworthy. From the ensuing debt structure emerged a latticework of interacting developments. The most significant structural change is the shift from government-to-government lending, which predominated until about 1974, to commercial bank lending to sovereign states. With it came the threat to the global financial system, the change in the purpose of the loans, the blatant IMF intrusions into economic policy, the threats to world trade, the perverse effect on monetary relations, currency exchange, and economic policy, and the impact on the world's population. The vast expansion of loans to sovereign states developed into a new dimension of imperialist relations and a situation that revealed the extremes of austerity and profligacy. Could these trends have been foreseen? And if so, would it have changed the policy of the countries involved?

In fact, both rising and floating interest rates, the fluctuating exchange rate of the dollar, the unstable terms of trade, and capital flight were the immediate causes that converted a chronic problem into the acute crisis of the 1980s. These conditions were not foreseen by states eager to take advantage of the exceptionally enticing loan terms to develop their economies or cover their balance-of-payments deficits in some cases or to facilitate corruption or capital flight in others. And the private borrowers, the TNCs that acquired most of the original state-guaranteed loans or the local corporations or importers of goods for the small elite, could not have cared less about such growing risks. The state generally guaranteed the exchange rate. Ultimately, others would pay the price. Lenders, too, such as corporations anxious to make a sale, official state lenders for exports determined to support their own economy, and, particularly, the bankers who found these loans highly profitable when they were eager for borrowers—they all never imagined, or simply refused to consider, the outcome. As the world debt situation worsened, countries wishing to avoid the IMF and its conditions, and lenders eager to avoid long-term commitment, turned to short-term debt and thus had to meet principal as well as interest repayments. Finally, not only has debt objectively restructured the economy as it interacts with all the other aspects of the crisis, but it is the precondition for the "restructuring" policies that I shall discuss in the following chapters.

A few figures can only highlight the transformation over a brief period. During the 1970s, when the debt had already reached startling heights, the World Bank estimates of world debt were purposely released late in order to avoid panic in the financial markets. But by the mid-1980s the world was more inured to the astronomical figures when the estimate of the LDC's total debt was $1 trillion. But despite a more calloused general attitude, the dangers continued to mount. Debt service, the so-called rigid element in the balance of payments, and the one most important to the banks, increased more rapidly than the debt, showing a 26 percent average annual growth and continuing to mount after 1982, as new lending declined.

Trade was affected in innumerable ways. Nations like Brazil can earn the foreign exchange to repay their debts only by exporting goods. But by the end of 1982, when Latin debtors, beginning with Mexico, could no longer meet their payments and the series of reschedulings began, the external debt service as a percentage of exports was 179 percent for Argentina, 129 percent for Mexico, 122 percent for Brazil, 95 percent for Venezuela, and 91 percent for the Philippines. Their manufactured goods are intensely competitive with those of the OECD industries. And as the indebted LDCs are forced to reduce their imports, the exports of the trade-dependent OECD countries are reduced. Implicit in this debt crisis, therefore, are trade conflicts and a struggle between financial and industrial capital in the OECD nations.

Falling commodity prices also changed the debt perspective of the Philippines, Thailand, Indonesia, and Malaysia and increased the demand for more debt. Malaysia's debt, 80 percent of it to private banks, had been growing at 30 percent a year. Its exports depended on commodities such as tin, rubber, oil, and gas. The contradictions of trade, debt, and political relations increased. American subsidies to its own rice exporters and protectionist barriers for its manufactured goods directly affected Thailand's economy and its ability to service its debt. Thailand is only an example of a general pattern. With the fall in the price of oil and the deteriorating terms of trade of the indebted OPEC countries, the IMF in 1986 anticipated a whole new group of nations with debt-servicing problems that would have major repercussions on world trade. In the preceding fall in the oil price, in 1982, the oil-exporting countries' current account had shifted in two years from a surplus of $95 billion in 1980 to a deficit of $26 billion in 1982. The 1982 fall in oil prices was generally considered too late for importers, and far too soon for exporters. Debt has become most devastating of all in the context of world deflation, when not even the illusion of repayment can be maintained.

The fall in the LDC's export prices also coincided with the rise in interest rates. Since by 1985 some 80 percent of the LDC's debt was dollar denominated, the severe cash flow problems of the 1980s were substantially due to the rise in dollar interest rates. The LDCs in the 1980s suffered an enormous capital drain in interest payments, falling terms of trade, and capital flight.[1]

CAPITAL FLIGHT

It has been estimated that one-half of the foreign borrowing of Mexico, Venezuela, and Nigeria and one-third of Argentina's had been transformed into capital flight, with the United States and Switzerland as the principal havens. The IMF asserted that the outflow was "particularly large in relation to GDP" in the years 1977–80 and that in general it increased the borrowing needs by two-thirds.[2] Between 1980 and 1983, $71 billion was shipped out of the seven biggest debtor nations. In 1985 the governor of the Bank of England estimated that the capital flight from the Latin debtors alone totaled $80 billion, an amount equal to the new borrowing of those countries since 1981. Other projections run as high as $130 billion. Many countries had no exchange controls until after 1982. Individuals, politicians, some small businesses, and, primarily, the TNCs sent the vast sums (not profits, but borrowed sums and operating costs) from the LDCs to the OECD during the first half of the 1980s. About $15–$20 billion of the Argentine debt was for the pet projects of the former military rulers, and a good part of it ended up in private foreign accounts. Marcos transferred at least $5 billion to safe havens over his years of misrule in the Philippines. "Capital flight is the great unspoken issue," asserted Robert Hormats, vice-president of Goldman Sachs and a former assistant secretary of state. "For countries that sought to maintain overvalued exchange rates, it is responsible for up to 25% of their debt problem."[3] But despite, or even because of, devaluations, the rich continued to export their funds, although the level has dropped somewhat since 1982.

It is also often difficult to distinguish capital flight from capital flow of speculative investment. Flight usually refers to illegal transfers to avoid currency controls, taxes, or other restrictions. But transfer of capital due to fear of the future (one frightened Hong Kong resident declared, "The only safe place for my money is in U.S. dollars, in a U.S. bank, on U.S. soil") is also termed capital flight, and it differs only in motive from financial speculation.[4]

Some $5–$6 billion left Mexico in 1985, and the finance minister in negotiating for a new loan in early 1986 indicated he had to cover an estimated $1 billion flight in that year. The banks played a major role in facilitating the transfer of capital, often as cash in suitcases, to their banks in the United States or Switzerland. Other funds were invested in property abroad. The IMF's prescription for stopping capital flight has been to make it even more profitable for capital to remain or be repatriated, and offer greater incentives to attract foreign capital.

DEFUSING THE DEBT CRISIS

For the first three years of the debt crisis the international organizations and the creditor nations focused on averting a world financial collapse through a banking crisis. The banks had regarded their loans to governments as "evergreen" since they would not go bankrupt and disappear, as loans to private entities could. On the other hand, there was no enforcement body to collect if they ever declared a moratorium. The crucial thing was to keep up the illusion of repayment so that the banks did not have to write off their loans as losses. A rollover of credits supported by the IMF would allow the banks to list at face value loans (and collect huge profits in the rescheduling fees and increased margins) whose market value had indeed collapsed and whose principal would never be repaid. And the financial market, as I discussed earlier, had already discounted those loans substantially.

In order to service these credits, the debtor countries increased their exports by squeezing the domestic economy. Per capita income fell, and real income in Latin America was less in 1985 than in the 1960s. Between 1982 and 1984 Latin America had a $26 billion trade surplus with the United States, reversing the deficit of the preceding eight years, even though its aggregate production fell 9 percent between 1980 and 1984. Success in export trade bred new obstacles. With the slowdown in the U.S. economy and increased protectionism in 1985, the trade surplus declined 42 percent in Mexico and 17 percent in Brazil. More comprehensive trade restrictions in their markets accompanied every gain in their export-oriented strategy.

Even many official bodies, such as the financial experts of the Commonwealth countries reporting on the LDC debt situation in September 1984, asserted that "severe adjustment strains are becoming economically and socially unbearable." It was "neither feasible nor desirable" for the debtor countries to amass the huge trade surplus to repay the debt.[5]

While the nominal interest rate in 1985 was half that of 1982, real interest rates from the debtors' perspective were rising with the deteriorating terms of trade and falling inflation. Debt service still absorbed the same or higher portion of export earnings. But interest repayment in dollars had to come from somewhere if the debtors did not call a moratorium on debt repayment. If the foreign exchange could not be earned through exports, it had to come through reduced imports and more bank lending, generating a circular process without a resolution. And in all cases it was extracted from the population in the form of increased misery. But access to new bank loans was no longer an option, since the LDCs were also being "crowded out" by the increase in loan demand from corporate megamergers as well as by the OECD nations' financing of their own government debt. By 1985 about 80 percent of the international loans went to the OECD countries.

The moment for a debt moratorium will arrive when the cost of repayment exceeds the benefit of new loans. The penalties can be severe if there is solidarity among the creditors against an isolated debtor state. The dependence of the indebted countries on essential foreign supplies has discouraged a unilateral or even a collective moratorium to date. But in a condition of generalized crisis, nations eager to continue trade may, in their own self-interest, ignore reprisals and continue to supply the defaulting country. As the finance minister of Pakistan pointed out, "developing countries' own payments of interest and principal are increasingly financing the so-called new assistance that they negotiate. . . ."[6] And that "new assistance" comes burdened with additional fees and conditionality. An American Express computer model showed capital flows reversing between 1982 and 1986, when banks would receive a net inflow of $12 billion a year; these flows would also reverse their "political leverage."[7] But the Latin debtors, rather than uniting in a moratorium, did in 1984 forge a rather perverse solidarity, which revealed the political complexities of united action against the creditors at the time. Brazil and Mexico pressured Argentina to meet the bankers' terms and, in fact, lent it money to do so, fearing that a default would reflect on their own ability to get better loan terms, since they themselves had earlier accepted usurious terms that would have been insupportable politically if Argentina had been able to extract better ones. But by 1985 there was increasing unilateral resistance on the part of all these nations as the internal political realities left little alternative. Peru declared that it would pay no more than a fixed percentage of its export earnings, and Brazil in 1987 rejected IMF terms and refused to pay interest on bank loans until better terms were negotiated. The Philippines insisted on the better terms arranged with Argentina.

After averting a world financial collapse by maintaining the illusion that the debt would be repaid, the IMF, as spokesman for the collective creditors, chose to focus on the internal economic policies of the debtor states or on the need for economic growth in the OECD countries that they hoped would create a market for the debtors' exports. These involved restructuring policies. In 1985 its stance was the same, but alarm over the situation and evidence that various Latin American debtors were resisting the IMF strictures and unilaterally changing the terms of repayment, if not calling for a moratorium, led to a renewed emphasis on increased lending. Given the growing struggle for investment funds among the OECD nations themselves and a turn toward recession, such proposals were irrelevant at best.

The poorest nations, particularly in Africa, until the 1980s had no significant debt to the commercial banks, since they were not considered creditworthy. The commodity exporters in black Africa first entered the commercial debt market in the early to middle 1970s, when commodity prices were rising, and then borrowed during the recession in the mid-1970s to ease the decline in their terms of trade. But as their situation worsened with the recession in the 1980s and/or as the political aims of the United States, France, or Britain dictated it, the IMF from 1981 on became the lender of first and last resort. By 1985 sub-Sahara Africa's forty-two countries owed $135 billion, or 35–40 percent of its exports, compared with 9 percent in the mid-1970s. Governments began to increase their production of commodities to meet their foreign-exchange demands for debt service and essential imports, and the overproduction drove prices down further. Over the same period their average per capita national income fell between 10 and 25 percent. By July 1983 fifteen countries had IMF agreements, and by 1985 one-fifth of all IMF loans were in Africa. With interest at 8–9 percent, repayment in 1985 exceeded all new funding. Zambia received one-third of these three- to five-year loans. Repayment to the IMF consumed 25 percent of that nation's export earnings by 1984 and 40 percent in 1985. Under these conditions the GNP in Zambia was 27 percent lower in 1984 than in 1974 and per capita income had fallen by two-thirds since 1981. Tanzania's president Nyerere noted in 1985, "Africa's debt burden is now intolerable. We cannot pay. All our . . . creditors know it."[8] In 1987 Zambia finally withdrew from the IMF after submitting to its restructuring austerity programs for twelve years. It then embarked on a policy of self-reliance, and the government reintroduced import controls and a price freeze.

The Bank for International Settlements (BIS), the so-called central bankers' bank, began to play a much more prominent role in the international monetary system than it had in the past. The so-called bridging loans made available in emergency situations, as to Brazil and Hungary, were also linked to the borrowers' acceptance of the IMF's policy prescriptions. By 1985, however, the president of the BIS concluded, "The time for bridging loans is over."[9]

The renegotiation of official government credits by the Paris Club of

government lenders accelerated as thirty-one countries rescheduled
their debt between 1983 and 1985. They also insisted that the debtor
countries turn first to the IMF for a restructuring of economic policies.
The private banks also rescheduled with another thirty-one countries
(not the identical list) over the same period, covering a total of $140
billion. In some cases it was a major undertaking from the creditor's
side. Argentina had 320 lenders, and each one had to be consulted for
rescheduling. Some of the major borrowers are, ironically, also significant lenders, such as Brazil.

POLITICAL RESPONSE

As the debt crisis reached a new height in 1985, in the context of
the other developments in trade and slowing industrial economies, the
Mexicans indicated to the U.S. Treasury that they would make a new
collective response to the problem. Gone would be the United States's
cherished "case by case" approach. "We think the industrialized countries are gradually coming to realize that the debt issue is not just an
economic problem, but a political problem, and it must be handled
politically," observed an official from Ecuador.[10] They had always
known it was political, of course, but they simply did not define politics
as negotiating at the behest of others. The U.S. government then
responded to the worsening situation and to the Mexican threats by
devising its Baker plan, which proposed $20 billion additional lending
from the banks and $20 billion from the World Bank and the Inter-
American Development Bank (IDB) and which it unveiled at the IMF
meeting. But debt is not stable. Mexico, seen to need $4 billion when
the plan was proposed in September 1985, required $8 billion less than
a year later as the price of oil, its chief export, plunged following Saudi
Arabia's increase in production. At that point Mexico, to pay its interest, needed 60 percent of the Baker's fund that was originally planned
for fifteen indebted nations. The threat that a unilateral "pay what we
are able" decision would spread around the world to other debtors
forced new ad hoc compromises with the IMF and the United States
and emergency funding with new loans, as well as new tactics of the
banks. But everyone understood that only a rise in the price of oil would
create relief for Mexico's creditors on the one hand and greater debt
burden for the oil importers on the other.

Finally, the critical point was reached by the mid-1980s, when the
debtor countries had every incentive to default. Their debt service
outweighed, by far, the funds they could expect to receive from rescheduling. And with world trade rising by only 2 percent, recessionary
trends in Japan and the United States, and commodity prices in a

freefall, there was no chance that they could continue to increase their exports to repay their debt. The contradictions between the interests of the banks and those of other capitalist exporters, both in their loss of markets to the indebted nations and in the new competition they offered in their effort to earn foreign exchange, became increasingly evident.

DEBT AND DEFICITS OF THE OECD COUNTRIES

Government debt to the commercial banks, besides the highly publicized one from the LDCs and CPEs, also includes significant debt from the OECD countries. Although these nations are usually able to acquire credit by selling their bonds, they must offer high interest, and the payments for both forms of debt weigh significantly on their budgets. With the intensifying fiscal crisis of the state, many of these loans also came into question. At the end of 1982, commercial banks held 60 percent of West European debt and had put Denmark on their "watch" list.[11]

The monumental government budget deficits of the United States and other developed capitalist countries have different implications in the process of restructuring the international economy. With the smaller and weaker countries, the international effects of their foreign debt were ultimately the threat to the financial system, by undermining the banks, and the aggregate debt's restrictions on world trade. Their internal budget deficits would have no international repercussions. Given the role of U.S. currency, the debt and consequent internal monetary policies of the United States have affected every other nation directly, both internally and externally.

By 1985 the U.S. national debt was growing faster than the economy, and the interest payments on the deficit were the fastest-growing component of the national budget. The federal debt, $914 billion in 1980, reached $1,841 trillion in 1985, or 37 percent of the GNP. (The total public and private debt grew in 1985 to over $8 trillion, a postwar record and amounting to nearly twice the GNP, and the rate of increase was the most startling of all. The debt in 1970 was $1.6 trillion and $4.6 trillion in 1980.) The most notable figures for comprehending the mounting federal deficits are those for military expenditures and debt service. National defense rose from $86.5 billion in 1975 to $253 billion in 1985. Net interest on debt rose from $23.2 billion in 1975 to $42.6 billion in 1979 and to $129.4 billion in 1985, or 13.7 percent of the budget. Interest payments as a percentage of the GNP rose from 2.2 percent in 1973 to 5.0 percent in 1984.

"None of us really understands what's going on with all these numbers," bemoaned Budget Director David Stockman in 1981. "The defense numbers got out of control and we were doing that whole budget-cutting so frenetically . . . so fast, we didn't know where we were ending up . . . just a bunch of numbers on a piece of paper. And it didn't quite mesh. . . ."[12] He reports in his memoir that a mathematical error in the process accidentally awarded the Pentagon an astounding sum, which it then refused to relinquish. The new funds in search of a project were eventually translated into the "Star Wars" program.[13]

On the one hand, the rise in government debt was one of the key countervailing forces that prevented the economy from sinking into a deep depression, as it had in the 1930s. In the United States the state provided 30 percent of the demand in the economy in the 1970s. But the contradictions inherent in the concept of debt to finance debt, even for the United States, have emerged as one of the chief factors in the economic crisis. Arithmetic projections show that interest payments will soon crowd out the other budget expenditures or require a large tax increase, either of which would have a serious recessionary impact on the economy. The alternative of printing money would probably lead to hyperinflation. Finally, in a mood of desperation, Congress at the end of 1985 tried to counter the disastrous implications of this trend by legislating a balanced budget, but the Supreme Court later nullified its key provisions.

The U.S. government has been able to avoid the alternatives of dealing with its debt only because of the vast influx of foreign capital. In 1982 about 26 percent of the capital inflow went into government securities, 15 percent into direct investment, and 14 percent into port-folio investment. By 1984 this foreign capital financed 40 percent of the budget deficit. Foreign investors, private and official, bought $53 billion in U.S. government securities in 1986, or 25 percent of all those issued. This inflow kept a lid on interest rates. According to Paul Volcker, the United States should not become "addicted, but for the time being, is dependent on them." The credit demand was "far in excess of our capacity to save."[14] By 1985 the United States was a net debtor to foreign creditors for the first time in 68 years. "[E]ven under favorable circumstances that net indebtedness will increase substan-tially in the years ahead," Volcker underlined in October 1986.[15] According to the BIS annual report, the U.S. fiscal deficit "has been almost identical to the increase in . . . net capital inflows."[16] And the new U.S. foreign debt was used mainly to pay interest on existing government debt.

In 1983 alone $150 billion in European capital flowed into the United States because of the high interest rates and rising value of the dollar. By 1984 a fierce competition had developed between the various European nations, the United States, and Canada for the world's liquid funds. The shift in the pattern of capital flows is striking, particularly for Japan. Net long-term capital outflow from the Asian power was $17.7 billion in 1983 and $49.8 billion in 1984.

Not only was the United States determined to hold the funds it had attracted, but in 1984 it was trying to entice an additional $85 billion of new funds. By drawing a huge inflow of interest-sensitive funds, it was able to finance its record deficit without shifting to an expansionary monetary policy or competing for domestic savings and "crowding out" the private sector. Beginning in 1986, as the dollar continued its plunge, governments once again began to finance the U.S. deficit as they tried to brake the dollar's fall. It also weakened other currencies and economies by forcing them to adopt similar monetary policies or suffer an even greater capital hemorrhage. Only the United States is able to finance its current account deficit, reaching 2–3 percent of the GNP, with its own currency. Others finance their deficit in foreign currencies; "the exchange risk was borne by the deficit country itself, not by the foreign saver. In the case of the U.S. . . . the exchange risk is mainly being absorbed by foreign investors," noted a report by the Federal Reserve Bank of New York.[17] As for the mounting foreign debt, it was effectively reduced by devaluing the dollar. There was also a form of "war" in the international equity markets, as the various governments abolished withholding tax on foreign investment in their attempt to attract capital. But, important for the future, the funds remained very short-term and volatile.

Government debt and interest payments for other OECD countries rose even more than for the United States, although the international impact was smaller. Japan's government debt in 1983 reached 39 percent of the GNP. Interest payments rose from 0.9 percent of GNP to 4.6 percent between 1973 and 1984 and composed 20 percent of the budget in 1985, rising 11.7 percent over the preceding year. By 1981 the German debt had risen over the decade by five times. Interest payments as a percentage of its budget rose threefold between 1973 and 1984, as they did for Belgium and the Netherlands.

In Italy in mid-1983 the budget deficit equaled 17 percent of the GNP. Interest payments experienced the greatest rise of all over the decade, from 2.5 percent of the GNP in 1973 to 9.8 percent in 1984. The Socialist party formed the government with a program of introducing austerity to reduce the deficit and inflation even while unemployment was rising. France's foreign debt in 1984 reached $37 billion plus

$7 billion owed by nationalized banks. It grew 70 million francs in six months solely because of the rise in the value of the dollar, in which 54 percent of its debt was denominated. In Canada, as well, interest payments reached nearly 8 percent of the GNP in 1984. This enormous percentage of the budget of all these countries reflected the extraordinary interest rates propelled by those in the United States. Compounding their debt, many European nations had to borrow to support their currencies, then had to repay at the devalued rate.

This fiscal crisis is made more severe by the transfer of profits by transnational banks and corporations to "offshore" havens, where taxes are nil or minimal, or through transfer pricing. In addition, stagnation and recession have reduced revenues from other sources. And as tax revenues have declined, expenditures have mounted. Denmark, for example, tried to maintain its welfare state through the 1970s by external borrowing. By the 1980s its foreign debt had reached $14 billion. Unemployment payments rose, and tax revenues from the workers fell. In Belgium unemployment benefits in early 1982 reached 3 percent of the GNP. In the United States various states had to borrow to pay unemployment compensation. Municipalities, especially in the depressed steel region, survived on bank loans until unable to pay interest; by 1985 some small towns had finally "closed down," in terms of all services.

Government spending as a percentage of national income by 1982 was 60 percent in Holland, 46 percent in the FRG and France, and 30 percent in the United States and Japan. The spending on social programs, on the other hand, did prevent the recession from being considerably worse. But the fiscal crisis worsens in recession, and the deficit becomes that much more intrusive on money available, which intensifies the national rivalries for available capital. Yet, while payment in welfare services and unemployment compensation have been cut back, state payments to capital were unaffected or even increased, as governments, from local to national, offered subsidies, tax holidays, and other incentives to attract or hold investment.

The IMF pointed out in its 1985 report, "Since the late 1970s, a central objective of governments in industrial countries has been the reduction of fiscal deficits. . . . Despite these aims, however, the combined deficit of the seven major . . . countries taken as a group was considerably higher in 1983–84 than . . . five years earlier."[18] After 1983 there were "historically unusual proportions of private saving being absorbed by the financing of government deficits . . . [and] significantly lower proportion absorbed by gross private domestic investment . . . than during earlier recoveries."[19]

Debt is ubiquitous in the world economy. It has obviously restructured the economy objectively, and it offers the IMF the leverage to implement its "restructuring" policies. But it remains an area of ever greater risk. As one European banker expressed it in 1984, the "outer limit" for defusing the debt bomb "is the outset of the next recession."[20] Debt, with all its ramifications, is clearly a key element in this economic crisis, at once threatening and sustaining the system.

CHAPTER 14

WORLD TRADE RESTRUCTURED

International trade has changed in so many ways that national balance of trade and other statistics can give only a very distorted image of reality. If one assesses them on the basis of value, especially in dollar terms, one enters a make-believe land, for values are determined by administered and transfer prices in intrafirm trade of the TNCs, currency fluctuations, subsidies, over- or underinvoicing to hide capital flight, and an endless array of other devices. While earlier conditions and forms of trade have radically changed, inertia continues to define official, and much other, discussion of broad categories even when the implications of the trade statistics are understood, creating a false impression that the old forms of trade still exist.

INTRAFIRM TRADE

The growth of intrafirm trade, or foreign trade between branches of one company, is a structural feature that makes obsolete or irrelevant whole categories in international trade. In order to exploit beneficial tax arrangements, firms notoriously distort the price structure; one result is that the trade figures used to guide government policy are unreliable at best. And this form of trade is increasingly dominant; 27 percent of all U.S. exports were to subsidiaries, and 56 percent of the total imports were from affiliates in 1982, most of them representing intrafirm trade. The so-called increasing dependence of the U.S. economy on foreign trade, reported to be 25 percent in 1980, double the 1970 level, really therefore reflects transfers within U.S. TNCs. Such figures on American corporate trade with its own affiliates are for the *value*, not the volume, of trade and thus are subject to the manipulation of prices implicit in intrafirm trade. Intrafirm trade is measured by recorded transfer prices rather than by market prices, which can be very different. Moreover, all factors of production are broken down in minute detail and "assigned" a price, including normal corporate interchange, such as phone calls, which are then listed as exports or imports.

Many excellent studies of the TNCs' control of foreign trade through their intrafirm transfers have shown that corporations consistently distort aggregate national trade and tax figures to their own advantage. In raw materials, for instance, the open market accounts for only a small part of the value of world trade. For nationally controlled commodity sales, the existence of oligopsony, control of the market by a few buyers, is of crucial importance. The TNCs market 70–80 percent of all global trade in primary commodities. Those independent suppliers not linked to the giant trading companies increasingly find themselves "suppliers of last resort."

The shift in the geographical pattern of U.S. trade, which has been noted by many, also really reflects intrafirm trade. Between 1972 and 1983, U.S. manufactured imports from the LDCs rose from 11 percent to 28 percent of the total imports, those from Japan rose from 4 percent to over 25 percent, while imports from Europe fell from 35 percent to 24 percent. The relocation by American companies in search of cheaper labor for the production of goods to be sold in the United States shows up as part of the trade deficit. "We are not taking away your manufacturers' business," the chairman of the Sony Corporation declared in 1986. "They are giving it up. If they move out factories [from the United States] and depend on the Far East," there is no reason to blame Japan.[1]

No discussion of intrafirm trade would be complete without a consideration of the giant Japanese trading companies—Mitsubishi, Mitsui, and nine others—especially since they have become the model for many American manufacturing and raw-materials companies. The latter have essentially converted themselves into trading companies as they contract for production, particularly commodities but also manufactured goods, in the LDCs; then they package, label, and market the product, be it computers or automobiles. Furthermore, one-third of the increase in U.S. manufactured exports between 1983 and 1985 were components of goods later imported.

Although formal trading companies in Europe and the United States largely disappeared before World War II, they continued to be of great importance in Japanese capitalism. Over the years they constructed a vast worldwide intelligence network, allowing them to assess trends and locate markets and the cheapest supplies, usually, but not necessarily, Japanese owned. Whether they make their own investments or take minority equity, or form joint ventures with other Japanese investors and local interests, their principal interest is to sign exclusive trading agreements for supplies (inputs) and marketing, rather than the profit from, or control of, production. The trading companies' role in exporting from Japan has diminished as the big manufacturing companies like Toyota and Sanyo export directly to their principal markets in North America and Europe, although the trading companies handle their sales to the CPEs, Africa, and the Middle East. Japanese companies have also set up what the Europeans term screwdriver plants, which import and assemble Japanese parts in Europe. As the EEC began to exclude the parts, the Japanese turned to joint ventures and relocating the parts companies; this seriously affected employment in Japan.

In addition to the fact that an ever growing proportion of world trade is intrafirm, innumerable layers of subsidies, state incentives, and other guarantees "artificially distort" market operations in the workings of the theoretical "comparative advantage" in international trade. In 1978 the OECD predicted that "the whole of international trade might develop an oligopolistic structure in which the main transactors would be governments, the multinational firms and diversified trading companies."[2] Its expectations were borne out.

COUNTERTRADE AND BARTER

Barter trade is the most rapidly growing form of international trade, and the reasons for it are obvious. In 1972 it represented 2 percent of all world trade but grew to 30 percent a decade later. Eighty countries are actively engaged in countertrade or are seeking to be. This form of trade takes several forms, but all obviate the need to use currencies and the usual means of exchange.

Payment in goods is especially important to the LDCs and CPEs, which are poor in hard currency. The OECD estimated that 15 to 20 percent of the trade between Eastern and Western Europe is countertrade. It is also widespread in France, Italy, Japan, and Canada. Examples include Iranian oil for New Zealand lamb, Japanese construction machines for Soviet timber, and Spanish buses for Colombian coffee. A Malaysian rubber trading company supplied a Mexican tire company and was paid in cocoa beans, which it sold to a U.S. candy company. McDonnell-Douglas has traded aircraft for canned hams. Iraq obtains most of its arms from France in exchange for oil. Sometimes the trade is bizarre, an outcome of desperation, or involves only a marketing function. Banks have begun to participate in it, bringing traders together for a fee. They have also developed their own countertrade or "swaps" in their loan portfolios.

The TNCs are deeply involved in barter trade and usually have subsidiaries to handle it. As a GE executive described countertrade, "half a loaf is better than none."[3] Exports of GE, America's leading manufacturing exporter, rose in a decade from $500 million to $4 billion in 1983. "Without countertrade we couldn't have expanded our exports," explained its vice-president for international trade.[4] India's countertrade clearing agreement with the USSR attracted to India Western investors who hoped to penetrate the Soviet market indirectly. And companies that accept countertraded goods frequently dump them in a third market, further undercutting "normal" trading relations.

Buyback trade, a form of countertrade that pays for turnkey plants, introduces considerable uncertainty and often extra marketing costs, since it extends over a period of years and often changes the price. The Soviets imported more than a hundred chemical plants in the 1970s with buyback agreements of payment in production. By the 1980s Western Europe was "awash" in chemicals from the USSR.[5]

The size and number of deals has increased steadily, reaching a $1 billion contract between Saudi Arabia and Boeing in 1984. The U.S. Department of Commerce has estimated that countertrade will account for half of all world trade in fifteen years, and it has issued guidelines to corporations on how to proceed with the transactions.

The IMF uses it leverage to discourage countertrade arrangements considering it a reversion to the forms of trade that prevailed during the 1930s depression. It pushes instead for devaluation and other fiscal and monetary policies.

CURRENCIES AND TRADE

Currency fluctuations—particularly of the dollar, which is used for 40–50 percent of all world trade—are *the* major cause of shifts in global trade patterns. With the cheap dollar in the late 1970s, according to Assistant Treasury Secretary Fred Bergsten, "our exports were growing at twice the rate of world trade, our share of the world market was better than at any time since the 1960s, and exports provided 25% of the growth of the GNP."[6] Exchange rates were decisive. The U.S. trade deficit fell from $55 billion to $24 billion between 1978 and 1980, then rose to $102 billion in 1984. By 1985, exports had declined in every category except military and automotive, and imports had increased in every one except raw materials.

In 1980 the United States had a $16 billion surplus in trade with the EC; in 1984 it ran a $13 billion deficit. With the strong dollar and economic "recovery" in 1983–84, imports flooded the market, bringing renewed calls for protection. German exports to the United States increased over 50 percent in 1984 and provided its second-largest export market. There was general agreement that until 1986 the dollar was overvalued by 40 percent, equivalent to a 40 percent subsidy on imports or to a tariff on exports. And looking at the vast expansion of worldwide competitive capacity, corporate interests considered the inflow only "the tip of the iceberg."[7] The strength of the dollar in the 1980s caused imports as a percentage of the domestic market to rise from 8 percent in 1970 to 19 percent in 1984. Machine tool imports, which supplied 27 percent of the U.S. market in 1982, had a 40 percent share one year later. Even the most efficient American industries— agriculture, electronics, and computers—were hit by the rising dollar in both import and export competition. In 1984, moreover, imports of telecommunications equipment (supposedly an American "comparative advantage") were greater than exports for the first time.

While the yen was weak against the dollar, it retained its value vis-à-vis the European currencies; so Europe's trade deficit with Japan did not grow significantly, whereas the U.S. deficit ballooned. Yet with the fall of the dollar, Japanese companies in less than a year became more than 50 percent less competitive. They sought to cut costs and to reduce profits in order to hold their market share in the United States. This, plus the crucial fact that half the U.S. trade is with the rest of Asia, Latin America, and Canada, whose currencies are linked to the dollar, meant that import prices by 1987 rose only about 5 percent.

Currency fluctuations also made for rapid and decisive shifts in unit labor costs. In 1980, for example, the United States ranked fifth among the OECD states, and in 1982 it was first by a wide margin. The Europeans, naturally, gained a major trade advantage thereby. Yet Morgan Guaranty Trust assessed that only one-third of the U.S. trade deficit was attributable to the dollar strength, another one-third to the continued slow growth among the industrial countries, and another third to the effect of the debt crisis on reducing exports and NIC competition. Although the currency issue was the key variable in trade, the various corporations and governments took the opportunity to wring further concessions from labor in order to restore competitiveness.

The appreciation of the U.S. dollar also proved devastating to the terms of trade of the commodity exporters, since their debt and imports were denominated in dollars. U.S. exports to Latin America declined by $21 billion between 1981 and 1983, because seven of the indebted nations in Latin America had accounted for 14 percent of all U.S. exports. For the Europeans, however, the fall of commodity prices kept import costs steady and lessened alarm over the dollar's strength, given the demand for their export industry. The head of the Bundesbank, Karl Otto Pöhl, said, "I have no reason to worry about the exchange rate, as long as our import prices are not increasing dramatically."[8] In fact, it protected German industry from American exports as well. With the fall of the dollar in 1986, the situation reversed for Japan and the FRG, but there was no immediate change in the U.S. trade deficit, since in value terms, a smaller volume of imports would still be a higher cost and vice versa for exports. Politically, given only the balance-of-trade statistics, tensions between the United States and Japan rose sharply in 1987.

This currency development also accelerated the trend toward the conversion of U.S. manufacturers from being producers to being distributors of goods made elsewhere. One machine tool company established marketing links with Japanese and European companies. "We have to import parts or complete lines of equipment, and everybody's doing it," reported the president of one U.S. company.[9] This accelerated an important structural shift of the TNCs, from production and ownership to marketing conglomerates dealing with the producers through contracts, particularly of commodities but also of manufactured goods in many LDCs.

Only the United States has never felt required to restrain its policies or amass reserves in other currencies. All other nations must pay for their imports with an accumulation of foreign-currency reserves. Obviously, the fact that the United States can pay with the dollar, which is printed rather than earned, is—its inevitable contradictions notwithstanding—an enormous lever of power that it is unlikely to relinquish without a struggle.

SERVICE TRADE

By the 1980s trade in the services was an arena of sharp contention. The United States believed it had the comparative advantage in this domain, which constituted 15 percent of its exports. Bank loans represented 55 percent of service exports by 1983. Leasing and insurance were second, followed by air transport, construction and engineering, data processing, communications, and franchising. In 1981 these service exports transformed a U.S. commercial deficit of $28 billion into a surplus of $7 billion. But the surplus in the service trade also fell, from $41.2 billion in 1981 to $18.1 billion in 1984, as the deficit in goods rose. One reason, according to one American executive, is that

many "exports," such as Americans' giving legal advice to foreigners
or managing hospitals abroad, are not counted, underlining the nebu-
lousness of this trade.

In 1983–84 the United States began its assault to secure "free"
trade in services within GATT, whose regulations and rounds of
negotiations apply only to the trade in goods. Its efforts met opposition
in 1985 when the LDCs, led by Brazil and India, refused to participate
in any GATT negotiations on services.

COMPETITION

Because of the size and power of the TNCs in world trade, there is
a tendency among some people to assume that they are able to exert
control. But while all the new forms of trade, especially intrafirm trade
and transfer pricing, are of great significance in the structure of world
trade and the fiscal problems of states, the real action continues to take
place in the realm of struggle, rivalry, and competition. The forces of
competition are as dominant in international trade as they are crucial
in domestic economies. And states, serving their most powerful nationals, play a major role in this respect. Unfortunately for a successful
execution of national policy, the interests of their diverse nationals
are often in contradiction with each other: the interests of some are
best served by promoting free trade; others require protectionist
measures.[10]

"A dangerous rigidity," according to the IMF, "is the tendency of
governments to provide various forms of subsidization or protection to
industries whose competitive positions have deteriorated."[11] Currencies, labor costs, subsidies, and credits are just a few of the many means
to compete in international trade. Competition in trade, as in the locale
of production, has reflected rapid changes. Before the late 1960s Japan
was perceived by other industrial nations as a competitor only in
textiles. But by 1985 the Japanese ambassador to the United States
described the new situation succinctly when he said that Japan was so
powerful economically that "the United States and Europe can't compete at all."[12] Nevertheless, and underlining the fact that all structural
conditions are transitional, the change in the value of the yen and the
mounting competition from the NICs had swiftly altered the prospects
of Japanese companies in the world market and those of Japan's internal economy as well.

"Even when the dollar was not overvalued in 1977–78 and early
1979 . . . we were losing market share in manufacturing to Japan and
others in the higher value-added products," noted a professor of busi-

ness at Harvard.[13] This was especially true in electronics. The United States's competitive position in the world market had shifted radically between 1960 and 1980. In the earlier year it supplied 25 percent of the world market and 98 percent of the domestic. By 1980 it had lost 39 percent of its world share. Similarly, its export market share in plastics fell from 27 percent to 13 percent; in drugs, from 27 percent to 15 percent; in agricultural machinery, from 40 percent to 25 percent; textile machinery, from 15 percent to 7 percent; and the like. Even in the high-tech industry category, the United States was by 1984 running a $6.8 billion trade deficit, and the deficit continued to expand at the same rate. In electronics, its deficit with Japan was $15 billion. Nevertheless, the dependence of the whole economy on exports had increased. In 1982, according to the Institute for International Economics, more than 20 percent of all U.S. industrial production was exported, along with 40 percent of the agricultural production, and trade accounted for one-third of all corporate profits.

Discussions of American trade are usually couched in terms that indicate a persistent bias and that give a wrong impression of the process and reasons for its deficit and falling share of world trade. One such opinion, for instance, asserts, "Japan subverted US industry by first supplying cheap parts, then subassemblies, and finally finished products labeled with US brand names."[14] In reality, it is more accurate to say that the U.S. corporations produced abroad or subcontracted for their own account for much of that production. Of the IBM personal computer's manufacturing cost of $860, three-fourths is for imported parts, of which a third is from U.S.-owned plants. As the chairman of Sony noted in 1986, "American companies have either shifted output to low-wage countries or come to buy parts and assembled products from countries like Japan that make quality products at low prices. . . . The U.S. is abandoning its status as an industrial power."[15]

The U.S. export dominance in world trade that existed after World War II began to shift in the early 1960s, as U.S. companies began to manufacture abroad what they had formerly exported. A major turning point came with the Vietnam War, when U.S. industrial production was insufficient for both the war and American demand. Imports then increased dramatically, and U.S. industry lost much of its market to others. America's first official trade deficit of the century occurred in 1971.

The growth, prosperity, and economic strength of Europe and Japan had largely depended on foreign trade since the 1950s, and they also took advantage of America's preoccupation with its wars in Asia. By the end of the 1960s there was a trend toward saturation in the industrial markets. Increasing competition and rising costs, especially those of labor, propelled corporations to seek lower labor costs on the periphery of Europe and in the Third World.

Some TNCs freely proclaim that they overcame the foreign competition simply by becoming part of it. In fact, while the U.S. economy's competitive position declined, that of its TNCs increased. In addition to establishing their own affiliates, some, especially the conglomerates like Litton Industries, also buy shares of existing competitors. But their growing control of international trade has forestalled, though not prevented, growing protectionism.

Other factors that have reduced America's share of world trade include U.S. government political policies, such as boycotts of the USSR. When Carter restricted wheat sales to the USSR in 1980, the U.S. market share fell from 74 percent before the embargo to 20 percent in 1983. Other political policies with negative effects on trade shares were the pipeline technology restrictions, a general boycott of soybean exports in 1971, monetary policies, and tariffs, protecting one industry and leading to retaliation against others—all have had a permanent effect on the U.S. export trade.

RIVALRIES AND CONFLICT

Agriculture has always been the major area of transatlantic trade conflict. Referring to the EEC's farm subsidies in 1982, the U.S. deputy secretary of agriculture said, "The world is not big enough for us to both operate, not with the policies we have today. . . . We're clearly on a collision course."[16] Washington then prepared to dump $3 billion worth of surplus dairy products on the world market to "retaliate" against EC policies.[17] The 1985 farm export bill provided for the systematic underpricing of the huge American agricultural stockpile in the world market. The tensions erupted again when Spain joined the Common Market, reducing its agricultural imports from the United States at a critical moment of oversupply of grain in the world market. National rivalries are also rife in the issue of the access and control of high technology.

The GATT meeting of November 1982, called to avert a trade war, was described at the time as "a near disaster" or as "good theatre" characterized by "inflamatory rhetoric" and threats of retaliation.[18] For Europeans these are vital issues. The strength of the dollar allowed export prices to increase faster than domestic prices in Europe. Between 1983 and 1985 U.S. demand for European exports provided the major source of recovery for European business and profits; when that market subsided, there was no domestic demand and no market in OPEC or the debt-ridden LDCs to replace it.

By 1985 the American government, frustrated by a lack of progress in GATT, had shifted from multilateral to bilateral trade negotiations, introducing selective free trade with some countries, starting with Israel and then Canada. In its negotiations with Canada in 1986, the United States essentially demanded a rollback in Canadian welfare legislation, claiming it gave a subsidy to Canadian business that American business did not have. But this step toward creating trade blocs was foiled by the protectionist moves in Congress.

Trade was linked to other political questions as well. In order to offset rising American sentiment for protectionism, the Japanese foreign minister in 1982 stressed Japan's cooperation on other questions of U.S. policy toward such areas as the Soviet Union, Asia, the Middle East, Central America, and the Caribbean and emphasized its role as a reliable ally. Although advocating "export restraint" from Japan, the United States in 1985 resisted the Japanese business association Keidanren's proposal of an export tax and instead insisted on a greater share of the Japanese market for U.S. exports. "[T]he trade relationship between Japan and the U.S. is at its worst since the war" and threatens to "cause a schism in our alliance," Shintaro Abe, the former foreign minister, said in 1987.[19]

The American practice of looking at the final balance of trade and then demanding that the other nation "do something" to reduce the surplus is a political gesture aimed at domestic constituencies suffering from competition. It has nothing to do with the realities of international trade. The so-called enormous trade imbalances reflect the impossibility of analyzing trade by means of the traditional categories. As one Japanese economist pointed out, if the calculations are based on the production of U.S. vs. Japanese companies, the balance is about equal. U.S. companies producing in Japan sold $44 billion worth of goods plus $25 billion imported from the United States. Japanese companies sold $69 billion, of which $12 billion was produced in the United States. And $15 billion worth of U.S. imports from Japan are components produced under contract expressly for American companies. Much of the trade imbalance comes from U.S. companies that produce abroad for export to the United States.[20] This accounts for nearly all of the $11 billion trade surplus of Taiwan, which Washington also pressed to open its market to correct the trade imbalance. But by 1987 there were clear indications that there would be a "hollowing" in Japan as well. Despite the American rantings at Japan over the auto trade, the worsening deficit was attributable mainly to Canada, where American companies completely control the industry. And in consumer goods the deficit increase was primarily with the Asian NICs. And ironically at one point, as economist Gerald Helleimer noted, "the U.S. actually attempted to induce Japan to impose 'voluntary *import* restraints' on particular U.S. . . . exports in pursuit of U.S. internal policy objectives."[21]

But the U.S. position has always been that all the responsibility for the American trade deficit should be placed at the door of other nations, that they must make basic adjustments and that no domestic solution was necessary, except for an offensive against the American workers in the form of demands for concessions to increase competitiveness. But much of the trade struggle was increasingly between its own capitalists, who often own the competitive imports and who distort their export prices for tax advantages, and those other interests that are adversely affected by the competition.

SUBSIDIES

State subsidies in 1980 financed a significant percentage of the exports of the industrial countries—the United States subsidized 18 percent; France, 34 percent; the United Kingdom, 35 percent; and Japan, 39 percent. The bulk of these subsidies went to aid the largest TNCs.[22] The OECD gave the following illustration of the chain of subsidies that it believes distorted world trade: "The developed country of origin gives its investment guarantee; the countries supplying the capital goods grant long-term credits on soft terms; the infrastructure is financed . . . by the host government or by development assistance; the host country grants tax relief and export aids [and all create] customs codes that facilitate sub-contracting abroad."[23] The OECD considered its members responsible for the resulting crisis of their own domestic industries, which could no longer compete either in the world market or at home.

But with the debt crisis in the LDCs, the export guarantees backfired on the deficit-ridden OECD governments. By the end of 1983 the FRG, Britain and France were losing hundreds of millions of dollars annually and suspended coverage in rescheduling countries. Japan had already eliminated insurance coverage for exports to Brazil. As the LDCs renegotiated, the export guarantees of the OECD contributed to the government deficits and fiscal crisis in the OECD countries. The governments raised the insurance premiums, yet most countries ultimately had no choice, given the competition, but to continue the subsidies to maintain their market share.

The TNCs had long practiced a form of subsidization in which one affiliate's profits underwrote losses elsewhere, usually in the process of gaining a greater market share in the subsidized area. During the debt crisis they were also forced to assist their branches in those areas requiring foreign exchange.

Although world trade expanded 9 percent in 1984, it grew by less than 3 percent in 1985. There was a clear capital shortage to finance trade in the indebted LDCs. Local banks usually underwrite export-import contracts, but by the mid-1980s many lacked the foreign exchange to do so. The seller must then finance the sale. Without the export guarantees of their own governments, the private export credits necessary for the indebted LDCs to finance essential imports disappeared or sharply declined, as did the volume of world trade.

In 1985 the United States introduced a $2 billion export bonus plan, lowering its price supports so that U.S. farmers could gain a larger share of the world market and giving an undisclosed amount of U.S. surplus to the giant agribusiness exporters at no cost. The move brought immediate accusations from other grain-exporting countries that the United States was dumping grain on the world market. U.S. rice subsidies, estimated at $1 billion annually, undermined the price of Thai rice, thereby threatening to reduce by one-fourth the market of Thailand, where peasants make up 70 percent of the population. The Europeans, especially the French, have subsidized their farm exports to the Middle East and Latin America. The Japanese government has subsidized turnkey plant exports to the LDCs, although they are frequently less willing to transfer the technology than the Europeans or Americans, and objectively, the economic development of the LDCs is most threatening to the interests of Japan. Originally its markets, the NICs rapidly emerged as its primary competitors. Yet the government encouraged export of plants, principally for assembly, while continually upgrading technology in Japan itself.

PROTECTIONISM

"In the end we are all nation states and the prime responsibility of nation states is towards their own people, not to the abstract ideal of free trade," the British trade secretary Edmund Dell warned the Japanese.[24] In Europe the president of the EC said in late 1982, "At a time when the unemployed in the community run into millions, no government can afford to be guided by theoretical models of . . . free trade at any price."[25]

New forms of restrictions to protect threatened sectors with nontariff barriers that some have dubbed neoprotectionism have emerged to supplement better-known means of defending national markets. By

1983 about 50 percent of all international trade was subject to some form of quantitative restriction. "Voluntary restraint" agreements on steel and unilateral shifts in textile and apparel are recent U.S. forms of neoprotectionism. All the bilateral negotiations that are tailored to the needs of particular industries politicize trade even more than do general tariffs.

Japan has high tariffs on value-added products and on many agricultural goods. Like most industrial nations, it had been strongly protectionist in the formative years of its industry, banning car imports until 1962 to protect the development of its auto industry. In a poll of the LDC representatives in GATT in 1984, all said that Japan was the most protectionist and that Europe stood midway between it and the United States, the least protectionist of the three. Despite this viewpoint, in the United States in 1984 roughly 45 percent of manufactured imports met some sort of trade barriers, compared with 22 percent for Japan. And demand from affected industries for additional protection increased greatly in the 1980s.

The various interests in the U.S. economy have always struggled over the issue of protectionism. An American Soybean Association official was quoted in 1984 as saying, "We export two-thirds of our wheat, one-half of our soybeans and cotton, and one-third of our corn. So we farmers potentially have more to lose from import restrictions than the protectionists have to gain."[26] The farmers have joined the importers to resist the textile, steel, and labor lobbyists. Since many of the protectionist targets are the nations most indebted to the commercial banks, the banks, too, have used their influence to oppose trade restrictions.

Despite the obvious linkage of the trade deficit to the exchange rates, the pressure in Congress, which saw some three hundred bills for protection in 1985, intensified. In trade negotiations the Americans continually uses the threat that Congress will impose the worst protectionist scenario in order to extract concessions from others. And although the Reagan administration was doctrinally committed to free trade, the pressures were such that it installed more import controls than any other administration since the 1920s.

The Japanese response to protectionism elsewhere was increasingly to invest in the protected area, either directly or through joint ventures. Not only the giants took this course; smaller companies that had previously produced only in Japan did so too. The restraints on exports also increase competition in the home market, and with the appreciation of the yen the giant corporations demand concessions from their subcontractors, greatly aggravating the latters' already tenuous existence.

THE NEW INTERNATIONAL DIVISION
OF LABOR

Both the industrialized countries and the Third World are dependent on trade with each other. About 28 percent of the OECD nations' aggregate exports in 1982 went to the Third World. German industry was sustained in the first two years of the decade by the LDC markets. In 1982 the LDCs imported 40 percent of all U.S. exports. The Americans sold more to the non-OPEC developing countries than to the EC and the CPEs combined. Seven of the most indebted Latin American countries had purchased nearly 14 percent of U.S. exports before 1983. And 42 percent of Japan's total exports were to the LDCs as an aggregate in the mid-1980s. It has been estimated that in 1981 the LDC market compensated by 40 percent for the recessionary contraction in the OECD trade.

The debt crisis and the enforced austerity programs of the past years have changed the LDCs' special role, except in the area of arms sales. Between 1981 and 1983 Argentina reduced its imports by 52 percent, Brazil by 30 percent, and Mexico by 66 percent. These declines, of course, contributed to the U.S. trade deficits. With Mexico alone, the United States had a drop of $12 billion in its exports between 1981 and 1983. Imports were purchased with debt, and then exports were used to repay debt. Between 1980 and 1982 the ten major debtors had a near balance of trade. The LDCs' exports to the United States advanced in nearly all sectors, capital goods making the greatest advance, as their industries became competitive in all domains. They achieved their balance-of-payments surplus by 1985 primarily by reducing imports. Most of the export gains were in 1983–84; however, this advantage was short-lived, since a shift in the terms of trade came with a fall in commodity prices and growing protection in the major markets.

Brazil's 40 percent increase in exports between 1983 and 1984 went nearly all to the United States. Yet, despite all these gains, their debt service still exceeded the total income from their exports. Since one-half of these exports faced protectionist restrictions in the OECD countries, Brazil also moved to establish closer links with the LDCs, including Cuba and Nicaragua. The slowdown in the U.S. economy in 1985 then cut Brazil's exports 7.5 percent and Mexico's by 15.0 percent. In 1985 there was no increase in aggregate Latin American exports to the United States and a sharp fall in those to Japan.

Industrial products now make up more than half of the exports of goods from India, Pakistan, and Brazil, and from 1970 to 1981 the

share of manufactured products for the LDCs in the aggregate, excluding oil, rose from 22 percent to 51 percent. If the four Asian NICs are
left out, the proportion doubled to 30 percent.

But the most important criterion for the LDCs, especially for the
commodity exporters, is the terms of trade—how many imports their
exports can buy. For the oil-importing LDCs in the aggregate, the terms
of trade declined between 1980 and 1985 by 13 percent, even though
the price of oil, a major import, declined over this period, a trend
canceled by the rising dollar.

All of these world economic developments increase the irreconcila-
ble contradictions in the system. While their economic development
poses a definite competitive threat to the economies of the OECD states,
the LDCs' borrowing and importing to achieve development has at the
same time also been crucial to the economic recovery in the industrial
countries.

EXPORT-ORIENTED STRATEGY

Export-oriented development became the rallying cry of the IMF/
World Bank, using the model of the NICs in Asia—South Korea,
Taiwan, Hong Kong, and Singapore. According to the head of the
Institute of Developing Economies, in Tokyo, the industrial growth in
East Asia was "unprecedented in world economic development."[27]
Almost one-half of all Third World exports in 1975 were from these
four countries. Of those, two are city-states. In nearly all cases, the
IMF/World Bank advised its members with balance-of-payments prob-
lems to adopt this policy. Like most capitalist strategies, it evolved out
of an ad hoc response to objective conditions. In reality, in the early
stages, import growth outweighed export growth in the "Four Drag-
ons," which later became the models for export orientation.

There are various types of export strategies. One is related to a
value-added strategy of those countries whose principal exports are raw
materials. They began to insist that the TNCs extracting the materials
build processing plants in the country. The companies at first opposed
this, but with the advent of pollution control laws in their home countries, certain industries encouraged it. Some states, such as Brazil and
South Korea, also built export-oriented capital goods industries in the
mid-1970s, offering new competition in the world market independent
of TNC control.

With the inception of TNC investment for cheap labor in manufacturing, at the end of the 1960s, there was a race in Asia to establish
the free-trade zones and export-oriented development strategies. This

occurred despite all the evidence that in the existing structure of world production it contributes nearly nothing to development, since the investment is so marginal, the process so fragmented, the employment so restricted, and the impact on the overall economy so distorted. At the same time, it creates great expense and, usually, a debt burden for the host country, which builds the infrastructure to service these investments. The electronics industry's investment did nothing for male unemployment, since the firms usually hire young women for the hazardous work, commonly discarding them as disabled after a few years and hiring others from the vast reserve of labor. Foreign-currency earnings were usually eradicated by the costs and concessions. Since prices and profits were manipulated within the TNCs, the capital drain was significant. And while national statistics listed these foreign firms as manufacturers of sophisticated equipment, in reality the process consisted of only a few semiskilled tasks on partial components for further assembly elsewhere for global sales.

The world market determines the form and extent of capitalist development of the individual nations, nearly all of whom should have learned that export-led development is beyond their control. The Vietnam War, and then the U.S. market from 1981 to 1985, because of the currency exchange, created a huge demand for the products of the Asian NICs. In 1985 the United States bought 50 percent of Taiwan's exports, 45 percent of Hong Kong's, 35–40 percent of Korea's. But the economic slowdown in the United States in that year reduced the growth in the Asian countries dependent on the U.S. market. The protectionist mood in the United States led to the removal of duty-free status in 1986.

Export orientation generally refers to the LDCs' development strategies, but in fact it is the economic strategy of most industrialized nations. World trade is crucial in their economies, and the expansion of this competition leads to rivalry and conflict. As competitive weapons, the various states use subsidies to promote their exports and various forms of protectionism against imports and, at times, a conscious manipulation of currency value to strengthen their trade position.

LABOR EXPORT

State-sponsored labor export became a prime source of foreign exchange for many LDCs over the past decade. The labor-exporting countries received $31 billion in worker remittances in 1980, compared with only $3.8 billion in 1970. For Egypt, Bangladesh, and Pakistan it represented over one-half of the total value of exports, and for Jordan

it is much greater than the sum of all other exports. The official remit-
tance figures are the lowest, since they represent only the recorded
transfer through the banking system, whereas a large proportion is
transferred by other means. Korea, the Philippines, Thailand, Bangladesh, and other Asian nations compete in exporting construction
workers; each country receives an average of $230 million yearly in
remittances. The labor exports of the 1970s were the outcome of the
oil price rise, as 2.8 million migrant workers went to Arab OPEC states.
The ILO estimated that 1.0 million were from Asia in 1981. West
European recruitment halted in the mid-1970s, and the exporting countries on the periphery of Europe were affected sharply. In Turkey, one
of the most dependent, remittances fell by over 60 percent in 1974–77,
and another 23 percent in 1978, and the economy plummeted into a
severe crisis and had to turn to the IMF for emergency aid. Immigration
to the Arab OPEC nations has fallen with the price of oil. The Middle
East labor-exporting nations are even more vulnerable to an end to
emigration.

The real disadvantages to those nations exporting labor are often
overlooked because of the importance of the migrants' remittances to
their BOPs and their reluctance to welcome the returnees—in part,
because of their high unemployment. Yet a number of studies of the
migrants in Europe showed that a third or more were skilled or semiskilled, especially compared with the remaining workers. Most had
been employed before they left their home countries, and a large proportion had worked in industrial jobs not easily filled by the remaining
workers. Given this drain of skilled workers in a number of countries,
the home countries had to import workers from still other countries. This
was true in the Middle East, Mexico, and the Ivory Coast.

Rural areas lose the most able-bodied workers, decreasing land use
and food production, and peasant families increasingly live on remittances. In the past, in Ireland and Italy, according to one study, "emigration did not shrink the labor surplus and hence unemployment; it
increased unemployment by shrinking the economic base of the
area."[28] Between the 1950 and 1970s, 40 percent of the migrants from
Turkey were skilled workers, and their emigration depleted the construction, shipbuilding, mining, and textile industries. In Greece, where
emigrants were not the unemployed but the younger and more skilled
workers, industrialization was retarded by their exodus. Yugoslavia and
Tunisia also lost a high proportion of their skilled workers. Some
45,000 to 60,000 Pakistanis emigrate every year, and a substantial
majority of them are skilled. A survey of the literature concluded, "All
the exporting countries have had their skilled labour supply, including

employed labour, negatively affected by labour exports."[29] Such emigration can actually aggravate unemployment by handicapping certain industrial sectors. There was a shortage of skilled workers in nearly all the exporting countries, while those who left supplied an industrial reserve army that made possible the period of high economic growth elsewhere. Moreover, there was not necessarily a match of a job to their skills, for many of the skilled or semiskilled performed the menial jobs that in a period of full employment were refused by local workers. It compounded the problem that any skills learned in the host country rarely matched those needed in the home country. But most of the migrant workers who returned were generally the unskilled, and since over 80 percent of the unskilled immigrant workers in Europe remained so, or remained in unskilled jobs, there was no transfer of skills to the home country when they returned.

Repatriation of migrant workers from the OPEC states began in the mid-1980s. "This migration has uprooted people as never before [in the Middle East]. But its end is even more dangerous," claimed an Egyptian political writer.[30] The problem was especially severe for Egypt, the source of 43 percent of all Arab migrant workers and officially the recipient in 1984 of $3.3 billion in remittances. Unofficially, this sum was assumed to be $6–$10 billion, and Egypt's chief source of foreign exchange. Some Egyptians were even working as mercenaries for Iraq in its war with Iran. The political implications of the migrants' return was the subject of a CIA study in 1985, which concluded that it posed a threat to political stability in the area, particularly in Egypt, Jordan, Sudan, and Yemen.

There has occurred an objective restructuring of world trade over the past decade that poses new challenges to governments everywhere. Intrafirm trade, countertrade, and the amorphous trade in services require different evaluations and responses. The goal of each nation has been to export more and to import less and to sharpen its competitive position in the world market. Policies to achieve this goal were put in place in the 1980s throughout the globe.

The trade theories of "comparative advantage" are, in reality, instruments of new forms of imperialism and involve the question of relative power. The reality, as opposed to the theory, would be protectionism for the center and free trade for the periphery. The LDCs depend on growth and developments in the OECD countries, but these economies are in turn dependent on their exports.

Ultimately, states can close their borders to international trade, but only at the cost of world economic collapse. Another alternative, trade blocs, is improbable, since the pattern of trade is global rather than regional. But in the neomercantilist environment where all nations have adopted an "export orientation," where competitiveness in the world market is the standard for restructuring the domestic economies, but where austerity policies and debt have steadily reduced the market, rivalry and conflict must increasingly shape international relations.

CHAPTER 15

RESTRUCTURING THE INDUSTRIAL CAPITALIST STATES

The investment decisions of capital *objectively* restructure the economy, as do developments in monetary relations, debt, and trade. States respond to their consequences with ad hoc measures and develop a strategy. And for the nations in the OECD the goal of the common policy of restructuring the macroeconomy is to renew or encourage the productive investment process in industries that are perceived as competitive and that offer prospects for growth. But state policies can restructure the economy only indirectly. Their efforts have become yet another factor in the political economy, interacting with all the others. The final outcome is rarely as planned. But by the 1980s governments of all political persuasions were questioning the whole spectrum of state intervention in the economy that had emerged in the postwar period, ranging from nationalizations to subsidies and regulations. The reasons for these reassessments reflected both political bias and certain objective realities.

The former chief economist of the OECD, Sylvia Ostry, claimed in 1983 that a country's ability to adapt to the new economic environment of slow growth and falling living standards and an end to "increasing income, good jobs and better and more forever" was the crucial question of this decade.[1] After concluding that a political choice had to be made between providing "social justice" and restructuring the OECD economies for competitiveness in the world market by reducing labor costs and lowering living standards, the OECD's *Interfutures* noted, "One thing is certain; the choice cannot ignore the fact that today's industrialized societies are becoming minority societies in a changing world."[2]

"The 1970s witnessed profound changes in commonly accepted views regarding the role the central authorities should play in the economy . . . ," the IMF wrote in its 1980 report. "One basic postulate concerned the 'fine tuning' view of economic policy, the failure of which became obvious in the course of the 1970s. . . . [I]t became clear that direction of fiscal and monetary policies toward the achievement and maintenance of unduly low unemployment rates can be very costly in terms of inflation. . . ."[3] Prolonged austerity with proposed statutory wage limits and tight monetary policies to assure growth rates low enough to crush inflation were required in the restructuring process. Once inflation was crushed, such policies were needed to prevent its resurgence.

There was by the 1980s a general consensus among government decision makers that the democratic nations had been too lax and had lacked the discipline to impose austerity in the early 1970s. The major difficulty is persuading democracies to accept long periods of unemployment, the BIS reported in 1980. One year later it concluded, "[M]any if not most governments now appear to believe that restrictive demand management offers the main—and perhaps the only—hope of a gradual return to more satisfactory levels of unemployment."[4]

Any survey of the OECD literature reveals that the key themes are structural adjustment, restructuring, rigidities, deregulation, privatization, and the like. There are new definitions of full employment and of "normal" unemployment. There are also proposals, particularly in the EEC, for new industrial policies to adapt the economies to the new structural changes through the development of high-technology industries to replace the older noncompetitive ones.

Restructuring took the form of the state's withdrawal from direct participation in some aspects of the economy, as in Britain, or an industrial policy to shift the economy away from certain industries and toward others—or a combination of both. Monetarists dominated policy-making in the conservative governments. As the free-market ideologues acquired powerful positions in the Reagan administration, the United States proclaimed fiscal conservatism for others but pursued a spendthrift policy of arms expenditures, creating a budget deficit that threatened the entire world's financial stability. But as a former head of the Budget Bureau, David Stockman, described it, politics inhibited the full implementation of the ideology, even though the administration was able to cut the already meager social benefits of millions of Americans and push them further into poverty.

In their anti-inflation policies, the various governments deliberately chose to ignore the real factors that caused inflation and instead used these policies as a weapon against the working class, reinforcing the efforts of capital to lower labor costs.

Restructuring became a dominant theme among European governments in their search for an exit from the economic dilemmas that have afflicted them all. The French government established its Interministerial Committee to Restructure; Helmut Schmidt developed *Strukturpolitik* in 1978, intending it to be high tech, market oriented, and financed by a proposed European investment bank. Governments, constrained by their fiscal crisis, as well as motivated by their ideology, moved to dismantle welfare provisions, deregulate the financial sector, and to sell off state enterprises. Deregulation has further encouraged extravagant financial speculation.

But the most important aspects of restructuring were the measures against the working class. In all cases it involved a conscious policy to shift national income shares from labor to enhance the profitability of capital. By April 1985 the Belgian prime minister was able to report to an international investment conference that the key to Belgium's "strategy for recovery" was parliament's decision to make it easier to hire and fire workers and its move away from the indexing of wages. The Dutch prime minister, for his part, indicated that all parties agreed on the need for wage restraint and for reductions in social welfare and government spending. European government leaders participating in the meeting all said they had "learned a lesson" regarding the negative effects of wage and welfare support in their competition for investment capital.[5] In fact, the labor share in the national income of all the OECD countries fell steadily after 1979.

The American Under Secretary of State for Economic Affairs Allen Wallis noted, "[M]y European colleagues identify structural problems as major reasons for Europe's failure . . . such problems as overly generous unemployment and employee benefits packages, rigid hiring and firing practices. . . ."[6] One official EEC study called for greater reliance on part-time jobs and homework.

But the contradiction remained that an unemployment rate of 13 percent for the EEC was excessive even as an instrument of wage control and was costly to the state in terms of compensation payments and falling tax revenue. European governments have therefore tried to encourage the "entrepreneurs," convening conferences of government economists in Europe in 1986. "Entrepreneurship increasingly is viewed as the way of helping us get out of economic difficulty," commented an official of the German foreign ministry.[7] France has paid the unemployed worker his or her benefits in a lump sum for start-up capital of a new business, organizing "business shops" to offer the know-how. Britain, with Italy and Ireland, proposed a formal policy to the EEC in 1986 to encourage one-person businesses and unemployed youth to start their own companies. Eliminating "Sabbath laws" and other protective labor "rigidities" is increasingly the means to promote the growth of entrepreneurship and to encourage "venture capital." "Europe has made a start on reforms that promote employers' flexibility . . . ," a Morgan Guaranty economist observed with satisfaction in June 1985, "making it somewhat easier for employers to lay off workers and to use part-time help."[8]

"Since the late 1970s a central aim of governments in most industrial countries has been to limit the share of government expenditure in GNP . . . and increase the share of saving available to finance investment by the private sector," noted the IMF in its 1985 report.[9] The IMF went on to summarize the restructuring policies of the industrial countries as

modifying or reforming many of the institutional arrangements that impede adjustments in real wages, raise the costs to firms of hiring and releasing workers, and reduce the incentive to work. Common modifications have been to reduce the extent to which incomes are . . . adjusted to price increases, to exclude items such as energy and indirect taxes from wage-regulating price indices . . . lowering of minimum wages, the limitation of unemployment benefits, the extension of occupational training schemes, reductions in subsidies, deregulation, and the "privatization" of some public enterprises.[10]

In Japan the government has always worked explicitly to set the framework for economic developments. In the 1950s it had already made the decision to move out of labor-intensive, simple technologies, such as textiles, and in the 1970s and 1980s it consciously defined the areas of specialization for the future. It never invested in the social infrastructure, as did the Europeans, and so it had few such policies to reverse. It did provide regulations and protection for the various industrial and agricultural interests to facilitate the accumulation of capital. These regulations were the target of much international pressure, particularly from the United States.

DEREGULATION

Deregulation of financial markets, telecommunications, and transport spread from the United States to other regions of the capitalist world as part of the restructuring in the 1980s. The timing of the international efforts at deregulation could not have been worse, as the threat of massive debt defaults, the trend toward recession in the two largest capitalist economies, a free-fall of commodity prices, and the dangers of deflation all moved the world economy closer to breakdown. Regulation of the financial markets had initially been to guarantee the safety of the banks and protect depositors. Deregulation only aggravated the existing chaos in capital flows, with their perverse effect on the currency exchange rates, and increased the risks to banking. It gave added license to financial traders, to the immense disadvantage of other capitalist interests and the entire world system. But while technology has been more instrumental than policy in the deregulation of the financial markets, many regulations now being deliberately dismantled, had bought time and provided the thin line separating anarchy from total chaos.

The United States applied considerable diplomatic pressure on the Japanese to deregulate their financial markets by eliminating interest rate ceilings on deposits and allowing the domestic banks to compete for foreign funds, in this way pushing up the value of the yen. Such changes made it more difficult for smaller banks to compete with the largest. It also was intended to open Japan to foreign banks eager to tap its huge pension funds.

Some countries, such as Austria, after a brief period desperately tried to restore regulations and undo some of the damage resulting from a series of deregulations. There were also hurried ad hoc meetings of the Group of Five to try to patch up the damage. States still had to rescue failed banks. And in early 1987 official alarm over the mounting risks in the banks led Washington and London to move to standardize their banking regulations that would allow regulators to set a minimum capital ratio for each individual bank based on an evaluation of risk. In a number of OECD governments, a textbook faith in competition in the internal economy was contradictory to a desire to have companies strong and large enough to compete internationally.

Deregulation of the financial sector implied an abandonment of policy-making or acknowledged the impotence of the state, given certain structural changes in the economy. It also contributed to a situation that got progressively out of control and was eventually feared by even the most ardent supporters of the policy. By 1986 the danger inherent in the multiple new forms of high-risk speculation was sufficiently alarming to convince the BIS of the urgent need for more controls. But it was too late. Between the new technology and the competition among states to keep the profitable business within their borders, the governments would not yield to the warnings of their central bankers before the inevitable calamity.

PRIVATIZATION

One ironic aspect of the present time is that, after a decade of failures, capital is being coaxed and cajoled everywhere to resume the unfettered operations of an economics textbook image of the economy. Historically, the state's role in a capitalist crisis was to assume the costs of the unprofitable economic sectors through subsidies or nationalization or to provide financing to important national companies when internal or bank financing was inadequate. Public sector enterprises grew with nationalizations after World War II, reaching a peak in the 1950s. The state's share of fixed capital ranged from 4 percent in the United States to 17 percent in the United Kingdom and Australia, the average in the OECD states being 11 percent in 1980. Most capitalist countries therefore have a mixture of state and privately owned industries, especially in steel, banks, transport, and arms—with crucial subsidies for others. The U.S. government in recent years rescued Chrysler and Lockheed and essentially nationalized Continental Illinois. One giant Canadian TNC, Massey-Ferguson, appealed for and got state aid in 1980. Research and development have been financed largely by the state in both the United States and Japan. In Europe the state's involvement in the accumulation process was considerably more extensive, especially in France, Italy, Spain, the United Kingdom, and Sweden. The state, in most cases, intervened either at the behest of capital or as an alternative to bankruptcy, not in conflict with the principle of private accumulation.

Contracting to private companies or licensing them to provide public services has been common in many nations in the past. The United States, as may be expected, uses this form more than any other country, and in 1980 state and local governments spent $68 billion on a variety of such services—from refuse collection and day care to urban transport. Scandinavian countries contract for fire and ambulance services. Such activities have generally been uncontroversial and been motivated by pragmatic rather than ideological justifications. Most significantly, as a number of studies have shown, such activities have no social welfare or redistributive function.

But many governments in the 1980s expected capital to assume a greater role, as they tried to "privatize" the public sector for both fiscal and ideological reasons. As the deficits grew and revenues shrank, governments everywhere began to scrutinize expenditures. Should the public sector be evaluated by social or profit criteria? Could countries afford the welfare state? Should the state finance its services with user fees rather than with taxation? The questions were political, of course. Basic public services do not return profits. In some cases such retrenchment efforts led to sharp cutbacks, and in a number of countries privatization has become a part of an aggressive ideological struggle and restructuring offensive against the working class. This latter viewpoint has dominated the international organizations, Britain, and the United States.

The Thatcher government in Britain began its program of privatization on a large scale in 1979, but in most cases it retained a significant interest in the companies. Other nations have followed. Japan is selling the national railway, one of the few state-owned companies, parts of Nippon Telegraph and Telephone, 35 percent of Japan Airlines, and the tobacco monopoly. France, the FRG, Italy, the Netherlands, and Canada are denationalizing many of their state industries. By 1986 fifteen states had announced plans to sell some 250 state-owned companies. As the IMF concluded in its 1985 report, "the longstanding tendency toward continual expansion of the role of the government in the major industrial economies is finally being arrested" and even reversed.[11] The French, even before the Socialists were defeated, were trying to denationalize many profitable companies whose internal structure had been rationalized, usually by job reductions, during the years of state ownership. But that there was not unanimity among businessmen on the desirability of this wave of privatization was revealed in a German bank's refusal to continue to finance KLM if the Dutch government reduced its ownership below 50 percent.

So many governments were trying to privatize such a large number of companies simultaneously that there were problems on some stock exchanges and alarm that they would "crowd out" the stock issues of existing private firms. In selling British Telecom for $4.5 billion, the United Kingdom had to use New York, Tokyo, and European as well as London exchanges. But by 1986 the Thatcher administration had realized $20 billion through its sell-offs. And the investment bankers underwriting such sales reaped fees in the hundreds of millions.

There are many facets to the vogue of privatization that has prevailed in the world economy during the 1980s. Among the elements stimulating it are the objective imperatives of debts and deficits, the ideological component, and the special interests that in some cases have been able to acquire "bargains," including the investment banks. But only successful industries are of interest to the private investors, who despite entreaties have stubbornly refused to buy unprofitable enterprises. Another goad, particularly in the United States, has been the tax "revolt" of the middle class. Beginning in 1978 in California, where the real estate industry mobilized frustrated home owners to back a referendum lowering property taxes by 60 percent, the movement spread to twelve other states and exerted important pressure on the political parties.

George Shultz, an economist before he was secretary of state, noted with satisfaction in December 1985 the direction most governments were moving in:

> . . .[P]erhaps the wise perceptions of Adam Smith two centuries ago are once again gaining practical prominence. . . . There is a new skepticism about statist solutions, central planning, and government control. . . . And this economic wisdom isn't culture-bound either. We see on every continent—Western Europe, East Asia, Latin America, and Africa—movement to decentralize, to deregulate, to denationalize, to reduce rigidities in labor markets, and to enlarge the scope . . . to interact freely in open markets.[12]

Beyond these generalities, the United States demanded that other nations adopt expansionary policies within this framework in order, presumably, to avoid an aggravation of the world debt, trade, and monetary crises. According to the U.S. representative to the OECD, Shultz has made reducing the "rigidities" in the labor market and general deregulation the centerpiece of America's economic relations with Europe and Japan.[13]

Washington has called for "structural adjustment" of the European economies in order to break down protectionist barriers and reduce subsidies in trade competition, particularly in agriculture, telecommunications, and steel. It has also criticized the state-guided industrial policy approach to restructuring, advocating instead deregulation and allowing the private market to determine investment priorities.

Ideologically, the process of privatization is obviously very desirable for the interests of capital, since it opens new areas to its exploitation and offers a wide choice of concessions to attract and hold investment. But, to repeat, capitalists do not invest because of exhortation or ideology, or even generous incentives; they invest because they expect to profit. Ironically, in the mid-1980s investors were turning to the bonds of sovereign borrowers and state-owned entities for a safe haven.

INDUSTRIAL POLICY: SCIENCE AND TECHNOLOGY

There is now in many nations a strategy to use science and technology to restructure the economy to resolve the crisis. But in a capitalist society this policy carries the seeds of a future impasse. Along with the myth that the new technology was somehow recession proof came the perception, shared by many local and national governments, that the new industries would replace the employment lost in the traditional "smokestack" industries. Some 4,500 communities in the United States, and many in Europe, began to compete for high-tech industries, defined by the state of Connecticut as "any industry that is going to create jobs in the 1980s and 1990s."[14] Four midwestern states in the United States spent $300 million between 1983 and 1985 on incentives to high-tech entrepreneurs.

Confounding their strategy, however, is the fact that, in the aggregate, high technology is contractionary, not expansionary, in employment—that is, it eliminates far more jobs in the general economy than it creates. For example, the robot industry is expected to create 3,000 to 5,000 jobs and eliminate 50,000 in the auto industry alone. The entire high-tech industry in the United States is expected to account for 4 percent of all nonagricultural employment in 1993, up from 3 percent in 1979.

The EEC has also created its cooperative science and technology program, ESPRIT, to prevent foreign dominance in what it perceived to be a strategic technology. Reagan's pipeline boycott fiasco in 1982 further deepened the EEC's concern over technological dependence.

In May 1983 Etienne Davignon, the EEC industry commissioner, urged the member governments to invest in the research effort for ESPRIT, originally proposed in May 1982, claiming it was Europe's last chance to remain competitive. Europe's share of the world integrated-circuits market had fallen to 7 percent, from 13 percent in 1979, and even had only one-third of the European market. Yet it was not until January 1985 that the EEC finally inaugurated ESPRIT, choosing 270 companies, universities, and research labs and allocating $1 billion over ten years. Their research is to focus on microelectronics, computers, office automation, and robotization. It is obviously a highly competitive area that all states are emphasizing simultaneously.

The French made another effort in 1985 to organize European cooperation in high-tech R & D, dubbed Eureka, and eighteen countries joined the effort. The French committed one billion francs at the first meeting in July 1985. In November the British and West Germans had made financial commitments, and the FRG is trying to lure new industry to its "rust belt" sector in the north and establish it as a site for the EEC cooperative Eureka projects. But the Italians, Dutch, and Belgians wanted protection against a "rich big-nation club" of France, Britain, and the FRG.[15] "The future competitiveness of all businesses operating from Europe is at stake in this clash between 'national versus European' in telecommunications," asserted the Round Table, an organization of twenty of the largest European corporations.[16] These companies had become the "most ardent supporters of a United Europe," according to EEC president, Jacques Delors.[17]

"The nations that develop the new planetary communications will command economic and even political power in the next century," warned the former French interior minister Michael Poniatowski in a European parliament report.[18] Telecommunications is an area in which Europe, the United States, and Japan are roughly equal and in which the EEC actually had a surplus in trade. But since all are seeking to specialize in the same products, as prone to intense and destructive competition as any capitalist industry, it further intensifies their rivalry. Davignon later said, "Europe deplorably missed a great opportunity when we omitted the military dimension from Eureka."[19] It was the only way, he believed, to mobilize the whole scientific community and the funds.

SOCIALISTS IN POWER

Turning back the clock in welfare and labor legislation was a logical outcome of the conservative perspective. Despite past evidence, however, there were great promises and expectations for the socialists parties in power. As one reviewer of the OECD's McCracken report wrote in 1978, "Calling for more sacrifices by ordinary people in order to increase profits and thus preserve capitalism hardly constitutes a brilliant rallying cry for a new majority." But he was sadly premature when he concluded, "It is difficult to imagine French socialists, Italian communists, or British trade unionists joining readily in a 'consensus' on the need for higher profits."[20] By the 1980s they were indeed.

In the mid-1970s the most distinctive aspect of the European social democrats was their commitment "first and foremost, and primarily [to] jobs, jobs and more jobs," as Chancellor Kreisky of Austria asserted.[21] But by the 1980s there was a virtual consensus among the conservative parties in the United States and the United Kingdom and the socialists and communists in Western Europe on austerity for the working class and on the need for greater profits as an incentive to investment in order to restructure the economy. The left parties neither perceived nor conceived of an alternative to the capitalist system. In fact, capitalist programs in their crudest form had regained hegemony everywhere, irrespective of ideology.

The would-be reformers in power decided that they, too, must "adapt" to the reality and the discipline of the world economy and restructure their national economies to survive within the system by obeying the same "laws" as their predecessors. Reformist restructuring they found to be undermined by the free flow of capital internationally. The laws of capitalism, to its former critics, had become "economic laws." The problems expanded in scope as they accepted the global integration, and the possibility of pursuing socialist goals was made more elusive.

One crucial feature of the current situation is that the former reformists have dropped even Keynesian reform, as they embrace the draconian restructuring prescriptions of their predecessors for the renewal of capitalist accumulation. "We used to think that you could just spend your way out of a recession. . . . I tell you in all candour that that option no longer exists and that insofar as it ever did exist, it worked by injecting inflation into the economy," the British Labour prime minister declared in 1976.[22] The Labour government subsequently slashed spending on social expenditures and channeled funds to the relief of industry, "recognizing," according to one Labour official, that an "adequate return on capital is a precondition to economic growth."[23] In the mid-1970s incomes policy meant protecting capital. The Swedish Social Democrats had managed to keep high employment through enormous subsidies to private corporations in the form of low taxes. The Swedish "welfare state" had been very profitable for foreign business. In 1973 Sweden's five most profitable companies were foreign owned, and some of them, such as Union Carbide, earned 43 percent on their investment.

In France by 1984 the rhetoric of "austerity" and "profitability" had replaced even the radical *vocabulary* of the Socialists' 1981 campaign. The finance minister remarked, "We want to have wages rise more slowly than prices in order to curb consumer purchasing power and increase profitability."[24] The same approach was articulated wherever the Socialists were in power in Europe. "There is no alternative. Austerity has no political color anymore," said the socialist governor of Portugal's central bank.[25] Under the IMF's direction, Portuguese real wages fell and food subsidies ended. "The road to socialism no longer passes through the welfare-statism of the 1950s and '60s. Today, socialist goals require restructuring the economy, improving competitiveness. Those are difficult, painful things," asserted the socialist finance minister of Greece.[26] But his adherence to wage indexing while import costs and the deficit and foreign debt were rising, particularly as a result of increased arms expenditures, led to his replacement with a more conservative minister. By mid-1986 the Greek government had introduced austerity measures, wage controls, and new incentives to attract foreign investment. The outcome was strikes from the working class and little new investment, as business insisted on more concessions. The Spanish Socialist economy minister reiterated, "I have consistently said that macroeconomics recognizes neither right nor left. When there is a negative balance of payments or inflation the government reacts in the same manner whether it is right or left. . . . In macroeconomics there's only success or failure."[27] On the other side of the world, in New Zealand, the Labour finance minister lowered income taxes on the upper bracket nearly 30 percent and added a 10 percent sales tax: "the business community has generally been favorable to the market-oriented approach taken by the [Labour] government," he said. He saw nothing incompatible between socialism and the free market but added, "It's a question, of course, of your definition of socialism."[28]

What the various socialist ministers were saying is, in fact, accurate. It is a real contradiction that the governments confront, for they have no way out *within* the system. In the real world of economic events, as opposed to economic models, there are no "hard" (orthodox) or "soft" (Keynesian or social democratic) techniques for management of the crisis in the capitalist system. This becomes much clearer in times of crisis, as does the role of the reformist state in the system. But the vigor with which the socialists of Europe have forced the working class to pay for this process in unemployment and sharply reduced living standards has often exceeded even that of the bourgeois parties that preceded them and has eliminated their electoral promise that they would at least attempt to protect the workers by reforming the system, if not by changing it.

FRANCE

France is the largest state in Europe that had a socialist government in the 1980s. The French Socialists came to power in coalition with the Communist party around the "Common Program" of social redistribution, nationalization, and other reforms. Hence it is useful to examine very briefly some of the dilemmas that it faced in implementing the program and that led to its well-known failure.

The policies of the left Common Program, what has been termed "Keynesianism with investment control," might have been implemented in France between 1950 and 1974, when there was an unprecedented economic growth rate. To a limited extent, Keynesianism had been characteristic of French governments since World War II. But the Left came to power, as always, during crisis conditions. In a period of

world economic crisis within a capitalist context, its program encountered fundamental contradictions.[29] Whether desirable or not, reforms
cannot alter the intrinsic features of the capitalist system.

The Socialists in France tried to implement the Common Program
during their first year by nationalizing the "commanding heights" of
the economy, including all the banks and nine industrial groups, and
they increased mass consumption somewhat with an enlarged welfare
program. The primary purpose of the nationalization was to direct
investment. Pursuing an expansionary program and introducing some
redistributive reforms, the government at first ignored international
conditions, except for its unwarranted assumption that a recovery
would begin in the United States in the spring of 1982 and that a
subsequent general world recovery would carry France along with it.
Contrary to their expectations, the recession became more severe in
1982—in the United States it was the worst since the Great Depression.
Naturally, the French capitalists had no inclination to invest and instead sent their capital out of the country. An enormous trade deficit
of 100 billion francs in 1981 was compounded by the falling value of
the franc and led to its devaluation within the EEC. Inflation wiped out
the effects of devaluation, imports rose with the increase in demand,
industrial production stagnated, unemployment rose, and France's international accounts were termed "disastrous." Some 54 percent of its
debt and 30 percent of its imports were denominated in the rising
dollar. As late as May 1982, in response to the call of other OECD
countries for uniform policies of austerity, the finance minister still
proposed that each country go its own way in economic policy.

In June 1982, however, the Socialists did a 180-degree turn and
followed the rest of the OECD with austerity policies. Planning Minister
Michel Rocard declared, "We have paid a high price to learn the
realities of living in a highly interdependent world economy."[30] The
response was austerity (euphemistically called solidarity), another
devaluation, wage and price controls, and the elimination of wage
indexing. "We are the first major industrialized country to successfully
fight indexation," boasted the finance minister.[31] In November 1982
one bank economist noted that the French Socialists had "turned into
the most conservative socialists in Europe."[32] They became more rigorous in restructuring, even initiating massive closures in the nationalized
industries, than the other capitalist countries. Their new goal was an
industrial policy to reindustrialize or restructure the French economy
along high-tech lines, building what they called corporate "winners" by
channeling investment funds through the nationalized banks. The state

would act as stockholder and financier, corporate planner and re-searcher, customer and salesman, but "let the managers decide what they want."[33] In 1982 the Socialists expected the new technology to lead to economic recovery, reduced unemployment, and competitive-ness in exports, making France the leader in the European race in semiconductors and computers. By May 1983 the high-tech dream was also postponed. Prime Minister Laurent Fabius commented that the government would "hold spending down in 1983 by cutting many social programs."[34]

But the financial pressures from the integrated world economy were not alone in operating on the government. Announcing in October 1982 that the 1983 budget would raise military spending 10 percent, in-crease nuclear arms procurement by more than 14 percent, and create an intervention force for the Mideast and Africa, the Socialists also revealed that during the summer of 1982 they had decided to proceed to build the neutron bomb at a gigantic cost, making it the only govern-ment beside the American to authorize production. "The government has decided to make economies elsewhere," for example, by cutting unemployment benefits.[35] In 1982, for the first time in many years, the French workers suffered a real income drop. Clearly, government poli-cies were not merely responding to the difficulties of "Keynesianism in one country." It was a question less of necessity than of priority.

In evaluating the Socialist government in October 1983, the head of the French Employers Association noted, "Let's face it, purchasing power must be forced downward. . . . It is an opportunity for important reductions in wages. . . . We shouldn't be saying this too loudly, but the government's strategy is going in the right direction for us—it represents an opportunity to get our costs down. . . ."[36] Or as another Parisian businessman noted with satisfaction in mid-1984, "Europe's political leaders now have a pro-business, anti-interference line whether they are Socialists or right-of-center."[37]

At a September 1985 meeting of the Group of Five (the United States, Britain, the FRG, France, and Japan), the French Socialists declared they would "curb public spending in order to reduce taxes, foster a private investment recovery, and intensify efforts to expedite structural adjustment through such measures as financial market liber-alization. . . ."[38] In France that translated again into a 1986 budget with substantial cuts in spending, except for increases in defense, education, and culture, and a cut in corporate and income taxes to stimulate investment.

Socialist planning was explicitly "the power to say to particular firms that particular activities are going to be developed while others are going to be phased out. This means major sectoral and structural change," according to Jacques Attali, one of the Socialists' principal economic advisers.[39] The government cut shipbuilding and steel by one-third and made comparable cuts for Renault and telecommunications, originally one of the "commanding heights" of the economy.

The nationalized companies' combined losses rose from 12.0 billion francs in 1981 to 19.6 billion in 1982 and were followed by a loss of 34 billion francs ($4.5 billion) in 1983. On coming to power in 1981, the French Socialist government, along with many other economic decision makers throughout the world, estimated that the new oil price would raise the demand for coal, and so it invested heavily in the French mines. By 1984 the coal industry had a deficit of $100 million despite a subsidy of $750 million. The deficit in the steel industry of well over $1 billion in 1984 was 60 percent higher than in 1983. These losses absorbed the budget allocation of $2 billion that had been destined for the "locomotives" of reindustrialization in science and technology. The government decided to cut coal production by 30 percent by 1983 and eliminate 25,000 jobs; and made a similar decision for the steel industry. Another cost-cutting measure was the decision to eliminate 100,000 more jobs in nationalized industries and simultaneously approve more private layoffs. Since the National Assembly blocked any considered denationalization until a new parliament was elected in 1986, the government, determined that they must be profitable by 1985, devised a plan to sell stock in the nationalized companies on the Bourse.

Finally, reformist restructuring in France meant increased unemployment. Between mid-1982 and mid-1984, it rose by 385,000. By the end of 1984 some 3 million were unemployed, or 10 percent of the labor force, and the number was increasing. The government even made resigned references to the need to wait for demographic change in order to resolve the problem, although even this passive response was belied by the fact that the working-age population was growing much faster than the general population. Ironically, the Employers Association's model was adopted as the new unemployment insurance program. The government emphasized the retraining of workers for new skills, but it was never clear for what or how it expected new jobs to be created, except through workers becoming "entrepreneurs." One CGT trade union organizer said, "[T]he fact is you have a government that is taking jobs away, and I don't see how you can explain this as being in the worker's interests."[40] Predictably, the Left began

to lose local elections in areas where they had held power since
1919.

In 1982 there were over 40,000 homeless persons in Paris alone,
compared with 20,000 in 1971, while 5–6 million people lived on less
than $180 a month in 1985, and without any supplemental welfare
benefits. One private businessman embarrassed the government in
1984 by opening soup kitchens for the hungry. And the president of
France decided that during extreme cold the homeless would not be
prevented from sleeping in the Paris subway.

Alongside these developments in the economy, the Socialists revived
an Atlanticism in foreign policy that their Gaullist predecessors had
opposed. More incredibly, in the 1980s capitalism won the allegiance
of many intellectuals, who engaged in a veritable exorcism of their
leftist past, befitting the world's capital of fashion.

Similar developments in economic policy took place in Spain, as the
Socialist government aimed to make its industries competitive in the
world market. After introducing wage controls, investment incentives,
and one of the lowest tax rates in the EC, and amid 20 percent unemployment, the government moved to privatize nine major government
industries, first closing the chronic losers; it then hoped to make profitable most of the healthy companies and sell them, retaining arms, some
steel, utilities, and coal mines. One Spanish banker expressed the
typical approval of many domestic and foreign businessmen: "González
has done what the conservatives could not do, and in many ways, did
not want to do."[41] As the Socialist economics secretary explained it,
"although the means are conservative, the ends are socialist, because
the ends are to provide more wealth for more people."[42]

The experience of the socialist governments in Europe in the 1980s
was disastrous politically. No party offered even an alternative project
or vision to the capitalist system. "Our message is that things will be
worse under the conservatives," said an official of the French Socialists
before their election defeat in 1986.[43]

In the United States some liberal Democrats also advocated an
industrial policy to resolve the problems of the economy in the 1980s.
Their economic advisers, such as Lester Thurow, Robert Reich, and
Felix Rohatyn, proposed policies comparable in some respects to those
of the social democrats in Europe—including the creation of an investment development bank to stimulate the high-tech sectors that promise
to be competitive, as well as relief for the plight of those victimized by
the dying industries. Such liberals in Congress formulated a new out-
line for government, business, and labor cooperation, increasingly, and
superficially, looking to Japan as a model. They have since buttressed

this program with revived human capital theories, which would require a greater investment in education and training as well as corporate tax credits for the retraining of workers. Abstractly, their emphasis on an infrastructure of an educated work force is of obvious importance in estimating the capital base of a nation. However, in a capitalist society, where the very process of accumulation progressively reduces the need for large numbers of workers with mental and physical skills, and in a system whose economic problems have nothing whatever to do with the educational base, such emphasis is irrelevant at best and reflects one more attempt to find a nonsystemic origin to the existing severe economic problems. This analysis, with its implications that retraining and education are keys to growth and a solution to the economic crisis of accumulation, has gained proponents in Europe as well.

Liberal Democrats have also proposed public works to rebuild the national infrastructure, to be paid for with user fees. But the tax revolt of the middle class, the crucial voting constituency in America, in the late 1970s has impressed America's liberal Democrats. They also plead, therefore, the cause of fiscal restraint, and to this extent even their out-of-power rhetoric tends to overlap the Reagan administration's economic policies.

DILEMMAS OF REFORMIST RESTRUCTURING

There were calls for reform and promises of it in the election of the various European socialist parties, and the working class expected it. But the successful implementation of the welfare provisions in Europe were made possible by the periods of expansion in the general economy. When capitalism enters a period of crisis, as it must, illusions of change or reform pass with the prosperity. Essentially, there is no escape for any nation integrated into the international capitalist system. The Keynesianism that was the essence of social democracy could be implemented only in precrisis conditions. Keynesianism failed, and some economists, such as Stuart Holland, blamed the TNCs for the failure, since they robbed the state of its tax base. Others insisted inflation was its Achilles' heel, which had brought the monetarist to political power. But even these conditions at this period were dependent on the war-generated expansion of the dominant American economy, with its stimulating effects on world prosperity.

There is a certain perverse validity in the apparent conclusion of the European socialists that if they are to be a part of the capitalist market system, their respective nations must be operated along capitalist principles. Expectations of profit must remain the incentive for investment in a competitive environment. If indeed a noncapitalist future is inconceivable to socialist politicians, then their policies followed a certain logic. Unfortunately for their plans, however, the revival of capitalism by the traditional means is not in their hands any more than is reform of the system; it depends instead on developments in the world economy utterly beyond their control.

CHAPTER 16

THE DEVELOPING COUNTRIES

There will be a frontier for capitalism until the whole world is organized to adopt its mode of production. But the bulk of the LDCs are already subjectively and objectively a part of the capitalist world, and their internal class structure reflects this fact, though the persistence of precapitalist feudal and military institutions, ideologies, and social structure can be dysfunctional to capitalist development or distort its character.[1]

More realistic recent analyses of the parallel class structures in developed and less developed economies alike have largely superseded the oversimplified and false dichotomy of rich versus poor countries, or industrial versus nonindustrial nations, that characterized the Third Worldist perspective of the 1960s and 1970s. It should always have been obvious that capitalist societies, whether industrialized or not, are riven by class antagonism and offer no basis for an alliance except to the disadvantage of the laboring classes. Obviously, for the worker it is no more desirable to be exploited by his own national than by a TNC. The national capitalist will struggle for his own advantage, against international capital or with it. Like capitalists everywhere, they follow the flag of profit. But if threatened by a challenge to property within, the capitalist soon makes his primary allegiance clear. This reality has sometimes been clouded by intellectual theories, often with calamitous results when they were the basis of action by political groups. But that the LDCs are a part of the capitalist world economy does not signify that they are able to achieve an independent national capitalist economic development at this time in history—or that the age-old intracapitalist competitive struggle does not proceed as always. Nor does it obviate the fact that there are weak and strong nations with relative power. This means that there are reasons to examine the LDCs separately and that the process of restructuring has a special character and importance in these societies.

For restructuring in the LDCs, while also taking the form of the reactionary prescriptions in which it is applied in the OECD countries, is imperialist. Imperialism implies the domination of the weaker nation by the stronger, which imposes new socioeconomic, and hence political, conditions beneficial to the latter and usually in conflict with the national accumulation of capital. Being weaker and indebted, the LDCs have been more vulnerable to the implementation of the logical extremes of the new adjustment policies and ideology, represented above all by the IMF, than has so far been possible in the stronger countries. But being weaker, they increasingly also have less to lose from resistance to their subservient status. And governments must concern themselves with debt, terms of trade, balance of payments, and the like—problems of no concern to the individual capitalist.

For all their multiple historical and cultural differences, the LDCs continue to share important characteristics that make them vulnerable to imperialist relations. All the traditional forms of superexploitation of the laboring classes and economic domination and dependence persist. Armed intervention to prevent or undo revolutionary changes that challenge imperialist interests is the most obvious and horrendous form of interference. Of the 215 instances of U.S. threat or use of armed force to secure its economic and political aims between World War II and 1975, 185, including two major wars, were in the LDCs—to which many more can be added since then. Britain and France have also used their military to protect their interests in the LDCs in recent years.

The UN Office for Emergency Operations in Africa, set up to deal with the famine conditions, in March 1986 blamed "externally supported insurgencies" in Mozambique and Angola that "have displaced hundreds of thousands of people, disrupted economic and agricultural activity and thus are the root cause of the continuing emergency." Since the drought had ended, the famine in those two countries was "clearly the result of aggressive South African policy toward its neighbors," with significant U.S. aid to the mercenaries.[2] Both in Cambodia after the war and in Nicaragua the consciously destabilizing direct American support of aggressive armed conflict has distorted the economic development efforts, with the crudest and most brutal forms of intervention.

Elsewhere in the Third World both foreign and domestic industries engage in superexploitation where repressive regimes are able to guarantee a cheap and submissive work force. Typical of this relationship is the comment of the manager of a joint venture in an African country who, when asked about the atrocious working conditions, responded, "[I]n a place like this we cannot expect to maintain European standards."[3] Western and Japanese firms, in addition to their traditional exploitation of labor at the lowest cost, have increasingly established their most dangerous production—asbestos, arsenic, zinc, mercury, pesticides—in the Third World to avoid the pollution-control expenses in their home country. The State Department responded to Bangladesh's effort to ban the sale of dangerous or worthless drugs already banned in the United States, with immediate pressure on Bangladesh and the comment "The State Department has a statutory responsibility for assisting American interests abroad."[4] Everyone knows that, in addition to the internal class exploitation in the LDCs, there are countless examples of the special imperialist relationship between capital and the state of the industrialized countries with those loosely referred to as the Third World—it is the rule, not the exception. The nature of the internal regimes is, more often than not, the outcome of that relationship. Needless to say, the laboring classes—wage earners, peasants, and the vast numbers of marginalized survivors in the so-called informal sector—bear the brunt of it all, as they do everywhere, but the magnitude of the conditions of poverty and exploitation and the numbers involved make the conditions in the LDCs that much more extreme.

A large number of the LDCs share a dependency on a few commodity exports for their foreign trade. In 1980 there were forty countries where two commodities, besides oil, accounted for 30 percent or more of all exports—and for many it was over 50 percent. These countries are vulnerable not only to a volatile demand for their products but also to a secular decline in the use of numerous raw materials, as technology has developed substitutes and new means of recycling and conservation. Objectively, therefore, the LDCs are always more susceptible to the commodity cycle: a rise in commodity prices, leading to development plans that require imports resulting in unfavorable terms of trade, which are met by foreign borrowing and increased commodity production, followed by a fall in export prices and cutbacks in production and an eventual shortage of commodity supplies. In the context of a world economic crisis, the impact of such instability is even more devastating.

Each nation, desperate for capital, produced as much as possible, and the more it produced, the lower the prices and the more it had, in turn, to produce. Brazil, to meet its debt repayments, increased its output of tin from 8,000 tons in 1983 to 22,000 tons in 1985, at the time when the world tin market had collapsed. As Malaysia lost its tin income, it increased its oil production. Falling prices invariably eliminate the marginal producers. Low prices then lead to mine closures and the abandonment of commercial crops, setting the stage for later shortages and rising prices.

Although many countries have made a significant shift toward manufactured exports over the past years, they have encountered increasing trade barriers. In the production of both raw materials and manufactured goods, profits usually accrue to the TNCs, either through the trading companies or through intrafirm trade. Capitalist penetration of the agrarian sector, among other factors, was instrumental in creating a range of disasters, from the famine in Africa to the huge numbers of displaced peasants who have multiplied the urban populations throughout the LDCs.

The differences between the LDCs are also of obvious importance. In Guatemala, Zaire, and El Salvador, for example, there are rightist neocolonial police states dominated by the military and/or a small, corrupt compradore elite; there is minimal state involvement in the economies, which are, in principle, open to foreign investment and which assign a dominant role to private enterprise. In Mexico or Peru, by contrast, there are mixed economies with a large role for the state sector, foreign investment with restrictions, and a politically dominant nationalist bourgeoisie, which sometimes must share power with the military. The question whether national elites are compradore or nationalist could determine whether the profits accumulated remain in a nation for economic growth or are exported, but profitability, not patriotism, determines the flow of capital. There are also a few states that have primary state planning in the economy and egalitarian goals that aim toward socialism.

FROM ECONOMIC DEVELOPMENT TO RESTRUCTURING

Since 1945 the Americans have been deeply interested in the form that economic development takes in the Third World, especially in Latin America, and this interest has become an important aspect of imperialism. The United States has vigorously opposed national capitalist development—in Brazil, the Philippines, Indonesia, Iran, and other countries—when restrictions were placed on its own citizens, frequently supporting an overthrow of the existing government. Because of this, countries that have chosen an independent nationalist or non-capitalist road have faced even greater obstacles from American hostility than were inherent in their underdeveloped status. Moreover, there was no doubt that the United States and many Western governments, as well as the bankers and the IMF/World Bank, welcomed military regimes like Brazil, Argentina, and Chile, regarding them as reliable credit risks to which they could "recycle" the petrodollars deposited by OPEC and as ideal investment outlets. But the evolution of even these regimes led to new contradictions with foreign economic interests.

The most obvious factor inhibiting development in the LDCs was the shortage of capital, which could be acquired in only a limited number of ways—by internal accumulation and exports, borrowing, aid, and foreign investment. Development also had to contend with the forces of decapitalization—repatriation of profits, capital flight, negative terms of trade, and the usurious terms of borrowing, to say nothing of such external "shocks" as the price of oil (rising or falling, depending on whether the country imported or exported), monetary developments, and world recession. It was, of course, the importing LDCs that suffered most from the price escalations of oil, which were compounded by the strength and shortage of dollars in which it is sold. Energy is fundamental to the early stages of industrial development and is linked to all sectors of the economy.

Before the 1950s there were scarcely any conscious national development "strategies" to develop the economy. There were not even many prescriptions from economists and others on how to develop a nonindustrial economy. Since then a massive library of writings has emerged on all its ramifications and from perspectives that range across the whole political spectrum. Those on both the right and the left shifted their positions as the world economic condition changed. During the 1950s and 1960s the emphasis of governments and the international agencies was on industrial development and import substitution, in keeping with both the nationalist aspirations of new nations and the private TNCs' investment interests. But given the limited nature of their internal market, production was oriented to meet the needs of the elite and often stagnated and the economies were afflicted by vast overcapacity until they were stimulated by such external factors as escalations of the Vietnam War. "Aid" was marginal to real needs, tied to conditions—that is, to source of supplies, projects, and technology—and often accompanied by economic and political interference. When not siphoned off in corruption, it was used in many areas to build the physical, institutional, and policy infrastructure essential for domestic

and international capitalist economic exploitation and for marginal
national development.

Foreign capitalists in the postwar period first invested for raw
materials to meet world demand generated by the Korean War and to
produce goods for the internal markets. By the end of the 1960s, the
impetus was the search for cheap labor to produce manufactured products for the competitive world market. Many countries' development
strategies, and those of the World Bank—from import substitution to
export-oriented enclaves and to agricultural development—followed
the interests of the foreign investors. The TNC affiliates also used the
concessional credits, sometimes to the exclusion of local national interests, and contributed to the debt crisis as well.

The state sector nevertheless grew, irrespective of the dominant
ideology, through the building of new industries or the nationalizing of
the existing ones, particularly in mining and oil during the 1960s and
1970s. Countries with oil revenues vastly expanded the public sector.
But capital alone is insufficient to develop an economy. There was a
huge infusion of capital in the OPEC countries in the 1970s, but
bottlenecks in labor and infrastructure restricted their ambitious development plans. Events during this period graphically demonstrated that
a nation could have extraordinary industrial growth, as did Iran between 1974 and 1977, without industrialization, which implies a condition that transforms and permeates the entire economy.

The state played the dominant role in economic development in most
of the LDCs. This was due less to ideology or desire than to the absence
of private investors with sufficient capital able or willing to take the
long-term risks in many large-scale industrial projects. A significant
portion of the LDCs' budgets therefore went for capital expenditure.
Even in 1980, capital outlays were 27 percent of total aggregate LDC
government budgets, falling to 23 percent in 1983, as debt service rose
over those years by 90 percent. Private local capital was frequently
restricted to light industry and the so-called informal sector. The state
built the infrastructure, subsidized the areas of high-growth potential,
and expanded state enterprises in the basic and heavy industries like
fertilizer and steel.

The provision of food at low cost for the population was the most
important state subsidy for a large number of the LDCs. Until the
1980s it ranged from a consumer subsidy of 40 percent, in Bangladesh,
to a sum equal to 2 percent of the GDP, in Peru. Also important in
agrarian countries were subsidies to the peasants for agricultural inputs
like fertilizers and pesticides. To varying degrees, countries subsidized
other basics like fuel costs, transport, water, and electricity.

For many countries the creation of new industries often followed plans for economic development and retaining the "commanding heights," or basic industry, in government control. But independent development was inevitably indebted development. Development "strategies," despite their titles, were in many cases shaped by the availability of cheap loans from the banks or suppliers' credits. Some state capitalist countries took advantage of the loans to initiate industrial projects independently of the TNCs but became dependent instead on the banks and, eventually, the IMF. This course would have had a certain rationality if it had been used to build the infrastructure essential for self-reliance, particularly in food and other basics, in order to survive the inevitable crises in the capitalist world market. This was generally not the case, however.

As exports fell with the exigency of debt repayment and the recession of the 1980s, numerous LDC development projects were abandoned and debt was rescheduled. The decline in growth in the 1980s was the greatest since 1945. In aggregate terms, the UN found, one-fifth of the population of the LDCs lived in nations with falling per capita output and another fifth in countries with no growth at all in the 1980s. For one hundred countries there was a "sharp deceleration" in capital formation during the first four years of the decade. The "impetus toward development was more sharply broken by the global recession than at any time since the Bank began operations," said a World Bank vice-president in 1983.[5] While this increases the misery, the vast mass of the population in most of these countries had never shared in the benefits from earlier periods of high growth. The congruence of all these conditions by the 1980s paved the way for the restructuring policies of the IMF and the World Bank.

Although the nature of the regime was obviously important in defining the development strategies that various nations chose, the world economic context imposed a certain uniformity on all of them. In fact, all of the LDCs with different regimes went through phases in their development strategies in response to the evolving world economic crisis. In the mid-1970s there was a consensus, including the most reactionary states, in the Group of 77 and the organization of non-aligned nations, which demanded that the world economy be restructured to create a new international economic order (NIEO). During this brief period, because of a strong world demand for commodities and because of OPEC's power, the LDCs possessed a momentary bargaining advantage.

In addition to the nationalization of natural resources, many nations sought such new types of foreign investment as joint ventures, turnkey plants, and production sharing instead of direct investment. A significant number of the TNCs had come to appreciate the advantages of these new forms, which were more profitable and carried fewer risks than did traditional direct foreign investment. But since marketing and inputs remained under foreign control, some governments began in the changing economic context to consider the disadvantages of the new forms. Because their desperate financial position after 1980 required investment with the lowest direct outlay from themselves, they once more offered numerous incentives to foreign capital. Barely five years after the proclamation of the NIEO, the most intense competition for direct foreign investment and submission to draconian and imperialist restructuring policies confronted the LDCs, including the most progressive countries.

DEVELOPMENT STRATEGIES

Among the most prominent capitalist "development strategies" that various LDC governments pursued were "import substitution," particularly in Brazil, Argentina, and Mexico, and accelerated industrial growth with the importation of the most modern technology, which was the strategy of Algeria. Always present in practice, emphasis on export orientation reached the highest level of ideological respectability when the IMF/World Bank adopted it as the development strategy to promote among all the LDCs during the 1970s and 1980s. The fate of these strategies, of course, depends on the regimes involved and the world economic context.

Import substitution in the capitalist context of a dual market—a small consuming elite and impoverished masses—meant industrialization to meet the demand of that elite, and it consequently perpetuated the nature of the market. The choice of products is determined by those with the money to buy them. The entire industrialization process was oriented toward meeting the demand of that tiny sector of the population—automobiles, appliances, cosmetics, steel, and rubber: all industries that are particularly capital intensive. In Brazil, the leading example, the luxury market of the upper class accounted for the exceptional growth of the economic "miracle." By 1974 the demand was saturated and there were large inventories of cars and appliances. The government tried to promote exports, but its efforts coincided with the world recession in the mid-1970s. Import substitution was acceptable to the TNCs during the period in which they were able to produce profitably for local sales. The IMF, in keeping with its essentially imperialist role, opposed the protectionist requirements of an import substitution strategy, especially after the interests of the TNCs had shifted to component production for

export, and advocated instead the export orientation of the newly industrializing countries (NICs). Since cheap labor was the attraction, these
industries tended to be more labor intensive.

But import substitution was crucial to industrial development, and
in the past both the United States and Japan developed only by protecting their budding industries from more advanced competitors, as did
the NICs in their early stage of development. The key to all these
"strategies" is the social system of which they are a part.

THE NICS

Both the OECD nations, with which they now compete, and the
developing nations, which hope to imitate them, have studied the
reasons for the incredible growth rates of the NICs—Hong Kong,
Singapore (city-states really are not at all similar to other LDCs), South
Korea, and Taiwan, and often, Brazil. While the IMF/World Bank and
the United States strongly endorse privatization of the state sector
among the LDCs, in the NICs most proclaimed as development models,
the state has ironically been the critical participant in economic development, and both Korea and Taiwan pursued an import substitution
policy in their development until the mid-1960s and relied on what was
anathema to the IMF—tariffs, import licensing, and overvalued exchange rates. The shift toward export orientation took place in the
mid-1960s, amid the escalation of the war in Vietnam, which provided
demand for their output. By the end of the 1960s industrial goods
accounted for 75 percent of their exports. The NICs provide further
evidence that, internally, both primitive accumulation and continued
economic "success" is determined at least as much by political as by
economic factors.

Foreign aid was also crucial. From 1951 to 1965 Taiwan received
massive U.S. aid—about $1.5 billion, 34 percent of its total gross
investment—to "make it the showcase of capitalist development."[6]
Korea received $4.5 billion, equal to one-half the government's reve-
nue in the 1950s and 1960s. Thereafter the war in Vietnam generated
the economic demand that created their "miracle" economies. As a
result, the average growth was 8 percent a year after 1965; even during
the recession in the 1970s, the NICs fared better than the rest of the
world. The 1980 recession in Korea was its first since the war in the
1950s.

Indigenous finance capital, meaning primarily state credit, financed
the bulk of production. The percentage of foreign-owned manufactured
exports has been relatively small—10.0 percent in Hong Kong, 18.7
percent in Korea, 20.0 percent in Taiwan—but it dominates the elec-

tronics sector. Twenty of the fifty largest companies in Korea are state owned, and they absorb 30 percent of all investment. In Korea the state completely controlled the banking system (until it privatized some banking in the early 1980s), which it used actively to direct investment and to transfer failing companies on to others, along with credit to organize the mergers. The production of autos was a disaster area until the Seoul government in 1980 allocated sectors to companies, making the industry profitable by 1984 and expanding production internationally in 1985. "In Korea they're trying to do in five years what took the Japanese 20 years," one TNC executive observed.[7] The so-called family-based companies were wholly dependent on the state for their rise to economic power. Ten companies provide 70 percent of the exports and 64 percent of the GNP. Despite a superficial semblance of success, these patriarchal, huge, inefficient conglomerates, operating in every sector, were built with credit and, with a debt-equity ratio of 4.5:1, were reportedly the "worst financially structured corporate bodies in the world."[8] The emphasis in the past was on volume rather than on profit. Eventually, the vulnerability of export growth began to affect even the NICs. Their exports, which accounted for one-third of their GNP, dropped in 1985. But the rise of the yen opened new, if temporary, opportunities for access to the Japanese market and for replacing Japan in the U.S. market. Because their currencies were linked closely to the dollar, their exporting companies increased their share of the European market. Economic growth for both Korea and Taiwan was near 10 percent in 1986.

As the NICs became more competitive, the World Bank "graduated" them to a new status of "Advanced Developing Countries," making them ineligible for International Development Association (IDA) loans and tariff concessions.

Other nations are being urged to adopt an export orientation in order to repeat the success of the NICs. But there is a high risk to applying economic policies and hoping for the same congruence of circumstances in the world economy that led to earlier successes. Economic development that could occur at one time will not necessarily happen again. The demand in the world market generated by such events as the Vietnam War had everything to do with the successful takeoff of the export-oriented "strategy" in the NICs. When the United States tried to make a "showcase" of capitalist development in Jamaica in the 1980s, in a different world context, it failed totally.

Most LDCs have shown an extreme dual market. Such economies have no basis for an alternative strategy when recession or protectionism afflicts the world market. Deflationary austerity policies as well as the class-imposed political inhibitions are decisive restraints on expanding the internal market.

The industrialization of much of the Third World has vastly increased the global surplus capacity in many industries. Much of this capacity is independent of the TNCs, and often state controlled; even when it is not, it enlarges the area of competition and heightens it in many industries. With the intensifying competition in trade, the industrial nations have moved to protect their threatened industries.

As national economies become further integrated into the capitalist world market, they are made increasingly vulnerable to its inherent instability. Once ensnared in the debt cycle of loans to repay loans, the countries face creditors who demand a restructuring of the economy, first to repay debt, then to mold the economy to the capitalist model enunciated by the imperialist states, primarily by the United States, working through the IMF and World Bank. Even though the governments of most of the indebted LDCs are in agreement with such aims in principle, they still see a keen contradiction between the means demanded and their own, internal capitalist development.

Autonomous state capitalist development is a threat to existing capital in the international system. It provides new competition in the export markets as well as new restraints on the TNCs in the internal market, with the imposition of national controls. U.S. policy has usually opposed national capitalist development that restricted their own citizens' opportunities to exploit any and every investment possibility. The United States has increasingly turned to the IMF/World Bank as the most effective instrument with which to pursue its imperialist aims in the LDCs—to restructure not only those countries that were oriented toward state planning and egalitarian social goals but also those like Brazil in which the state increased its role and put pressure on foreign companies. Whether declared or not, the state-capitalist moves of independent development present a competitive threat that the IMF/World Bank adjustment and privatization strategies are in the process of reversing.

Although originally political in origin, regional development banks emerged to perform functions that parallel those of the World Bank. The Inter-American Development Bank was created in 1959. President Johnson promoted the Asian Development Bank (ADB) in 1965, although Japan was later to dominate it, to offset the negative impact of his Vietnam War policies. And the United States reluctantly supported the Africa Development Fund in 1975, after radical political changes began to occur on that continent. But the IMF and the World Bank have remained the preferred institutions. A leading State Department official told one expert on the topic, "The world is full of all sorts of challenges and proposals for new economic institutions. We are trying desperately to get them under the aegis of the World Bank, where we have some confidence they will be run in ways amenable to our interests. The alternatives are too horrendous for us to accept."[9]

CHAPTER 17

THE IMF AND
THE WORLD BANK

Despite its present deep involvement in developing countries, the IMF was never intended to be an agency of economic development or an aid-dispensing institution. Created as a reaction to the currency blocs that paralyzed world trade in the 1930s, it was designed to promote the free movement of capital through the convertibility of currencies. It has evolved to its current role in response to the objective developments in the international economy and has emerged as the vehicle of a centralized international economic imperialism, with an unprecedented power. The IMF is able to force comprehensive economic policies on numerous indebted LDCs, and even on a few European countries, to enable them to pay interest and repatriate profits in the short run, but also to restructure their national economies to make them compatible with the long-term needs of international investment.

Historically, the United States has tried to orient economic development in the direction of orthodox capitalist ideology, as with the European Recovery Program (Marshall Plan), the occupation of Japan after 1945, and wherever it has had leverage. But the ideology and purpose of the system transcend specific nations. The role of the IMF is another step in an international effort, the most successful to date, to homogenize economic policy among nations. The Cold War, which did much to reorient the IMF/World Bank, is now increasingly an impediment to incorporating an ever greater area of the world into the international capitalist system.

The IMF's effort to impose policies detrimental to national development began in the 1950s. It caused most countries, if they had any option at all, to turn elsewhere for capital. They did so, despite their own commitment to capitalism, because the IMF's draconian constraints on their internal development, with the purpose of repatriating investors' interest and profits, conflicted with their own national capitalist development.

Debt and the desperate shortage of capital in due course gave the IMF the leverage to "restructure" the economies of the developing countries on a vastly increased scale. As balance-of-payments problems worsened and debt became unmanageable in the generalized economic crisis of the 1970s and 1980s, the IMF performed a crucial supranational imperialist role. It could do this although between 1974 and 1980 the Fund provided only 3 percent of the LDCs' financing requirements. By 1985 the IMF was a net recipient of capital from the LDCs (including some $750 million from the poorest sub-Saharan countries of Africa) and expected to remain so unless commodity prices fell so low as to reactivate its compensatory financing provision. But as the banks, including the World Bank and the BIS, insisted that borrowers turn first to the IMF for policy review, it became the lender of first resort. Most debtor states had no option. During the global recession of the early 1980s, the number of new IMF agreements rose from twenty-four in 1979 to seventy-four in 1983. It allocated nearly $43 billion between 1980 and 1984, or about the same amount it had provided over the preceding twenty years. But the allocated funds were not the distributed funds: 30 percent of them were blocked because countries did not comply with the conditions or canceled their agreements. In 1984 the IMF began to increase its lending in sub-Saharan Africa in cooperation with the World Bank. As an IMF official explained, "Fund-Bank coordination is a code phrase. It means calling in the Bank to help the IMF get its money back."[1]

When the Latin American debtor states call for political dialogue on the question of debt, the United States recommends that they turn to the IMF, for it is essential that sovereign nations enter the debt trap in order to undergo the draconian restructuring program for which the IMF is now renowned. The IMF's ability to impose it is all a question of relative power. The IMF staff no doubt strongly desires to be able to apply the same discipline to the U.S. economy that it applies to that of the Dominican Republic. As the official history of the IMF in the 1970s pointed out, its conditions for Britain and Italy were equally strict. However, among the poorer nations it has the greatest leverage.

The ideology of the IMF/World Bank is now well known. The terminology, charged with ideological bias, is a direct descendant of Adam Smith and nineteenth-century British liberalism. "Anyone," the

IMF's research director observed in 1985, " . . . should find that oft-neglected work, *The Wealth of Nations,* both so relevant and so modern."[2] While its policies usually directly benefit the TNCs, it cannot be said that the well-paid staff seeks only to service their needs. The professional employees evince an almost religious conviction that their prescriptions are correct, that they are ultimately for the good of all. Anyone without these convictions would not long endure in the position. The high salaries, too, are a salve for any painful doubts some may develop. The IMF and the World Bank have also established a training institute for administrators from the LDCs; there they endeavor to portray the ideological bias as strictly scientific and technical expertise. Despite its reputation for capitalist orthodoxy, the IMF has steadily increased its ranks of member nations, drawing them more and more from the CPEs.

Aside from playing its lending role, the IMF staff conducts periodic reviews of the members' policies in connection with its "surveillance" of the exchange rate system. At this time it also offers "guidance" to those not yet in the debt trap. As the IMF director emphasized, *"The Fund has a central responsibility to encourage member countries to make the right policy choices."*[3]

CONDITIONALITY

Conditionality is the IMF/World Bank's crucial tool in enforcing its restructuring policies in the indebted nations. Put simply, it releases usually desperately needed funding, contingent on specific policy changes in the members' economy. John Maynard Keynes, one of the founders of the IMF, opposed giving it the authority to intervene in members' economic policy. Conditionality was introduced in the 1950s at the behest of the United States.

Under criticism from all quarters, the IMF in March 1979 introduced new conditionality guidelines, replacing a single policy with a range of policies. When a member nation is forced by its debt to ask for assistance, the IMF negotiating teams always arrive with the prepared "letter of intent" for the finance minister to send to the IMF. The policy prescriptions rarely waver, regardless of the situation. Such uniformity makes it virtually unnecessary for the technicians to know anything about the country in question. Nevertheless, the mission team usually stays two to three weeks for "fact finding" and "policy-oriented discussions."[4]

The adjustment recipe is best described by two of its economists who studied the relationship of the Fund's programs and economic growth, using the classic terms of supply and demand. While acknowledging that exogenous factors, such as deterioration in a country's terms of trade and rising international interest rates, may have something to do with its plight, the authors, and all the Fund's staff, quickly ignore them and invariably turn to the area they can more readily manipulate, given their relative power, even if their prescriptions can scarcely do more than seriously aggravate the problems. When one agreement expires, another succeeds it. The two IMF economists noted that their focus is always on "inappropriate domestic policies that expand aggregate domestic demand too rapidly." They added, "[T]he need for a stabilization typically reflects excess demand, all programs must involve some degree of restraint of aggregate domestic demand . . . and simultaneously to cause a shift in its composition away from current consumption and toward fixed capital formation. . . . Fund policy leans heavily in the direction of eliminating controls and restrictions on trade and payments."[5] Uniformly, the programs are designed to reduce the consumption, direct and indirect, of the bulk of the population. One means to this end is to force the reduction of government social expenditures and subsidies.

The IMF's adjustment programs regularly call for devaluation, elimination of subsidies, import controls, low wages, reduction of state expenditures, restrictions on credit, greater export orientation, sales tax, and measures to improve the business climate to attract capital. A primary objective is to secure and liberate foreign exchange for the payment of interest.

Primarily under the aegis of the IMF, country after country, whatever its political system, has in the 1980s reduced or abolished its subsidies for the basic needs of the population. Bangladesh removed food subsidies between 1980 and 1983; Tanzania dropped subsidies on all food except cornmeal in 1980; Sri Lanka eliminated its subsidy on imported rice, causing local prices to rise; Peru had abolished all food subsidies by 1984. Other subsidies were eliminated by 1983 in Ghana, Indonesia, Bangladesh, Pakistan, Zambia, Benin, and other countries. In the aggregate, subsidies fell over 22 percent between 1980 and 1983, all in the context of living standards severely worsened by other factors.

Devaluation, of course, makes it necessary to increase the volume of exports to earn the same exchange. It thereby also raises the price of all imports and increases inflation, whereas selective tariffs would curtail the nonessentials. Foreign debt expressed in local currencies is multiplied with devaluations. But IMF credit is usually available only on the condition of a devaluation and the maintenance of free exchange.

These are fundamental political decisions made by technicians responsible to no one in the affected nations.

The IMF admonishes states to "adjust" to the realities of the world economy. But adjustment by whom and to what? To rising energy costs or falling energy costs, to an expanding market or protectionism, to rising commodity prices or falling commodity prices? These objective "realities" change in a few years, and the policies pressed on the recipient of the IMF/World Bank guidance have themselves helped reverse structural conditions in the world economy. Significant capital expenditures, to say nothing of the price paid by the population in lower living standards, are often made in "adjusting" to one or another shifting structural condition. For years the IMF insisted that the LDCs adopt an export orientation and attacked import substitution policies. But when commodity prices plunged in 1985–86 and manufactured goods faced protectionist restrictions and stagnating or declining markets, one World Bank vice-president wrote in early 1986, "[I]n the second half of the 1980s, there appears to be a new challenge on the horizon—the need to adjust to a less favorable export environment[!] . . . It is important, therefore, that the policies pursued should emphasise not just export growth but also efficient import substitution."[6] Yet the IMF and World Bank continued to urge their bankrupt programs of export-led development on China, Indonesia, and other nations.

Programs that offer the same solution to every situation have generally led to recession, deindustrialization, inflation, aggravated imbalances of trade, unemployment, further concentration of income, and political repression. The enforced cutbacks in what economists call human-capital formation—education and training—seriously undermine future development of any sort. The examples are endless and readily found in the now vast literature on these institutions. Whether intentionally or not, the IMF has effectively decapitalized the recipient countries.

For a nation to "fall from compliance with an austerity program" is to have its loan disbursement terminated—in other words, "countries are not able to make drawings for as long as they are out of compliance."[7] Brazil, Peru, and Nigeria rejected recession as the price of compliance in 1985. The latter two simply decreed the percentage of their export earnings they would allocate to debt service. Between the mid-1970s and 1984, of the IMF's thirty-three most conditional "extended facilities," sixteen were canceled and five left large undrawn balances.[8]

By the mid-1980s the IMF's policy-making committee, led by the United States and France, was pressing for even more rigorous public surveillance, in order to persuade countries to conform to the chosen policies. But the French called for the same criteria to be applied to America's deficit-ridden economy.

The IMF's strategy is totally incompatible with economic development. Unlike that of the private bank or corporation, the IMF's aim is not profit but restructuring of the economies in ways compatible with *international* capitalist interests. But rather than being subjugated at the point of a bayonet, governments often approach the IMF as the sick turn to a doctor for bitter medicine, which the staff administers with a missionary zeal. However, the IMF's economic strategy advice, even for capitalist development, is imperialist. This is an essential contradiction in the IMF's role, for while the fund increasingly uses its leverage to establish general orthodox capitalist policies in as many nations as possible, it serves primarily as an imperialist agent by promoting external interests at the expense of national capitalist development.

Historically, the capitalist development of nations like the United States and Japan required protective tariffs and import substitution. Economic development requires controlled imports, especially if past imports have been for the luxury market or inappropriate technology. Until development is well under way, a chronic deficit is inevitable. The usual IMF demand of devaluation is always disastrous, especially for essential imports like food. The higher cost of imports is passed on to exports, whose price in any event is often a "transfer price" within a TNC rather than one fixed by market forces. Suspension of subsidies for basic commodities—food, fuel, public transport—only increases the suffering of the most exploited.

The IMF's impositions have also played a significant objective role in stimulating social revolt and political instability. They have led to social and political upheavals in many nations and to silent or repressed suffering elsewhere. Headlines like "Dominican Republic Death Toll Is 43 in Rioting over Food Price Increases" are recurrent.[9] The toll in Guatemala, Zambia, Brazil, and elsewhere during protests over IMF-ordered price rises on basic necessities, in dead, wounded, and arrested was high. The IMF again ordered Egypt in 1985 to cut its subsidies on the price of bread, even though in 1977, when the IMF demanded a cut in food imports and reduction in subsidies in basic staple foods, a virtual uprising for two days forced a modification, but not a revocation, of its policies. The list of incidents—some of them smaller in scale and suppressed before making world headlines—continues to grow, as the populations resist these measures. Such instability led the former assistant secretary of state Charles Maynes to write in September 1983, "The extraordinary recent increases in arms sales to Africa and Latin America—in Africa the increase has been 13-fold in the last decade—reflect elite fears of internal insecurity more than of external aggression."[10]

Even some bankers recognized the shortsightedness and absurdity of the policy. "It's insane for the IMF to say to 36 countries 'All you have to do is cut imports and push exports,' " exclaimed one.[11] Finally, the Reagan administration acknowledged that increased economic growth was needed to avert catastrophe or at least maintain American exports. In 1985 the United States and the international institutions sought a means of promoting "growth" in the indebted LDCs in order to maintain payments to the banks and renew a market for their own exports. In a desperate effort to put off a collective debt moratorium, the Treasury broke from its "case by case" policy and prepared a collective proposal for the fifteen most indebted nations, subsequently called the Baker plan. But the specifics at the IMF meeting in 1985 translated into more debt and more conditions.

The IMF insists, "The Fund never chooses where expenditures cuts are to take place. . . . We leave the priorities, the political priorities, entirely to the government."[12] However, its "guidance" in "making the right policy choices" leaves no doubt where the IMF expects the cuts to be made, and it retains the power of the purse to enforce its preferences. The IMF is not the only villain. Some governments do make their own selection. Chile, Brazil, Indonesia, Nigeria, and Venezuela introduced draconian austerity measures on their own, not merely because they were preconditions for talks with the IMF but also because the governments were committed to such policies.

CONTRADICTIONS

Although the IMF austerity program is shortsighted and reduces the world market, it is a typical example of the myopia intrinsic to capitalist restructuring. In whose interest, then, are the programs? Devaluation, elimination of tariffs and subsidies, and the other IMF demands are compatible with the short-run interests of some TNCs and the banks. At the same time the fundamental contradictions in these policies create new structural dilemmas. Devaluation for a trade advantage also raises the debt-service account and makes the suddenly competitive exports a target for protectionism.

Another contradiction is between IMF policies and U.S. political-strategic interests. The IMF can apply its academic orthodoxy in the Third World only if the United States does not demand leniency for strategic reasons, as it has in Chile, El Salvador, and South Africa, to name a few examples. In these cases, and often despite the opposition of the other member countries, the IMF suspended all of its usual criteria. In July 1981 it issued a loan of $36 million to El Salvador; in 1983 it gave South Africa a $1.1 billion credit. The IMF staff must modify or suspend its own rules when the American voting power requires it to follow U.S. interests. In some areas, such as South Africa, European and Japanese interests coincide, but it is American voting power that determines the decisions.

In August 1982, for example, the World Bank praised Grenada for its innovative planning, which had since the revolution in 1979 led to consistent economic growth, despite the world economic recession. Washington stopped an IMF loan of $17 million in 1983 as part of its implacable hostility, which culminated in an invasion of the tiny island in October of that year. In the case of Nicaragua, an internal World Bank study in February 1982 recommended that the bank link aid to Nicaragua's agreement to make more concessions to the private sector.

WORLD BANK

The World Bank lending strategy has closely followed the interests of the TNCs. In the 1950s and 1960s it made project loans to build the infrastructure, essential for profitable investment in developing countries. With the growth of transnational agribusiness, the bank altered its agricultural lending policy and strategy to aid in the orientation of LDC food production for the world market. Its programs were also often a substitute for American aid when the U.S. Congress refused to appropriate sufficient funds.

In the 1980s, when it introduced its long-term structural-adjustment loan (SAL), the World Bank's emphasis moved from the financing of projects to economic strategy. The SALs, like the IMF's balance-of-payments support, are conditional on changes in macroeconomic policy and usually force a country to make an explicit commitment to the IMF as well, and the two programs are usually administered with close ties. But the policy demands on governments have often been contradictory. In the Philippines, for instance, the Bank insisted that the government use its counterpart funds for expansionary investment, whereas the IMF was demanding a cut in services to contribute to a different conditionality. Earlier charitable rhetoric concerning basic needs and the eradication of poverty has receded and been supplanted by more protection of private banks through cofinancing and cross-default loans as well as by the promotion of export-oriented policies. Project loans have become increasingly loaded with blatant policy conditions designed to move economies toward a reliance on "market criteria."

In order to maximize its influence, the World Bank also engages in "dialogue" with government officials to build a consensus for the policy the bank deems desirable. "Policy changes are sometimes the condition for project appraisal, approval, or disbursement," a bank official observed, and reluctance to accept the bank's advice has frequently put the entire lending program in jeopardy.[13] By cofinancing projects with governments or requiring "matching funds," the bank can also determine how a government spends its own money.

The World Bank and other multilateral development banks, according to the U.S. Treasury, "follow neo-classical economic lines emphasizing open trading systems, realistic exchange rates, use of market forces to determine appropriate resource allocation, realistic pricing policies," and the like.[14] For the United States it was important that the World Bank's better lending terms gave it the leverage to mold the borrowing countries' economic policies. The Treasury report in 1982 stressed that "the willingness of the borrowing countries to adopt and implement appropriate policies should be a prime consideration in the country allocation."[15]

A. W. Clausen, the World Bank's president, said in 1983, "The fundamental philosophy of our institution is to help countries diversify their exports . . . and to have an export orientation."[16] In 1982 the World Bank in its *Report on Sub-Saharan Africa* still emphasized export-oriented agricultural production as a solution to the region's development problems, ignoring the highly volatile world market. As the minister of economic development of Sierra Leone criticized at the time, "such a strategy underplays the vital need for self-sufficiency in food production."[17] The World Bank financed a coffee plantation in Africa when coffee prices were declining and the land was needed to grow food whose import costs were rising, in great part because it had to be purchased with a devalued currency. Naturally, the LDCs had no control over the demand for their exports. When production of commodities increased, the prices fell; when manufacturing export prices were cheapened by devaluation, protectionism increased in their former markets. But even when there was a market for all the LDCs could produce, the World Bank advocated devaluation; this aided the buyer, which was invariably a TNC marketing oligopsony. Recognizing the bankruptcy of these policies for the countries being "restructured" is not a matter of hindsight; it was always obvious. The World Bank has also supported the agribusiness TNCs in their shift from plantations to contracting to peasants around a nucleus of a processing plant owned by one of the giant companies.

In 1985, after the policy had helped create a famine in Africa, the World Bank made another shift in emphasis. Scarcely acknowledging the monumental errors in its earlier requirements, the bank now demanded that the state encourage the market forces by allowing urban food prices to rise as an incentive to the peasant to produce food. The conditions for bank lending continued to be devaluation and the elimination of price controls and subsidies.

The World Bank lending commitment actually declined nearly 5 percent between June 1984 and June 1985, and loans from the concessional IDA, for the poorest nations, fell over 15 percent—although the bank was the largest nonresident borrower in the world's capital markets. Reflecting a shift in emphasis, its commitments to finance the private sector through the International Finance Commission (IFC) rose 35 percent. The World Bank's profit for the same period was a record $1.14 billion, and its interest and terms were then higher than those of the commercial banks.

The World Bank also gave the SAL greater emphasis. Its president, Clausen, stated, "Those who make an effort to manage their economies are those very countries which we want to help. More of our lending has become policy-based. Four years ago 3% of our lending was [SAL]. . . . Now it is 18%. . . ." The new criterion for the IDA was to shift its resources from the poorest (with a per capita income of $400 or less) to those "making the greatest efforts to restructure their economies," according to Clausen.[18] The World Bank is also engaged in "assisting over a dozen countries in the design and implementation of comprehensive restructuring programs and strategies both at the industry and enterprise level."[19] By 1986 all new World Bank loans were essentially policy oriented.

Despite the debt disaster of the early 1980s, both the IMF and the World Bank were in 1986 urging China and India to increase their development debts. All their strategies assumed that capital markets for the LDCs would soon return to "normal," supposedly meaning the situation that had existed in the 1970s.

PRIVATIZATION

The increasing privatization of the state sector after 1980 became both a response to the fiscal crisis in the OECD countries and a crucial aspect of restructuring in the LDCs. Selling off government-owned industries was not only an answer to the intractable debt crisis but one compatible with the underlying conservative ideology in Washington and in the IMF and the World Bank. "The big issue for the developing world is that the days of bank lending are over. They are going to have to generate capital internally or through foreign investment," the vice-president of a major New York bank maintained in 1985.[20] The solution, in the eyes of the creditor governments and the international-development institutions, was that equity had to become the alternative to debt for both governments and corporations in the LDCs, and the easiest way to obtain it was for governments to sell off the state industries and commercialize public services. In the United States the Reagan administration has incorporated conservative academic economists to help develop a strategy for the privatization policy thrust of American foreign aid. Associates of such think tanks as the American Enterprise Institute and the Cato Institute are now allowed to project their free-market fantasies into the real-world political economy. And in 1986 Reagan was able to appoint Barber Conable, Jr., a former congressman and associate of the American Enterprise Institute, as president of the World Bank and thus to reinforce the existing policy direction.

In Asia the ideology of privatization has been widely accepted, particularly in India, where, with the introduction of new policies, a stock market boom took place in 1985. Stocks and bond issues rose six times from 1980 to 1985. And the stock market activity doubled over that year, the number of investors tripled, and the market was opened to foreign sales in 1986. The Indian government has also proposed joint ventures with merchant banks. Pakistan and Bangladesh have returned industries to their former owners and privatized other industries previously reserved for state control. South Korea and the Philippines have denationalized some banking and some state-owned industries. Sri Lanka, China, and other nations have moved rapidly to establish a stock exchange, although the effort in China was finally shelved in 1987. Even in remote Nepal the stock exchange won a much publicized visit from a deputy secretary of state and the head of the SEC, as part of the U.S. campaign to encourage privatization. By 1986 Singapore, Malaysia, Turkey, and Nepal were selling their national airlines. Brazil had chosen a hundred companies to denationalize. Ecuador, Jamaica, the Ivory Coast, Kenya, Mexico, and Peru had joined the parade.

There is "greater willingness to see a role for multinational corporations. . . . There's a climate that's better for international business," the secretary-general of the British Commonwealth noted in 1983.[21] Tanzania, Zimbabwe, and Mozambique, African states that earlier rejected private capitalism, have attempted to attract private capital into areas once reserved for public control. They compete with generous foreign-investment laws. The reasons are not ideological but dictated by desperate economic conditions, natural calamities, and significant political pressures and, in the case of Mozambique, military destabilization.

Direct American foreign aid, administered throughout the LDCs by the AID, has naturally always advocated the development of private enterprise. In 1981 the new administration introduced the so-called private sector initiative to guide all future foreign aid. It has defined the private sector to include any "for profit" business—including corporate farming, but excluding family farms, co-ops, and all nonprofit organizations. However, since "dialogue" to persuade a government may not be enough to make the changes in policy, the AID staff is instructed to "direct . . . actions to eliminate legal, regulatory and other constraints to private enterprise development."[22] Leverage to force the implementation of market-oriented policies on the recipient nations has included linkages to World Bank loans and trade concessions for those that comply. The Americans have also been able to direct counterpart funds, the local currency equivalent of all U.S. aid, which in countries like India reach enormous sums, to promote this strategy.

The debt crisis and the ideological predispositions reinforced each other, as both the U.S. government and World Bank officials concluded that equity should replace loans for future nonleveraged growth. Their program extended from aid to the existing private sector to divesting state enterprises or services and to developing the physical and institutional infrastructure. "Our goal is for AID to be involved in an average of at least two privatization activities in each of these [forty] principal countries by the end of 1987," claimed an AID administrator in 1986.[23]

The IMF/World Bank message also was to "privatize" as many state-operated functions or enterprises as possible. "We are working with country after country in looking at their public investment programmes. . . . The losses are enormous. We must clean them up, make them efficient and [in some cases] privatize them," noted Clausen in 1985.[24] By 1986, under Washington's aegis, the IMF and the World Bank were using their increased leverage to insist on free-market policies as the condition for new loans. World Bank staff members are investigating just how far they can go in privatizing what have traditionally been considered public services. One staff member even developed a program for the private sale of water after the state builds the infrastructure.

The IFC, "the multilateral agency that finances private-sector business in developing countries," is being primed for a new, expanded role. Established in the 1950s, it was never before of great importance.[25] It now plans to invest $7.4 billion over the period 1985–89, but in 1986 its own investment was about $1 billion a year, to which it attracts only an additional $3 billion in private investment spread out over thirty-eight countries. "We like to have [only] 15% of the equity in a project," said its vice-president.[26] The aim for the future is to "catalyze" portfolio investment, particularly that of pension funds and insurance companies. It also invites banks and other financial institutions to participate in its loans. In March 1986 the IFC introduced an Emerging-Markets Growth Fund, initially endowed with $50 million from ten institutional investors and run by a U.S. mutual-fund company to invest in LDC stock markets. Investment started in such markets as India, Brazil, Argentina, Chile, the Philippines, and Thailand. The IFC estimated total foreign equity investment in LDC stock markets to be $600 million, or less than 1 percent of these markets' total investment. The IFC in 1985 was also the "catalytic partner" in encouraging foreign investment in Hungary. And in order further to aid the banks, the IFC plans to try "to convert some bank claims on LDCs into obligations in investment trusts which could be traded abroad."[27] The World Bank also set up an investment insurance agency, linked to the IFC, to guarantee foreign investors against risk of currency losses, nationalization, repudiation of government contracts, and armed conflict or civil unrest.

The Asian Development Bank (ADB) and the Inter-American Development Bank also have been actively promoting and coordinating capital-market development in their respective areas. The ADB completed an eighteen-month study of the capital markets of its member states in January 1986, concluding that governments dominated the financial sector and did not appreciate the potential "pivotal role in economic growth" of the private capital market. Pension funds and insurance companies are usually required by law to invest in government securities. "[M]ost financing has been channeled through the non-securities market as government-guaranteed and subsidized loans. . . . This has led to unbalanced development and a hazardous over-dependence on debt finance," the ADB study maintained.[28]

The ADB proposed that governments allow interest rates to reflect real costs of capital, reduce their role in offering concessional credit for income redistribution purposes, make changes in fiscal policy so that investment profit "properly reflects investment risk," and offer greater incentives for foreign portfolio investment. It also advocated a shift away from regulation to a positive promotion of capital-market development.[29] Under strong American pressure to promote private enterprise and encourage privatization, the ADB in its 1986 report pressed member countries to "become more market-oriented, rather than remain protected by high import tariffs or saddled with avoidable social costs."[30]

The Inter-American Development Bank set up its investment corporation with initial capital of $200 million in early 1986, and the ADB followed shortly thereafter. While the private corporations welcomed this new emphasis, they were anxious that it not replace project lending from the World Bank itself. "Unfortunately, the expansion in private-sector support is being accompanied by scaled-back programs of the development banks themselves. Investment corporations will . . . be limited in size and scope of operations. Their emergence and growth can nowhere near compensate for declines in World Bank and regional bank lending," commented *Agribusiness Worldwide,* in an opinion reflecting the concerns of its constituency and shared by other sectors of private capital.[31]

In Latin America domestic investment was lower in 1984 than a decade earlier. The decline in real investment began in 1981 and in 1982 reached 12 percent in real terms for the region as a whole, as fifteen countries reported disinvestment and the rest experienced stagnation. In Argentina, for example, gross capital formation fell from over 25 percent of the GNP in 1980 to 16 percent in 1985. The adjustment programs have slowed investment or brought it to a standstill among all LDCs, with far-reaching implications for the future.

In the ten indebted nations where private enterprise was expected to resolve the debt problem, net private savings fell drastically and, in the aggregate, investment fell 7.5 percent in the 1980s. More capital flowed out of these countries than into them, with minor exceptions. The private sector in most LDCs was overwhelmed with debt, and many firms were bankrupt. The state has been forced, willy-nilly, to intervene to save the banks from collapse—sometimes, as in Mexico, by nationalizing them. Similar situations occurred in foreign trade and the management of enterprises. In a situation of force majeure, there was no time for ideological musings on the benefits of the market. It takes no great economic insight to recognize the fantasy of this privatization project. The policies did provide a few real bargains for members of the ruling class or the TNCs, and a UN study reported that "state owned enterprises have been sold at prices far below their real value," contributing "to the concentration of economic power in the hands of a few."[32] As for the state enterprises with large losses, which the IMF/World Bank, the AID, and others castigated as a drain on the budget, they found no buyers in the private sector, domestic or foreign. The Argentine government introduced a program of massive privatization, but an adviser to the president noted, "[W]e don't have any buyers. Who wants to buy something that loses money? Nobody wants to take risks."[33] With so many competitive incentives worldwide, and in an environment of little or no growth, foreign investors have been loath to invest in the troubled economies. Some do, of course, particularly in Mexico because of its proximity to the American market, but such investment is small compared with that nation's estimated $17 billion in capital flight between 1983 and 1985.

While the ideologues with the AID waxed lyrical about the magic of the market, assuming that investors would rush to depressed economies as soon as government services were put up for sale, the IFC was rather more realistic. In its 1985 report it observed:

It is ironic that the private sector is coming more into favor just when private firms in so many countries are weakened from the events of the past few years. Indeed, in some cases this weakness has led governments to intervene in decapitalized industry and shaky financial intermediaries, actually increasing the public sector's share of the economy. . . . [A]usterity and recession are poor bases for long-term investment in productive assets. Structural adjustments . . . saps the financial strength and ability of business to adjust.[34]

Of direct foreign investment it noted, "[I]t alone can never be the panacea for shortages of other international capital flows. For private business in the majority of the developing countries the outlook continues to be one of slack demand, expensive credit, uncertainty and low confidence."[35]

CHAPTER 18

RESTRUCTURING THE CENTRALLY PLANNED ECONOMIES

Restructuring is now a global effort. In the centrally planned economies (CPEs) of Eastern Europe and of Asia, as in the OECD states and the less-developed capitalist countries, the states are engaged in certain fundamental structural changes. Mikhail Gorbachev in his address to the party congress in 1986 called for a full "restructuring" of the Soviet economy.[1] This insistence was but a continuation of an effort of over two decades to try to compensate for the economic failures in the centrally planned economies. In each of these countries during the 1980s there were both economic and political reasons for restructuring in some fashion, and many of them paralleled those in the rest of the world economy. While not minimizing the importance of Gorbachev's policy of cultural 'openness' as a welcome contrast to the oppressive conditions of the preceding decades, in this chapter I will focus on a number of questions on the direction of the economy and the contradictions in restructuring. This focus in no way implies that, in my view, the traditional form of Soviet economic organization was a preferable one.

No one was more aware of their deficiencies than many of the managers of the system. They looked admiringly toward the economies of the OECD states and sought to restructure their own, in large part, by imitating them. Their primary focus over these years was to increase productivity and "modernize" the economy by way of a "scientific and technological revolution." In order to attain this goal rapidly, they sought both to borrow from and to trade with the capitalist nations, intending to participate in what they perceived as a new international division of labor.

In their general tendency toward convergence with the capitalist economies, many in the CPEs, particularly the economists, have also proclaimed an ever growing number of aspects of the capitalist system to be objective economic "laws," which transcend capitalism and are valid at all times and in all places. One Soviet study asserted, "State monopoly capital establishes a system of economic management. . . . The proletariat must utilize this mechanism. . . ."[2]

TRADITIONAL CHARACTERISTICS
OF THE CPEs

None of the Communist parties have ever achieved a unanimity on the policy of "restructuring"; rather, all of them have experienced a consistent struggle between what the Western press has labeled the "conservatives" and the "reformers." The conservatives are those who seek to preserve the traditional characteristics of central planning and who reject changes that introduce new capitalist ingredients into the society as well as moves toward political liberalization.

Traditionally, with some variations, the CPEs have had certain economic characteristics beyond state ownership of the means of production that distinguished them from capitalist economies. Among these are the role of the central plan and a centralized direction of all the factors of production, macro- and micro-investment decisions, the allocation of resources, foreign trade, and the distribution of the surplus. Quantitative targets were established for each enterprise, and production was measured in volume. Administered prices were stable and separated from those in the world market; they served essentially an accounting function rather than as "signals" like those alleged to operate in a market economy. Also typical of the CPE model were high rates of investment, full employment, and limits on income inequality, for equity was an important aspect of the ideology, if not of the reality. Wages were based on a principle of equal pay for equal work and established centrally, prices were generally formulated on a cost-plus basis, and those essential products that could not yield profits were subsidized. Labor was comparatively immobile and assigned where required by the state plan.

But the position of the advocates of change, the "reformers," grew in the party and the bureaucracy because, as one UN report concluded, "the increased complexity of the economies has been making them less amenable to the traditional methods of centralized planning, with their emphasis on detailed quantitative and meticulous administrative controls."[3] These economies needed to use scarce resources more efficiently and to introduce new technology. An ever present contradiction in the USSR was severe shortages accompanied by overproduction of unwanted goods.

PRODUCTIVITY

To increase productivity is the principal motivation for the restructuring of the CPEs. Although one Western study found that labor productivity does not lag behind that of the capitalist economies—in fact, the "contrary is true"—the managers of the CPEs have perceived productivity as the great dilemma facing their system.[4] This perception and the attempt to increase productivity have led the Soviet bloc to turn increasingly toward capitalist measures. The primary changes the CPEs have sought are in the areas of mechanization, decentralization, and incentives. Their policies in each area have introduced new contradictions.

While the arguments on productivity and wages parallel those in the capitalist countries—with exhortations against "laziness" and calls for increased work discipline, piecework wages, and the like—one former Soviet economist pointed to underinvestment in machine building, compared with investment in raw-materials extraction (40 percent for oil and gas), and "an unprecedented decline in manufacturing producer goods and machinery for the energy, metallurgical, chemical, and agricultural sectors," as two of the chief restraints on productivity growth.[5] "The result has been an abysmally low level of mechanization of even the simplest tasks," he elaborated. "Almost half [40 percent] of the workers in industry, more than half the workers in construction, and more than 70 percent of the workers in agriculture and other branches of the economy are reportedly occupied with unmechanized physical labor."[6] The new call for labor discipline, he added, did not address these problems or the disruption caused by shortages of fuels and raw materials. Gorbachev also emphasized mechanization in order to increase output. To secure the new technology to increase productivity, many states went deeply into debt to the Western banks. And as the result of a calamitous misperception of a new international division of labor, they oriented investment plans toward the capitalist world market rather than toward the needs of their own societies.

The Polish government, for example, with one of the worst planning records in Eastern Europe or, at least, now the most exposed to scrutiny, purchased a color TV factory from RCA in 1975 for over $68 million. By the 1980s it was considered a total loss, since the Poles could not afford them and no one outside Poland in the hard-currency area would buy them. They also exported golf carts to the United States until the American industry demanded protection, leaving Poland with no other market. These are only instances of a widespread effort.

In addition to the perennial problems of low productivity, therefore, the CPEs also had to confront the new requirements of foreign-debt service and the demands of foreign trade. The countries of Eastern Europe were dependent on energy and raw-materials imports for their economic growth, and the USSR continuously required food and desired imports of high technology. As in the LDCs debt financing, especially from the commercial banks, was attractive in the 1970s, since the rate of inflation and the declining value of the dollar led to low and often negative real interest rates.

But the inflationary recession in the capitalist economies, by increasing the cost of imports and reducing the market for exports, sharply altered the terms of trade for the COMECON countries. Their collective trade deficit in 1975 was a record $12 billion, more than doubling that of 1974. To finance the deficit and to retain a choice of suppliers for their imports, they continued to borrow from the commercial banks rather than rely on government export credits. Competition was intense among the banks that gave them the best terms as preferred credit risks. By 1976 many CPEs were forced to borrow for debt service.

Both the bankers and the governments with export credits took the initiative in urging them to borrow. They assumed that the economic fundamentals were healthy and that the USSR was the umbrella in case of trouble. In 1985 Poland's chief negotiator with the Paris Club of creditors, to whom it owed $27 billion, ruefully admitted that borrowing had been "very risky and one can say catastrophic. It has proved so, unfortunately."[7] The ability of a few officials to commit the nation to onerous debts contributed to Poland's social crisis in the early 1980s.

Mechanization nevertheless remains a principal goal in Soviet restructuring. The current plan calls for an 80 percent increase in machinery investment and for scrapping half of the existing facilities by 1990, when it is planned that two-thirds of all production will be by new machines. But the government anticipates that this process of restructuring will also leave 13 to 19 million workers unemployed.[8]

DECENTRALIZATION

The objective factors of foreign debt and the consequent need to export accelerated the trend toward restructuring, and decentralization was an important feature. Hungary, with the longest experience with economic "reforms," was the model among the Comecon nations, but experiments had been made in the USSR since Khrushchev's efforts to decentralize economic decisions in the late 1950s.

The sheer size and complexity of the economies made the old, centralized form of all decision making unwieldy for any bureaucracy. Many officials advocated decentralization of decision making; but decentralization can take many forms. To whom and how decisions are delegated are critical questions. A World Bank study differentiated two types of decentralization among the CPEs. One *modifies* the system of central planning by transferring to local managers decisions on the composition of output and production methods and other micro decisions while retaining macro policy planning in the center. The other is a systemic change: "market forces," including competition from imports, are introduced, and "enterprises are coordinated horizontally through market links rather than vertically along an administrative chain of commands."[9] The state then takes on the role it has in other capitalist countries by dealing with taxes, credits, and subsidies. Both Hungary and China in the 1980s have systematically moved to introduce the latter, as did the USSR in 1987. But the state and the party remain in the background in all these countries as the ultimate arbiters.

Soviet reforms began in 1957 when Khrushchev abolished most of the industrial ministries and established regional councils to which the individual enterprises were subordinate. It was believed that the councils would be more responsive to local needs, but the organization replicated the centralized system on a regional basis. Khrushchev's successors eliminated the regional councils in 1965, on the grounds that they created unnecessary duplication, and introduced a new "reform" based on the ideas of the economist Yevsei Liberman. This reinstated the industrial ministries but gave more decision-making powers to the managers of the enterprises and increased the role of profit as a criterion for allocating resources and bonuses as an incentive for production.

Although Western analysts tend to emphasize the ideological dimension and struggles between "reformers" and "conservatives" in the USSR and elsewhere, pragmatic factors were significant in policy shifts away from this program under Brezhnev. After a review of the obstacles to the implementation of the Liberman "reform" of economic planning, a former state planner concluded, "Planners found that, once again, only direct regulation could bring an improvement for any individual indicator. This sequence rather than some wish by planners to turn the clock back . . . was, in my view, the chief cause of the retreat from the 1965 reform."[10] He added, "I have first hand knowledge of Soviet planners and have considerable respect for their attempts to improve the Soviet economy."[11]

Continuing their efforts in 1981, some four years before the ascendancy of Gorbachev, the Soviets set up a large-scale economic experiment that included 700 enterprises in five industries. It introduced greater autonomy for decisions in the enterprise, emphasized contract fulfillment, and increased material incentives. Gorbachev, as is well known, has pushed this program further. Cost accounting and responsibility for the profit of each enterprise were made a question of individual management. Beginning in 1986 the Soviets introduced a limited program of joint ventures with Western companies, retaining 51 percent ownership but allowing unrestricted profit repatriation. They also permitted the managers of state enterprises to negotiate directly with foreign companies on trade and investment matters and to use part of the foreign currency they acquire as they choose. The managers of enterprises continue to be the focus of the decentralization, as more and more functional decisions on investments, on what is produced, on prices, and on distribution of profits are passed to their hands.

INCENTIVES

The decision to augment material incentives through increasing income inequality is another principal feature of the reform effort to raise productivity in the CPEs. Higher wages to enterprises that are successful is replacing the policy of equal pay for equal work. Gorbachev asserted, "It is necessary for the size of an enterprises wage fund to be directly tied to revenues from the sales of its products. . . ."[12] And although the workers never decided what to produce, he went on, "We can no longer reconcile ourselves to the fact that the workers of enterprises of unsuitable products are living without particular cares, receiving in full both their wages . . . and other benefits."[13] But they faced an additional dilemma, described by one official who reported, "[E]conomic managers claim that in recent years this incentive [more money] has been working less and less and many workers have no serious interest in extra money. Why? . . . The essence of the matter is that economic conditions now allow . . . workers to exist comfortably. . . . [This] reduces the economic need to work intensively in order to have the means for existence."[14]

In their search for means to increase productivity, state bureaucrats have readily chosen to focus on "egalitarianism" as a barrier to greater productivity, arguing, in effect, that equity and efficiency are incompatible. The differentiation of income as an incentive to production is therefore the most widely advocated reform in the CPEs. But a frustrated Soviet economist wrote in 1985, "[T]he traditions of leveling are tenacious; just as soon as there is an appreciable differentiation in wages, . . . an apprehension arises—is this permissible?"[15] Such contradictions are more obvious in countries where the ideology was oriented to equity and the reforms have increased class differentials.

THE CONTRACT SYSTEM IN THE CPEs

In their search for new modes for the organization of production, the Soviet Union and a number of other CPEs have been experimenting with contracts—between the state and either private entrepreneurs, brigades of workers, or peasants—shifting from an emphasis on quantitative goals to contract fulfillment. Since 1983 the Soviets have been experimenting with the contract system in agriculture, based on the Hungarian model, contracting for a fixed quantity and allowing the excess for private sale. In the same year a contract system was applied in the factories, which pay a brigade of twelve to fifty workers who contract to do certain functions and are paid for the end result rather than individual wages or for piecework. They are also financially responsible for damages or losses from the underfulfilling of contracts. The members of the brigade decide among themselves how the payment is allocated. The impetus of this new form of work organization came at the end of 1980, in response to the events in Poland.

The 1986 "individual labor" law in the USSR allowed individuals to contract to run small businesses for profit, particularly in the services, legalizing the moonlighting that was already widespread. The state would provide the credits, and a contract would require the enterprise to pay a fixed sum out of profits. The managers would buy their supplies directly from the producers and set their own prices. Initially, it extended from small service and family tailor shops to seventy large state enterprises set up in conglomerate form and organizing their own marketing, pricing, and purchasing strategies, including foreign trade.

Although internal factors dominated the restructuring efforts, the pressures of debt service and the requirements of trade with the hard-currency countries also affected them. As the UN *World Economic Survey* of 1985 noted, "The external pressures for adjustment were most pronounced in Hungary, Poland and Romania . . . which had to embrace restrictive adjustment policies. . . ."[16] In part, therefore, the move toward capitalist restructuring in some of these countries coincides with the increasing intrusion of the IMF into their economic policy.

CPEs AND THE IMF/WORLD BANK

By 1986 Hungary, Romania, Yugoslavia, Poland, Vietnam, and China, half of the CPEs, belonged to the IMF/World Bank. The Romanian and, particularly, the Yugoslav economies, under IMF guidance, have been crippled for many years. Vietnam inherited its membership with its victory in 1975 and has since adopted much of the IMF recipe for its current economic policies, even using a former IMF functionary from the old regime as a key adviser. Hungary joined in November 1981, after it was already well advanced on an economic program that met with the approval of these two institutions. Poland tried to join the IMF at the same time as Hungary did but was blocked by the United States after it imposed martial law, and it was not able to join until five years later. Finally, by the end of 1986 even the USSR was expressing interest in joining the IMF and World Bank.

In November 1982 an IMF loan of $580 million to Hungary was linked to the Fund's traditional austerity program. The IMF staff asserted that its objective in Hungary was to restructure "the entire industrial sector [and introduce] policy and institutional reforms . . . to enhance internal and external competition, resource mobility, and the market-responsiveness and financial discipline of enterprises—the three aspects identified as fundamental for effective restructuring in that country."[17] " 'Rationalization' of the consumer price system could reduce or eliminate prevalent subsidies for some basic consumer goods and services such as food, mass transportation, heating fuel and housing. Such a process is taking place today in Hungary," noted a World Bank study in 1983.[18]

As in the LDCs, using the leverage of debt, coupled with the government bureaucrats' credulousness and lack of interest in, or commitment to, an alternative, the IMF technicians are able to apply textbook economics as if on a tabula rasa, proposing measures that were long ago circumvented or superseded in the capitalist nations of the OECD. "Of particular interest [to the IMF and World Bank] are the various changes in ownership in the means of production, the locus of decision making, price formation, incentives to workers and managers, and the degree of competition," observed one World Bank staff member.[19] Under IMF guidance, the criteria for evaluating an enterprise changed from volume of production to profit. Decisions on what to produce, the use of inputs, including labor, and the nature of new investment are transferred to the

manager, whose incentives are based on profit. Prices are determined
by supply and demand rather than by a rational plan or social needs.
Bankruptcy and liberalized imports will increase competition. When
failures in these guided economies occur, the IMF attributes them to
the persistence of central planning or, particularly, to a residual "conservative" commitment to equity, which one of its economists called the
strongest barrier to the essential "reforms."[20]

HUNGARY

János Kádár introduced the "New Economic Mechanism" in Hungary in 1968, long before it joined the IMF, and began the gradual shift
to a market capitalist economy. Since then, it has been the model for
other CPEs, including China.

There was a struggle, however, among party leaders, even in Hungary. Some feared the inevitable consequences of the "reforms," in the
form of unemployment, inequality, inflation; others desired some of
these same results, thinking they promised an increase in efficiency and
effective work incentives, particularly the moves toward greater inequality of income. The planners underestimated how strongly the
industrial workers resented the idea of managers' being rewarded at
their expense. As one analyst pointed out, inequality is considerably
more "transparently" a political decision in the CPEs than in the
capitalist countries.[21] Those opposed to the capitalist restructuring and
the emergence of a new bourgeoisie—and the opposition was always
an internal one—were able to arrest the moves in 1973. There emerged
a compromise by which income differentials at work were balanced by
increased family allowances. However, the government borrowed heavily in the West until 1978 in order to maintain a growth rate of nearly
6 percent. In 1979 with the subsequent debt crisis, and after 1981 with
IMF guidance, restructuring began once more.

The major shift came in 1979, with a drastic increase in prices. The
state had determined that at least 20 percent of all production was being
sold at a loss. Factories were henceforth required to pay world prices
for their materials, and the state decided that within four years the
prices of two-thirds of the commodities would be set by supply and
demand. The state auctioned off leases of many small-scale enterprises
to private "socialist entrepreneurs." Assembly line workers were transferred to piecework, and wages in Hungary for the same work soon
differed markedly, on the basis not of work performed but of the
enterprise's profitability, which, of course, involved other factors than
the effort of the workers.

The reforms worked out in conjunction with the IMF in Hungary and in other member nations "have sought to increase income differentials to stimulate the economy," said a World Bank economist in 1983. The Hungarian officials have tried to redefine equality in a manner quite acceptable to capitalist ideology, as "equality of opportunity."

All the characteristics of a market capitalist economy have sequentially been put into place. Profit-oriented competing banks and enterprise managers, using bank loans and retained profits, increasingly make the investment decisions. Managers decide what to produce and set their prices to meet the demand of those with money or to suit the export market. It is obviously more profitable to produce for the demands of the newly rich. Scarce resources are allocated to the profitable enterprises. Prices rise to reflect scarcities, even for basic needs, and are linked to world prices. Yet even the World Bank, while urging such a policy, recognized the difficulties in this effort:

The principle of linking domestic prices of industrial commodities with their international counterparts is a move in the right direction. . . . The problems arise in part from the difficulties in arriving at a strict concordance between a domestically produced commodity—for example an article of clothing or a specialized machinery item—and a comparable internationally traded commodity and its price.[22]

The state has permitted enterprises to issue stocks and bonds to raise investment funds and, since Hungary had no income tax, absorb hidden money reserves. Banking in Hungary had by mid-1987 acquired all the features of a capitalist banking system, including foreign competition with interest rates and loans granted on the basis of expected profitability. Piecework and managers' bonuses are the usual production incentives. When piecework is possible, the basic wage is set at the lowest end of the scale. Managers' bonuses reach 30–35 percent of their salaries. The differential in income establishes demand in nonessentials, creating the signals to managers on what to produce.

As in the indebted LDCs, there is in Hungary also the burden of foreign-debt service and the need to export in order to acquire the raw materials with which to produce the exports to earn the foreign exchange with which to pay the debt. This circular trap has been a persistent drain on the country's resources.

The argument is always made that there is a struggle between the "conservatives," or ideologists, who cling to the ideology and resist change, and the "reformers," or "pragmatists," who recognize the paralysis in the economy and advocate changes in the direction of the

market capitalist economies. Since the "reformers" emphasize growth
and development, not the formal adoption of a capitalist ideology, it is
important to look at the "pragmatic" outcome of the restructuring of
the Hungarian economy.

There has been recession or stagnation since the beginning of the
1980s, when the restructuring really got under way. At the end of 1986
the Communist party newspaper reported that one-third of the population had a lower living standard, with a fall of 7 percent since 1983,
and that it could "see no basic improvement ahead."[23] While a small
elite prospered, 80 percent of the working population had two jobs,
inflation was 8 percent, and the foreign debt per capita was the highest
among the CPEs.

Stores are well stocked, but only a minority can afford to buy the
goods. The average wage in 1986 of the equivalent of $137 per
month—and the young and the old made much less—obviously did not
go far when prices were aligned to world prices. Prices were aligned,
but wages were not. And as always in capitalism, those with money
increasingly determined what was produced. During the 1980s there
was growing resentment in the general population at the rising prices,
falling living standards, and the new rich.

The new bankruptcy law was expected to close many "unprofitable"
factories, creating "temporary unemployment," while the workers were
admonished to find work in the services. "Job opportunities for young
people have worsened," reported one official in early 1987.[24] Yet, as
elsewhere, the official press continued to point to worker "laziness" as
a cause of the economy's problems.[25]

A recession in 1985, with a decline in both agricultural and industrial production, was followed by stagnation in 1986. The trade balance
shifted from surpluses in 1984 and 1985 to a deficit of over $539
million in 1986, and the hard-currency debt rose from $5.0 billion in
1985 to nearly $7.8 billion in 1986. The government devalued the
currency by 8 percent in early 1987, at which time the deputy prime
minister reflected, "[I]t is a real truth that we cannot endure without
consequences another year like 1986, because we might approach the
edge of the abyss."[26]

But Hungary proceeded with its restructuring although, as even a
World Bank study noted in 1983, "if the benefits of the reforms cannot
be demonstrated in a tangible manner, and the costs are apparent to
all," political opposition would emerge.[27] It proceeded because, from
its managers' point of view, there was nowhere else to go. The chief
of the National Planning Board and a high official in the party admitted,
"We have to clarify the matter of principle. If we continue to proceed

pragmatically, we will fail to resolve the question of what is socialism and how is it different from Western capitalism."[28] But by 1987, with economic failure evident, internal criticism was widespread. One prominent Hungarian writer interviewed in the Western press observed, "The mood of the whole country is turning to discontent. It's becoming common wisdom that the country is in crisis and the government is not able to solve it."[29]

POLAND

In Poland after the military coup d'état, against the Communist party as well as the population, and after the declaration of martial law in December 1981 that lasted until July 1983, the Military Council quadrupled the prices of basic needs, devalued the zloty, and lengthened the work week. By 1986, Warsaw economists found that 30 percent of all families had an income below what the government defined as the minimum for the purchase of necessities.

Pressed by foreign creditors and anxious to arrange IMF credits, the government announced a further austerity program to eliminate the remaining subsidies, including a new increase in food prices in 1987. "The whole leadership of the Polish economy and its management will be replaced," said a government spokesman, and the state will sell shares of industry to the public; "this definitely means stepping out of the system of centrally subsidized industry [to allow] the outdated and unprofitable parts of industry to go bankrupt."[30] Summing up the new perspective, one of Poland's economists in the State School of Planning, asserted, "[T]he dream of an economic system better than capitalism is dead."[31]

The National Trade Union Alliance, the official union designed to replace Solidarity, warned in March 1987, "We will undertake all actions to prevent the shrinking of society's real income." It insisted that price increases of up to 500 percent in 1982, of 25 percent in 1983, and of 18 percent in 1986 meant a "systematic lowering of living standards," which workers would no longer tolerate.[32]

CHINA

The IMF/World Bank's greatest success, however transitory it may be, has come in China. Moving a nation with one-quarter of the world's population into a form of leasehold capitalism, complete with production for profit, prices fixed by supply and demand, export processing zones, and commodification of labor, and the like, in four years' time is certainly a phenomenon for which they modestly claim considerable credit. The IMF has trained China's "modern" economists and even publishes its journal in Chinese. A joint project of the U.S. and Chinese governments set up a business school in Dalian in 1982. The change was swift. The 1977 party congress committed the party to "eliminating the bourgeoisie and other exploiting classes" and to continuing the revolution. The current Chinese leaders under Deng Xiaoping have zealously thrust such archaic notions as egalitarianism (which the *People's Daily* called "copied from a foreign country") and planned economic production for social need into the dustbin of history in their march toward "modernization."[33] The reformers continue to advocate a rapid end to the remaining aspects of central planning. "China is in transition . . . to a new system of a planned commodity economy," a government memorandum prepared for GATT declared.[34] The goal was a full capital and labor market and distribution by supply and demand.

The process began in 1978, with 6 enterprises in Sichuan Province under Zhao Ziyang, and expanded to 6,600 in 1980. In 1983 half of the nation's enterprises operated on the "responsibility" profit system. In October 1984 the party officially decided to extend it to the whole of China, so industrial enterprises had to compete in all ways to survive, and committed the party to a whole panoply of market capitalist policies.

Between 1980 and 1987 the living standard rose sharply for some Chinese, but life became considerably harder for most others, as wages failed to keep up with prices. Food prices rose 50 percent in May 1985 alone when decontrolled, and small traders soon dominated distribution. Factories began to drop the production of cheap, everyday items because of the low profitability. Stable and subsidized prices for basic needs had in the past equaled security for the mass of urban dwellers. But according to the deputy prime minister in charge of prices, the operation of the law of supply and demand is the key to modernization. By 1987 the market set the price for 65 percent of agricultural goods, 55 percent of industrial products, and 40 percent of raw materials.

By 1985 "modernization" had gotten out of hand. Widespread corruption, profiteering, and speculation, a fall of foreign exchange for the importation of luxury goods, with a trade deficit of nearly $8 billion, production of low-quality goods, and shortages and illegal trading of raw materials and other state-sector goods highlighted the contradictions in the policies pursued. The experiments with the free-trade zones were also alarming by 1985. The model zone adjacent to Hong Kong that had been expected to attract foreign investment and generate export earnings was instead a drain on foreign exchange, and only one-third of its production was exported. The zones were also centers of corruption. Officials then appeared surprised when the contradictions inherent in their policies emerged. Petty capitalist traders exploited the people with price-gouging, hoarding, corruption, and speculation. Those who did not participate were bitter, forced into panic buying and hoarding because of the fluctuating prices. Significantly, these policies are advocated by economists and goverment officials who cannot personally profit; on the contrary, they belong to the group on a fixed low income and will actually suffer from the inflation the policies entail. Theirs is an ideological conviction that reveals little understanding of the workings of capitalism.

In the countryside, a Chinese party official said, "rich peasants give hard-up ones something to look forward to."[35] He elaborated, "Our government promotes the policy that some people get rich first, then we will have the other people get rich."[36] China in effect reinstated private agriculture under the façade of the state's leasing the land for thirty years, allowing the land to be passed from father to son and sold to enterprising peasants, with the likelihood that the latter would concentrate landholding in a number of years. The free-market policies were followed by peasants who shifted from grain to cash crops and conversion to fish ponds. Although this produced higher profits, it also resulted in lower grain production, raising the fear of shortages by 1990, even without a natural calamity. The Chinese people are dependent on grain for over 90 percent of their calories and proteins. Peasants did not fulfill state contracts to provide a fixed supply of grain, and production in both 1985 and 1986 fell below the targets. The 1985 decline in the harvest was the greatest since 1949. The state tacitly reduced the contracts to increase the incentives to plant more grain for free-market sales. However, while the free-market price was well above the contract price, the cost of inputs was also high and profit remained low.

Opposition to the economic reformers was already evident by the beginning of 1987, as party leaders committed to traditional central planning, and the vast bulk of the people, who have not gained in the new reforms, mounted their resistance. The rhetoric focused on "bourgeois liberalization," but at stake was the direction of the economy itself. Reports from China of internal party documents indicated Deng's fear that the workers would follow the students into the streets in early 1987 and that a Solidarity-like movement would develop. He expressed admiration for the "cool-headed" response of the Polish authorities. Chinese and foreign observers in Beijing were of the opinion that at this point the army would have intervened.[37]

Because of the pendulum swings in policy in that volatile land, one is hesitant to generalize about China's future course, for fear that between the writing and the publication of these words another radical shift in direction will have taken place.

CUBA

Between 1976 and 1986 the Cubans also experimented with techniques like a free farmers' market, profit criteria for enterprises, joint-venture laws for foreign investment, and the buying and selling of property whose ownership had been transferred from the state. The head of the planning commission was a Moscow-trained technocrat who since 1976 had pushed for Hungarian-style reforms in the economy, although in practice Cuban planning was closer to the post-1965 Soviet system. In 1980 Fidel Castro advocated the policy, but the absence of pragmatic accomplishments coupled with ideological repugnance led to a sharp reversal, and in mid-1985 those advocates of "market socialism" were replaced. Since then the Cuban leader has attacked the trend toward capitalism and personal enrichment and has reversed many of the regulations that made it possible. "From the moment we have so-called businessmen who worry more about the enterprise than the interests of the country, we have out and out capitalism," he observed.[38] In 1986 the government closed the peasants' free market, suspended pay bonuses based on productivity, and eliminated private sales of property. But many Cuban economists continue to advocate the reforms. The struggle parallels that in other CPEs, but Fidel Castro himself is leading it against other party leaders who still favor the Hungarian path.[39]

What has happened in Cuba can happen elsewhere. The political developments in China beginning at the end of 1986 reveal the potential for a swift reversal of policies that were once declared fixed. Foreign investments fell 50 percent in 1986, and reportedly investors were "cautious," "few showing interest in doing business in China."[40] As the CPEs are eager to achieve economic growth through capitalist enterprise and foreign investment, are not the contradictions equally clear—as the developments in Cuba and China appear to illustrate? Private capitalists can never be certain that there will not occur a swift reversal of the "reforms," and this uncertainty affects their actions, especially given the competitive enticements for their capital worldwide. If "reforms" are introduced only on a temporary or emergency basis, or if the goals of socialism are retained, the foreign investors the governments are trying to attract and the domestic capitalists will both be oriented toward speculation, a quick profit, neglect of maintenance, and so on. The result is all short-term, primitive accumulation, extracting the maximum for repatriation. These changes may create a short-run increase in production, but they quickly introduce other capitalist contradictions that were minimized by state planning. This form of mixed economy is the most difficult to manage, since the introduction of market forces creates its own set of attitudes and institutions. Within the milieu of the CPEs over the medium and the long term, these policies can have only the most negative "pragmatic" consequences. There will be ambiguity unless the CPEs renounce the ideology altogether and openly declare themselves capitalist states like all the others.

There was naturally a struggle on these issues in all of the CPEs. Many Russians, and opponents of the restructuring elsewhere, are convinced that Gorbachev's proposed "reforms" along the lines of those in Hungary would aggravate income differentials, raise prices of basics like food and rent, and increase unemployment and that the call for austerity and hard work would fall most heavily on the working class. Workers in some Soviet factories have indeed protested their being asked to bear the cost of problems created by the management in the restructuring process, and opinion polls revealed deep opposition. Other officials have resisted the planned restructuring of the Soviet economy, claiming that it could eliminate the jobs of 13 to 19 million workers. Other interests have also opposed these changes, of course, such as state bureaucrats who fear they will be replaced by managers or those who fear a weakening of the hegemony of the Communist party.

The perceived *political* requirements for restructuring were also compelling after 1980. The struggle in Poland created a sense of urgency elsewhere. For some government officials it underlined the imperative of achieving a higher standard of living, which they presumed would be an outcome of increased productivity. Academics and policymakers discussed the situation and likened it to that of 1921, the year of the Kronstadt uprising, which some compared to the Polish events, and Lenin's introduction of "state capitalism" with the NEP. Such analogies with the NEP have been used by reformers to justify changes they desire.[41]

That many Soviet officials understood the nature of the crisis and were concerned about the developments of new "antagonistic contradictions" in their social system is obvious from their writings and debates. A discussion of the possibility that the struggle in Poland would spread to other countries was aired in the press and economic journals. Some openly discussed the prospect of "antagonistic contradictions" between "managers and managed."[42] A sector chief of the Institute of the Economy of the World Socialist System, in Moscow, argued after the Polish events that the "fundamental contradiction . . . between productive forces and production relations" is "the source of all economic, social, political and ideological problems of socialism."[43] He discussed "state bureaucratic property alienated from the workers" and attempts to "replace the workers' own power by the activity of the state apparatus, in the name of the working people but not in their interest."[44] If managers "lose contact with the managed, if they begin to implement their own selfish group interests at the expense of public interests and working peoples interests," the two "become mutually exclusive interests that acquire in this regard the nature of antagonistic contradiction."[45]

The distinction between "reformers" and "conservatives" that has colored reports of this struggle outside of these countries only further confuses the issues. The ambiguity lies in the fact that political liberalism—advocating civil liberties and intellectual freedom, greater "openness" and political democracy—is invariably linked in the discussion to moves away from central planning and toward a market capitalist organization of the economy. Indeed, there is often such a political lineup among officials in the CPEs.

But the arguments are distorted and artificially made to appear ambiguous, as if greater freedom and civil liberties, cultural "openness" and political democracy, must be linked to a capitalist restructuring of the economy while resistance to such restructuring is linked to political and cultural authoritarianism. In reality no such dichotomy exists, and there are clearly alternatives to either of these two combinations.

While the "reformers" called for greater income differentials and the establishment of nearly all the institutions of a capitalist economy, the Polish workers, like workers everywhere in periods of mass self-mobilization called for greater equality and the leveling of income and privilege. "There is a profound egalitarian impulse at the heart of the Solidarity movement. One valuable legacy of 35 years of communist rule: people have been exposed to these slogans for so long that now they want to make them real," a Warsaw sociologist told one Western reporter in 1981.[46]

We shall press for the realization of egalitarianism in society. . . . Social justice demands that the cost of the crisis and the necessary reforms be distributed among all citizens, that is in proportion to their means. Poland is a country with a wide range of income levels among social groups. . . . The costs of the program to restore equilibrium should fall on the shoulders of the most well off groups. . . . [I]n the 1970s there began a sharp rise in social inequality, and the privileges of those in authority swelled to even greater dimensions. And yet this very group is responsible for the current state [of the economy]. . . . [T]hey are divorced from the realities of the . . . population.[47]

Solidarity called for a tax to equalize income, a tax on wealth, and restrictions on privilege: "The measures for redistribution of income . . . will make possible both the elimination of the inequalities that society will no longer accept and the financing of the most essential social programs."[48] As the way to improve productivity and efficiency, Solidarity proposed improved safety conditions and a shorter workday. It also advocated submitting broad programs of economic reform or changes for public discussion and consideration and a general democratization of the system.[49] The Polish workers, in their early political demands, wanted some authority over the critical questions of what to produce and what happens to it, what and where to invest, and how to determine wage levels. Cultural and intellectual freedom and political democracy were also prominent in their demands, and artistic and intellectual creativity flourished widely before the movement was crushed. There were also many ambiguities in the movement, but the thrust of the demands were egalitarian and democratic and were an assertion that the working class was not a mere commodity in the production process that would passively bear the brunt of the calamitous decisions of a few bureaucrats, but the subject of its own history.

Obviously, the real questions are not whether a "market" decides consumer preferences in styles, how much freedom of choice there is in types of music or art forms (all obviously desirable), or whether services like cafés are provided by individuals or by a collective. Such diversionary issues avoid the real questions of transferring from a centralized bureaucratic "commandism" of state planning to introducing market determinants in the economy, promoting greater differentiation of income, basing production on profit—in short, progressively bringing in the whole panoply of capitalist relations and institutions while continuing to call the system "socialist." By attributing what is inherently linked to the capitalist mode of production to neutral economic "laws," the CPEs incorporate new contradictions into their own system. And economic organization carries its own logic and the formation of the sociopolitical institutions, attitudes, and class relations. Any moves toward political liberalization will be undermined by the accentuation of class differentials in the social sphere.

The real political and economic questions in the CPEs, as elsewhere, are the basic ones. The fundamentals remain the same everywhere. Who controls the surplus and how is it allocated? What is produced and for whom, and is the criterion use or exchange? Is the distribution of scarcities determined by price or by rational planning? Does the fulfillment of needs or of profits determine decisions? And who participates in these decisions?

It is the answers to these basic questions that determine the nature of the society. By trying to combine a capitalist organization of the economy, even to the extent of subjecting the nation to the directives of the IMF, with the ideology and goals of socialism, and by making radical shifts between the market and central planning, these economies will only aggravate their internal contradictions.

CHAPTER 19

CONCLUSION TO PART III

A basic tenet of the existing system is that when the incentive for capital to invest breaks down, the state must renew or restore the process once more by restructuring the world economy to provide the incentive. Individual states have adopted a uniform perspective on their role in this process. As the evidence has shown, this has been reinforced by the objective fiscal crisis that afflicts them all and that forces and makes possible their leanest, and meanest, response. Their solution to the economic crisis is simple, if crude—to increase profits and reduce wages and labor costs for both capital and the state.

These are the boundaries within which all political parties move, since the capitalist system supersedes the state, which conforms to its needs. Governments everywhere are competing for capital and trying to restore the investment incentives by reducing the cost of labor. They have been largely successful in the offensive against labor but have failed in their principal aim of restoring productive investment. The orthodox capitalists, the socialists, and the CPEs have failed on a global scale.

The perceptions of policymakers play an important role. By misperceiving the origin of economic conditions, they commit great errors in state policy. France, for example, looked at the American "recovery" in 1983–84 and drew the wrong conclusion, and the CPEs in their moves toward market determinants in the economy misperceive the origin of the flaws in their own economy that they are trying to correct and the efficacy of those they are trying to imitate, and so forth.

Still, that the monetarists and other bourgeois economists have been

able to proceed as far as they have is striking. The near religious
adherence to the "market forces" has gone well beyond the rational
pursuit of special interests. Inevitably, the ideology that the market will
be the exclusive regulator had to retreat in America, where its rhetoric
was most prominent, when it collided with powerful interests long
accustomed to special state subsidies. The government in the United
States, in fact, has seldom had a greater presence in the economy—
through subsidies, budget deficits, and bank rescues—than when it
declared its fervent advocacy of getting the state "out of the economy."
Politics, defined here as struggle within the class that rules, determined
the outcome. The administration could implement the austerity measures only against the powerless. Indeed, the market is always regulated, and the only question is by whom and for whom?

The ideology of the private versus the public sector has been all the
more ludicrous in the context of the economic reality of the 1970s and
1980s. So-called market forces are everywhere being endowed with a
new credibility and hegemony at the very moment when their contradictions are most apparent and acute. Notwithstanding these blatant contradictions, other states, including the CPEs, rush to embrace the
market system.

Privatization is proclaimed at a time when capital is showing little
interest in investing except to shuffle assets and speculate in the financial markets. But that the state provision of basic services—water,
education, health—should be under scrutiny and attack indicates how
far to the right the boundaries of dialogue and policy have been extended over the past decade. Nationalization of industry was once a
path by which to emerge from crisis, but state-owned industry must also
conform to the exigencies of the capitalist system. State industries
compete in steel, chemicals, banks, and arms. But formal ownership
proved to be less significant in the operations of the system, since the
intrinsic features of accumulation, competition, and struggle with labor
prevail regardless of formal ownership. The major losses in state industries spurred governments to insist that they operate to maximize profit
and/or be sold to private interests.

All the industrial states are pursuing the same strategy: competing
for capital and aiding the development of the same industries in new
technology, preparing the way for a new wave of devastating competition. The new technology aroused utopian hopes among government
planners for new products that would resolve the crisis in the industrial
countries, in their quest for a new competitiveness and a comparative
advantage in the new international division of labor. Armaments is the
other industry with a steady market and intense competition. And the

potential for future conflict is greater, as austerity shrinks the world market still further.

The nitty-gritty issues of trade conflict in protectionism and subsidies undermine all grand strategies for free trade. All nations are "export oriented" as a new form of mercantilism is ascendant, since their internal markets are subject to their austerity policies. States struggle to be competitive in trade, even though, under the new conditions, foreign trade has lost its former meaning, except to generate conflict.

States are both withdrawing from their direct participation in the economy and becoming more engaged. They remain ready to rescue the largest corporations that face financial crisis. The IMF restructuring policies of massive political interference in the economies of the LDCs have only increased the chaos and misery in these countries.

Unfortunately for those who would like to resolve the crisis with their "structural adjustments," other laws remain in operation. The shrinking market that is the outcome of the austerity programs, unemployment, and falling real income further inhibits investment and deepens the crisis. A strengthening of nominal profits with fiscal measures in the context of declining profitability from investment in production and shrinking markets creates additional conditions for speculation in financial assets. For beyond the interest of the collective system, but fundamental to its very nature, each individual looks toward his or her own profit or loss.

Meanwhile capitalists will scarcely object to the fact that governments everywhere will continue to woo them with ever greater concessions, even in countries where they were once maligned, as in some of the LDCs and the CPEs. But because the concessions are costly, in economic, political, and social terms, the goals of economic development will be further set back. If the suitor is successful in attracting investment, the outcome, given the evidence of the past, is likely to be worse. Not only will the governments have invested in the infrastructure, which at least represents capital formation, but they will also be subject to continual capital drain by the foreign investor, since the subsidiaries finance themselves by absorbing local funds, in the form of capital flight and the repatriation of profits, intrafirm manipulation of prices, and numerous other techniques. Ironically, as the governments rush toward private equity, many corporations move toward new forms of nonequity investments requiring less capital outlay.

But the states have not gone far enough in their restructuring strategies to induce capital to invest sufficiently for renewed and sustained growth in the world economy. Having achieved its aims in regard to income shares and labor costs and having offered an array of incentives,

they failed to attain the renewed investment growth that they all competed for in vain, since, as always, the very means of lowering the cost
of labor undermined their goal. This again demonstrates one of the core
contradictions of the system. Meanwhile, the state's own dilemmas of
a fiscal crisis continued to grow. Recessions were closer and more
severe and recoveries weak and only partial. Cumulatively, the interaction of all these structural and intrinsic features were bringing closer
what all hoped to avoid—a world depression.

Some officials in the EEC in the late 1970s expressed hope for a
mass market in the Third World to save the system from crisis in the
same way that they believed the proletariat in Europe had expanded
the market in the late nineteenth century. It is a major question, one
separate from this study, why a mass market developed in Europe and
North America, denying (or delaying?) Marx's immiseration theory. I
can only allude to the implications of the fact that there were four major
wars in this century, with an immense impact on the world economy.
A mass market is in the long-term interest of capitalism, but because
of one of its basic contradictions, it cannot create such a market except
as a by-product of other factors. Indeed, crucial to the restructuring
strategies of capital and the state is the compulsion to cut labor costs
by whatever means, and crucial to those of the IMF, in the LDCs as
elsewhere, have been the austerity policies that have further impoverished the populations and shrunk the market.

A dim recognition of this contradiction emerges as other interests of
industry and trade in the OECD countries, directly affected by the effort
to squeeze every dollar out of the indebted states for debt repayment,
assert themselves in order to achieve their own gains. The overall
economy needs the massive stimulus that in the past came through war.

There is indeed a strategy, and an old one, to organize the world
economy, both its industrial and its nonindustrial sectors. A vast effort
has been made to expand the reserve army of labor on an international
scale to eradicate the effect of rising wages and falling productivity,
which capitalists everywhere view as the inhibition on the expansion
of private capital investment. Government attempts to intervene and to
"plan" the economy will be variations of the current schemes, and these
gestures will indeed have their impact, as they interact with multiple
other forces in the private sector and create new conditions in the
economy and relations between states.

The dynamic is that though the supranational organizations and even
the most powerful states can formulate policies, and even implement
them in selected cases, they cannot impose their world order—for
competitive forces remain inherent in the economic system. All forces

contribute to the development of the economic crisis, and while many may try to manipulate it, none can control it.

Obviously, wherever possible, national economies have been subjected to a counterreformist wringer—either voluntarily, under pressure from creditors, or with a police state—to install a certain type of draconian economy. In the Third World it has often rested on terror; in other parts of the world, it has so far been based on austerity to the limits of acceptance. In many of the LDCs these efforts are an aspect of the class struggle in its crudest form, involving torture and systematic liquidations of those who dare to resist or who are even suspected of having the capacity or intent to do so. Elsewhere, restructuring has entailed varying degrees of hunger and misery, imposed by policies calculated to shift income shares and repay debt through unemployment and systematic reduction of the living standards of the working class.

PART IV

LABOR

CHAPTER 20

RESTRUCTURING AND THE WORKING CLASS

Speculations and generalizations about the nature of the working class in the last half of the twentieth century, in both the industrial nations and the LDCs, have flourished but rarely resolved the main analytic issues. However, a discussion of "restructuring" as it pertains to labor should begin with a definition of labor as a class. As in considerations of capital and the state, it is important to distinguish the systemic from the structural features in such a definition for, again, most of the generalizations about the "new" working class are based on transitional structural conditions.

Whether the nature of work is industrial or service, whether workers are employed as clerks or as miners, in transport or in construction, are skilled or unskilled, organized or not, well paid or earning subsistence wages, composed of minorities, natives, or migrants, or are unemployed are all important *structural* factors to examine. These structural features change and are restructured, but they are all subject to the *systemic* components, which determine the nature of the working class in the capitalist system at any time and place, whether in conditions of crisis or of "prosperity." These features include labor as a commodity in the production process; its vulnerability to immiseration; exploitation; and the class struggle (objective and/or subjective). One of the most important factors, other than the workers' role as producers, is their vulnerability as an expendable commodity.

Some analysts have emphasized the difference between productive and nonproductive workers. But workers must survive by selling their labor, not their production, and they may sell it in a factory or a

305

restaurant one month and in a home as a domestic the next. More important is the whole web of class, family, and community relationships that transcend individual cases and occupations.

Two persons from different classes may meet on the same job, for example, as clerical workers. Some individuals may identify subjectively with classes other than that of their origin. But it is not necessary to be concerned with each individual. It is the broad structures that count and that shape institutions and attitudes. Harry Braverman's point is well taken in this regard that "the term 'working class' properly understood, never precisely delineated a specified body of people, but was rather an expression for an ongoing social process."[1] He sought to avoid a precise definition and suggested that the definition was in fact his whole study of labor, with all its ramifications. That approach has validity, especially given the convoluted debate on the definition of class over the past decades. Nevertheless, I find it useful to delineate the constant features of the working class in formulating a definition, for as with the other categories, one can in this way avoid the tendency to generalize on and extrapolate the structural features. This delineation is less urgent today than in the recent past, because social reality is starker under the condition of prolonged economic crisis, and there is now less inclination to dwell superficially on the appearance of prosperity and what it may mean for a changing working class.

The working class clearly extends beyond the occupational category of the industrial proletariat, which by the 1980s was less than half of the wage earners. Paul Mattick rightly pointed out, "It is then not its *occupational character* that characterizes the proletariat but its *social position* as wage labor. The diminution of the industrial working class implies the growth of the working class irrespective of the type of employment [or unemployment] it is engaged in."[2] Its essential trait is the sale of labor for wages, productive and nonproductive.

In agrarian societies, as they are increasingly penetrated by the capitalist mode of production, the peasantry, traditionally a class that both owned its means of production and sold its produce, divides into the owners of the means of production—land, equipment—and those with only their labor to sell.

A distinction should also be made between the working class and the "poor." In recent decades many writers have tended to focus on the poor. The bourgeois analysts defined the poor in sociological and not economic terms, and some on the left hoped that they would perform the revolutionary role that the working class had failed to fill. But poverty *by itself* is not a mobilizing force for change. What has been termed a resurgence of militancy and class conflict erupted in Europe at the end of the 1960s, not in a time of economic crisis and not among the "poor," but in a time of prosperity and among workers generally experiencing a rising standard of living. In a time of prolonged economic crisis, however, poverty becomes the lot of an increasingly large sector of the working class.

Hence a definition of class is based not on income but on the origin of income, be it wages or property, and is linked to the relations of production. In America part of the ideology has been to define nearly the whole of society as "middle class" and to use the terms *upper, middle,* and *lower,* not to indicate income distribution but to exclude the terms *capitalist* and *working class* or *bourgeoisie* and *proletariat.* The ideologists thus made a part of the working class "middle class," on the basis of a family income of a certain level, usually with more than one earner. When a number of economists recently concluded that one result of the restructuring of the economy was a shrinking of the middle class, with higher income at the top and growing numbers at the bottom, there were widespread expressions of genuine consternation.

Income distribution is one critical aspect of class, of course, and the figures say much about a society's susceptibility to a crisis of underconsumption. Even when it was widely claimed that American capitalism had achieved a more equitable distribution, the empirical evidence revealed a contrary story, as Gabriel Kolko demonstrated in 1962, when the prevalence of this illusion among economists and others was at its height.[3] And the maintenance of a certain level of consumption during the periods of full employment and rising inflation increasingly depended on more than one earner in a household and the use of credit.

The conclusion of many writers that the working class becomes "bourgeoisified" by owning commodities or a house, or by having a high nominal income, or that elements of the bourgeoisie become "proletarianized" as their conditions of work change and they are vulnerable to unemployment, was highly superficial. Except over time and with generational change, there is far more to class than is measured by income. More income for workers does not change their relations of exploitation or their vulnerability as a commodity. Their enhanced bargaining position reached in the cyclical peak and near full employment as in France and Italy in the late 1960s, crumbles in times of crisis. The downward mobility of the bourgeois usually produces not solidarity with the working class but bitterness: such individuals retain the cultural and ideological baggage of their class. Working-class identity is determined by a whole matrix of associations in an individual's life, not merely by his or her income or occupation. It is crucial to emphasize the important systemic factor—the worker's vulnerability as an expendable commodity in the capitalist system. A worker's middle-class living standard has never been secure.

The conceptual myth that the working class would steadily become more affluent and an aristocracy of labor formed the basis of multiple generalizations, and it was rudely shattered in the recent condition of the world economy. It was also an example of the tendency to extrapolate current structural conditions rather than to focus on the systemic factors of capitalism. To be vulnerable, expendable, and increasingly superfluous has always been a reality for labor. And in this context the International Labor Organization (ILO) estimated that in the last twenty years of the twentieth century, one-third more people will enter the labor force each year, at a time of shrinking employment worldwide, than between 1950 and 1975, when employment was expanding.[4]

The OECD's 1979 report, *Interfutures,* declared, "On the whole, Western civilization has, during the last 150 years, succeeded in integrating its internal proletariat [which it attributed to an expanding middle class]. . . . However, this civilization is now confronted by the problem of its external proletariat. . . ."[5] Putting aside the fact that these nations in the OECD were in the process of dis-"integrating" their "internal proletariat," the structural conditions of the laboring classes in the less-developed capitalist countries have deteriorated rapidly as they are forced to bear the brunt of the restructuring of their society, seriously worsening the special "problem of its external proletariat."

CHAPTER 21

RESTRUCTURING EMPLOYMENT

The decade since the mid-1970s has seen fundamental changes in employment that are crucial to the restructuring of the economy and the nature of work. As has been widely noted, the most significant new characteristics for the entire industrial capitalist world, in addition to the export of jobs in search of cheap labor, have been the shift from relatively high-wage factory work in heavy industry to low-wage service occupations, the importance of part-time and temporary employment, and the predominance of lower-wage women workers in the occupations with expanding employment. These changes were largely the outcome of the objective operations of the system. But their advantages for capital and for the state were quickly apparent, and they were adopted as part of a conscious strategy to restructure the economy. The contradictions in these developments are all too evident as well.

In the United States, where 4.0 million jobs were added between 1958 and 1968, the Labor Department found in 1985 that 2.3 million manufacturing jobs had disappeared since 1980, some 90 percent of them probably permanently, and most of these were in high-wage, organized heavy industry. Its studies argued that the economy was moving on two paths—service producing and goods producing. The workers in the fast-growing service industries were earning, on the average, $5,000 less than those in the industries with a shrinking work force. In the factories of the new industries, such as electronics, assembly jobs are few and low paying.

In the organized heavy-industry sector, business has demanded concessions and a rollback of previously won wage and benefit gains as part of its general offensive to cut costs and to take advantage of the economic crisis to change the relations with labor that had developed over the preceding thirty years. Union concessions on wages and benefits in settlements with U.S. employers numbered 159 in 1982 and 430 in 1983. In 1982 some 38 percent of the unionized workers took wage cuts, and 15 percent had no increase. These concessions did not diminish layoffs. The most common form of wage concession accepted by the unions, usually under the threat of closure and relocation, was the dual wage and benefit system for new and old workers. The airline, auto, trucking, copper, and aerospace industries negotiated new-worker wage cuts of $4–$5 per hour in 1983. Frequently, the old workers were fired, so the two-tier system soon became the major grievance.

In addition to wage concessions, there were many other "givebacks" pertaining to work rules and working conditions in the labor contracts negotiated in the 1980s. Often the savings gained by union concessions intended to maintain employment and production were spent by management on more automation or financial speculation. Inevitable workers' resistance to these trends led in the mid-1980s to an increase in local strike action over company reductions in job security and benefits. Workers soon realized, especially in the steel industry, that when they made concessions the company often closed the plant anyway. Black male workers suffered most in the shift of employment away from manufacturing, for it was in the factory that they had been able to secure relatively high-wage jobs since World War II.

When industries close or restructure with automation, the change is dramatic. Workers habituated to high wages, benefits, and continued rises are confronted with falling wages and worsening conditions, if they are lucky enough still to have a job, or unemployment and the admonition to find a job in the low-paying services.

SERVICE WORK

According to an OECD report, "since the beginning of the 1970s [the service sector] has been the *only* sector to create jobs in most member countries" in the OECD.[1] The U.S. Bureau of Labor Statistics estimated in 1985 that the most rapidly growing sector in the American economy until 1995 would be janitors, fast-food workers, nurses' aides, and clerical workers. They expected a demand for only 120,000 computer programmers. By 1986 fully 81 percent of the new jobs in the United States were in services, compared with 66 percent in 1985 and 52 percent in 1984, and the vast majority of them were near the bottom of the wage ladder. The trend accelerated in 1987 when 94 percent of new employment was in the services. Three-fifths of the 8.1 million new jobs, service and nonservice, since 1979 have paid $7,000 a year or less.

The initial growth in service was linked to the expansion of the public sector. But the government sector, which accounted for one-third of the growth before 1975, accounted for only 15 percent of the growth between 1976 and 1982 and has since contracted further because of the fiscal constraints. Services in the *private sector* in the OECD countries, by contrast, are considered the only expanding employment sector in the economy. It was estimated in 1984 that up to 65–70 percent of the jobs in Europe were in the services of all sorts and that three out of four American workers were.

But service work is a heterogeneous category. In the United States health services were by 1981 the largest component, with 29.5 percent of all service workers, and 80 percent of them were women. Next is the category of business services, with 16.9 percent. Work in the business services increasingly consists of feeding data into computers, an extremely boring task, performed in nearly total isolation from other workers, usually on a piecework pay scale, and under constant electronic surveillance by supervisors. In "wholesale and retail trade," the number of workers rose from 8.7 million in 1950 to over 18.0 million in 1982. In the "recovery" beginning in 1983, all of the employment growth was in the private sector services, primarily in new small retail trade enterprises. Service workers' wages fell over the decade, and the new employment came in what were considered "dead-end" jobs. On the average, service sector pay was two-thirds that of manufacturing. In all the services there was a higher than average proportion of women, blacks, and part-time workers.

In manufacturing, as well, the percentage of service as opposed to production workers increased. In 1978 the figure was 23 percent in the United States, 35 percent in the FRG, 27 percent in France, and 25 percent in Sweden. In the 1980s such nonproduction workers made up 80 percent of the *new* employment in U.S. manufacturing.

When employment statistics in North America and Europe are compared, the gain of 18.0 million jobs in the United States and the loss of 1.5 million in Europe since 1973 has been attributed by government officials and businessmen to the "rigidities" of wages and other social benefits in the European economies that are absent in America. And in good part, among other factors discussed later, it does reflect the differing social attitudes in America and Europe. In the United States unemployment benefits are both shorter and lower; this forces workers to take any job and makes it mandatory for child-rearing women to seek work to supplement the family income. Their work is invariably in the service sector.

But service workers are now as vulnerable to automation as production workers. Employment in banking doubled between 1968 and 1983, but the new technology has helped halt or reverse that trend. By the 1980s even the computer programmer's work was being automated. Automation is increasingly evident in those industries where labor is the important component of cost, such as the insurance industry, where labor is 60 percent of business expenses. And clerical and other white-collar workers in the manufacturing industries were also susceptible to unemployment in the great industrial cost cutting over this decade. White-collar work fell 40 percent in the steel industry, and 15 percent in the auto industry, totaling one million lost jobs since 1979. Other industries, such as oil, were also rapidly automating clerical jobs in the mid-1980s. While the cyclical pattern of service joblessness in manufacturing has matched overall unemployment, in the recession employment also increased, as women reentered the labor force for new forms of service work.

There is another factor behind these statistics of growth and decline of jobs in services and manufacturing. In the OECD nations business services have had the highest growth, and personal services as well as transport and communication have declined. This is because manufacturing companies, which once produced their own services, began to contract them to specialized companies and temporary manpower firms and because the same jobs are listed differently in the statistics. And it also explains why the service sector is smaller in the FRG, where manufacturers have not followed this trend and still produce their own services, giving a different employment picture. The classification of "personal services" has declined with machinery, whether it is a matter of household machines replacing laundries or of vending machines, or the workers are part of the "underground economy" and not listed statistically.

THE NATURE OF WORK

In addition to sectoral shifts in employment, work itself is being restructured. Part-time, homework, temporary, and other forms of "cost-free" labor are replacing traditional employment in both service and production. Such forms account for the expansion of employment in the United States because of the absence of the so-called rigidities in the labor market that existed in most of the European economies. The official celebration of the growth of employment in the United

States in the 1980s, compared with that in other industrial countries, ignored the fact that it was part-time work that had increased while the number of hours worked and weekly earnings had declined. A worker is statistically employed in the United States if he or she works at least three hours a day for three days a week or if the work is temporary. What used to be a recession tactic has now become a structural feature of the economy. This fragmentation of the work force is a crucial dimension of the restructuring of the economy. "Personnel is not a fixed cost anymore," proclaimed the satisfied head of a temporary-employment agency, summing up this important trend in employment.[2]

Since 1980 the number of part-time workers in the United States has grown 58 percent, to one-fourth of the total of those employed. While such work is preferred by many, 17 percent of all American workers were part-time workers who desired full-time work, the number having doubled since 1980. One-third of the jobs in retail trade and the service sector are part-time, although most part-time work is in production. The workers in these realms are in circumstances scarcely better than those of the unemployed, and they naturally make up the bulk of the "working poor." Their advantages to the employer are obvious: there are no costs such as sick pay, health insurance, or vacations. Wages are usually nearly one-half those for a full-time worker, and a transient labor force is usually unorganized. This expansion of part-time work obviously depends on a large reserve army of unemployed.

Part-time work is especially prevalent in the new high-tech sector of the economy, in those very industries that are allegedly the great hopes for replacing the employment disappearing from heavy industry. In California's Silicon Valley, the labor force is unorganized and as flexible as the automation. The workers are hired for short periods adjusted to the frequent peaks and slumps in the industry, and the part-time employees are frequently 30 percent of the total.

Part-time work is the trend in the rest of the OECD states as well. It has increased 50 percent in the FRG since the early 1970s, to 12 percent of the workers, and in Sweden it composes 25 percent of all jobs. In Japan the use of part-time workers has been termed the "second secret weapon" of its competitive success.[3] (The first was workers' acceptance of long overtime hours.) And many in Japan work full-time hours for part-time wages and no benefits. Part-time jobs and temporary work increased over the 1970s, but it did so exponentially after 1980, when there was only one temporary-employment agency in Tokyo. By 1985 there were nearly 150. Some large companies had begun to hire out their own permanent workers to other companies needing temporary employees. It was a natural corollary to the system of lifetime full-time employees and shifting demand in manufacturing. So-called lifetime employment, in any case, has never affected more than 25 percent of the Japanese workers. More and more companies have forced these workers into early retirement during the 1980s. And because there are minimal social services in Japan and the cost of living is exorbitant, the government developed a plan to export its elderly to low-cost countries. According to a Tokyo businessman, Japanese corporations concluded by 1983 that "the removal of people [permanent employees] is the only way to make money."[4] Japanese business prefers the part-time flexible work force for the same reason that capitalists elsewhere do—it lowers costs.

Temporary work is similar to part-time. The director of staffing at Citibank said, "Face it. Labor costs are a major item. You are not paying the same fringe benefits to temporaries, and this is one way for industry to keep costs within reason."[5]

Many industries have restructured to a much smaller "permanent" work force, and temporary or "contingent" workers have become an integral part of their adjustment to cyclical changes and of their efforts to lower costs. Over the 1980s the number of jobs defined as temporary grew at 20 percent a year in the United States. Temporary workers are most prevalent in office work and are a major restraint on labor's organizing efforts. In Japan contract temporary workers used seasonally to expand manufacturing production are not listed statistically, but in steel, for instance, they constitute up to 40 percent of the labor force. Temporary and part-time workers earn 30–50 percent less than permanent workers. But this structural factor in Japanese capitalism is also emerging in U.S. industry, where the unions and companies increasingly agree to permanent employment for a small group of core workers to be supplemented by part-time or temporary workers.

Also increasing over the past decade in the United States has been the old technique of homework and sweatshops, made possible by an increase in the number of illegal migrants. These are often linked with workers spending nine hours in the shop and taking the work home for additional hours of piecework. The home computer has also made it possible for much office work to be done in the home. The number who work at home rose fourfold since 1980, to nearly nine million.

All these factors mean that in Japan, and increasingly throughout Europe and North America, there is a trend toward a duality in the work force: a shrinking number of full-time permanent employees and a growing number of temporary or part-time workers for the giant industries, and the bulk of the workers in low-paying, insecure jobs with the thousands of small subcontractors to industry or in the services.[6]

WOMAN'S WORK

Throughout the OECD countries low-wage jobs are performed by women, minorities, and immigrants. Both objectively and intentionally, this situation is lowering the general wage level of all these economies. And the growth of women in the work force has paralleled the growth of service work in the economy. Some 60–85 percent of the employed women in the OECD states are in the services.

As inflation increased and real wages began to fall, two earners maintained family income and the growth of credit sustained consumption beyond income by nearly one-fifth. In the United States the percentage of women in the labor force jumped from 36.5 percent in 1960 to 54.0 percent in 1985, the chief growth being among married women between twenty-five and thirty-four, whose participation rose from 28 percent to 65 percent. In over 50 percent of the families with children, both parents work, including nearly half of all women with children under six years. The gap between the wages of men and women declined after 1978, but falling wages for male workers were the origin of the change. Yet, despite more than one income earner, household spending power fell in the 1980s, and in 1986 it was below that of 1979, and continued to fall in 1987.

The new factories in high-tech and service industries in Europe also moved toward the greater use of part-time, migrant, and women workers. This trend became their means to restructure the economy and increase employment. In Japan the part-time workers, increasingly crucial to the operations of the Japanese economy, have been predominantly women, whose participation has increased 7–8 percent a year since 1980 and accounted for 90 percent of those part-time workers who are statistically counted. In trade they already outnumber full-time workers.

In the LDCs, in every country with free-trade zones, over 80 percent of the workers are young women between the ages of sixteen and twenty-four, who are particularly prevalent in the electronics and garment industries. Their wages are often half of those of men, and a dearth of options forces them to work the longest hours. Many studies have chronicle the marginally subsistence wages and dangerous working conditions that wear out the health of these workers in a few years. Either they are replaced from the local labor reserve or the company

moves elsewhere, as many aspiring nations advertise the young women
in their labor force at competitive terms.[7]

In addition to the changes in the nature and type of work in the
visible or legal economy, there has been an expansion of the "underground economy" in the OECD countries—that is, work outside of the
state social security, minimum wage, and other legal labor standards.
Mounting unemployment has only favored its growth. In Britain it is
estimated to be 5–15 percent of the GNP. In the United States the
comparable figure is reputed to be somewhere between 4.5 percent and
6.0 percent of the GNP, rising, not surprisingly, since the mid-1970s.
The estimate is largest for Italy, at 30 percent. Such illegal labor
parallels the LDC economies' vast "informal sector," where massive
unemployment and extremes of exploitation are hidden. There one of
the principal causes has been the displacement of the peasants, with
the mechanization of agricultural production oriented toward the world
market and with the increasing penetration of capitalist organization
into the countryside, transforming many peasants into agrarian wage
workers or into migrants to the urban areas in search of work.

Great diversity of activity characterizes the informal sector in the
LDCs. That sector includes petty sales, services, such as shoeshines,
pedicabs, and domestic work, as well as manufacturing and repair.
Various bureaucrats in the international organizations have called the
informal sector an example of enterprise and ingenuity and urged
governments to provide credit to its various "entrepreneurs." In many
large cities in Asia and Latin America, it is the activity of 50–70 percent
of the total "employment"; in Africa it absorbs 40–60 percent of the
urban labor force. For the most part, this large mass barely ekes out
a subsistence at the bottom income layer of the urban society, living
in squatter dwellings devoid of elementary services like water and
sanitation in and around the vast urban sprawls that now make up the
cities of the Third World.

However, as a number of analysts have demonstrated, a substantial
part of this sector is really integrated into the industrializing, so-called
formal sector and serves as "underground" labor for much of the work
in that part of the economy, thereby allowing capitalists to avoid the
extra cost, minimal as it is, and the labor relations problems of regular
employment. This is especially true of the clothing, furniture, and
handicrafts industries, where established companies supply materials
on credit. Garbage pickers for recycling are in this way also part of the
"formal" industrial economy. And the "informal" workers are impor-

tant in the circulation of goods, as the ubiquitous street peddlers in Third World cities are often controlled by companies on an informal basis. They earn a bare subsistence margin in sales, out of which they also usually pay interest on credit from the supplier of whatever goods they sell. The informal-sector worker is vital for the profitability of many companies, large and small.

Evidence shows that this sector loses, whatever the condition of the economy. When there was high growth of the GNP, in countries like Brazil, this segment of the population actually became poorer, although it was an important component of that growth. In periods of recession and austerity, their ranks are swollen by those who have lost regular jobs, the "visible" unemployed. And there is always a vast rural reserve enlarging this informal sector, as the process of displacing peasants continues. During the period from 1981 to 1984 agricultural employment rose in most Latin American countries—in Brazil by 4 percent a year—with depression in the urban formal sector as would-be migrants clung to the land because of yet worse conditions in the cities.[8]

WAGES

The restructuring of employment in the industrialized countries achieved its principal aim of a generalized lowering of wages. As the OECD economists noted in 1985, a chief feature of the recovery was the "widespread fall in labor share of national income and the associated rise in the profit share and profits. Another related development has been the decline . . . of real wages in many countries."[9]

According to the IMF:

From about 1969 through 1975, real wages of manufacturing enterprises in industrial Europe rose by about 6½ per cent annually, while manufacturing output per labor hour was increasing at a rate of only 4 ½ per cent. . . . [T]his difference was very damaging to the profit position. . . . [R]estoration of adequate profit margins is likely to require that real wage increases be kept below productivity gains for some time to come.[10]

In a perspective typical of the one that dominates government policies throughout the OECD countries, the IMF continued:

In particular, it must be recognized that the legitimate scope for real wage increases has become more limited than it once was, because of (a) the marked slowing of productivity gains. . . . (b) the substantial changes in external terms of trade . . . and (c) the squeeze on business profits, with its implications for investment incentives. . . . [T]here is also a need to re-examine the practical effects of the minimum-wage laws or regulations. In addition, a reassessment of the costs of social transfers and unemployment benefits under contemporary conditions is called for. . . .[11]

In the United States there was growth in real income until the beginning of the economic crisis in 1974. Real wages then began to decline, fell significantly in 1980, remaining at the point attained in the early 1960s and more than 12 percent below the 1972–73 peak, and were expected to fall in 1987 for the fifth year of the decade. Real income fell 5 percent between 1978 and 1986 in manufacturing, as companies cut costs. Cutbacks or a freeze in even nominal wages took place in the recession in 1981 and continued for the following three years. According to *Business Week*, it was "the first major deceleration since the massive wage cuts in the largely nonunion economy of the early 1930s."[12] The first negotiated wage cut was the UAW agreement with Chrysler in 1980 to trade a 12 percent pay cut for job security. Unions, such as the IUE and UAW at GM factories, have bargained for a two-tier work and wage structure to protect the jobs of their existing members. The OECD, in noting all the concessions during the 1980s, commented, "What is novel is continuing union acquiescence . . . despite a comparatively strong recovery in activity and profits."[13] Only in the FRG and in Japan did the unions demand to share in the rising profits. By 1986 American rank-and-file workers had begun to resist the union's readiness to make concessions.

By sector of the economy, the differential in wages is also outstanding. The average hourly wage of a service worker in the private sector is significantly less than that of a manufacturing worker. And in the competitive high-tech industry, as in the garment industry of old, wages are low.

The wage differential between blacks and whites and men and women in the same occupation widened in the United States in the 1980s. But U.S. consumption continued to be higher than wages would indicate in the mid-1980s, since many workers turned to credit. In 1986, consumer debt amounted to a record 19 percent of all take-home pay, a pattern that portended much greater problems for the future.

The same pattern in wages prevailed in the rest of the OECD countries after 1980. In Europe real wages rose until 1982, except in Germany, where workers in 1981 took their first cut in real wages since World War II. In France the Socialist austerity program required a 2–3 percent real-wage cut for those workers still with jobs. Denmark imposed a strict wage ceiling and no indexation. In Japan real wages have risen an average of 1.3 percent per annum since 1979, compared with

5.7 percent in the 1970s. But in 1985, Japanese wages were higher than those in the United Kingdom and Italy and equal to those in France. An overall decline in the wage level in the OECD economies occurred, as the high-wage industries not only secured concessions from the unions but also diminished in size, and the growth industries were those with low wages.

Wages were indexed to the cost of living in most of the European countries during the inflationary 1970s. A coordinated government offensive against wage indexing began in 1979, after the second rise in the oil price, when the EC agreed that the increase would be excluded from the index for wages. "What's certain is that the OECD, the IMF and management are trying to bring about a reallocation of wealth within the industrialized countries, leading to higher profits," one international union official noted.[14] Socialist governments in France in 1982 and in Italy in 1984 set a limit on the index, which no conservative governments had dared to do. Milton Friedman said, "The major reason countries are backing off on indexation is that they seek a way to cut real wages."[15] The minimum wage in most countries has also fallen or been ignored altogether. In the United States the minimum wage of $3.35 an hour was at the lowest point in purchasing power in over thirty years. Over 5 million workers, or nearly 9 percent of the total, worked at or below the minimum. If raised by $1.00, it would cover one-fourth of the hourly workers, or 13.5 million, more than half of them over twenty-five years old. This assault on the wages of those still working has been a successful systematic effort in restructuring the economy. In order to drive the point home, some governments in the OECD states have applied a "general squeeze on public sector wages" and proposed "schemes to tax excessive wage increases" in other industries.[16]

In Japan, and to a lesser extent elsewhere, the system of subcontracting for parts allows various levels of wages to exist in tandem. The Japanese auto industry, for example, subcontracts for 60 percent of its parts, whereas its U.S. counterpart subcontracts 40 percent, and wages in these small factories are 30 percent lower than those in the auto companies. And, as I noted earlier, contracting out for low wages is increasingly the pattern in other industries.

Prolonged unemployment at a high level was the major cause of the decline in wages. The OECD concluded that in the United States "wage moderation has been so pronounced as to suggest that there may have been an underlying change of behavior" in wage demands.[17] In fact, they found that the evidence was clear in the United States that wages follow rather than lead price inflation and that there was "little empirical support" for a prospective catch-up demand in wages, even where profits were high and rising. The statistics showed that, in the decade following 1973, average nonagricultural real wages in America fell 16 percent and average household income by 11 percent.

Since there was a sharp decline or stagnation in real wages in most countries, government officials could observe that this major goal in restructuring their economies had been successfully achieved either through the direct struggle between capital and labor or through state policies. Because bargaining positions depend on the condition of the general economy, real wages may rise at various times, but they are always vulnerable to a reversal and to the perpetual struggle to lower labor costs. The outcome of the gains of labor, in the context of other developments in the economy, was an acceleration of international investment in low-wage areas and investment in automation and other countermoves opposing labor in the late 1970s and 1980s, against a background of rising unemployment.

In the LDCs, of course, barely subsistence wages of a couple of dollars a day in many countries and less than three dollars an hour in the NIC's modern factories have been the major "comparative advantage" in the international division of labor for the labor intensive assembly tasks. These low wages have fallen drastically in real terms in the 1980s, for example, by 33 percent in Brazil and over 28 percent in Mexico in 1981–85, because of the restructuring policies in many nations, as the price subsidies for basic needs have been reduced or eliminated.

PRODUCTIVITY

Productivity revolves around the question of how much more can be produced with a given amount of labor or, in a capitalist economy that cannot sell what is produced, how labor cost can be reduced for a limited production. Productivity, then, is the rate of exploitation. Increases can be achieved by maintaining the same output with fewer workers, more labor per worker, or the introduction of new technology.

Bourgeois economics and government and corporate policies generally hold the productivity of labor responsible for stagflation, lack of competitiveness unemployment, falling real income, deficits—for virtually all the problems of capitalism in crisis. And although that productivity is usually dependent on factors over which the workers have no control, those in power place the problems of productivity squarely on their shoulders. Yet, as an ILO report put it, "when total ouput is stagnant any increase in labour productivity from whatever source will add to unemployment. . . ."[18] Since a rise in productivity may come with the firing of workers, U.S. government economists interpreted the decline in employment in manufacturing as "a sign of relative productivity growth, not of industrial demise."[19] Labor productivity generally rises in a recession. It is obvious that if capital cannot sell what is produced, a rise in productivity means there is less need for labor.

As an example of blaming the worker even when the industry is operating at low capacity, a Brookings Institution economist made the astonishing assertion that if productivity—as though it were the only variable in the economy—had kept rising at "its old 3% trend rate . . . through the 1970s, . . . output in 1981 would have been 20% greater."[20] While this is only one of many examples of the bourgeois analysts' ideological leap from the evidence, this perspective is often translated into policies, and even some economists on the left have also attributed the failure of the economy to work at capacity to the decline in worker productivity.

Samuel Bowles and his collaborators wrote in 1982, "[W]hen productivity growth declines, [from the mid-1960s on] the struggle over the distribution of a more slowly growing economic pie intensifies; this exacerbates inflationary pressures and encourages the Federal government to pursue restrictive unemployment–generating fiscal and monetary policies. . . . We argue, in short, that the productivity slowdown lies at the heart of the U.S. economic crisis."[21] Harry Magdoff cogently exposed their assumption that the Department of Labor can measure productivity on the basis of price or that the market can measure the physical volume of production, pointing out that the changes of productivity are an outcome of the operations of the capitalist system, not vice versa.[22] Later addressing themselves again to the productivity "puzzle," the radical economists declared they had "largely succeeded in cracking the case," by focusing on the factors of work intensity (or motivation and management control) and innovative pressure on business.[23] They pointed to a lack of motivation among workers because of the adversary conditions in the factory—as, indeed, do many bourgeois economists who have developed the "quality of work life" programs. Their proposals for reform, however, call for a democratic workplace, high minimum wage and guaranteed employment, and elimination of corporate taxes except when prices exceed price ceilings; these and their other reformist measures are, in essence, no more "realistic" or "relevant" than a call to abolish the capitalist system altogether.

Because of the high rate of mechanization across the economy historically, the United States still has the highest absolute productivity, although the rate of growth is one of the lowest in the industrial

countries. But even of the ten *official* causes of low productivity growth
in the United States, only three relate to workers—the so-called declining work ethic, equal opportunity laws, and union "featherbedding."
The rest are attributed to government fiscal policies and regulation that
diverts investment funds that (supposedly) would go into automation.
One politically motivated advocate of deregulation even did a semiofficial study (for the Brookings Institution) that sought to demonstrate
that government regulation was the most important cause in the decline
of U.S. productivity in the period 1968–78. Many capitalists attributed
the decline in productivity to a lack of investable capital, because of
high taxes, wages, and falling profit. According to this viewpoint, as
productivity depends on "incorporating new technology into new production facilities," business takeovers, rather than new investment,
have become one of the greatest barriers to improved productivity.[24]
The crude measure of productivity is output divided by hours worked;
a more informative measure is output related to all factors of production. And some economists did conclude in 1980, "[T]he slow growth
of investment has probably been the major cause of inadequate productivity growth."[25]

Much of American management now views the rigid Taylor organization of production as a barrier to increases in productivity with the new
technology. Changes in work rules for many companies, even more than
lower wages, are the most sought-after concessions from their workers.
They need "flexible" workers and flexible work rules to accompany
their flexible automation. Many companies have merged job classifica-
tions, eliminating "superfluous" workers and lowering costs. In many
cases, it is now the unions that demand strict job assignments and work
segmentation in order to protect jobs. This was especially true of skilled
workers, who were increasingly being reclassified as "helpers." Change
in work rules, rather than wages, was the most frequent cause of strikes
in the early 1980s.

There has also been more experimentation in what is termed quality
of work life or worker participation or productivity teams, in many
cases modeled on Japanese factory organization, in an attempt to raise
productivity and lower costs. "Teamwork" and a profitable manipulation of "job satisfaction" impulses are supposed to replace the old
assembly line. These measures have usually been linked to a reduction
of the work force around a core group, to be extended seasonally by
part-time and temporary workers. But a 1981 review of such efforts
between 1975 and 1980 found that 75 percent did not last more than
two years. For the workers, in a time of high unemployment, wages and

job security are the critical factors. In more prosperous times the boredom and pace of the assembly line rise in importance.

One of the outcomes of the drive for increased productivity and reduced costs has been a large increase in industrial accidents. U.S. statistics show injuries in manufacturing to have been 12 percent higher in 1984 and 1985 than in 1983, with bigger increases in steel, machine tools, metal fabrication, and meat packing.

In other sectors of the economy, productivity rose. Farm productivity continued to grow over the decade by 2 percent a year, and further advances were expected. In service, increased productivity in the use of computers led banks to cut their work force and to close branches with automatic teller machines.

Harry Braverman accurately discussed the reductio ad absurdum of seeking productivity improvement even while plants lie idle, as "a frenzied drive which approaches the level of a generalized social insanity."[26] Indeed, from a rational perspective, the discussion of productivity is often nothing less than astounding. In *The 1983 Economic Report of the President,* for example, economists attributed the fact that the GNP per capita was $12,780 instead of $16,128 to a decline in productivity of 26 percent over the preceding fourteen years. On the basis of this common enough statistical reasoning, the document went on to assert, "The consequences of reduced productivity growth for our standard of living over the long run are greater than those of any other current economic problem."[27] Such analysis swept aside all the complexities and implications of the preceding decade's generalized economic crisis.

Productivity questions in the capitalist industrial economies are merely a foil with which to extract greater concessions from the workers. The system's perennial problem is not inadequate productivity but overproduction.

The earlier U.S. advantage in productivity over the LDCs had diminished by the 1970s. Labor productivity in the foreign subsidiaries in electronics assembly was 92 percent of that in the United States; in some it was even higher by the early 1970s, because of the intensity (long hours) of work—ten or more hours a day and often seven days a week. And according to the OECD, "the technologies transferred tend to be the most efficient ones and, in many cases, the most capital-intensive . . . because in some developing countries with very disciplined manpower the capital equipment can be operated longer per day or per year, and therefore the original investment can be recovered more rapidly."[28] The work week is generally 20–30 percent longer than the OECD average. Needless to say, there is a little concern with health or safety standards. One of the most successful of the NICs, South Korea, has the world's longest average work week, varying over recent years from fifty-four to sixty hours, one of the worst health and safety records—*officially,* there were 1,728 deaths and over 140,000 serious injuries in work-related accidents in 1985. The extreme regimentation of work in South Korea is usually compared to that in an army, and workers commonly stand at attention and salute their supervisors. High productivity is achieved in the process of superexploitation and absolute repression.

MIGRATION

Labor migration has always existed in the world as a response to unemployment and economic difficulties, and it has changed the face of nations and had a profound impact on economic development. The workers have been either self-motivated, spurred by unemployment, recruited by companies, or encouraged by states. Over the past decade significant changes in the pattern of migration have contributed to the general restructuring of the world economy.

Emigration was a safety valve in some societies in the past, alleviating unemployment that might have produced political agitation. It also offered the nations recruiting workers a supply of cheap labor at crucial periods of economic expansion, restraining wages that would otherwise have risen in response to labor shortages. The option of migration to relieve unemployment throughout the world has now been nearly eliminated. And many of those recruited earlier face hostility both in the nations where they are working and in their home countries.

Migration to the European industrial economies depended on the demand for a subproletariat. But the restructuring process in these economies, by increasing unemployment, led to intense competition between national and foreign workers for the limited number of jobs. An estimated 20 million economic migrant workers were laboring in nations other than their own in 1985, of which 12 million were from the LDCs working in the industrial countries or OPEC. These figures exclude the nearly 9 million refugees in the world in 1981, which is the UN high commissioner for refugees' rough estimate of the numbers, but one that indicates the magnitude. Some of these refugees are really economic migrants. About 6.2 million workers, excluding refugees and illegal immigrants, were in the labor-importing countries of Europe in 1980. Concentrated in the recession-prone industries and the least-desirable jobs in the host countries, migrant workers are also the most vulnerable to automation.

Migrants were often recruited from rural areas, with the expectation that they would be a docile and easily exploited work force. Experience in most countries in Europe proved this to be an illusion. Migrants were more permanent and more militant than expected. In Italy, the FRG, and France, they turned out to be among the most militant in the late 1960s and early 1970s. Migrants participated fully in the events of May 1968 in France, and they were frequently the leaders of strikes in West Germany before 1968, as well as in the auto factories in France in 1984.

While the function of migration in the OECD countries was to increase the supply not merely of labor but of cheap labor, in the OPEC countries labor of all kinds was in demand, and migrants now make up half of the total employment. In both cases, labor was actively recruited during the periods of peak demand.

Migration is a form of competition among the world's workers, particularly among those at the bottom of the labor force, who must compete not only for jobs but for housing and social services as well. Migrants also changed significantly the demography of nonimmigrant societies like that of the FRG, where 20 percent of the fifteen- to nineteen-year-olds will be of non-German origin by 1995. By the mid-1980s they were already 25–30 percent of the students in the primary and secondary schools of the largest German cities. Xenophobia is often native labor's reaction, and it is frequently invoked by demagogic politicians in periods of high unemployment.

Immigration to the United States amounted to over one million annually in the late 1970s. Half the workers in Silicon Valley are women migrants, primarily from Mexico, the Caribbean, or Asia, working for the minimum wage and under dangerous working conditions. The lot of the estimated more than eight million illegal migrants in America, as elsewhere, is superexploitation in the sweatshops and in home piecework, principally for the garment industry. There was always an advantage to capital everywhere in maintaining an informal subsistence sector, drawing in workers and then allowing them to fend for themselves when they were old or sick, because that arrangement avoided all the social security overhead that native labor had secured over the years. In the United States the large numbers of illegal immigrants from Mexico serve this function, particularly for the agricultural sector.

Labor-importing nations succumbed to the myth that migrants could be called when needed and would return voluntarily when superfluous to the needs of the economy. Since most migrants have preferred to stay, a growing number of states have introduced inducements and pressures to leave. The FRG, for example, makes it almost impossible for migrant workers to get another job once laid off. But only 1.2 million immigrants in Europe returned home between 1973 and 1977. Their departure, however, did not create sufficient jobs for the unemployed natives.

The pattern of migration changed after the mid-1970s. As the European recruitment of labor mainly from the periphery of Europe ceased, recruitment began for the OPEC nations, especially from the Arab countries (2.8 million) but also from Asia, principally through "contract migration" teams that large construction companies mobilized. For political reasons, Saudi Arabia preferred the unassimilable Asians to Palestinian or Shiite Moslem workers. South Africa was also a major importer of workers, employing 400,000 from Mozambique.

Large engineering companies have been in the forefront in hiring skilled construction workers from various Third World nations, much as shipping companies flew flags of convenience in order to hire low-wage seamen. In turn, a growing number of governments have "packaged" teams of workers for export. South Korea has been the leading nation to do so, its experience dating from the Vietnam War, when, organized in a paramilitary fashion, it contracted to the U.S. Army. Their numbers were enlarged by the uncounted workers illegally recruited by agencies.[29]

Within the industrial countries during the 1960s, internal migration was from the backward rural areas to the booming industries. But listed among the "rigidities" in the European economies in the 1980s is the lack of worker mobility, the reluctance to migrate internally to find work.

Some companies recruited from, or built plants in, the rural areas in the expectation that young rural workers would be more pliable than the organized city workers. Fiat and Citroen both learned to their regret that they were, if anything, more militant than their urban counterparts. A similar rationale for recruiting workers from the surrounding farms inspired GM to build an ultramodern factory at Lordstown, Ohio, and the angry reaction of the workers to conditions on the automated assembly line gave social scientists a new term—the "Lordstown syndrome." In the United States at the end of the 1970s, workers migrated in great numbers from the so-called rust bowl in the Midwest and from depressed New England to the booming Southwest, prompted in large part by the ending of their unemployment compensation in their home cities. Within a couple of years the collapse in the energy industry in the Southwest put thousands of American workers on the move again in a largely futile search for work.

UNIONS

With the restructuring of employment have also come major changes in labor organizations in the industrialized countries. The OECD wrote in December 1985, "Labour power as measured by union membership and strike activity has fallen to post-war lows in most countries. . . ."[30] This situation clearly reflected the restructuring of employment in general, especially the highly organized heavy-industry sector, as well as the enormous increase in unemployment throughout the OECD countries, which especially affected the unionized industries. But it also was a response in many countries to two subjective factors— an all-out effort by capital to smash the unions and a growing recognition on the part of the workers that unions could not protect their interests.

During the twenty-five years of the precrisis "golden age," union strength grew and wages and benefits were secured regularly. Unions had rationalized the system of wages with industrywide bargaining and provided regularity and order in labor management in prosperous times. This was particularly true for the unions in capital goods and other oligopolistic industries, such as automobiles, where increased labor costs were passed on to the buyer. Certain concentrated industries allowed a union strength not available in the less concentrated and more competitive industries, where the market conditions did not permit price administration. When demand for their product was high, the companies were loath to lose sales in prolonged labor disputes.

By 1980 the negotiating environment had been transformed. In a time of increased competitive pressures, falling profits, and the other conditions of the economic crisis, even the unions' narrow goals, and willingness to offer concessions, were not enough. By 1983 the corporate appetite had been whetted by the concessions, and an all-out struggle for more began. U.S. corporations had resisted the initial organization of unions, but in times of high demand the oligopolistic industries tolerated and even found the unions useful, as long as they could pass on their costs. They also accepted them if they were able to secure wage cuts and other concessions. But their relationship was wholly dependent not only on the nature of the industry but also on the condition of the general economy. The very industries where unions

had had their greatest strength were those with the highest unemployment in the 1980s.

In the restructuring of the 1980s industrywide wage bargaining in
many industries where it had been the rule collapsed and reverted to
the company or plant level. All the gains of previous decades began to
crumble, as unions made concessions in order to prevent a threatened
bankruptcy or to gain the promise of job security for a core of the
existing work force. The unions remained useful to the industries as
they negotiated these concessions. The companies secured two-tier
wage scales, pay cuts, contingent workers, new work rules, and subcontracts, while the unions won pay raises of 1.2 percent in 1986, a rate
that had been falling steadily since 1980.

During the recession of the 1980s, many U.S. unions agreed to
freeze or cut wages and benefits and change work rules, enlarge jobs
by adding duties, and restrict seniority in most of the basic industries.
This form of bargaining continued into the so-called recovery, especially in industries like steel that remained depressed. But it became
increasingly evident to the workers that concessions did not forestall
what they were intended to and that concession bargaining had evolved
into a pattern. However, in response to the call from the membership
for renewed militancy, the AFL-CIO council declared, "Today's economic and political climate makes it imperative that unions follow
realistic bargaining strategies . . . not 'all-or nothing' stances. . . ." It
also advocated community pressure as an alternative to strikes, as well
as experiments in labor-management cooperation.[31]

Unions began their own staff layoffs and raided other union territory
to sustain their income. National unions' servicing of locals declined
sharply. As safety conditions deteriorated, protests to the government
regulatory agency diminished. The ILO complained in 1985 about
cutbacks in safety regulations that were increasing the number of
accidents throughout the OECD. The American union bureaucracy's
leadership, calloused as always by its high salaries and affluent life-style
to the needs of the rank and file, nevertheless feared a complete disintegration of its dues-paying base as workers began, out of necessity, to
act independently on a local level.

There has been a marked shift in the American workers' attitude
toward unions over the past three decades. In 1950, unions won 73
percent of the elections to organize new locals. By 1970 the figure had
dropped to 58 percent, and in 1982 only 46 percent agreed to unionize.
In addition, the number of elections to decertify an existing union from
representing the workers rose from 216 in 1959 to more than 900 in
1980. Between 1980 and 1984 union membership fell 2.7 million

among employed workers, to just under one-fifth of the labor force, down from a peak of 35.5 percent in 1945. A larger percentage of black workers are organized, but with the changing job structure the number of organized workers has fallen among all ethnic groups. The drop was largely due to the employment decline in basic industry. This rate of membership is relatively low compared with that in Europe and Japan. And the length of the U.S. contracts—over half of them are for three years—is also exceptional by international standards and was especially damaging to workers' real income during the inflation of the 1970s. In each of the first three years of the "recovery" in the 1980s, union wages rose less than inflation and nonunion pay.

By 1986, American companies were demanding changes in all work rules—from washroom breaks to seniority. A number of firms, particularly in steel, threatened closures to gain rule changes. Most of the strikes in the mid-1980s were over changes in work rules and, increasingly, against union-negotiated contracts. The Japanese foreign investors in the United States, on the other hand, try to prevent organization of their plants, often by paying wages higher than the going rate and introducing other so-called nonadversary, consultative working conditions. But, as in Japan, the work pace is faster and soon creates conflict.

The attempt to organize clerical workers has been relatively unsuccessful. Only 14 percent were organized in 1986, in large part because of the growing role of temporary and part-time workers. In Japan, as well, unions have been unable to organize service workers.

Socialists in power have had an important effect in reducing labor protest against the austerity policies. One union official in France exclaimed in 1984, "Ten years ago, if we had seen the kind of layoffs we're seeing now or the cuts in purchasing power, we would have shut down the big companies and waged war on the capitalists—and tried to change the government to boot. Today there's an appreciation that a reaction like that doesn't fit the times."[32] And an official of the Trade Union Institute in Brussels observed with resignation in 1985, "Somehow governments in Western Europe of whatever political coloration feel now that they ought to be tougher. Many of the problems would exist even if there were socialist governments in every capital, because the economic crisis cannot be escaped."[33]

The situation varied only slightly from country to country, because economic conditions were fairly uniform. In Italy, after the "hot autumn" of 1969, the unions experienced a rapid growth in numbers, legal rights, and influence until 1977. But, as elsewhere, a parallel development that interacted with and responded to the growing strength of labor was rapid technological change (robotization) in the factories. Over the following five years the labor movement suffered multiple checks, one of the most important being the antiterrorist campaign in Italy. The Red Brigades were sometimes centered in the factories, and the unions were involved in the antiterrorist efforts at the same time when they were the target of an antilabor campaign of capital and the state. The Fiat strike in 1980 over the company's plan to fire tens of thousands of workers was the symbol of defeat. The company did fire 50,000 workers and eliminated the work councils. The retaliatory strike was broken by a march of 40,000 other workers demanding the right to work. This defeat was of great importance for the following years, as capital and the state demanded a rollback of the gains labor had made over the preceding decade. Subsequently, the unions collaborated with the austerity policies of the state. As one Italian analyst noted, "Since the 19th century employers have affirmed during negotiations that the cost of labor is too high and that profits are too low; labor unions asserted the contrary. In Italy, since the end of the '70s . . . , the directors of the unions have accepted the conservative theory that the greatest Italian problem is the cost of labor."[34] The Left was unable to take the initiative. Against the background of unemployment, the rank and file, usually more militant than the leadership, was by 1982, at least for the moment, apathetic toward the concessionary contracts.

The highly centralized German unions won a shorter workweek in 1984, after eight weeks of strikes in the capital goods and auto industries. The outcome was not more jobs, however, but more overtime work. And the government introduced policies to permit more firings.

In Japan the key institutional forms of labor relations—enterprise unions, lifetime employment security, and wages and promotion linked to seniority—were established between 1945 and 1949. Unions at that time had power in the midst of the economic devastation after Japan's defeat and in the context of the initial democratization policies of the occupation. Since about 1955 the unions have functionally been company unions, which deal with the companies on a consultative basis and whose demands do not exceed the consensus of the employers' association. Collective bargaining for the whole nation has become ritualized in the annual "spring offensive," in which the unions accept predetermined national wage adjustment. Young workers have increasingly recognized the unions' ineffectiveness, and membership has been on a decline in the 1980s.

As usual, during recessions and with high unemployment, the number of strikes diminished greatly in the OECD countries as a whole. The fear of unemployment led many workers to try to negotiate either individually or at a local level. And in the mid-1980s an OECD report noted with considerable satisfaction, "Labour power as measured by union membership and strike activity has fallen to post-war lows in most countries, with little prospect of immediate reversal."[35] While the observation did describe the situation in the first half of the 1980s, it was rash indeed to make predictions, for scarcely had the ink dried on their report than workers in Spain, Greece, France, and Holland, and in other places on a smaller scale, called major strikes and/or demonstrations independently of their trade unions.

The ILO, in its 1985 study of the global labor situation, observed that although unions everywhere were weakened as far as their ability to represent the workers' interests was concerned, "in fact, unions have never been so much a part of economic and social life." It added, "They are being given ever-increasing responsibilities at all levels."[36] In Europe their trustability was commensurate with their support of the restructuring of the economy. And in the United States, as usual, they served the same function in the economy without receiving official responsibility. Workers have been increasingly forced to resist this collusion.

The majority of trade unions in the LDCs are government-sponsored or company unions, factional rival groups, or gangster-ridden business unions, all of which must be classed with the other institutions of oppression. There are also legitimate unions, which cater to the interests of a tiny minority of full-time workers in large industires, where there are frequently two tiers of labor in the same factory, some organized and others not. U.S. and European organizations are also active in aiding particular unions or keeping labor disunited. Some unions, however, are a part of a genuine labor movement that must be political in its orientation, and these, along with spontaneous action among workers, have played a significant role in workers' responses to their worsening conditions.

Although strikes are forbidden in most of these countries, workers' organizations exist in some form nearly everywhere despite the weight of repression. Women workers, who have been much in demand by the TNCs and exploited throughout the LDCs, in the 1980s are among the most militant in organizing strikes and confronting repression. This is very evident in Korea, especially in the textile industry, and in Brazil, where women played a crucial role in the great expansion of the workers' movement after 1977. In the Philippines, suffering a sharply falling real income, the workers engaged in a record number of strikes. The new labor federation, May First Movement (KMU), founded in 1983 and linked to the revolutionary movement, three years later claimed 600,000 members, organized in both industrial and agricultural unions. In Brazil the military regime's suppression of the official and traditional trade unions opened the way for the creation of an entirely new, militant, and autonomous workers' movement rooted in the factories and emerging directly from the ranks. In many ways it resembled the Solidarity movement in Poland, which it supported. The creation of this movement after 1977, representing over 4.3 million workers, and their organization of a workers' party in 1980, with over 400,000 members within two years, was a highly significant development in the politics of Brazil.[37] And in South Korea in 1987, genuine workers' organizations emerged from the national strike movement that shattered the illusion of a quiescent working class.

CHAPTER 22

UNEMPLOYMENT

Unemployment in the capitalist countries is both an objective outcome of the operations of the system and a subjective strategy of many states to prevent inflation, meaning rising wages. As Harry Braverman contended, "the mass of employment cannot be separated from its associated mass of unemployment. Under conditions of capitalism, unemployment is not an aberration but a necessary part of the working mechanism of the capitalist mode of production. It is continuously produced and absorbed by the energy of the accumulation process itself."[1] This is the *objective* condition of the operation of the system. Unemployment is deplorable at all times and in all ways, but here it is its special features in regard to the restructuring of the economy that I wish to examine.

As those in power in the industrial nations have increasingly accepted high rates of unemployment as permanent, the issue of the decade according to the director of the Bank of Italy in 1983, is "unemployment management."[2] The proposition that millions should be out of work so that prices will not rise is now officially accepted in the OECD nations, and the only question remaining is *how many* millions are essential for a "healthy" economy?

The OECD held that the unemployment in its member countries was "the consequence of a long-term trend," beginning in the mid-1960s.[3] Prior to 1974 the average unemployment for the OECD nations was 2 percent; that of Canada and the United States exceeded the average considerably, while Japan and Sweden had lower rates. Many of the OECD countries encourage the existence of an industrial reserve army since 1974 to control inflation by putting downward pressure on wages and "dampening" consumer demand. "[I]t would be imprudent to use macroeconomic policy to reduce the unemployment rate below its inflation threshold of 6 to 7 percent," the U.S. *Economic Report of the President* blandly asserted in 1983.[4] In Europe this strategy is termed "non-accelerating inflation rate of unemployment (NAIRU)."[5] European policymakers rejected "expansionary policies" in 1984, since they then chose to interpret the NAIRU as being equal to the existing unemployment rates. What followed instead was a systematic attack on the minimum wage and on unemployment compensation; in effect, many governments held these measures responsible for the high rates of unemployment.

The problem of unemployment had reached the point by 1983 that the OECD economists concluded, "20,000 extra jobs will be required every day [over 15 million] during the last five years of this decade if OECD unemployment is to be cut back to its 1979 level of 19 million."[6] Their persistent argument that higher labor costs were the origin of unemployment was undermined by their own statistics. In 1986, governments found that the unemployment rate had exceeded the NAIRU, rose while real wages fell and productivity increased, and far exceeded the capacity utilization slack in the economy.

Full employment had been a U.S. goal only rhetorically. Under President Kennedy the government aimed at an unemployment rate of 4 percent; in 1974 a rate of 5–6 percent was considered a minimal level to avoid inflation. The *Economic Report of the President* in 1983 explained, "The lower limit on unemployment below which inflation will tend to increase is referred to as the *inflation threshold* unemployment rate. . . . [I]t probably lies between 6 and 7 percent."[7]

Until the 1980s unemployment was always considered more politically tolerable in the United States and Canada than in other industrial countries. In the United States work contracts were in effect from day to day or even hour to hour. Many European nations had "security of employment" agreements, created in the 1950s and 1960s and reinforced in the recession in 1975; these pacts limited an employer's freedom to dismiss workers. In France one to two months' notice was required and in the FRG two weeks to three months. But by the beginning of 1983 unemployment in the large European economies was twice as high as in 1975 and growth in total employment turned negative in Europe for the first time in 1982, with a drop of 1 percent. This was attributed to a decline in the growth of the work force and also to the growing number of "discouraged workers." The number of employed workers in Europe was the same in 1983 as in 1968. The governments, meanwhile, began to reverse their employment-security policies and to permit or directly implement massive layoffs, particularly in the basic industries. By January 1987 unemployment in the EC, excluding Spain, Portugal, and Greece, had reached 17.1 million. In the United States employment grew in the 1970s and 1980s, but the *type* of that employment, as I discussed in the preceding chapter, was the most significant new factor.

In the 1960s the OECD governments' emphasis was on such sociological causes of unemployment as race, sex, or other noneconomic factors that supported the "human capital" theory in economics, emphasizing endowments in education and skills. The policy orientation was toward training services and measures to alleviate discrimination, while the economic assumption was that the general economy would continue to grow. Today, however, unemployment is termed "structural" and officially amounted to over 35 million in the OECD countries in the mid-1980s. Unemployment grew and with it a new ideological rationale. Throughout the OECD countries there was a general resignation that the high levels would persist into the future. The German labor office predicted 16 percent unemployment between 1990 and 1995. While they keep raising the figures for an acceptable "minimal unemployment," the various governments have taken an increasingly punitive policy toward the unemployed.

Unemployment has always been a part of the experience of the U.S. worker, even in "prosperity," especially among younger workers and blacks of all ages. But even in that socially backward nation, the situation was considerably worse than in earlier periods. At the depths of the 1982 recession there were more than 12 million officially listed as unemployed in the United States, up to 6 million involuntary part-time workers, and nearly 2 million "discouraged" (unemployed but having lost hope of finding a job and therefore not listed statistically) workers. Unemployment was highest in the basic industries—at over 18 percent in steel and other metals—and in the auto industry. With each business cycle the percentage of unemployment rose, and the remaining unemployed during the "recoveries" also reached new highs. There were still 8.5 million officially unemployed, plus 1.2 million "discouraged" workers at the end of 1985—after three years of "recovery."

Reflecting the racism endemic in American society, unemployment continues to be disproportionately high among black workers. In 1984 the unemployment rate for black men was 16.4 percent, compared with 6.4 percent for white men. The figures were nearly the same for women workers. For men aged sixteen to nineteen the differential was more extreme—42.7 percent for blacks and 16.8 percent for whites. Given these conditions, the number of black discouraged workers is obviously much higher.

One change noted by the IMF and the OECD in their 1983 reports, and also by the head of the U.S. Bureau of Labor Statistics, was the new character and duration of unemployment. Since 1980, according to the IMF, "a substantial portion of the increase in unemployment has occurred in the core group of male heads of household. . . . In general, some of the largest increases in joblessness . . . have been among groups whose unemployment rates previously had been low and stable. . . . The range of occupations seriously affected by unemployment has also broadened . . . and the average duration of unemployment has lengthened considerably. . . ."[8] In the United States the growth of this core group was almost twice as large as that for youth or women. As for the duration of joblessness, the official figure for the average period was eleven weeks in 1979 and eighteen in 1982. But "official statistics systematically understate the length of time a person is unemployed," a Federal Reserve Board report noted, since they measure only the beginning and "fail to accurately depict . . . the growth of long-term unemployment."[9] In fact, the FRB's experts calculated an average in 1982 of twenty-six weeks, rather than eighteen. Others estimated eight months to a year. And these were national averages. In areas where plants closed or industries were radically restructured, unemployment was permanent, especially for middle-aged workers.

Similar, or worse, conditions existed in Europe. Long-term unemployment for a year or more in 1986 reached 46 percent of the unemployed for the EC as a whole, with 25 percent over two years. By country it was over 45 percent of the unemployed in France, more than 40 percent in Britain, and 30 percent in the FRG. The longer a worker is unemployed, the greater the probability that he or she will never find work. Only Japan had a different statistical report. But the measurement of unemployment differs significantly in Japan. The term *unemployment* in Japan refers to those who have lost full-time employment, not to those who have never had a job. Other significant differences in its measurement include the following: laid-off workers are counted as employed, workers who worked more than one hour of the last week of each month are also considered employed, and soldiers are counted in the labor force. Furthermore, between 1973 and 1979 employment in manufacturing fell by 12 percent. Even before the rise of the yen, there had been a steady growth in the unemployment figures through the 1970s and 1980s. According to official criteria, by the end of 1985 unemployment in Japan had reached a record 2.9 percent, the highest since January 1953, when records were first collected. And the duration of unemployment in Japan is longer than in the United States or Canada. With the rise in the yen, manufacturing industry lost 260,000 jobs between November 1985 and November 1986, and there was general anxiety that the situation would approach that of the rest of the OECD countries. For the core of permanent workers, the companies tried numerous means to avoid firings, like transfers to other affiliated companies and early retirement.

In 1983 around 44 percent of the unemployed in the OECD states were under twenty-five. Some 20–30 percent of the youth in all the European countries were unemployed by 1985. Most have never had a job and expect never to find one. This reality has, of course, great implications for their entire lives and for the economy as well. A young worker is now lucky to be able to sell his or her labor for any task.

Unemployment also hits hard at the other end of the age spectrum, at those over the age of fifty. Corporations have increasingly forced rule changes in seniority, and the skills of older workers have been made obsolete by the developments in technology. There was a concentration of older workers in the dying industries of steel, mining, transport, and marginal farming. Once unemployed, the worker over fifty has little chance of finding work again. Many countries, by offering early retirement, have kept large numbers of older workers out of the statistically counted unemployed.

In Europe overall employment fell in the 1980s recession by 2.7 percent and in manufacturing by 11.7 percent. Put another way, it is estimated that 4.5 million blue-collar jobs disappeared between 1979 and 1984. Unemployment would have been even higher had it not been for the large increase of early retirement and of "discouraged" older workers who dropped out of the labor market. Among unemployed women, generally, the rates are greatest among married women whose husbands are also unemployed and among single women who head households.

Rather than the development of employment-expanding new products, the impetus of the new technology since 1974 has been the replacing of labor. In the United States between 1980 and 1985, some 2.3 million jobs in manufacturing disappeared through the "restructuring" of industry.[10] As the cost of robots declined, their installation became more widespread. To compete with Japan, the French auto industry moved rapidly toward robots, eliminating thousands of jobs. The French computer industry created some tens of thousands of jobs and eliminated 200,000 by the end of 1985. A British study forecast that microelectronics would be important in raising unemployment to 16–25 percent in 1990. In the FRG automation was the major factor in both productivity growth and rising unemployment. "The people who are displaced . . . are pretty much permanently displaced," noted a management consultant for the German auto industry.[11] After fearing automation for many years, many trade unions were unwilling to recognize that it had arrived. It particularly hit the skilled machinists.

There is no question that the new technology has far-reaching implications for employment as it substitutes for both physical and mental labor. This is particularly true of the expansion of microelectronics in many products and industries. Most significant is the almost parallel threat to service jobs, which were the only growing employment sector in the OECD countries. The generally stagnant or declining conditions in the economy that have existed over the past decade accentuate the impact of technology's negative effect on employment.

One response to plant closures during the crisis was worker buyouts of companies. There were about one hundred of these over the 1970s in the United States, and they have been credited with saving 50,000 to 100,000 jobs. These buyouts involved little change in management decision making and often were followed by layoffs that unions had earlier prevented and "a widespread tendency for [labor] conflict to re-emerge some months after the transition," according to one study.[12] In France there were widespread worker occupations of closing factories during the 1970s. These quixotic and desperate attempts to establish worker-managed islands in a capitalist sea were usually defeated either by police expulsions or by attrition.

One political response to unemployment was an increase in xenophobia among workers. In nations like France, Switzerland, and the FRG, the large immigrant communities were the closest scapegoat for many natives. Job loss due to competition in the new international division of labor first affected industries with a high proportion of unskilled and women workers, such as textile, apparel, furniture, rubber, and plastic goods. By the 1980s competition from the capital-intensive industries of shipbuilding, steel, machinery, and services was creating job losses. Yet trade with the LDCs and investment relocation were of less importance in creating unemployment than was the aggregation of the many other critical features in the world capitalist economy.

The duration and extent of unemployment compensation quickly became a focus of governments intent on reducing their expenses. In 1981 a comparative study revealed that benefits as a proportion of

wages amounted to 80 percent in Holland, 70 percent in France, 65
percent in Japan, 47 percent in the FRG, 45 percent in the United
Kingdom, and 34 percent in the United States. But its duration was
limited and also varied by nation. The proportion of the unemployed
still receiving benefits had fallen generally in the OECD "in order to
widen the gap between compensation for activity and inactivity," as an
OECD report expressed it.[13]

After reducing employment with their sundry restructuring policies,
between 1983 and 1985 the various governments sought to make the
workers pay further by reducing their compensation, by 36 percent in
the United Kingdom, and freezes, cutbacks, or taxation in the FRG, the
Netherlands, Denmark, and France. In 1975 about 78 percent of the
unemployed in the United States were covered by unemployment compensation. In 1982 only 45 percent of the 10 million unemployed
received compensation, largely because payments had been limited to
26 weeks. Of the 8.5 million unemployed at the beginning of 1986, 65
percent received no compensation at all.

Officials increasingly concluded that the retraining of workers for
new work was not only costly to the state but often utterly ineffective.
"A steel worker over 40 is almost incapable of being retrained for a
new kind of work," said a union leader appointed by the French
government to work on the unemployment problem in Lorraine.[14]
Retraining an unemployed worker from steel or auto factories for the
new high-tech jobs, even if there had been enough of them, was always
a mirage. Not only low-paid, "the semi-skilled worker of the high-
technology industry sits with a doily on her head . . . and fiddles with
a piece of wire. This is very different than an auto worker who bangs
on a car. . . . [T]he great majority of [these] jobs are going to new
employees," a researcher for a community and regional development
project noted in 1983.[15] As cyclical unemployment becomes en-
trenched, it becomes structural since the unemployed are not able to
acquire new skills. It is the skilled jobs, with their high labor costs, that
are in the process of being automated. In the United States the National
Commission on Employment Policy estimated in 1986 that over the
next decade over 400,000 workers a year would need to be retrained.
With middle-income-producing jobs disappearing in any case, retraining is ultimately irrelevant.

RESTRUCTURING STRATEGY

The de facto policy in the OECD countries is to place the blame for
unemployment on the working class. In precrisis conditions the Right
and much of the rest of the bourgeoisie dismissed the unemployed as

either lazy or—for noneconomic, sociological reasons—unable to get work. Governments as well as the OECD, IMF, and other groups now rank the minimum wage, unemployment compensation, state "welfare" legislation, and the like as causes of unemployment, although significant aspersions on the personal character of the unemployed continue.

Toward the end of the 1970s there prevailed a consensus that growing unemployment is due to the "rigidity" in labor costs and that *"[c]ertain forms of social protection* in the developed countries . . . are no doubt helping to increase structural unemployment."[16] The IMF attributed unemployment to the generous unemployment benefits and to a "substantial increase in the *relative cost of labor,"* which directed investment to labor-saving equipment.[17] U.S. government economists in 1983 asserted that "increased wage rigidity is likely to raise the economy's inflation-threshold of unemployment."[18] The OECD proposed "offering marginal investment subsidies to firms which reach agreement with their unions on wage moderation, thereby linking wage moderation to the maintenance . . . of employment."[19] Yet in 1985 the OECD reported that wages had not fallen far enough, for the "sluggish response of wages to post-war record unemployment in many countries is often regarded as the root cause of continuing unemployment."[20]

There was general agreement that much of the unemployment was not cyclical but *"the consequence of a long-term trend."* "Rates in the biggest boom years have increased from one cycle to the next and also between periods with the same capacity utilization rate," an OECD study observed.[21] And in the mid-1980s, another study held, the "rates are far above levels observed at comparable stages of previous cycles."[22]

SOCIAL CONSEQUENCES

Unemployment "wreaks havoc in the present lives of . . . working class families whereas it interferes with the future of middle class families," as one study in Britain noted.[23] Accompanying the restructuring of employment to a lower income level and the long-term unemployment are all the characteristics of increased poverty—hunger, soup kitchens, homelessness, drug abuse, racism, and suicides—while the politicians speak of cutting back the "safety net" and permitting the homeless to sleep in the subway. Beggars are found in places where they were not a decade ago. The aggregate statistics of falling living standards are depressingly accurate here. This was especially true in the United States, which is not encumbered with the social "rigidities" that persist in Europe. Five million additional Americans fell below the poverty level between 1980 and 1982 alone. Drug addicts rose six-tyfold between 1960 and 1985. Homelessness by the end of 1985 was estimated to be 312,000 in fifteen of America's largest cities, and up to 3 million in the nation as a whole, 140,000 in Britain, and uncounted hundreds of thousands in the rest of Europe.

Unemployment or underemployment of over half the labor force prevailed in most of the LDCs, and this situation became even more acute in the 1980s, with the world economic crisis and the various government "adjustment" policies. And the unemployed who had re-cently lost full-time work expanded the informal sector of the cities, leading in every country to falling income in this segment of the population, to accompany the decline in real wages of those still em-ployed. The street economy and family workshops absorb labor in the LDCs that would elsewhere be counted as unemployed. But since there are no "rigidities" in the form of a social safety net in these societies, such marginal activities are the people's only option. As one IMF economist put it, "very few people can afford to be openly unem-ployed."[24] In fact, this process, existing in its extreme form in the LDCs for many years, is becoming more common in the industrialized parts of the world with the growth of contracting out and the use of irregular and "contingent" labor.

Official unemployment, which counts those who have lost full-time work in the urban areas, rose 3.5 times in Egypt between 1973 and 1980 and doubled in Brazil between 1978 and 1981. In Indonesia, Thailand, and India, that listed in employment offices grew 140 per-cent. In the Philippines, official figures listed 3 million unemployed and another 8 million underemployed out of a labor force of 20 million. Since 1980, given the condition of the LDC economies, the situation worsened by many times, especially in Latin America. As a UN survey stated between 1981 and 1983, unemployment in Latin America reached "proportions without recorded precedent."[25] The primary new causes were the world recession and the various, usually IMF-imposed, "adjustment" policies.

Clearly, capitalism could not long accept the goal of full employment enunciated at the end of World War II and in large part realized in Europe between 1955 and 1975. Creating a reserve army, not just in the periphery, where it appeared limitless, but also in the center, has become a fundamental aim of restructuring. But once it had achieved the goals of redistributing shares of the national income, broken the link with inflation, sufficiently reduced wages, and weakened labor organizations, official economists began to worry after 1985 about the loss of human capital for the future, about the continuing job loss in the economies in excess of what they required, and, worst of all, about the growing possibility of a spiraling deflation and worldwide depression.

CHAPTER 23

CONCLUSION TO PART IV

A crucial consequence of the entire restructuring process in the OECD countries has been to reverse the position that labor had attained over the preceding decades. This restructuring—both objective, as the outcome of the operations of the capitalist system, and as a subjective offensive of capital and the state in the class struggle—created a basically new condition for labor in the 1980s.

The changes in the nature of work have tremendous implications for the future development of capitalism, as technology aggravates a trend toward unemployment and lower living standards in the context of all the other crisis features in the world economy. While offering the potential, in a different social system, of strengthening the forces of production and liberating workers from dangerous and monotonous work, the technological changes, now as in the past, are used as a weapon against labor. Technology has made possible the reduction of the cost of labor in production—in an increasing number of cases, by eliminating labor altogether. The introduction of new technology in industry's cost-cutting efforts in order to compete in the world market has sharply polarized incomes and jobs, shrinking middle-income employment. And if the costs of labor-substituting technology fall as fast as the cost of labor, it will continue to replace high-wage workers. The contradiction to this trend is that the technology must be used and amortized, whereas living labor can be hired and fired at will.

Unemployment at levels unprecedented since the Great Depression has persisted with little change during the so-called cyclical recoveries, and it has been accompanied by shrinking state support in terms of compensation. The option of migration has closed in the OECD countries and is closing in the OPEC states as well. Workers are the targets everywhere, as states struggle to renew investment incentives and compete for capital. The labor force is being "restructured" to a lower level of income and skills, and part-time and temporary work has become increasingly common.

The workers' conditions in the developing countries deteriorated on all levels, as the various factors of the crisis in the world economy increasingly bore in on them from all sides. Unemployment, worsening wages and working conditions for the minority of full-time workers, increased cost of living for all, as subsidies of basic essentials are removed, increased harassment in the squatter settlements, and a greater influx from the countryside, as conditions there continue to fall, determined the life experience of the vast majority.

All these structural changes have made relevant once more Marx's prognosis of growing immiseration with growing concentration of wealth. This is developing disastrously in the LDCs and increasingly in the OECD nations as well. For a period during the 1970s the standard of living in many countries in the OECD was maintained by two income earners in a family, or through the use of credit that raised the income bracket and consumption level of many working-class families for a brief period, but those factors are no longer sufficient. New jobs for the working class are low-wage jobs, and two earners now may make less than one did a decade ago—and unemployment increasingly strikes both earners as well. At the other extreme, in the United States after the mid-1970s, there was a sharp acceleration of the concentration of wealth. One study for the U.S. Congress concluded that the holdings of the top one-half of one percent of the population rose from about 15 percent of total wealth in 1976 to approximately 38 percent in 1983.[1] Yet the contradictions for capitalism in all these developments are equally evident. This struggle with labor at the point of production costs shrinks the market that capitalists must have in order to realize profits.

Class conflict between capital and labor in the relations of production and for greater shares of national income, an essential aspect or systemic feature of capitalism, exists even when a political consciousness regarding the direction of that struggle is absent or when it is suppressed. The class struggle is always waged more or less vigorously against labor. In the late 1970s and 1980s it was a reaction against the significant gains of labor during the period 1968–72, especially in Europe, gains resulting in higher wages at a time when competition was gathering momentum among most capitalists in the world economy. The struggle is now being waged relentlessly by capital and the state to reduce systematically the cost of labor and its share in the national income, to weaken the working-class organization and movement, to restructure the work process globally, and to compensate for the state's fiscal crisis by further reducing expenditures for health and welfare.

But labor must resist or remain a victim. In many LDCs there has been worker resistance to government austerity programs and worsening conditions. Inevitably, by 1987, after over a decade of absorbing the systematic reduction of living standards and the threat of permanent unemployment, workers in France, Spain, and Greece, independently of the trade unions, had made it known through mass strikes and/or demonstrations that it was no longer possible to proceed with the restructuring policies without mounting opposition. In other parts of the world, too, there is evidence of growing resistance. Workers acted against an array of institutional forces committed to the preservation of the status quo or, in most cases now, to a reversal of even the modest gains in social welfare won over the preceding decades. These actions evoked surprise at the time and place, yet they should not have, for labor militancy and class struggle are also systemic in capitalism. They can be expected in general even if they are usually unexpected in the specific; the potential is always there.

Of one thing we may be sure: there will be renewed periods of militancy and spontaneous active struggle on the part of the working class in the industrial nations. When and where one cannot predict. But there can be no illusion. The process of restructuring is well advanced, and radical social change for the benefit of labor will not come about without active resistance and mobilization.

CONCLUSION

The world never really emerged from the economic crisis that began in the mid-1970s and has been characterized by both the new structural conditions I have described throughout this book and the ultimately determining systemic features of capitalism. Inadequate profit incentives for productive investment; acute inflation that eventually yields, by way of high unemployment and intense competition, to deflation; stagnation; sectoral depression; debt; austerity; unemployment; falling living standards; and excess capacity in all economic sectors and in most countries—these are but a few of the features of the integrated world economy today. All are the outcome of, and contributors to, a process of restructuring, creating problems unprecedented in magnitude since the Great Depression. In Latin America such a depression already existed by the mid-1980s.

The long-term IMF restructuring programs forced on the LDCs are juxtaposed with the extremely short-term calculations and actions of capital. Socialists in Europe have managed capitalism in ways that their conservative predecessors never dared to try. And the CPEs are moving to embrace the market system at a time when it is evident that all the remedies for the crisis in the market economies—be they monetarist, Keynesian, or social democrat—have been tried and failed. Exposed are the bare essentials of the system; all the illusions that the capitalist state has a neutral or "autonomous" role in class relations melt away, revealing the state everywhere, regardless of the party in power, as the promoter of profit and the antagonist of labor.

At this stage the basic, profound challenge to the bourgeoisie comes from the workings of, and contradictions in, the system itself and their inability to manage it. While various states offer increasing incentives to invest, capitalists respond only to profit expectation, not to exhortation. Unless there is evident opportunity for profit, investors will not solve the debt crisis by investing in debt-ridden countries, no matter what the incentives, or resolve the fiscal crisis by rescuing state industries. It was, after all, usually because of their unprofitability for capital that the state nationalized the industries in the first place.

The new structural conditions make the state of world capitalism in many respects as fragile today as at any other time in its recent history. There is constant, dynamic instability. Each recent resolution of a threatening condition, whether inflation, energy cost, or monetary dilemmas, became another crisis—deflation, debt and bankruptcy, trade struggle, and so on. The so-called recovery in the United States after 1983 was dependent on an extraordinary budget deficit, and the growth of employment was linked to a general restructuring of the job market, with deflationary consequences.

General perceptions of trends have been reversed during the past decade. The tendency toward a greater role of the state in the economy, providing ever expanding social security and regulating the economic cycle, was widely discussed after World War II as a permanent characteristic of Western economies, but the fiscal crisis has brought contradictions and retrenchment. At the same time there has been an *objective* privatization of many former state functions, such as money creation by the banks, as well as *subjective* policies, such as the denationalization of previously nationalized industries; in the CPEs there has occurred an increasing shift away from central planning and toward the introduction of market determinants in the economy.

The idea of an ever increasing standard of living also became incorporated in certain industrial countries after World War II as another permanent feature and goal of economic and social policies. Now, however, the retrogression in living standards for the masses in the industrial countries, as well as in the LDCs, and the official acceptance of high levels of unemployment present a new scenario, and with it a new social attitude, and reveal once more the predominance of the essential features of the capitalist system. There is increasingly immiseration on a world scale as there is simultaneously an exaltation of acquisitiveness for others.

The interacting parts of the system are dynamic but, though all the disparate elements are linked and interact, they are not susceptible to a coherent global strategy. The contradictions that come out of their objective interaction and integration engender a disintegration in the economy. The relation that emerges is therefore a dialectic of acts, perceptions, and reactions by individuals, classes, and states—a dynamic of perpetual struggle.

Without external stimuli, the economy tends toward stagnation or depression. Overcapacity in all sectors continues to characterize the world capitalist economy. A resolution of a crisis of overproduction may come in the destruction of capital, or what Joseph Schumpeter called the market's "creative destruction," which restructures the economy until the weak are eliminated and the cost of all the so-called factors of production are lowered, allowing the accumulation process to begin once more from a new foundation. But what most alarms those who expected this cyclical result from the restructuring of the economies is that the deflationary spiral has continued downward. Commodity prices have fallen with overproduction, but for many raw materials the market is disappearing altogether. More fundamentally, labor costs have fallen with unemployment, and jobs have disappeared and no new ones have emerged for which to retrain.

A traditional solution in capitalism is to destroy the surplus. But how much "creative destruction" can the world endure before it generates political struggle, which in the past too often led to war? Technology has escalated the dangers inherent in capitalist crisis, because its new changes have the potential to create consequences far more serious for humanity than any in previous epochs or crises.

The world economy is snarled in its contradictions, both those intrinsic to the system and those new structural conditions created by the dynamic interaction of these diverse forces historically. Both have shaped the political economy and will continue to shape it for years to come. Objectively, the world system is integrated and reform is not possible in a national context. Finally, who is to pay for the restructuring of the world economy, in the LDCs, in the OECD states, and in the CPEs? It is a rhetorical question. The answer is those who always pay and always will until the structure of power relations is changed and until the systemic features of capitalism are eliminated.

It is indeed redundant! History is tirelessly repetitive in this sense. And one must, just as repetitively, discuss the irrationality and destructive nature of this system, its resistance to reform, and the urgent dangers for mankind, given the nuclear age in which we live, of capitalism's continuing on its egotistical and relentlessly destructive course.

No new theory is needed; despite the changes, it is the same old story, in a different structural guise. All of the evidence in the preceding chapters has underscored this fact. There has been a vast effort to expand the reserve army of labor on an international scale, in order to

eradicate the effect of rising wages and falling productivity that capitalists everywhere have viewed as the origin of the crisis. Competition
among capitalists has intensified globally. Restructuring the world
economy, both objectively and subjectively, is a form of class and
imperialist struggle with winners and losers, waged systematically by
the capitalist states for capital and against labor on an international
basis. Words that hide or disguise this fundamental reality can only do
a disservice to an understanding of the existing capitalist social system.

Less than a decade ago the parameters of discussion of the world
economy would have been different. It would have been necessary to
make a critique of the still influential Keynesian paradigm, and there
were general illusions about the potential for socialist parties to effect
radical change. But as the system has returned to the fundamentals of
orthodoxy, the dominant ideology has increasingly reverted to the past.
Acquisitiveness is more openly and proudly acclaimed. There is no
effort to mask it as "people's capitalism" or "affluent society"; scarcely
even a "dribble-down" notion is any longer proclaimed. Even promises
of better to come are now missing. This generation is worse off than
the preceding one, and the official prognosis is that living standards will
be yet worse for the next generation. States accept high levels of
unemployment and formulate policies to restructure the world economy
further by eliminating yet more jobs to raise productivity and profits,
and they then move to cut off even the minimal compensation for the
unemployed. In the LDCs the restructuring policies have substantially
worsened their already serious economic plight. The orthodox capitalist
ideology is now so pervasive that few people any longer even conceive
of other than a capitalist future, including branches of the socialist
parties and many in those nations that call themselves socialist. And
others would declare that capitalism has been transformed into something else at the very time when its essential features are most exposed
and universal.

One can even say that the system has had more than its share of luck
or that capital has won this phase in its perpetual struggle with labor.
For what is the response to this condition of permanent economic
crisis—to stagnation, depression in large areas, or growth with immiseration—whose developments can only lead to greater catastrophes for
the world's people? The struggle is now being waged fiercely on one
side. As yet there have been only isolated responses from the victims.

But perceptions play an important part in history, and this may
change with a growing consciousness of the existing system's inability
to emerge from its crisis, except with a radically altered landscape, one
with significantly lower living standards for the population. Such new

perceptions *could* alter the political habits of decades and, if conditions worsen, may of necessity elicit a response. By 1987 some resistance was already evident. There is a real *need* to resist, since these efforts at "restructuring" have advanced very far. The *urgency* will come with a culmination of the contradictions and with a breakdown in depression.

Bureaucrats or men of power everywhere, from the United States to Poland, from South Korea to Latin America, relying on the appearances of power, technology, and repression, have had their surprises over the past decade. In the coming years those who rely on the political habits of the past may confront surprises as well, for the facade of power is usually deceptive, and the tendencies in science and technology, the moves in the international division of labor, and all the various attempts to restructure face constant contradictions.

Capitalism continues with significant structural changes; but it will not pass away without a struggle. This is as true in the 1980s as it was in the 1870s, or as it will be in the year 2000. There is no reason to conclude that while a breakdown may be inherent in the system's contradictions, these workings alone will bring it to an end, let alone introduce a socialist alternative.

It may be reassuring for successive generations of writers to envision, on the one hand, that the end of capitalism is near because it is "late" or "mature" or, on the other, that the time has not yet approached for the end, which will evolve in the future through the inevitable march of history. Both, I fear, are illusions. The inevitable crises arising out of the contradictions in the operation of the system create the vulnerable moments for it. But there have been many crises of capitalism that could have been seized for revolutionary change.

Like the notion of "mature" capitalism, that of "late" capitalism is relative and has little utility as an analytic framework, except to give one the satisfaction that we must be nearing the end. For Marx, capitalism was mature, even late, compared with the earlier periods. The year 1870 was "late," compared with 1790, as was 1930, compared with 1870. Capitalism has persisted through major catastrophes and has been reconstructed. One new feature in the world today, however, is the near universality of the capitalist mode of production and the formation of a world market. This carries important new implications.

But the reality remains that the vast majority of the world's people will remain victims of the operations of the capitalist system until *they* act to take power. This reality is the outcome of both the objective operations of the capitalist system and the subjective policies of states that react in a uniform manner, underlined once more by the actions of the socialists in the various European states, to resolve its economic crises. Socialism is not capitalism by another name nor "capitalism with a human face," but the negation of capitalism—that is, of its systemic features, its "laws"—and the affirmation and construction of a different system altogether.

The final and most important questions must remain unanswered. But of one thing we may be sure. Capitalism, in its primal form, is very much the dominant system, and it will continue and lead inexorably to more severe calamities. It will persist without the intervention of organized political movements dedicated to abolishing it in its essentials. And socialism can exist *only* where the systemic features of capitalism no longer define society.

SOURCES

The problem in writing about the contemporary economy is to choose from too many sources the essentials that will best express the reality and the process of development and change.

The publications of the IMF/World Bank, the OECD, the U.S. government and Congress, and the various divisions of the United Nations were of primary importance. The business press is an indispensable source of information. For general business coverage, *Business Week* and the *Far Eastern Economic Review* have been especially valuable for information. For individual sectors of the economy, I have used specialized journals dealing with various industries.

Journalists are the gathers of contemporary information, and their interviews provide statements by the various actors in the political economy. And many are outstanding analysts of the news they report. I would particularly mention Carl Gewirtz in the *International Herald Tribune*; his perception of what is important makes his reporting especially useful. A large proportion of my references to the *IHT* in the notes are to his reports.

In addition, there are individual scholars everywhere who have produced significant studies on these topics of vital concern to everyone. I appreciate them all for their serious and important work.

The notes represent only a very small fraction of the material consulted and usually refer only to sources for specific data. As in my previous books, for the sake of economy of space, I have footnoted the quotations and then listed the sources of information since the preceding note.

NOTES

Abbreviations

BIS	*Bank for International Settlements*
BW	*Business Week*
EROP	*Economic Report of the President*
FBIS	*Foreign Broadcast Information Service Daily Report*
F & D	International Monetary Fund, *Finance and Development*
FEER	*Far Eastern Economic Review*
ICR	*International Currency Review*
IHT	*International Herald Tribune*
JCA	*Journal of Contemporary Asia*
JES	*Japanese Economic Studies*
NEER	*New England Economic Review*
WEO	International Monetary Fund, *World Economic Outlook*
WES	United Nations, *World Economic Survey*
WFM	*World Financial Markets*

CHAPTER 1. Interaction of Events and Policy, 1974–1980

1. *F & D*, Sept. 1980, 9.

2. Paul Volcker, "The Dilemmas of Monetary Policy," *Federal Reserve Bank of New York Monthly Review*, Dec. 1975, 275. See also Gabriel Kolko, *Anatomy of a War: Vietnam, the United States, and the Modern Historical Experience* (New York, 1985), 283–93, 312–20.

3. *Swiss Credit Bulletin*, Summer 1975, 14.

4. "What Has Gone Wrong with Economic Performance," *OECD Observer*, July 1977, 8. See also *WES, 1983*, 8; *WES, 1975*, 14; *WES, 1975, Supplement*, 3; *Swiss Credit Bulletin*, Summer 1975, 14–16; Joyce Kolko, *America and the Crisis of World Capitalism* (Boston, 1974), 25–28; Angus Maddison, *Phases of Capitalist Development* (Oxford, 1982), 66, 126.

5. *WES, 1979–1980*, 94. See also *EROP, 1984*, 51; *WES, 1981–1982*; UN, *Economic Survey of Latin America, 1977* (New York, 1977), 2.

6. *WES, 1975, Supplement*, 1. See also *WES, 1975*, 88; *WES, 1976*, 26; *WES, 1976, Supplement*, 10; Philip H. Trezise, "The Evolution of United States-

Japan Relations," in *Japan and the United States: Economic and Political Adversaries*, ed. Leon Hollerman (Boulder, 1980), 152.

7. *WES, 1976, Supplement,* 25.

8. Ibid., 72.

9. *Journal of Commerce,* Nov. 13, 1978.

10. *BW,* May 26, 1975, 58. See also U.S. Congress, Joint Economic Committee, *The Business Cycle and Public Policy 1929–80: A Compendium of Papers* (Washington, 1980), 34–37; *EROP, 1979,* 92; Maddison, *Phases of Capitalist Development,* 66.

11. Such terms are found in all IMF documents, and in those of other official and semiofficial organizations as well.

12. Karl Marx, *Capital,* vol. 2 (New York, 1967), 411.

13. *WES, 1975,* 93.

14. *F & D,* Sept. 1980, 9.

15. "What Has Gone Wrong," 8. See also ibid., passim; *WEO, 1983,* 123.

16. *WES, 1977,* 2. See also *WES, 1979–1980,* 3.

17. BIS, *47th Annual Report* (Basle, 1977), 15.

18. *BW,* July 11, 1977, 29.

19. *WES, 1977,* 1, 4. See also *BW,* Oct. 17, 1977, 77.

20. *WES, 1981–1982,* 11. See also ibid., 26; *WES, 1976 Supplement,* 24, 29, 33–34; *WES, 1978,* 10; Michael Moffitt, *World's Money: International Banking from Bretton Woods to the Brink of Insolvency* (New York, 1983), 144–48; *Euromoney,* Oct. 1978, 115–24; Joyce Kolko, "Vers un renouveau de la planification capitaliste en Europe," *Monde Diplomatique,* Dec. 1979, 6; *BW,* Aug. 29, 1977, 22–24; April 4, 1983, 64–67.

21. Quoted in *FEER,* Aug. 22, 1980, 64.

22. See in this regard Karl Sauvant, "The NIEO Programme: A Framework for Restructuring the World Economy?" in *The New International Division of Labor,* ed. Dieter Ernst (Frankfurt, 1980), 110–36.

CHAPTER 2. The 1980s.

1. *WEO, 1983,* 14.

2. *WES, 1983,* 66, 71.

3. IMF, *Annual Report, 1983,* 14.

4. *IHT,* Dec. 7, 1982.

5. U.S. Department of the Treasury, *United States Participation in the Multilateral Development Banks in the 1980s* (Washington, 1982). See also *FEER,* March 26, 1982, 131–32.

6. *IHT,* May 5, 1982. See also *FEER,* Sept. 17, 1982, 67–74.

7. *EROP, 1984*, 56. See also "Financing the U.S. Current Account Deficit," *Federal Reserve Bank of New York Quarterly Review*, Summer 1984, 39–47.

8. *WEO, 1985*, 46.

9. *IHT*, Feb. 29, 1984. See also *WEO, 1984*, 83.

10. *IMF Survey*, Aug. 12, 1985, 247–49; Aug. 26, 1985, 266.

11. *WEO, 1985*, 192. See also ibid., 1983, passim; *WES, 1984*, 2; IHT, June 19, 1987.

CHAPTER 3.   Accumulation, Competition, and the Class Struggle

1. *IHT*, Aug. 8, 1982.

2. *Fortune*, Oct. 3, 1983, 63.

3. *BW*, Dec. 27, 1982, 26.

4. Ibid., March 21, 1984, 237. See also ibid., 236–50.

5. *IHT*, Aug. 8, 1982. See also *BW*, March 21, 1984, 236–37; Dec. 3, 1984, 139–41; Dec. 17, 1984, 70; Dec. 30, 1985, 49; *Fortune*, Oct. 3, 1983, 63.

6. Sadayuki Sato, "Japanese Multinational Enterprises: Potential and Limits," *JES*, Fall 1980, 101.

7. U.S. Congress, Joint Economic Committee, *The Business Cycle and Public Policy, 1929–80: A Compendium of Papers* (Washington, 1980), 243–44. See also ibid., 234–35.

8. David Felix, "Reaganomics: An Appraisal of Its Long Run Impact on US Stagflation" (Unpublished paper, July 6, 1982). See also *BW*, May 31, 1982, 87; *WES, 1981–1982*, 25; *EROP, 1983*, 258; *EROP, 1986*, 278–79; *WFM*, Dec. 1984, 4; *FEER*, Jan. 16, 1986, 91; *Survey of Current Business*, Jan. 1987, 11.

9. *BW*, March 19, 1979, 110–12.

10. Ibid., 111.

11. OECD, *Interfutures: Facing the Future: Mastering the Probable and Managing the Unpredictable* [1st Revision Edition] (Paris, 1979), 335. See also *BW*, Oct. 17, 1977, 66; *EROP, 1984*, 234–35; *Fortune*, May 2, 1983, 226; *Federal Reserve Bank of New York Quarterly Review*, Summer 1984, 40.

12. See the discussion of Daniel Saint-James, *De l'usage de Marx en temps de crise* (Paris, 1984), 56ff.

13. Daniel Holland and Stewart Myers, "Trends in Corporate Profitability and Capital Costs," in *The Nation's Capital Needs: Three Studies*, ed. Robert Lindsay (Washington, 1979), 105. See also *EROP, 1984*, 234.

14. *WFM*, Dec. 1984, 4. See also OECD, *Interfutures*, 123; Barry Bluestone and Bennett Harrison, *The Deindustrialization of America* (New York, 1982), 147; *BW*, Nov. 3, 1980, 50.

15. *WFM*, June 1985, 5.

16. See Robin Murray, "Transfer Pricing and Its Control," in *Multinationals Beyond the Market: Intrafirm Trade and the Control of Transfer Pricing*, ed. Robin Murray (Brighton, 1981), 157 and passim; also *BW*, Jan. 13, 1986, 46–47.

17. *BW*, Jan. 12, 1987, 76. See also *Federal Reserve Bulletin*, April 1987, 253; Barry Bosworth, "Taxes and Investment Recovery," *Brookings Papers on Economic Activity* (1985): 2–6.

18. *BW*, Feb. 18, 1985, 118. See also *EROP, 1983*, 78; *BW*, Oct. 17, 1977, 60–70, 105–16; March 19, 1979, 108–12; Jan. 30, 1984, 66.

19. Robert Reich, "The Next American Frontier," *Atlantic*, March 1983, 50. See also *BW*, Oct. 17, 1977, 67; *OECD Observer*, Sept. 1981, 9–15.

20. Reich, "Frontier," 54. See also *BW*, Nov. 24, 1986, 75; Jan. 12, 1987, 38; June 3, 1985, 88–100; May 21, 1979, 75; June 7, 1982, 88–93; Dec. 30, 1985, 148–59.

21. *BW*, March 4, 1985, 84.

22. *EROP, 1985*, 191, 197. See also *BW*, March 4, 1985, 82.

23. *BW*, March 4, 1985, 82. See also ibid., June 16, 1986, 32–34; Aug. 25, 1986, 72–74; Sept. 8, 1986, 76–77; March 2, 1987, 28–35; *IHT*, Nov. 19, 21, 28, 1986; *Corporate Finance*, March 1986, 57–64; *BW*, Dec. 1, 1986, 28–35; Jan. 12, 1987; U.S. House, Committee on Energy and Commerce, *Hearings: Corporate Takeovers*, 99th Cong., 1st sess., Feb. 27–May 22, 1985 (Washington, 1986), 296–400, 414–24, 444–50.

24. *Euromoney*, April 1982, 35. See also *BW*, Sept. 16, 1985, 78–90; *Federal Reserve Bulletin*, April 1987, 253.

25. Leon Grunberg, *Failed Multinational Ventures: The Political Economy of International Divestments* (Lexington, 1981), 4–5, 12–14, and passim. See also *EROP, 1985*, 193–95; *BW*, Nov. 24, 1986, 92–93.

26. Bluestone and Harrison, *Deindustrialization*, 154. See also *BW*, Sept. 16, 1985, 78–90.

27. *IHT*, July 6, 1983.

28. *Wall Street Journal*, March 23, 1981.

29. *BW*, July 1, 1985, 50.

30. Ibid., Nov. 24, 1986, 96.

31. Ibid., Oct. 19, 1983, 106.

32. U.S. Congress, *Business Cycle*, 240.

33. Felix, *Reaganomics*, 29. See also *BW*, Dec. 27, 1982, 16.

34. *Euromoney*, Sept. 1986, 120.

35. *BW*, Oct. 29, 1984, 101. See also *BW*, Oct. 16, 1978, 67–111; *IHT*, March 5, 1982; *Chase Economic Observer*, July/Aug. 1984, 3–5.

36. *BW*, June 24, 1985, 108.

37. *Euromoney*, Sept. 1984, 153.

38. *BW*, Dec. 2, 1985, 44.

39. Ibid., April 7, 1986, 33.

40. Ibid., 35.

41. Ibid., Nov. 24, 1986, 96.

42. Ibid., Dec. 30, 1985, 22. See also *WFM*, Jan. 1986, 7–8; *IHT*, Jan. 1, 1985.

43. *BW*, Sept. 16, 1985, 78. See also *FEER*, June 12, 1986, 57; *BW*, May 12, 1986, 30; *IHT*, Nov. 24, 1986.

44. *Euromoney*, Jan. 1986, 29.

45. *BW*, Jan. 13, 1986, 46–47.

46. Ibid., 47.

47. Ibid., Nov. 1, 1982, 89.

48. OECD, *Interfutures*, 159–60.

49. See Benjamin Cohen, *Multinational Firms and Asian Exports* (New Haven, 1975), 137; *OECD Observer*, Sept. 1981, 9–15; Sato, "Japanese Multinational Enterprises," 71, 91; Hideki Yoshihara, "Research on Japan's General Trading Firms: An Overview," *JES*, Spring 1981, 70–82; *BW*, June 9, 1986, 47; May 11, 1987, 68.

50. Charles Oman, *New Forms of International Investment in Developing Countries* (Paris, 1984). See also Frederick Clairmonte and John Cavanagh, "Transnational Corporations and the Struggle for the Global Market," *JCA* 13 (1983): 446–80 (this is one of a number of exceptional studies by Clairmonte and Cavanagh on various aspects of the global economy); *BW*, Aug. 18, 1986, 50–51; March 3, 1986, 57.

51. Sato, "Japanese Multinational Enterprises," 71. See also Kiyoshi Kojima, "Japanese Direct Investment," *JES*, Spring 1986, 73–76.

52. Michael Sharpston, *International Subcontracting* (Washington, 1975), 94.

53. *BW*, March 31, 1980, 83.

54. Ibid., June 4, 1984, 104; *IHT*, March 1, 1986. See also *WFM*, Jan. 1986, 6; *BW*, Feb. 3, 1986, 84–86; July 14, 1986, 45–46; June 4, 1984, 103–4.

55. *IHT*, Feb. 21, 1984.

56. *BW*, March 24, 1986, 118. See also *EROP, 1983*, 56–57.

57. *IHT*, Dec. 10, 1985. See also Kojima, "Japanese Direct Investment," 75; *Euromoney*, Oct. 1985, 321–23.

58. *IHT*, Aug. 15, 1980. See also *OECD Observer*, Sept. 1981, 9–15; Clairmonte and Cavanagh, "Transnational Corporations," 459.

59. *BW*, Sept. 16, 1985, 34.

60. Naohito Suzuki, "Japanese-style Management and Its Transferability," *JES*, Spring 1984, 67.

61. Ibid., 75.

62. *IHT*, Dec. 10, 1985. See also for management, *BW*, May 18, 1987, 102–9.

63. Albert Z. Carr, "Can a Businessman Afford a Conscience?" *Harvard Business Review*, July–Aug. 1970, cited in Ernest Mandel, *Late Capitalism* (London, 1975), 512.

64. *BW*, Sept. 24, 1984, 84, 88. See also the important study of Edward Herman, *Corporate Control, Corporate Power* (New York, 1981), 203–12, 236–39; *BW*, March 19, 1979, 110; May 23, 1983, 170; *Wall Street Journal*, March 23, 1981; Frederick Clairmonte and John Cavanagh, *World in Their Web* (London, 1981), 17; *BW*, Dec. 26, 1983, 42.

65. OECD, *Interfutures*, 152.

66. *BW*, June 14, 1982, 72. See also *EROP, 1984*, 244; OECD, *Interfutures*, 153–55.

67. *IHT*, June 27, 1987.

CHAPTER 4. The Service Sector

1. Ryuichiro Tachi, "The 'Softization' of the Japanese Economy," *JES*, Spring 1985, 67–88.

2. Quoted in Richard Kirkland, Jr., "The Changing Job Market," *Current*, Dec. 1985, 21. See also Tachi, "Softization," 69; Ronald Kent Shelp, *Beyond Industrialization: Ascendency of the Global Service Economy* (New York, 1981), 10–15, 21, 33; Frederick Clairmonte and John Cavanagh, "Transnational Corporations and Services: The New Frontier," *Trade and Development*, no. 5 (1984): 233.

3. Thomas Stanback et al., *Services: The New Economy* (London, 1981), 15. See also *IHT*, Nov. 5, 1983.

4. *Fortune*, Sept. 21, 1985, 168. See also Courtney Slater, "The (Business) Service Economy," *American Demographics*, May 1985, 6–7; *EROP, 1986*, 265.

5. Dieter Ernst, "Restructuring World Industry in a Period of Crisis—The Role of Innovation (Draft of study prepared for UNIDO, Vienna, 1981), 1:8. This excellent study was later published as *Restructuring World Industry in a Period of Crisis—The Role of Innovation: An Analysis of Recent Developments in the Semiconductor Industry* (New York, 1981). See also *BW*, March 18, 1985, 20.

6. *BW*, March 3, 1986, 59. See also ibid., 61–62, 79, 81.

7. Ibid., 66.

8. See Frederick Clairmonte and John Cavanagh, "Transnational Corporations and the Struggle for the Global Market," *JCA* 13 (1983): 461; *Economist*, Oct. 5, 1985, 81; Nov. 30, 1985, 63.

CHAPTER 5.   Banking: Changes in a Pivotal Sector

1. *IHT*, Oct. 1, 1984. See also Edward Herman, *Corporate Control, Corporate Power* (New York, 1981), 157.

2. *IHT*, Nov. 25, 1985. See also *BW*, Sept. 6, 1982, 80–86; Jan. 12, 1987, 109; W. P. Hogan and I. F. Pearce, *The Incredible Eurodollar* (London, 1982), 63; Hyman Minsky, *Can "It" Happen Again?* (Armonk, N.Y., 1982), 86; Albert Wojnilower, "The Central Role of Credit Crunches in Recent Financial History," *Brookings Papers on Economic Activity* (1980): 286.

3. *IHT*, Nov. 25, 1985.

4. *BW*, Oct. 29, 1984, 103. See also ibid., 100; *Euromoney*, Oct. 1985, 28; *BW*, Sept. 16, 1985, 87–90; *IHT*, Nov. 24, 1986; *Federal Reserve Bulletin*, April 1987, 253.

5. Walter Wriston, "The Information Standard," *Euromoney*, Oct. 1984, 92. See also *IHT*, Nov. 25, 1985; *Federal Reserve Bank of New York Quarterly Review*, Summer 1984, 28.

6. Wriston, "Information Standard," 92.

7. Wojnilower, "Central Role," 314, 326. See also Anthony Sampson, *The Money Lenders* (London, 1981), 228; *BW*, Sept. 16, 1985, 83.

8. *Euromoney*, Sept. 1986, 121.

9. *IHT*, Nov. 25, 1985. See also *BW*, Nov. 4, 1985, 24–25; *IHT*, Oct. 8, 1984.

10. Jack Guttentag and Richard Herring, "Crisis Scenarios" (NSF Project Working Paper, n.d.), 7. See also *Euromoney*, June 1984, 7; Seung Kim and Stephen Miller, *Competitive Structure of International Banking* (Lexington, 1983), 95.

11. *BW*, June 18, 1984, 21.

12. Steven I. Davis, *The Management of International Banks* (London, 1983), 21.

13. *Euromoney*, Oct. 1985, 76. See also Frederick Clairmonte and John Cavanagh, "Transnational Corporations and the Struggle for Global Market," *JCA* 13 (1983): 450.

14. *Euromoney*, Oct. 1985, 76.

15. Quoted in ibid., Sept. 1986, 121.

16. *BW*, June 25, 1984, 53. See also Davis, *Management*, 31, 177; Kim and Miller, *Competitive Structure*, 94; *BW*, June 25, 1984, 53.

17. *Euromoney*, Feb. 1986, 94. See also *BW*, Dec. 5, 1983, 144; Jan. 12, 1987, 108; *Euromoney*, Aug. 1986, 70–75; *Banker* (London), Feb. 1987, 18–20; *IHT*, Dec. 22, 1984.

18. *BW*, July 2, 1984, 72. See also *IHT*, May 16, 1984.

19. *IHT*, June 23, 1986.

20. *Euromoney*, April 1982, 32. See also *BW*, April 16, 1984, 176.

21. *BW*, Feb. 20, 1984, 59.

22. *Euromoney*, Jan. 1986, 34. See also *IHT*, Oct. 3, 1984.

23. *IHT*, Nov. 24, 1986.

24. *BW*, Nov. 24, 1986, 83.

25. *Euromoney*, Jan. 1986, 34. See also *FEER*, Nov. 21, 1985, 63–68.

26. *IHT*, April 3, 1986.

27. *Euromoney*, Jan. 1986, 31. See also ibid., 30; *FEER*, Nov. 21, 1985, 63–68.

28. *BW*, May 16, 1983, 125. See also *IHT*, April 14, 1979; Michael Moffitt, *World's Money: International Banking from Bretton Woods to the Brink of Insolvency* (New York, 1983), 150–58; *Federal Reserve Bank of New York Quarterly Review*, Summer 1984, 39–47; *IHT*, March 13, 1987.

29. *Euromoney*, Oct. 1985, 77.

30. *BW*, May 16, 1983, 125. See also *IHT*, Dec. 24, 1985; *FEER*, Nov. 21, 1985, 63–68; Jack Guttentag and Richard Herring, *A Framework for the Analysis of Financial Disorder*, Wharton School Working Paper no. 7-81, (Philadelphia, 1981), 27.

31. *BW*, May 16, 1983, 124.

32. Ibid., 126. See also *FEER*, Sept. 24, 1982, 51–56.

33. Ken Auletta, *Greed and Glory on Wall Street: The Fall of the House of Lehman* (New York, 1986), 176.

34. *IHT*, Nov. 25, 1985. See also Davis, *Management*, 109; *BW*, Sept. 16, 1985, 83, 92; Nov. 4, 1985, 25; *Euromoney*, Nov. 1985, 67; *IHT*, Oct. 8, 1984, Oct. 29, 1985.

35. *IHT*, Nov. 24, 1980. See also *BW*, Jan. 13, 1986, 32; Sept. 6, 1982, 80–86; *FEER*, Sept. 24, 1982, 51–56; Davis, *Management*, 121; *Euromoney*, Sept. 1986, 122.

36. *Euromoney*, Nov. 1982, 36.

37. *BW*, Sept. 6, 1982, 86. See also Kim and Miller, *Competitive Structure*, 97; Richard S. Dale and Richard P. Mattione, *Managing Global Debt* (Washington, 1983); *BW*, May 16, 1983, 126; Davis, *Management*, 178–80; *Euromoney*, Nov. 1982, 34–37.

38. *IHT*, Nov. 30, 1982.

39. Robert Devlin, "Renegotiation of Latin American Debt," *CEPAL*, Aug. 1983, 101–7. See also Dale and Mattione, *Managing Global Debt*, 16; *BW*, Sept. 6, 1982, 80–86; Dec. 3, 1984, 130–41; *WFM*, Aug. 1984; *IHT*, March 1, 1982; Davis, *Management*, 122–24; Carlos Diaz-Alejandro, "Latin American Debt," *Brookings Papers* (1984): 355–57.

40. *IHT*, Nov. 25, 1985.

41. Ibid., July 11, 1983. See also ibid., Dec. 12, 1983.

42. *IHT*, Dec. 12, 1983.

43. *IHT,* Oct. 17, 1983. See also ibid., Nov. 28, 1983, Nov. 25, 1985; *WFM,* Jan. 1986, 7; *BW,* Feb. 14, 1983, 50–53; Sept. 27, 1982, 66–69; *FEER,* May 8, 1986, 53–54.

44. *IHT,* Jan. 27, 1986.

45. *Euromoney,* Aug. 1986, 70. See also Dale and Mattione, *Managing Global Debt,* 39; *BW,* Nov. 21, 1983, 71–74; Sept. 16, 1985, 108; *Toronto Globe and Mail,* April 9, 1984; *IHT,* Nov. 28, 1983.

46. *Euromoney,* Nov. 1982, 35.

47. *IHT,* Nov. 14, 1984.

48. Ibid., April 18, 1983. See also *Euromoney,* Aug. 1982, 47.

49. *BW,* May 16, 1983, 125. See also Sampson, *Money Lenders,* 299–300; Jose J. Villamil, ed., *Transnational Capitalism and National Development: New Perspectives on Dependence* (Sussex, 1979), 252.

50. *BW,* Jan. 9, 1984, 47.

51. *IHT,* Oct. 16, 1985. See also Dale and Mattione, *Managing Global Debt,* 20, 31.

52. Wojnilower, "Central Role," 299.

53. *BW,* Nov. 21, 1983, 71. See also Jack Guttentag and Richard Herring, *Lender of Last Resort Function in an International Context,* Wharton School Working Paper no. 9-81 (Philadelphia, 1981), 22–31; Wojnilower, "Central Role," 299.

54. *BW,* June 4, 1984, 109. See also Davis, *Management,* 97; Guttentag and Herring, *Lender of Last Resort,* 8.

55. *BW,* June 4, 1984, 110.

56. *Banker* (London), Aug. 1984, 8.

57. Ibid., July 1984, 21.

58. Ibid., June 1984, 8.

59. Ibid., Jan. 1985, 11. See also U.S. Congress, House Committee on Banking, *Financial Services Industry–Oversight Hearings,* pt. 1. 98th Cong., 1st sess. (Washington, 1983), 136–37.

60. Quoted in *Euromoney,* Sept. 1986, 123.

61. See Guttentag and Herring, *Lender of Last Resort,* passim.

CHAPTER 6.   The Industrial Sector: Steel

1. Donald F. Barnett and Louis Schorsch, *Steel: Upheaval in a Basic Industry* (Cambridge, Mass., 1983), 4.

2. *BW,* Sept. 17, 1979, 79.

3. Cited by Pierre Judet, "Iron and Steel Industry and the Transfer of Technology" in *The New International Division of Labor,* ed. Dieter Ernst (Frankfurt, 1980), 312. See also Barnett and Schorsch, *Steel,* 53, 79; *IHT,* Sept. 13,

1983, Nov. 29, 1984; Barry Bluestone and Bennett Harrison, *The Deindustrialization of America* (New York, 1982), 88–89; *BW*, Jan. 12, 1987, 81.

4. *BW*, Sept. 14, 1974, 152. See also ibid., Sept. 19, 1977, 66–68. June 13, 1983, 84–94; Sept. 24, 1984, 144f–44h; Joel Hirschhorn, "Troubles and Opportunities in the United States Steel Industry," in *Industry Vitalization*, ed. Margret Dewar (Elmsford, N.Y., 1982), 11; *Wall Street Journal*, Jan. 24, 1985; *IHT*, Dec. 30, 1983, Feb. 17, 1984, Jan. 24, 1986, April 21, 1978; Barnett and Schorsch, *Steel*, 27, 79; Stephen Woolcock, "The International Politics of Trade and Production in the Steel Industry," in *National Industrial Strategies and the World Economy*, ed. John Pinder (London, 1982), 60; Les Aspin, Speech in U.S. Congress, *Congressional Record*, April 27, 1981; William T. Hogan, *World Steel in the 1980s: A Case of Survival* (Lexington, 1983), 162 and passim; *IHT*, June 4, 1985; *FEER*, July 19, 1984, 46–47; Bela Gold, "Pressures for Restructuring the World Steel Industry in the 1980s," *Quarterly Review of Economics and Business*, Spring 1982, 45–66.

5. *BW*, June 13, 1983, 90, 94. See also Barnett and Schorsch, *Steel*, 43; Hogan, *World Steel*, 4, 96, and passim; *BW*, Sept. 27, 1982, 23–24; June 1, 1981, 44–45, 58–59; Oct. 1, 1984, 40; Hirschhorn, "Troubles," 13–24.

6. Hirschhorn, "Troubles," 9.

7. *BW*, March 5, 1984, 77. See also ibid., Feb. 7, 1983, 38–39; Jan. 14, 1985, 84; Jan. 12, 1987, 81.

8. *IHT*, Sept. 13, 1983. See also OECD, *Interfutures: Facing the Future: Mastering the Probable and Managing the Unpredictable* (Paris, 1979), 158–60; *IHT*, Sept. 13, 1983; *BW*, Oct. 3, 1983, 132–36.

9. *BW*, Oct. 3, 1983, 132–36.

10. *BW*, Oct. 1, 1984, 40. See also ibid., May 31, 1982, 87; *IHT*, April 2, 1979; Hogan, *World Steel*, 48, 83–85, 201, 210; *Vision*, Feb. 1977, 29–32; Barnett and Schorsch, *Steel*, 228; Robert W. Crandall, *The U.S. Steel Industry in Recurrent Crisis: Policy Options in a Competitive World* (Washington, 1981), 21; *BW*, Oct. 3, 1983, 47–51; *FEER*, Oct. 25, 1984, 72; Woolcock, "International Politics," 69–84.

11. *BW*, Oct. 3, 1983, 51. See also *IHT*, March 9, 1981, Jan. 30, Feb. 22, March 24, 1984; *Asian Wall Street Journal*, Feb. 23, 1987.

12. *BW*, Sept. 19, 1977, 82. See also ibid., Oct. 17, 1977, 128–30; Oct. 1, 1984, 39–40; Lynn E. Browne, "Steel—An Industry Beset on All Sides," *NEER*, May/June 1985, 35; *IHT*, Oct. 4, 1977, Jan. 14, 1984; Trilateral Commission, *Industrial Policy and the International Economy* (London, 1979), 59–61.

13. *BW*, Jan. 30, 1984, 85. See also ibid., Oct. 25, 1982, 114–18; Aug. 30, 1982, 40; April 8, 1985, 38; Feb. 25, 1985, 56; *Toronto Globe and Mail*, June 7, 1982; *IHT*, Feb. 8, 1984, Sept. 13, 1983, March 6, April 3, 5, 1984; July 18, 1984; Hirschhorn, "Troubles," 7.

14. *Le Monde*, Oct. 14, 1980. See also ibid., March 3, 1981; *IHT*, Nov. 30, 1985; Woolcock, "International Policy," 62; *BW*, May 26, 1975, 58; July 17, 1978, 40.

15. *Economist,* Jan. 16, 1982, 37–38. See also *BW,* Nov. 10, 1980, 36; Hogan, *World Steel,* 21–22.

16. *IHT,* Dec. 23, 1983. See also ibid., June 30, 1983.

17. Ibid., April 6, 1984. On reports of state policy see ibid., March 22, April 30, 1982, Oct. 31, 1985, Jan. 24, 1986, Nov. 30, 1977.

18. *BW,* March 5, 1984, 76; Jan. 12, 1987, 81. On merger reports see also *IHT,* Feb. 5, 1982, Feb. 2, 3, April 3, 1984, Nov. 30, 1985.

19. *BW,* Sept. 17, 1979, 84, 89. See also ibid., May 31, 1982, 87; March 24, 1984, 68; Jan. 9, 1984, 28–29; Jan. 23, 1984, 145; Barnett and Schorsch, *Steel,* 53; Hogan, *World Steel,* 92, 210.

20. For diversification see Bluestone and Harrison, *Deindustrialization,* 156; *IHT,* Feb. 2, 1980, May 27, Oct. 31, 1985, Nov. 27, 1984; *BW,* Oct. 4, 1982, 90–91; Dec. 2, 1985, 132; April 16, 1984, 57–58; Feb. 24, 1986, 42; Oct. 22, 1984, 40; May 13, 1985, 102–4.

CHAPTER 7. The New-Technology Industries

1. Wassily Leontief, "Technological Advance, Economic Growth, and the Distribution of Income," *Population and Development Review* 9 (1983): 405.

2. Quoted in Gerd Junne and Rob van Tulder, *European Multinationals in the Robot Industry: A Pilot Study* (Amsterdam, 1984), 7. This study was the forerunner of the authors' important book *European Multinationals and Core Technologies* (New York, 1987). See also Gene Bylinsky, "The Race to the Automatic Factory," *Fortune,* Feb. 21, 1983; Joyce Kolko, "Vers un renouveau de la planification capitaliste en Europe," *Monde Diplomatique,* Dec. 1979, 6.

3. *BW,* March 3, 1986, 72.

4. Ibid., Oct. 22, 1984, 152.

5. Bylinsky, "Automatic Factory," 54.

6. Significant discussions of the possible implications for the industrial structure are found in Dieter Ernst, *Restructuring World Industry in a Period of Crisis—The Role of Innovation: An Analysis of Recent Developments in the Semiconductor Industry* (New York, 1981); Gerd Junne, "World Crisis, State Rivalry, and Company Cooperation" (Paper presented to Conference of International Peace Research, Gyor, Hungary, Aug. 1983); Annemieke Roobeek, "The Crisis of Fordism and the Rise of a New Technological System (Department of Economics Research Memorandum no. 8602, University of Amsterdam, Feb. 1986); Pierre Grou, *The Financial Structure of Multinational Capitalism* (Warwickshire, 1985), 58ff.; UN, *1985 Report on the World Social Situation* (New York, 1985), 43–57.

7. Junne and van Tulder, *Robot Industry,* 7, 11–12.

8. OECD, *Interfutures: Facing the Future: Mastering the Probable and Managing the Unpredictable* (Paris, 1978), 341.

9. *BW*, June 16, 1986, 108. See also ibid, Nov. 16, 1956, 56; *FEER*, Dec. 19, 1985, 51.

10. *BW*, June 28, 1982, 120. See also *FEER*, June 6, 1985, 69–74; *BW*, March 11, 1985, 56–67.

11. *BW*, June 28, 1982, 113.

12. Ibid., 115.

13. Ibid., 113.

14. Ibid., Sept. 8, 1976, 46–47. See also *FEER*, Nov. 21, 1985, 138–39.

CHAPTER 8.   The Arms Industry and the Economy

1. J.-B. Pinatel, "Sécurité et développement économique: Deux impératifs conciliables," *Problèmes Économiques*, Oct. 4, 1978, 17. This article, reprinted from the official French military journal *Défense Nationale*, cogently analyzes the role of the arms industry in the economy. See also *IHT*, May 16, 1984; Andrew Pierre, *The Global Politics of Arms Sales* (Princeton, 1982), 5; Jacques Gansler, *The Defense Industry* (Cambridge, Mass., 1980); 89, 209; OECD, *Interfutures: Facing the Future: Mastering the Probable and Managing the Unpredictable* (Paris, 1979), 378; Norman Fieleke, "The Foreign Trade Deficit and American Industry," *NEER*, July/Aug. 1985, 46, 49–51; Michael Klare, *American Arms Supermarket* (Austin, 1984), 1–2; Mary Kaldor, *The Baroque Arsenal* (New York, 1981), 150.

2. *IHT*, March 31, 1984. See also ibid., July 30, 1979; Pierre, *Global Politics*, 97; Klare, *American Arms*, 204.

3. *IHT*, March 31, 1984. See also ibid., May, 15, 1985; Alfredo Valladao, "Le tiers-monde se déstabilise," *Monde Diplomatique*, April 1982, 20; *BW*, Dec. 29, 1986, 46.

4. *IHT*, March 31, 1984.

5. *BW*, May 27, 1985, 144–45. See also Pierre, *Global Politics*, 26–27, 97–99; *BW*, Sept. 20, 1982, 74–75; Jan. 27, 1986, 116–18; Les Aspin, Speech in U.S. Congress, *Congressional Record*, April 27, 1981, E1852–E1855; Gansler, *Defense*, 13–14, 61, 209–10; *IHT*, June 2, 1982, Oct. 13, 1983, March 31, 1984, Oct. 8, 1985.

6. *IHT*, April 2, 1984. See also *BW*, July 8, 1985, 48–50; May 27, 1985, 144–49.

7. *BW*, Sept. 20, 1982, 80. See also Gansler, *Defense*, 170–71; *BW*, Sept. 20, 1982, 76; Jan. 27, 1986, 116.

8. See my discussion in *America and the Crisis of World Capitalism* (Boston, 1974), 5–6.

9. *BW*, July 15, 1985, 72.

10. Quoted in Valladao, "Le tiers-monde," 20. See also ibid., 19; Saburo Kugai, "Nakasone increases military spending," *END Journal*, March–April 1987, 18–20; Klare, *American Arms*, 7–9, 18, 206; Pierre, *Global Politics*, 5, 13, 131; *BW*, March 24, 1980, 62–69; April 2, 1984, 48; Dec. 29, 1986,

46; Wassily Leontief and Faye Duchin, *Military Spending: Facts and Figures, Worldwide Implications, and Future Outlook* (New York, 1983), 3, 56.

11. Valladao, "Le tiers-monde," 20.

12. See Amnon Kapeliouk, "Israel: Un pays possédé par son armée," *Monde Diplomatique*, April 1982, 22; Shuja Nawaz, "Economic Impact of Defense Expenditures," *F&D*, March 1983, 34–35; UN, *Economic and Social Survey of Asia and the Pacific, 1982* (New York, 1982), 114ff.; OECD, *Interfutures*, 378.

CHAPTER 9.   New Developments in Raw Materials and Agriculture

1. Charles Oman, *New Forms of International Investment in Developing Countries* (Paris, 1984), 43, 46. See also *South*, Feb. 1982, 9–12; *Africa News*, Jan. 25, 1982, 11.

2. *FEER*, Nov. 14, 1985, 64. See also Oman, *New Forms*, 68–69; *IHT*, July 27, 1985; *BW*, March 31, 1986, 20.

3. I argued this perspective in my *America and the Crisis of World Capitalism* (Boston, 1974), 139–48. Alfred E. Eckes, Jr., *The United States and the Global Struggle for Minerals* (Austin, 1979), later provided considerable historical and empirical documentation. See also *WEO, 1986*, 139, 145; *WEO, 1987*, 94–97.

4. *BW*, April 21, 1986, 23. See also Michael Tanzer, *The Race for Resources: Continuing Struggles over Minerals and Fuels* (New York, 1980), 110 and passim; *BW*, July 26, 1982, 16–20; Sept. 27, 1982, 66; Dec. 13, 1982, 26; Michael Tanzer and Stephen Zorn, *Energy Update: Oil in the Late Twentieth Century* (New York, 1985), 38; *WFM*, March 1982, 1–8; *WEO, 1985*, 150–51; *BW*, Aug. 1, 1983, 23; March 14, 1983, 25; Dec. 23, 1985, 24–26; Feb. 3, 1986, 26; April 7, 1986, 39; April 21, 1986, 22–23; *IHT*, Nov. 3, 1982, Feb. 8, April 16, 1986.

5. *IHT*, April 8, 1986.

6. *BW*, Aug. 9, 1976, 47. See also *IHT*, March 2, 1983.

7. Oman, *New Forms*, 42.

8. *IHT*, March 28, 1982. See also ibid, special energy supplement, Sept. 1982; *BW*, March 30, 1981, 44.

9. *BW*, Dec. 17, 1964, 70. See also ibid., May 3, 1982, 80.

10. Tanzer and Zorn, *Energy Update* 38. See also ibid. for one of the best concise discussions of these developments, and also Tanzer, *Race for Resources*, for the role of the basic minerals in the economy; *BW*, Dec. 17, 1984, 64–70, for a report on the depression in the American mining industry; ibid., Dec. 10, 1984, 38; Dec. 20, 1985, 61; *IHT*, Nov. 29, 1984.

11. *BW*, May 13, 1985, 24. See also ibid., 24–25.

12. *WFM*, March 1982, 1–8; *BW*, July 18, 1983, 52–53; *WEO, 1983*, 144–46.

13. *BW*, Dec. 17, 1984, 64–70. See also ibid., Feb. 27, 1984, 27–28; *IHT*, Oct. 18, 1984.

14. OECD, *Interfutures: Facing the Future: Mastering the Probable and Managing the Unpredictable*, 51. See also *BW*, Dec. 17, 1984, 67; Oman, *New Forms*, 36, 46.

15. OECD, *Interfutures*, 53.

16. *BW*, Nov. 25, 1985, 38. See also *WEO*, *1986*, 62, 145; *ICR*, Dec. 1985, 13.

17. *IHT*, Sept. 16, 1986. See also *BW*, April 21, 1986, 25–26; *ICR*, Dec. 1985, 18; *WEO*, *1986*, 62; *IHT*, Dec. 5, 1985; *FEER*, Nov. 14, 1985, 64–72.

18. *IHT*, March 24, 1987.

19. Ibid., April 21, 1984. See also ibid., March 2, 1983, Feb. 4, 1986, June 20, Nov. 5, 1985; *WEO*, *1986*, 142; OECD, *Interfutures*, 252–53; Speech of Under Secretary of State Allen Wallis, March 7, 1986, State Department Current Policy Release, no. 804.

20. *EROP*, *1986*, 360, 364; *IHT*, Feb. 4, 1986.

21. *BW*, Jan. 14, 1985, 60. See also *EROP*, *1986*, 133, 158; Harold Breimyer, "Agriculture: A Return to the Thirties," *Challenge*, July–Aug. 1982, 35–41; *BW*, Feb. 18, 1985, 124–26; March 22, 1985, 242; Aug. 19, 1985, 31; *IHT*, April 3, 1985; June 2, 1986.

22. *EROP*, *1986*, 131, 132. See also *Washington Post*, April 13, 1986; *IHT*, April 7, Aug. 13, 1986; *BW*, June 1, 1981, 52.

23. *BW*, May 18, 1987, 46. For sources of data on U.S. agriculture see also *BW*, Sept. 30, 1985, 91; June 17, 1985, 32–33; July 14, 1986, 24–25; *IHT*, June 20, 1985; Jim Longmire and Art Morey, *Strong Dollar Dampens Demand for U.S. Farm Exports*, U.S. Department of Agriculture Report no. 193 (Washington, 1983); *EROP*, *1986*, 120–21; U.S. Department of Agriculture, *1984 Handbook of Agricultural Charts* (Washington, 1984), 4–26, 52ff.

24. John Tinker, of Earthscan, in London, quoted in *IHT*, April 21, 1984. See the important study by Robert G. Williams, *Export Agriculture and the Crisis in Central America* (Chapel Hill, 1986); also C. A. Miró and D. Rodriguez, "Capitalism and Population in Latin American Agriculture," *CEPAL Review*, April 1982, 56–58; "Honduras," *NACLA Report on the Americas*, Nov.–Dec. 1981, 20–25; Cheryl Payer, *The World Bank: A Critical Analysis* (New York, 1982), 225–26; Agribusiness Council, *Agricultural Initiative in the Third World* (Lexington, 1975); *FEER*, May 1, 1986, 69.

CHAPTER 11.   The Role of the State in Restructuring the Economy

1. J. LaPalombra, cited in Ralph Miliband, *The State in Capitalist Society* (London, 1969), 184. Miliband's book remains, along with his collected essays *Class Power and State Power* (London, 1983), one of the most valuable discussions of the subject.

2. Brian Showler and Adrian Sinfield, *The Workless State* (Oxford, 1981), 36–37.

3. OECD, *Towards Full Employment and Price Stability* [Report of the Paul McCracken Commission] (Paris, 1977), 130.

CHAPTER 12.   Monetary Relations

1. Quoted in Adam Smith, *Paper Money* (New York, 1981), 109.

2. *Euromoney*, October 1985, 35.

3. *IHT*, March 12, 1983. See also *ICR*, May 1985, 3–5.

4. *IHT*, March 12, 1983.

5. *Financial Times*, May 24, 1982. See also *BW*, April 28, 1986, 72–76; Frank E. Morris, "The Changing World of Central Banking," *NEER*, March/April 1986, 3–6; *ICR*, July 1984, 8; *IHT*, March 13, 1987.

6. *IHT*, March 27, 1982. See also *Financial Times*, May 24, 1982.

7. *Euromoney*, October 1985, 38. See also *Institutional Investor*, Nov. 1985, 121–29.

8. *EROP, 1984*, 51.

9. *Euromoney*, Oct. 1984, 57.

10. Ibid., 55.

11. *BW*, March 23, 1981, 34. See also *ICR*, Dec. 1985, 4–7; *BW*, Oct. 14, 1985, 37; June 1, 1981, 15–16; July 20, 1981, 80.

12. *IHT*, Feb. 21, 1984.

13. See *BW*, Feb. 20, 1984, 86; Feb. 13, 1984, 44; *FEER*, Jan. 5, 1979, 36–37; June 13, 1985, 68, 89; *ICR*, Sept. 1985, 84; *Euromoney*, Sept. 1982, 98–102; Oct. 1984, 61; C. Fred Bergsten, "The Second Debt Crisis Coming," *Challenge*, May/June 1985, 17; *IHT*, Sept. 17, 1984; Hans-Peter Nising and Klaus Behling, "Effects of the Flexible Exchange Rate System on Developing Countries," *Intereconomics*, Nov./Dec. 1981, 281–86.

14. *IMF Survey*, July 1985, 8. See also Suzanne de Brunhoff, *The State, Capital, and Economic Policy* (London, 1978), 49, on SDRs as a form of credit; *FEER*, July 4, 1985, 79; John Williamson, *A New SDR Allocation?* (Washington, 1984), 12–13.

15. *IHT*, March 5, 1983.

16. Hyman Minsky, "Finance and Profits: The Changing Nature of the Business Cycles," U.S. Congress, Joint Economic Committee, *The Business Cycle and Public Policy, 1929–80: A Compendium of Papers* (Washington, 1980), 211. See also *IHT*, March 5, 1983.

17. *IMF Survey*, July 1985, 8.

18. Morris, "Changing World," 5. See also *BW*, April 4, 1983, 64–67; Aug. 4, 1986, 71–72; *Chase Economic Observer*, May/June 1983, 1–8.

19. *ICR*, Sept. 1985, 23.

20. See *IHT*, Nov. 4, 1985, April 21, 1986.

CHAPTER 13.   The Dilemmas of World Debt

1. See *OECD Observer*, Nov. 1981, 9–12; *BW*, Dec. 27, 1982, 24; *IHT*, Nov. 29, 1982, April 25, 1986; *WEO, 1986*, 49, 69; *WEO 1985*, 60; *Euromoney*, Sept. 1982, 80.

2. *WEO, 1986*, 89. See also *BW*, Oct. 3, 1983, 144; *IHT*, April 29, 1982, March 7, 1986.

3. *BW*, Oct. 3, 1983, 132.

4. Ibid., 133. See also *IHT*, Jan. 28, March 7, 1986; *WFM*, March 1986, 14–15.

5. Lord Lever et al., *The Debt Crisis and the World Economy* (London, 1984), iii, 5. See also *IHT*, March 7, 25, 1986.

6. *FEER*, Sept. 17, 1982, 72. See also *WFM*, Sept./Oct. 1985, 4; *BW*, May 27, 1985, 52; *IHT*, Nov. 25, 1985.

7. *FEER*, Sept. 17, 1982, 72.

8. *South*, July 1985, 35, 32. See also *BW*, April 16, 1984, 48–49; Sept. 23, 1985, 35; *IHT*, Sept. 26, 1985, Nov. 28, 1983.

9. *Euromoney*, Oct. 1985, 40.

10. *IHT*, Nov. 26, 1985. See also *WEO, 1986*, 92; *Euromoney*, Oct. 1985, 383; *Federal Reserve Bank of New York Quarterly Review*, Autumn 1982, 49; *BW*, June 23, 1986, 42–43; *ICR*, Dec. 1985, 8–11.

11. *Wall Street Journal*, Dec. 14, 1982.

12. William Greider, "The Education of David Stockman," *Atlantic*, Dec. 1981, 27, 51. See also *BW*, Sept. 16, 1985, 79; *EROP, 1984*, 304–5; *EROP, 1985*, 317; *EROP, 1986*, 341; *IMF Survey*, July 15, 1985, 215–17.

13. David Stockman, *The Triumph of Politics* (New York, 1986), 106–9. This book is very revealing of the chaotic and surrealist decision making of the men of power in other areas as well.

14. *BW*, Feb. 20, 1984, 29. See also Howard Sherman, "Inflation, Unemployment, and the Contemporary Business Cycle," in *The Faltering Economy*, ed. John Foster and Henryk Szlajfer (New York, 1984), 112; *EROP, 1984*, 56, 304–5; *EROP, 1985*, 317; *IHT*, Feb. 21, 1984.

15. *IHT*, Nov. 24, 1986.

16. *IMF Survey*, July 15, 1985, 216.

17. *Federal Reserve Bank of New York Quarterly Review*, Summer 1984, 29. See also *IMF Survey*, July 15, 1985, 217; *ICR*, July 1984, 7–11.

18. *WEO, 1985*, 99. See also *Euromoney*, Oct. 1985, 59; *ICR*, Oct. 1985, 52; *BW*, Dec. 7, 1981, 50–56; Jan. 21, 1980, 78–87; *IMF Survey*, July 15, 1985, 217; *IHT*, Nov. 29, July 29, 1983; *WEO, 1985*, 108–9; Sarah Bartlett, "Transnational Banking: A Case of Transfer Parking with Money," in *Multinationals beyond the Market: Intrafirm Trade and the Control of Transfer Pricing*, ed. Robin Murray (Brighton, 1981), 102; *OECD Observer*, May 1982, 14; *BW*, Sept. 13, 1982, 35–36.

19. *WEO, 1985,* 102–3.

20. *IHT,* April 12, 1984.

CHAPTER 14. World Trade Restructured

1. *BW,* March 3, 1986, 58. See also *EROP, 1986,* 368; U.S. Department of Commerce, *U.S. Direct Investment Abroad: 1982 Benchmark Survey Data* (Washington, 1985), 332, 335; Frank E. Morris, "The Changing World of Central Banking," *NEER,* March/April 1986, 3; Robin Murray, "Transfer Pricing and Its Control," in *Multinationals beyond the Market: Intrafirm Trade and the Control of Transfer Pricing,* ed. Robin Murray (Brighton, 1981), 152–57; Gerald Helleiner, *Intra-firm Trade and the Developing Countries* (London, 1981), 22, 45, 52; Frederick Clairmonte and John Cavanagh, "Transnational Corporations and the Struggle for the Global Market," *JCA* 13 (1983): 455; *Le Monde,* June 5, 1984.

2. OECD, *Interfutures: Facing the Future: Mastering the Probable and Managing the Unpredictable* (Paris, 1979), 388. See also Hideki Yoshihara, "Research on Japan's General Trading Firms: An Overview," *JES,* Spring 1981, 68–83; Eleanor Hadley, "Japan's Export Competitiveness," in Center for International and Strategic Studies, *World Trade Competition* (New York, 1981), 308–11; Clairmonte and Cavanagh, "Transnational Corporations," 460–61; *BW,* July 28, 1986, 25; Feb. 9, 1987, 47.

3. *BW,* July 19, 1982, 122. See also ibid., 118ff; *IHT,* Jan. 17, 1983, Sept. 23, 1985; *New York Times,* July 26, 1981.

4. *IHT,* Jan. 17, 1983.

5. *BW,* July 19, 1982, 122. See also ibid., Feb. 7, 1983, 53; Kung Mo Huh, "Countertrade," *F&D,* Dec. 1983, 14–16.

6. *BW,* Nov. 1, 1982, 97. See also *IHT,* April 26, 1982; *Chase Economic Observer,* May/June 1983, 1–8.

7. *BW,* Feb. 6, 1984, 31. See also Norman Fieleke, "The Foreign Trade Deficit and American Industry," *NEER,* July/Aug. 1985, 46; *BW,* Sept. 24, 1984, 35–36; April 1, 1985, 31; C. Fred Bergsten, "The Second Debt Crisis Is Coming," *Challenge,* May–June 1985, 19.

8. *BW,* Sept. 24, 1984, 35. See also *WFM,* Sept. 1984, 2–5; *BW,* Nov. 1, 1982, 19; Jan. 19, 1987, 30; *IHT,* Jan. 26, 1982; *FEER,* April 6, 1979, 44–48; *EROP, 1984,* 47.

9. *BW,* April 1, 1985, 31.

10. See *BW,* Nov. 1, 1981, 96–100; Marie-France Toinet and Hubert Kempf, "Guerre commerciale en occident," *Monde Diplomatique,* Jan. 1983, 5; *IHT,* Nov. 5, July 20, 1985; *FEER,* Oct. 25, 1984, 70–88.

11. *WEO, 1982,* 34.

12. *IHT,* Feb. 22, 1985.

13. *BW,* Aug. 29, 1983, 66.

14. *Ibid.,* March 11, 1985, 60. See also ibid., 56; *IHT,* Nov. 30, 1982.

15. *BW*, March 3, 1986, 57.

16. *IHT*, April 12, 1982. See also *NBER Reporter*, Winter 1985–1986, 17–20; *BW*, April 1, 1985, 31; Aug. 29, 1983, 67.

17. *BW*, Nov. 22, 1982, 32.

18. *Ibid.*, Dec. 13, 1982, 26–27.

19. *Ibid.*, April 20, 1987, 37. See also *WFM*, June 1985, 5; *BW*, Nov. 12, 1984, 34–35; *IHT*, March 22, 1982, Sept. 19, 1985.

20. Kenichi Ohmae, in "Special Economic Report on Japan," *IHT*, Sept. 16, 1985.

21. Helleiner, *Intrafirm Trade*, 81.

22. Clairmonte and Cavanagh, "Transnational Corporations," 467. See also *FEER*, April 6, 1979, 44–48.

23. OECD, *Interfutures*, 160. See also ibid., 159.

24. *IHT*, April 19, 1977. See also *BW*, Oct. 10, 1983, 42–43; *IHT*, Feb. 22, 1984, Nov. 26, June 12, 1985, April 3, 1982, June 25, 1986; Clairmonte and Cavanagh, "Transnational Corporations," 459; *FEER*, May 1, 1986, 66; *Bangkok Bank Monthly Review*, March 1986, 148.

25. *FEER*, Oct. 25, 1984, 84.

26. *BW*, Sept. 17, 1984, 40. See also *IHT*, June 1, 1982, Dec. 12, 1985; Clairmonte and Cavanagh, "Transnational Corporations," 472; *BW*, June 9, 1986, 30–31; May 5, 1986, 24–25; *FEER*, Oct. 25, 1984, 70–87; Jan. 16, 1986, 95.

27. Miyohei Shinohara, in *FEER*, April 28, 1983, 66. See also *WFM*, Sept. 1984, 2–12; *BW*, Feb. 7, 1983, 48; June 4, 1984, 104; Oct. 3, 1983, 132–136; April 2, 1984, 48; *IHT*, Nov. 29, 1982; *Le Monde*, June 5, 1984; *EROP, 1984,* 47, 78; *WFM*, Sept. 1985, 3.

28. Saskia Sassen-Koob, "Internationalization of Resources and Development," *Development and Change* 8 (1977): 534–35. See also Clive Hamilton, "Capitalist Industrialization in East Asia's Four Little Tigers," *JCA* 13 (1983): 35–72; Folker Fröbel, Jürgen Heinrichs, Otto Kreye, *The New International Division of Labor* (Cambridge, 1980), 295–338; *IHT*, Nov. 25, 1985, Jan. 22, 1986; *BW*, Dec. 20, 1982, 72–74; *WES, 1983, Supplement,* 35–40; Charles P. Kindleberger, *Europe's Postwar Growth: The Role of the Labor Supply* (Cambridge, Mass., 1967), 97; Kathleen Newland, *International Migration: The Search for Work* (Washington, 1979), esp. 14. UN ECAFE, *Economic and Social Survey of Asia and the Pacific,* (New York, 1982), 150.

29. Sassen-Koob, "Internationalization," 537. See also Fred Halliday, "Migration and the Labour Force in the Oil Producing States," *Development and Change* 8 (1977): 287–91; Jonathan Power, *Migrant Workers in Western Europe and the United States* (Oxford, 1979), 55; *Courier* (UNESCO), Sept. 1985, 39; *Le Monde,* Aug. 8, 1979.

30. *IHT*, Oct. 7, 1985.

CHAPTER 15. Restructuring the Industrial Capitalist States

1. *IHT*, July 30, 1983.

2. OECD, *Interfutures: Facing the Future: Mastering the Probable and Managing the Unpredictable* (Paris, 1979), 170.

3. *F & D*, Sept. 1980, 9.

4. BIS, *Annual Report* (Basel, 1981), 34. See also *IHT*, June 10, 1980.

5. *IHT*, April 30, 1985. See also *BW*, July 24, 1978.

6. Speech of Under Secretary of State Allen Wallis, State Department Current Policy Release No. 804. See also OECD, *Economic Outlook*, 1985, 30; *IHT*, April 18, 1986.

7. *IHT*, Nov. 28, 1985.

8. *WFM*, June 1985, 3. See also *IHT*, Nov. 28, 1985, Sept. 23, 1986.

9. IMF, *Annual Report, 1985*, 3.

10. *Ibid.*, 3, 5.

11. *WEO, 1985*, 108. See also Speech of Wallis, March 7, 1986; U.S. AID, *Front Lines*, Feb. 1986, 9; UN, *Report on the World Social Situation* (New York, 1985), 97; *Euromoney*, Feb. 1986, 59.

12. State Department Current Policy No. 771 release, Dec. 10, 1985. See also *ICR*, Oct. 1985, 32–37; *Euromoney*, June 1986, 76–93; *IHT*, Jan. 9, 1987; Pierre Grou, *The Financial Structure of Multinational Capitalism* (Warwickshire, 1985), 90, 145–51; Popular Economics Research Group, "The Great Tax Revolt," in *Crisis in the Public Sector*, ed. Kenneth Fox et al. (New York, 1982), 93–97.

13. *IHT*, March 1, 1986.

14. *BW*, March 28, 1983, 85. See also *Euromoney*, June 1986, 70; Feb. 1986, 59–67.

15. *IHT*, Nov. 6, 1985. See also ibid., Dec. 24, 1985; *BW*, March 28, 1983, 84–90; May 20, 1983, 45; Dec. 10, 1984, 57–60.

16. *IHT*, Nov. 28, 1985.

17. Ibid.

18. Ibid., Dec. 4, 1985.

19. Quoted ibid., Nov. 19, 1986.

20. Robert O. Keohane, "Economics, Inflation, and the Role of the State," *World Politics*, Oct. 1978, 123.

21. *BW*, Dec. 22, 1975, 25.

22. Quoted in John H. Young, "Toward a Consensus on Inflation," *F & D*, March 1977, 13.

23. See also Colin Crouch, "The Intensification of Industrial Conflict in the United Kingdom," in *The Resurgence of Class Conflict in Western Europe since 1968*, ed. Colin Crouch and Alessandro Pizzorno (London, 1978), 1:212.

24. *BW*, Jan. 10, 1983, 67.

25. *IHT*, Nov. 6, 1983.

26. Ibid. See also *BW*, April 16, 1984, 68.

27. *Euromoney*, July 1984, 16. See also *IHT*, Oct. 22, Nov. 4, 1985, Jan. 8, April 30, May 13, 14, 1986.

28. *Euromoney*, Oct. 1985, 60.

29. See the excellent analysis of the first years of the Socialists in power by George Ross and Jane Jenson, "French Socialism in Crisis," *Studies in Political Economy*, Summer 1983, 71–103. Also Pierre Dubois et al., "The Contradictions of French Trade Unionism," in *Resurgence of Class Conflict*, 54.

30. *BW*, Jan. 10, 1983, 66. See also Ibid., June 28, 1982; *IHT*, May 11, Nov. 26, 1982, Nov. 29, 1983.

31. *BW*, Jan. 10, 1983, 69.

32. *Euromoney*, Nov. 1982, 155.

33. *BW*, Jan. 10, 1983, 55.

34. Ibid., 67. See also *IHT*, May 19, 1983; *BW*, May 31, 1982, 39; *Le Monde*, Oct. 13, 1982.

35. *New York Times*, Oct. 8, 1982.

36. *IHT*, Oct. 24, 1983.

37. *BW*, May 14, 1984, 55.

38. *IMF Survey*, Oct. 7, 1985, 289, 295.

39. Stuart Holland, ed., *Beyond Capitalist Planning* (Oxford, 1978), 40.

40. *IHT*, March 9, 1984. See also *BW*, March 5, 1984, 43; Oct. 24, 1983, 58–59; Feb. 20, 1984, 42; *IHT*, March 9, 1984; UN, *World Social Situation*, 91, 97; ECE, "Labour Force and Employment in Western Europe: The Prospects to 1985," *Economic Bulletin for Europe*, 30 (1985): 14.

41. *IHT*, Jan. 8, 1986. See also Jean-Pierre Garnier and Roland Lew, "From the Wretched of the Earth to the Defense of the West: An Essay on Left Disenchantment in France," in *Socialist Register 1984*, ed. Ralph Miliband et al., 299–323; *Economist*, Jan. 4–10, 1986, 35.

42. *Economist*, Jan. 4–10, 1986, 35.

43. *IHT*, Jan. 31, 1986. See also ibid., Oct. 22, Nov. 4, 1985; *Euromoney*, Oct. 1985, 68.

CHAPTER 16.   The Developing Countries

1. There is a vast world library dealing with the economies of the LDCs, including schools of theories and analysis, controversies, and debates on nearly every aspect. To examine them adequately is beyond the scope of this book. My discussion in this chapter is prefatory to the restructuring strategy represented by the IMF/World Bank.

2. Quoted in *IHT*, March 28, 1986. See also Barry M. Blechman and Stephen S. Kaplan, *Force without War: U.S. Armed Forces as a Political Instrument*

(Washington, 1978), 16, 547–56; J. W. Sewell and J. A. Mathison, "North–South Relations," in *Setting National Priorities: Agenda for the 1980s*, ed. Joseph A. Pechman (Washington, 1980), 506; *IMF Survey*, March 4, 1985, 66–69.

3. *Africa News*, Oct. 25, 1982, 4.

4. *IHT*, Aug. 20, 1982.

5. UN, *Report on the World Social Situation* (New York, 1985), 6. See also ibid., 12, 95–96; *FEER*, Nov. 14, 1985, 64, 70; Feb. 27, 1986, 68–69; Oct. 2, 1981, 45–52; David Stephen, "The Political Setting," in *Latin America and the World Recession*, ed. Esperandza Durán (Cambridge, 1985), 10; *IHT*, Sept. 20, 1982; Sept. 16, 1983; Charles Oman, *New Forms of International Investment in Developing Countries* (Paris, 1984), 32, 34.

6. Clive Hamilton, "Capitalist Industrialization in East Asia's Four Little Tigers," *JCA* 13 (1983): 43. See also ibid., 48–58; Oman, *New Forms*, 35; ILO, *Report to a Symposium on Employment, Trade, Adjustment and North-South Cooperation* (Geneva, 1985), 73–74; Guy Pfeffermann, "Economic Crisis and the Poor in Some Latin American Countries," *F & D*, June 1987, 34.

7. *BW*, Oct. 3, 1986, 124F. See also ILO, *Report to a Symposium*, 53, 64; *FEER*, Sept. 26, 1985, 106; *Euromoney*, Sept. 1982, 33–34.

8. *FEER*, Dec. 12, 1985, 71. See also ibid., Sept. 26, 1985, 99–106; *IHT*, Oct. 8, 1985; *BW*, March 28, 1983, 64, 68; June 25, 1984, 42–43; Aug. 11, 1986, 41, 44; Dec. 15, 1986, 72–73.

9. Quoted by Jonathan E. Sanford, *U.S. Foreign Policy and Multilateral Development Banks* (Boulder, 1982), 28–29. See also ibid., 9, 49–51.

CHAPTER 17.   The IMF and the World Bank

1. *South*, July 1985, 35. See also *IHT*, May 5, 1982; *FEER*, Oct. 10, 1985, 87; UN, *Report on the World Social Situation* (New York, 1985), 9.

2. Deepak Lal, "The Misconceptions of Development Economics," *F & D*, June 1985, 13. See also *IHT*, Sept. 27, 1985; Robert Solomon, "The IMF in a Period of Turbulence," *F & D*, March 1986, 43.

3. *IMF Survey*, July 15, 1985, 213. See also G. G. Johnson, "Enhancing the Effectiveness of Surveillance," *F & D*, Dec. 1985, 2–6.

4. Edward Brau, "The Consultation Process of the Fund," *F & D*, Dec. 1981, 15.

5. Mohsin S. Khan and Malcolm D. Knight, "Do Fund-Supported Adjustment Programs Retard Growth?" *F & D*, March 1986, 30–31.

6. *FEER*, Feb. 27, 1986, 69. See also UN, *World Social Situation*, 9, 92–93; Charles Sisson, "Fund-Supported Programs and Income Distribution in the LDCs," *F & D*, March 1986, 34.

7. *IMF Survey*, Oct. 7, 1985, 300.

8. UN, *World Social Situation*, 9.

9. *IHT,* April 26, 1984.

10. *Ibid.,* Nov. 21, 1983.

11. *BW,* Jan. 10, 1983, 81.

12. David Finch, "The Push for Fiscal Balance: An IMF Response," in *Banking on Poverty: The Global Impact of the IMF and World Bank,* ed. Jill Torrie (Toronto, 1983), 300. See also UN, *World Social Situation,* 9–10.

13. U.S. Department of the Treasury, *United States Participation in the Multilateral Development Banks in the 1980s* (Washington, 1982), 31. See also *IHT,* Dec. 26, 1984; *Toronto Globe and Mail,* Sept. 13, 1982; Walden Bello and David Kinley, "America's Financial Policeman," *Africasia,* Jan. 1984, 55–58.

14. *Participation in the Multilateral Development Banks,* 54. See also Cheryl Payer, *The World Bank: A Critical Analysis* (New York, 1982), 18.

15. *Participation in the Multilateral Development Banks,* 68.

16. *IHT,* July 4, 1983.

17. *Africa News,* May 10, 1982, 3.

18. *FEER,* Oct. 10, 1985, 53, 52. See also ibid., 58; Sept. 27, 1984, 80; *South,* June 1981, 7–12; *Africa News,* May 10, 1982, 11; Payer, *World Bank,* 225–26; *IMF Survey,* Oct. 7, 1985, 297.

19. Anil Sood and Harinder Kohli, "Industrial Restructuring in Developing Countries," *F & D,* Dec. 1985, 49.

20. *FEER,* Oct. 10, 1985, 88.

21. *BW,* Feb. 7, 1983, 53. See also *FEER,* Jan. 30, 1986, 44–45; July 25, 1985, 63, 67; Oct. 10, 1985, 91; UN, *World Social Situation,* 97; Dick Wilson, "The Privatization of Asia," *Banker,* Sept. 1984, 47–65; *Euromoney,* Feb. 1986, 59–67.

22. U.S. AID, *Policy Paper: Private Enterprise Development* (Washington, 1985), 10. See also *IHT,* June 19, 1985.

23. AID, *Front Lines,* March 1986, 1. See also AID, *Private Enterprise Development,* passim; AID, *A Review of AID's Experience in Private Sector Development* (Washington, 1985).

24. *FEER,* Oct. 10, 1985, 53. See also *Participation in the Multilateral Development Banks,* 129–31.

25. *FEER,* Oct. 10, 1985, 82. See also Gabriel Roth, "The Role of the Private Sector in Providing Water in Developing Countries," *Natural Resources Forum,* Aug. 1985.

26. *FEER,* Oct. 10, 1985, 82.

27. Cited in Cheryl Payer, "The World Bank and the Debt Crisis," *Third World Quarterly,* April 1986, 671. See also *F & D,* June 1986, 23; IFC, *1985 Annual Report* (Washington, 1985), 26; *BW,* Feb. 17, 1986, 66.

28. *FEER,* Jan. 30, 1986, 46.

29. Ibid., 47.

30. *IHT,* April 21, 1986.

31. *Agribusiness Worldwide,* Dec. 1985, 1.

32. UN, *World Social Situation,* 97. See also ibid., 7; *WFM,* Sept./Oct. 1985, 1–14; April/May 1986, 2; Victor Tokman, "The Unemployment Crisis in Latin America," *International Labour Review* 124 (1985): 596–97.

33. *IHT,* June 6, 1986.

34. IFC, *1985 Annual Report,* 9. See also *IHT,* May 28, 1986.

35. IFC, *1985 Annual Report,* 10, 7.

CHAPTER 18.   Restructuring the Centrally Planned Economics

1. *FBIS, Soviet Union,* March 28, 1986.

2. M. K. Bunkina, *Current Problems of Contemporary Capitalism* (Moscow, 1982), 111.

3. U.N., *Report on the World Social Situation* (New York, 1985), 98.

4. Jan Drewnowski, ed., *Crisis in the East European Economy: The Spread of the Polish Disease* (London, 1982), 74.

5. Boris Rumer, "Structural Imbalance in the Soviet Economy," *Problems of Communism,* July–Aug. 1984, 28.

6. Ibid, 29.

7. *IHT,* Sept. 16, 1985. See also Lawrence Weschler, *The Passion of Poland* (New York, 1982), 5.

8. See *FBIS, Soviet Union,* March 19, 1986, S-5; Jan. 13, 1986, S-1. See also A. G. Agarbegyan, "The New Economic Strategy of the USSR and its Social Dimensions," *International Labour Review* (1987): 95–109.

9. Peter T. Knight, *Economic Reform in Socialist Countries,* World Bank Staff Working Papers, no. 579 (Washington, 1983), 23.

10. Fyodor I. Kushnirsky, "The Limits of Soviet Economic Reform," *Problems of Communism,* July–Aug. 1984, 37.

11. Ibid., 43.

12. *FBIS, Soviet Union,* March 28, 1986, 0-16.

13. Ibid.

14. *FBIS, Soviet Union,* Jan. 9, 1986, R-2.

15. R. Ivanova, "Curtailment of Manual Labor," *Problems of Economics,* Aug. 1985, 53. See also E. Iakovleva, "Overcoming Social and Economic Differences in Labor," *Problems of Economics,* Dec. 1985, 3–9.

16. *WES, 1985,* 89.

17. Anil Sood and Harinder Kohli, "Industrial Restructuring in Developing Countries." *F & D,* Dec. 1985, 47–48.

18. Knight, *Economic Reform,* 21.

19. Ibid., 2.

20. Ibid., 81.

21. Henryk Flakierski, "Economic Reform and Income Distribution in Hungary," *Cambridge Journal of Economics* 3 (1979): 16–19.

22. Quoted in Knight, *Economic Reform*, 72–73. See also Leslie Colitt, "Hungary Opts for Bank Competition," *Banker*, Feb. 1987, 45–46.

23. *IHT*, Oct. 31, 1986. See also *Euromoney*, May 1986, 62–68; *IHT*, Dec. 4, 1982.

24. *FBIS, Eastern Europe*, Feb. 4, 1987, F-6. See also *IHT*, April 2, 1985, Aug. 18, Oct. 31, Nov. 4, 1986.

25. *IHT*, Aug. 18, 1986.

26. *FBIS, Eastern Europe*, Feb. 10, 1987, F-7. See also *IHT*, March 12, 1987; *Financial Market Trends*, Feb. 1987, 37–38.

27. Knight, *Economic Reform*, 82.

28. Quoted in *IHT*, April 7, 1987.

29. Ibid., March 3, 1987.

30. Ibid., April 7, 1987.

31. Ibid.

32. See ibid., March 9, 1987, Jan. 25, 1986, April 7, 1987.

33. Quoted in *Banker*, Sept. 1984, 57.

34. *Mainichi Daily News*, Feb. 27, 1987.

35. *Banker*, Sept. 1984, 60. See also *FEER*, March 19, 1987, 64, 75; Oct. 10, 1985, 36–41; *BW*, Oct. 18, 1982, 80, 82.

36. *Banker*, Sept. 1984, 60. See also *IHT*, Dec. 24, 1985.

37. *IHT*, April 8, March 10, 1987.

38. Quoted in Jorge Pérez-Lopez, "Cuban Economy in the 1980s," *Problems of Communism*, Sept.–Oct. 1986, 33.

39. For recent discussions of the various aspects of the planning process in Cuba, see Andrew Zimbalist, ed., "Cuba's Socialist Economy toward the 1990s," *World Development* 15 (1987).

40. *FEER*, March 19, 1987, 88.

41. Ernst Kux, "Contradictions in Soviet Socialism," *Problems of Communism*, Nov.–Dec. 1984, 23–24. See also *BW*, Feb. 2, 1987, 45; Rumer, "Structural Imbalance," 25.

42. Kux, "Contradictions," 17.

43. Quoted ibid., 17–18.

44. Ibid., 15.

45. Ibid., 20.

46. Weschler, *Passion of Poland*, 44.

47. "Program of the Polish Trade Union—Solidarity," trans. in *Forward*, Sept. 1981, 5.

48. Ibid.

49. Yet Solidarity's own proposals and program for economic change were a rather contradictory mix of workers' interests and the absorption of some of the economic views of the "reformers," for in no way are the designs of the IMF ever in the workers' interest; but they were, in fact, compatible with the that of the Polish government, which by 1986 was adopting the IMF austerity program.

CHAPTER 20.   Restructuring and the Working Class

1. Harry Braverman, *Labor and Monopoly Capital* (New York, 1974), 24.

2. Paul Mattick, *Marxism: Last Refuge of the Bourgeoisie*, ed. Paul Mattick, Jr. (Armonk, N.Y., 1983), 117–18. This significant book is the last work by this important Marxist. It and his other works are of enduring value in studying the contemporary capitalist system.

3. Gabriel Kolko, *Wealth and Power in America: An Analysis of Social Class and Income Distribution* (New York, 1962). See also Gabriel Kolko, "Working Wives: Their Effects on the Structure of the Working Class," *Science and Society* 42 (Fall 1978): 257–77; Katherine Bradbury, "The Shrinking Middle Class," *NEER*, Sept./Oct. 1986, 41–55; Robert Kuttner, "The Declining Middle," *Atlantic*, July 1983, 60–72; Barry Bluestone and Bennett Harrison, *The Great American Job Machine* (Study Prepared for the Joint Economic Committee, U.S. Congress) (Washington, 1986); Mary Jackman and Robert Jackman, *Class Awareness in the United States* (Berkeley, 1983).

4. Cited in Richard Barnet, *The Lean Years* (New York, 1980), 258. See also *OECD Observer*, April–May, 1987, 14, which declared the annual increase in the LDCs alone was 60 million people.

5. OECD, *Interfutures*, 8.

CHAPTER 21.   Restructuring Employment

1. OECD, *Employment Outlook*, Sept. 1984, 40. See also Janet Norwood, Testimony to U.S. Congress, Joint Economic Committee, *Hearings: Employment-Unemployment*, 98th Cong., 1st sess., Feb. 4–June 3, 1983 (Washington 1983), 7, 28, 82; Barry Bluestone and Bennett Harrison, *The Great American Job Machine* (Study Prepared for the Joint Economic Committee, U.S. Congress) (Washington, 1986), 3; *BW*, Jan. 16, 1984, 23; Nov. 21, 1983, 41; June 14, 1982, 66–81; Aug. 29, 1983, 18–19, 54–56; Oct. 31, 1983, 40–42; April 8, 1985, 70–71; May 16, 1983, 100–10; *IHT*, May 15, June 10, 1985.

2. *BW*, April 1, 1985, 63. See also ibid., Sept. 29, 1986, 26; May 18, 1987, 34, 38; Bluestone and Harrison, *Great American Job Machine*, 17; *IHT*, June 10, 1985, June 20, 1984; Robert Kuttner, "The Declining Middle," *Atlantic*, July 1983, 60–72; M. Uquart, "The Services Industry: Is It Recession Proof?" *Monthly Labor Review*, Oct. 1981, 15–17; Richard Hyman, "Occupational Structure, Collective Organization, and Industrial Militancy," in *The Resur-*

gence of Class Conflict in Western Europe since 1968, ed. Colin Crouch and Alessandro Pizzorno (London, 1978), 2:41; OECD, *Employment Outlook*, 1984, 39–49; *IHT*, Jan. 27, 1984, March 11, 1986, June 27, 1984; Pierre Dommergues, "Les travailleurs américains victimes de la restructuration," *Monde Diplomatique*, March 1982, 13; Emma Rothschild, "Reagan and the Real America," *New York Review of Books*, Feb. 5, 1981, 13–14; *BW*, May 2, 1983, 126–27; *OECD Observer*, April–May 1987, 14.

3. *FEER*, Dec. 19, 1985, 57.

4. *BW*, Sept. 5, 1983, 96. See also ibid., April 1, 1985, 62–63; *IHT*, Aug. 17, 1983, March 17, 1986, Sept. 13, 1982, March 24, 1987; *FEER*, Dec. 19, 1985, 57.

5. *IHT*, Oct. 28, 1985.

6. See *FEER*, Dec. 19, 1985, 57; *BW*, July 17, 1978, 82–83; Dommergues, "Travailleurs américains," 13; Jeremy Brecher, "Crisis Economy: Born-Again Labor Movement?" *Monthly Review*, March 1984, 1–23.

7. For women in the labor force see Gabriel Kolko, "Working Wives: Their Effects on the Structure of the Working Class," *Science and Society* 42: (Fall 1978): 257–77; Liba Paukert, *The Employment and Unemployment of Women in OECD Countries* (Paris, 1984), 10–11, 47–81; *BW*, June 23, 1986, 68–70; Nov. 26, 1984, 81; Bluestone and Harrison, *Great American Job Machine*, 6, 24–25; *FEER*, Dec. 19, 1985, 55, 57, 73; Folker Fröbel, Jürgen Heinrichs, and Otto Kreye, *The New International Division of Labor* (Cambridge, 1980), 339–64; *BW*, Aug. 10, 1987, 180.

8. For the underground economy see Russell L. Ackoff, Paul Broholm, and Roberta Snow, *Revitalizing Western Economies* (San Francisco, 1984), 4–11; Vito Tanzi, "The Underground Economy in the United States: Annual Estimates, 1930–1980," *IMF Staff Papers*, June 1983, 302; UN, *Report on the World Social Situation* (New York, 1985), 76–77; Bryan Roberts, *Cities of Peasants: The Political Economy of Urbanization in the Third World* (Beverly Hills, 1978), 152–57, 165–69, and passim; Alejandro Portes, Silvia Blitzer, and John Curtis, "Urban Informal Sector in Uruguay," *World Development* 14 (June 1986): 727–41.

9. David Coe and Francisco Gagliardi, *Nominal Wage Determination in Ten OECD Countries*, OECD Working Papers, no. 19 (Paris, 1985), 27.

10. *WEO, 1982*, 36.

11. Ibid., 34.

12. *BW*, June 14, 1982, 66. See also *EROP, 1986*, 301; *IHT*, July 19, 1986; *BW*, Jan. 16, 1984, 23; OECD, *Economic Outlook*, Dec. 1985, 39; Robert Kuttner, "The Declining Middle," *Atlantic*, July 1983, 71; *EROP 1986*, 103.

13. OECD, *Economic Outlook*, Dec. 1985, 39. See also *BW*, April 1, 1985, 62–63; May 16, 1983, 100–10; *IHT*, Aug. 5, 1980.

14. *IHT*, Sept. 5, 1979. See also *BW*, March 3, 1986, 79–80; June 23, 1986, 30; Katharine Bradbury and Lynn Browne, "Black Men in the Labor Market," *NEER*, March/April 1986, 30–41; OECD, *Economic Outlook*, Dec. 1985, 72; *WFM*, Dec. 1985, 10; *BW*, Aug. 10, 1987, 20.

15. *BW*, Nov. 14, 1983.

16. OECD, *Economic Outlook*, Dec. 1985, 40–41.

17. Ibid., 42. See also *BW*, July 17, 1978, 83; Coe and Gagliardi, *Nominal Wage Determination*, 27.

18. ILO, *Report to a Symposium on Employment, Trade, Adjustment and North-South Cooperation* (Geneva, 1985), 44.

19. *EROP, 1984*, 88.

20. *BW*, Feb. 13, 1984, 94.

21. Samuel Bowles, Thomas W. Weisskopf, and David M. Gordon, "Falling Productivity," *Nation*, July 10, 1982, 46.

22. Harry Magdoff, "A Statistical Fiction," *Nation*, July 10, 1982, 47–48.

23. Samuel Bowles, Thomas Weisskopf, and David M. Gordon, "U.S. Productivity," *Challenge*, March–April 1984, 42.

24. *Wall Street Journal*, Jan. 29, 1979. See also *IHT*, Jan. 27, 1979; *Federal Reserve Bulletin*, April 1987, 247.

25. *WES, 1979–1980*, 27.

26. Harry Braverman, *Labor and Monopoly Capital* (New York, 1974), 208, 206. See also *BW*, June 14, 1982, 66–81; May 16, 1983, 100–10; Feb. 20, 1984, 32; *Le Monde*, Nov. 13, 1979; Michael Sharpston, *International Subcontracting* (Washington, 1975), 101.

27. *EROP, 1983*, 83.

28. OECD, *Interfutures*, 159. See also *IHT*, April 9, Dec. 27, 1986; Fröbel et al., *New International Division of Labor*, 353–55.

29. For migration see *UN Chronicle* 22 (1985): 12; *Courier* (special issue on migration) Sept. 1985, 4–7, 20; Mark J. Miller, *Foreign Workers in Western Europe: An Emerging Political Force* (New York, 1981), xv, 202; *BW*, May 3, 1982, 44; Jan. 23, 1984, 49; *WES, 1983, Supplement*, 36; Hilary Partridge, "Italy's Fiat in Turin in the 1950s," in *Capital and Labour: Studies in the Capitalist Labour Process*, ed. Theo Nichols (London, 1980), 416–33; Jonathan Power, *Migrant Workers in Western Europe and the United States* (Oxford, 1979), 55–57; Crouch and Pizzorno, *Resurgence of Class Conflict*, 1: 273–97, 2: 245ff.; Kathleen Newland, *International Migration: The Search for Work* (Washington, 1979), 19; Dommergues, "Travailleurs américains," 12–13; Alejandro Portes and John Walton, *Labor, Class, and the International System* (New York, 1981), 49; Fred Halliday, "Migration and the Labour Force in the Oil Producing States in the Middle East," *Development and Change* 8 (1977): 263–91.

30. Reported in *IHT*, Jan. 23, 1985.

31. *IHT*, May 5, 1986.

32. *BW*, Nov. 26, 1984, 84. See also Larry T. Adams, Changing Employment Patterns of Organized Workers," *Monthly Labor Review*, Feb. 1985, 25–30; Dommergues, "Travailleurs américains," 14; Brecher, "Crisis Economy," 1–23; Edward Kokkelenberg and Donna Sockell, "Union Membership in the

United States, 1973–1981," *Industrial and Labor Relations Review* 38 (July 1985): 540; ILO, *Report to a Symposium,* 29; *Wall Street Journal,* June 4, 1986; *IHT,* Dec. 11, Oct. 28, 1985; *BW,* July 8, 1985, 72–75; Feb. 24, 1986, 116; *FEER,* Dec. 19, 1985, 78; Adams, "Changing Employment Patterns," 25, 30.

33. *IHT,* Jan. 23, 1985.

34. Giorgio Galli quoted by Fabrizio Tonello, "Les syndicats italiens et le recul de la démocratie ouvrière," *Monde Diplomatique,* May 1983, 19. See also *BW,* Feb. 15, 1982, 38.

35. OECD, *Economic Outlook,* Dec. 1985, 41.

36. *IHT,* Jan. 23, 1985.

37. Gilberto Mathias and Michael Lowy, "Brésil: Émergence d'un nouveau prolétariat," *Monde Diplomatique,* Dec. 1982, 28.

CHAPTER 22.   Unemployment

1. Harry Braverman, *Labor and Monopoly Capital* (New York, 1974), 386.

2. *BW,* Jan. 31, 1983, 40.

3. OECD, *Interfutures: Facing the Future: Mastering the Probable and Managing the Unpredictable* (Paris, 1979), 162.

4. *EROP, 1983,* 41.

5. *WFM,* Dec. 1984, 8.

6. OECD, *Employment Outlook,* Sept. 1983, 7. See also *EROP, 1983,* 45–50.

7. *EROP, 1983,* 37. See also OECD, *Economic Outlook,* Dec. 1985, 30.

8. *WEO, 1983,* 35. See also Brian Showler and Adrian Sinfield, *The Workless State* (Oxford, 1981), 39, 203–5; *EROP, 1984,* 64; *EROP, 1983,* 29–30; *IHT,* Dec. 3, 1982, March 17, 1986; OECD, *Employment Outlook,* Sept. 1983, 7–11; Janet Norwood, Testimony to U.S. Congress, Joint Economic Committee, *Hearings: Employment-Unemployment,* 98th Cong., 1st sess., Feb. 4–June 3, 1983 (Washington, 1983), 3–141; Edward Yemin, ed., *Workforce Reductions in Undertakings* (Geneva, 1982), 4–5, 191.

9. John C. Ries, "Unemployment in 1982: Beyond the Official Labor Force Statistics," *NEER,* May–June 1984, 29, 36. See also Lloyd Kenward, "Unemployment in the Major Industrial Countries," *F & D,* June 1983, 24–27.

10. *IHT,* Sept. 4, 1985. See also *BW,* March 30, 1981, 16; March 9, 1987, 57–58; *IHT,* Nov. 22, 1984; Jan. 22, 1987; Akira Ono, "On Recent Studies of Unemployment in Japan," *JES,* Fall 1985, 4, 21, 75, and passim; OECD, *Standardized Unemployment Rates* (Paris, 1985), 35; *WFM,* 1984, 2–7; *OECD Observer,* Jan. 1987, 13–14.

11. *BW,* May 23, 1983, 170. See also *IHT,* June 10, 1985; Showler and Sinfield, *Workless State,* 176; UN, *Report on the World Social Situation* (New

York, 1985), 69–70; *WFM*, Dec. 1984, 2; *BW*, Nov. 26, 1984, 80; Liba Paukert, *The Employment and Unemployment of Women in OECD Countries* (Paris, 1984), 58–61.

12. *Economist*, March 13, 1982, 25. See also Jeremy Brecher, "Crisis Economy," *Monthly Review*, March 1984, 5; *BW*, March 26, 1979, 94–95; UN, *World Social Situation*, 79–80.

13. OECD, *Economic Outlook*, Dec. 1985, 41. See also *BW*, May 3, 1982, 44; Ian Hamilton, "International Dimensions of Industrial Restructuring," *Economist Intelligence Unit*, no. 4 (1984): 10; *IHT*, March 12, 1981.

14. *IHT*, Jan. 24, 1986. See also ibid., Sept, 12, 1983, 60; Jan. 31, 1983, 39–40; OECD, *Economic Outlook*, Dec. 1985, 41; *IHT*, March 17, 1986.

15. *BW*, March 28, 1983, 90.

16. OECD, *Interfutures*, 168–69. See also OECD, *Economic Outlook*, Dec. 1985, 66.

17. *WEO, 1983*, 36.

18. *EROP, 1983*, 39.

19. OECD, *Employment Outlook, 1983*, 10.

20. OECD, *Economic Outlook*, Dec. 1985, 41. See also UN, *World Social Situation*, 68.

21. OECD, *Interfutures*, 162.

22. OECD, *Economic Outlook*, Dec. 1985, 66.

23. Showler and Sinfield, *Workless State*, 160.

24. Guy Pfeffermann, "Economic Crisis in Some Latin American Countries," *F & D*, June 1987, 33. See also Victor E. Tokman, "The Unemployment Crisis in Latin America," *International Labour Review* 124 (1985): 591; UN, *World Social Situation*, 74–76, 82; *IHT*, Oct. 16, 1985; *New York Times*, July 20, 1986.

25. *WES, 1983*, 69.

CHAPTER 23.   Conclusion to Part IV

1. U.S. Congress, Joint Economic Committee, *The Concentration of Wealth in the United States: Trends in the Distribution of Wealth Among American Families* (Washington, 1986), 44.

INDEX

ABOUT THE AUTHOR

Joyce Kolko is the author of *America and the Crisis of World Capitalism* and (with Gabriel Kolko) of *The Limits of Power: The World and United States Policy, 1945–1954.* She lives in Toronto, Canada.